# Internet and E-mail for Seniors with Windows 8

## Studio Visual Steps

# Internet and E-mail for Seniors with Windows 8

*For senior citizens who want to start using the Internet*

This book has been written using the Visual Steps™ method.
Cover design by Studio Willemien Haagsma bNO



Edited by Mara Kok and Rilana Groot
Translated by Chris Hollingsworth, *1st Resources* and Irene Venditti, *i-write* translation services.
Editor in chief: Jolanda Ligthart

First printing: November 2012
ISBN 978 90 5905 128 7



**Resources used**: Some of the computer terms and definitions seen here in this book have been taken from descriptions found online at the Windows Help and Support website.

**Do you have questions or suggestions?**
**E-mail: info@visualsteps.com**

**Would you like more information?**
**www.visualsteps.com**

**Website for this book:**
**www.visualsteps.com/internet8**

# Table of Contents

## Appendices

# Foreword

The Internet has ushered in a whole new era. Before that most computers were isolated from one another. Since the emergence of the Internet, people are able to communicate with other connected computer users on a worldwide basis. The Internet has gradually become so vast that you can browse in even the most obscure libraries and communicate with people and organizations no matter where in the world they are.

More and more applications are being created that have advantages for computer non-experts as well. For example, e-mail is increasingly replacing the telephone, regular e-mail and the fax.

The purpose of this book is to acquaint you with the Internet. Then we will teach you the essential skills needed to take full advantage of what the Internet can offer. We have also given a lot of attention to Internet safety and privacy. We will alert you to potential dangers when using the internet. Finally, we will show you what kind of measures you can take to protect your computer.

We have created a special website to accompany this book, where you can safely practice what you have learned before you set out on your own on the Internet.

We hope you enjoy this book and wish you a pleasant journey on the Internet.

The Studio Visual Steps authors

P.S. Your comments and suggestions are most welcome.
Our e-mail address is: mail@visualsteps.com

# Introduction to Visual Steps™

The Visual Steps handbooks and manuals are the best instructional materials available for learning how to work with the computer. Nowhere else can you find better support for getting to know your *Windows*, *Mac*, iPad, iPhone, the Internet and other computer topics.

Properties of the Visual Steps books:

- **Comprehensible contents**
  Addresses the needs of the beginner or intermediate user for a manual written in simple, straight-forward English.
- **Clear structure**
  Precise, easy to follow instructions. The material is broken down into small enough segments to allow for easy absorption.
- **Screen shots of every step**
  Quickly compare what you see on your computer screen with the screen shots in the book. Pointers and tips guide you when new windows or alert boxes are opened so you always know what to do next.
- **Get started right away**
  All you have to do is have your computer and your book at hand. Sit some where's comfortable, begin reading and perform the operations as indicated on your own computer.
- **Layout**
  The text is printed in a large size font and is clearly legible.

In short, I believe these manuals will be excellent guides for you.

dr. H. van der Meij
Faculty of Applied Education, Department of Instruction Technology, University of Twente, the Netherlands

# Visual Steps Newsletter

All Visual Steps books follow the same methodology: clear and concise step-by-step instructions with screen shots to demonstrate each task.
A complete list of all our books can be found on our website **www.visualsteps.com**
You can also sign up to receive our **free Visual Steps Newsletter**.
In this Newsletter you will receive periodic information by email regarding:
- the latest titles and previously released books;
- special offers, supplemental chapters, tips and free informative booklets.
Also, our Newsletter subscribers may download any of the documents listed on the web pages **www.visualsteps.com/info_downloads**

When you subscribe to our Newsletter you can be assured that we will never use your e-mail address for any purpose other than sending you the information as previously described. We will not share this address with any third-party. Each Newsletter also contains a one-click link to unsubscribe.

## What You Will Need

To be able to work through this book, you will need a number of things:

The primary requirement for working with this book is having the US or English version of *Windows 8* installed on your computer or laptop. *Windows 8* comes equipped with all the programs you need to work with this book.

**Please note:** The screen shots shown in this book have been made using a local user account. It is also possible to login with a *Microsoft* account. Since this is a book for beginning computer users, we have chosen to not to use this type of account. If you are working with a *Microsoft* account, you will sometimes see different windows and other options.

A functioning Internet connection. For the settings for your Internet connection, please see the software and information supplied by your Internet Service Provider.

The following is useful. But it is not a problem if you do not have them. You can read through the sections where this item is used.

A printer is required for some of the exercises. If you do not have a printer, you can skip these exercises.

## The Website Accompanying This Book

At the website that accompanies this book, **www.visualsteps.com/internet8**, you will find some Bonus Online Chapters and more information about the book. This website will also keep you informed of changes you need to know as a user of the book. Please, also take a look at our website **www.visualsteps.com** from time to time to read about new books and gather other useful information.

# How To Use This Book

This book has been written using the Visual Steps™ method. The method is simple: just place the book next to your computer and execute all the tasks step by step, directly on your computer. With the clear instructions and the multitude of screen shots, you will always know exactly what to do. This way, you will quickly learn how to use the various programs or services, without any problems.

In this Visual Steps™ book, you will see various icons. This is what they mean:

**Techniques**
These icons indicate an action to be carried out:

 The mouse icon means you need to do something with the mouse.

 The keyboard icon means you should type something on your keyboard.

 The hand icon means you should do something else, for example, turn on the computer or carry out a task previously learned.

In addition to these icons, in some areas of this book extra assistance is provided to help you successfully work through each chapter.

**Help**
These icons indicate that extra help is available:

 The arrow icon warns you about something.

 The bandage icon will help you if something has gone wrong.

 Have you forgotten how to do something? The number next to the footsteps tells you where to look it up at the end of the book in the appendix *How Do I Do That Again?*

In this book you will also find a lot of general information, and tips. This information is displayed in separate boxes.

**Extra information**
Information boxes are denoted by these icons:

 The book icon gives you extra background information that you can read at your convenience. This extra information is not necessary for working through the book.

 The light bulb icon indicates an extra tip for using the program or service.

# Prior Computer Experience

This book assumes a minimum of prior computer experience. Nonetheless, there are a few basic techniques you should know in order to use this book. You do not need to have any prior experience with the Internet. But you do need to be able to:

- click with the mouse;
- start and stop programs and apps;
- type and edit text;
- start up and shut down *Windows*.

If you do not know how to do these things yet, you can read the book **Windows 8 for Seniors** first:

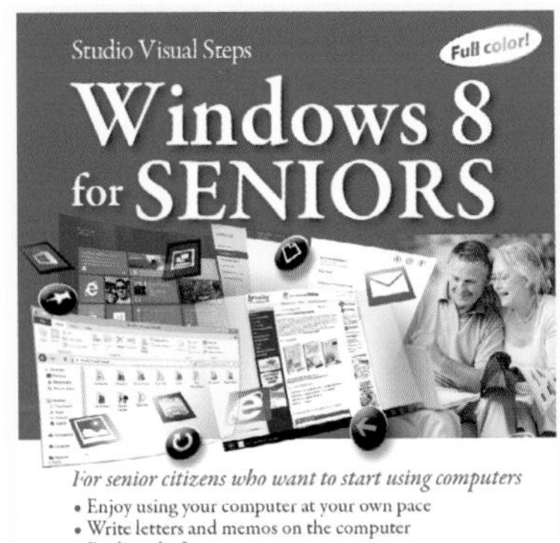


*Windows 8 for Seniors* has been specifically written for people who are taking their first computer steps at a later age. It is a real "how to" book. By working through this book, you will learn all the techniques needed to operate your computer. You will gradually become more confident and comfortable using the computer. The step-by-step method makes instruction easy to process so you quickly gain basic computer skills.

ISBN 978 90 5905 118 8

For more information, visit
**www.visualsteps.com/windows8**

# Test Your Knowledge

After you have worked through this book, you can test your knowledge online, on the **www.ccforseniors.com** website.

By answering a number of multiple choice questions you will be able to test your knowledge about Internet and e-mail as well as other topics regarding computing. After you have finished the test, your *Computer Certificate* will be sent to the e-mail address you have entered.
Participating in the test is **free of charge**. The computer certificate website is a free service from Visual Steps.

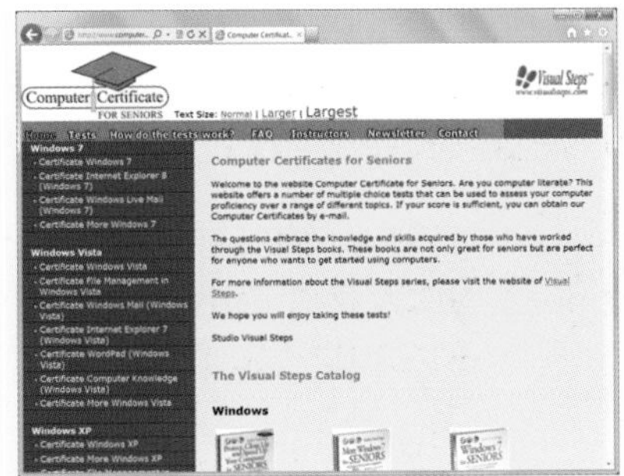

# For Teachers

This book is designed as a self-study guide. It is also well suited for use in a group or a classroom setting. For this purpose, we offer a free teacher's manual containing information about how to prepare for the course (including didactic teaching methods) and testing materials. You can download this teacher's manual (PDF file) from the website which accompanies this book: **www.visualsteps.com/internet8**

# The Screen Shots

The screen shots used in this book indicate which button, folder, file or hyperlink you need to click on your computer screen. In the instruction text (in **bold** letters) you will see a small image of the item you need to click. The black line will point you to the right place on your screen.
The small screen shots that are printed in this book are not meant to be completely legible all the time. This is not necessary, as you will see these images on your own computer screen in real size and fully legible.

Here you see an example of an instruction text and a screen shot. The black line indicates where to find this item on your own computer screen:

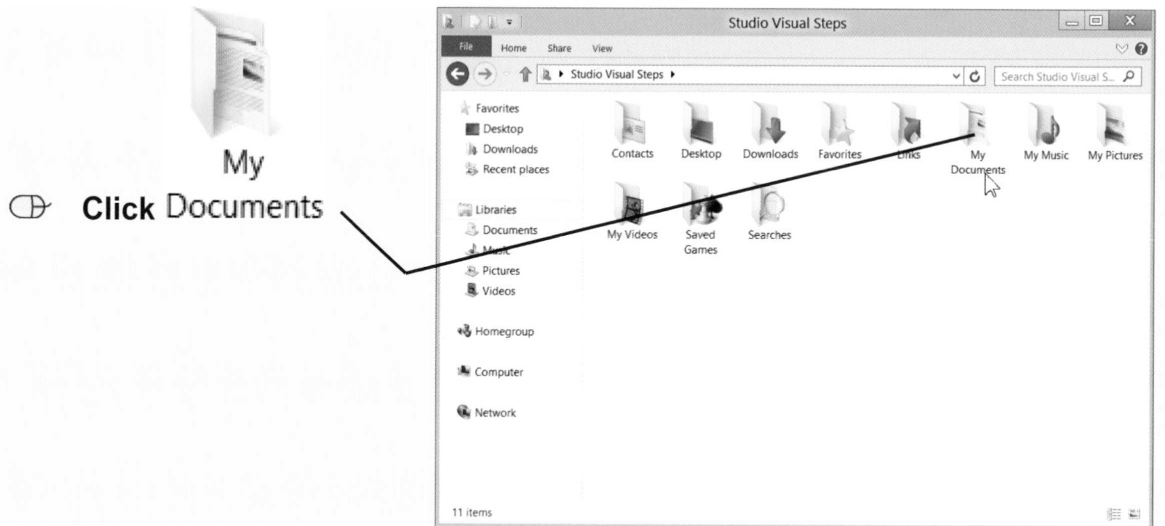

Sometimes the screen shot shows only a portion of a window. Here is an example:

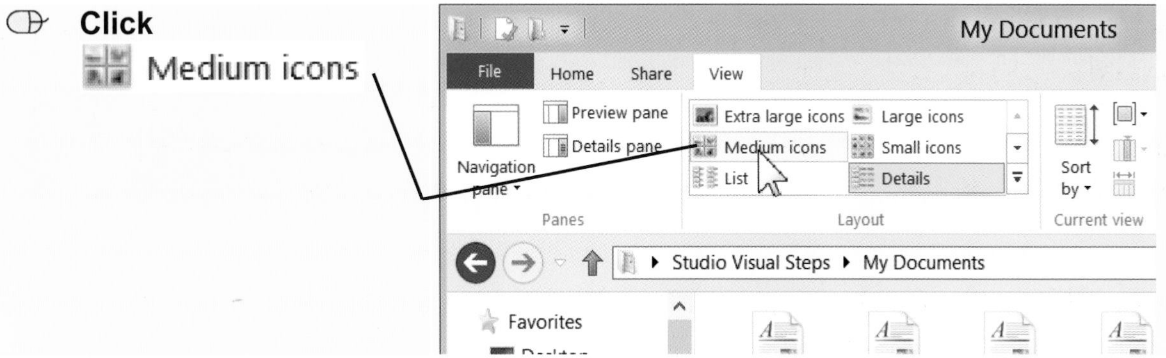


It really will **not be necessary** for you to read all the information in the screen shots in this book. Always use the screen shots in combination with the image you see on your own computer screen.

# 1. Surfing the Internet with the Internet Explorer App

The Internet consists of millions of computers that are all interconnected. This is also known as the *World Wide Web* and is one of the most exciting parts of the Internet. *World Wide Web* means exactly what it says: a web of computers where an infinite amount of information is located regarding every imaginable topic. No matter where you are in the world, you can access that information with your computer.

On the Internet, a source of information is called a *website*. It is a site somewhere on the web. Within the website, you can browse from one page to another by clicking with your mouse. You can even jump from one website to another. This is called *surfing*. The type of program you need to surf the Internet, is called a *browser*. *Internet Explorer* is an example of a browser.
In *Windows 8* you can both use the *Internet Explorer* app or the full version of the program. In this chapter you will learn how to use the app.

In order to get on the Internet, you must initiate a connection with a computer that is permanently connected to the Internet. This is done by means of an *Internet Service Provider* (ISP). If you want to use the provider's services, you must subscribe to them or pay for them in another way. The provider then assigns you a *user name* and a *password*. The user name and password will give you access to the Internet.

If you are connected to the Internet, you are *online* and able to surf the Internet. In this chapter you will learn how to *surf*.

In this chapter, you will learn how to:

- start *Windows*;
- open the *Internet Explorer* app;
- use a web address;
- browse forward and backward;
- use tabbed browsing;
- switch between multiple open apps;
- close the *Internet Explorer* app.

 **Please note:**

You must have a working Internet connection in order to use this book. This connection should already be set up on your computer. Contact your Internet Service Provider or your computer supplier if you need help.

 **Please note:**

This book assumes that you are working with a computer mouse. If you are working on a laptop with a touchpad, you may want to purchase an external mouse to be able to follow the steps in this book more easily.

# 1.1 Starting Windows

*Windows* automatically starts up when you turn on your computer.

 **Turn on your computer**

After a while you will see a screen that may look like this:

This is called the *lock screen*.

**Click somewhere on the screen**

Probably there are some user accounts set up on your computer. Such an account provides access to your settings. It is likely you will first need to log on, to gain access to your account:

If you see a screen like the one in this example:

**Click the icon of your user account**

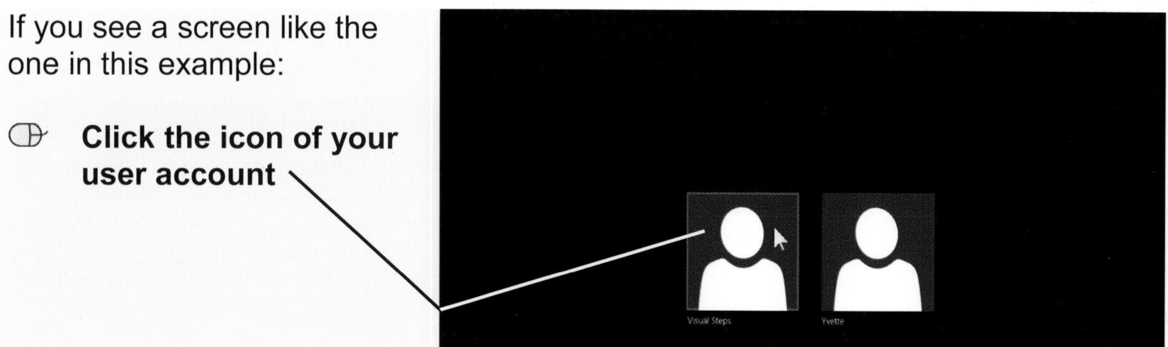


If you have set up a password for the user account, you will have to type it in the white box Password:

**Type the password**

**Click**

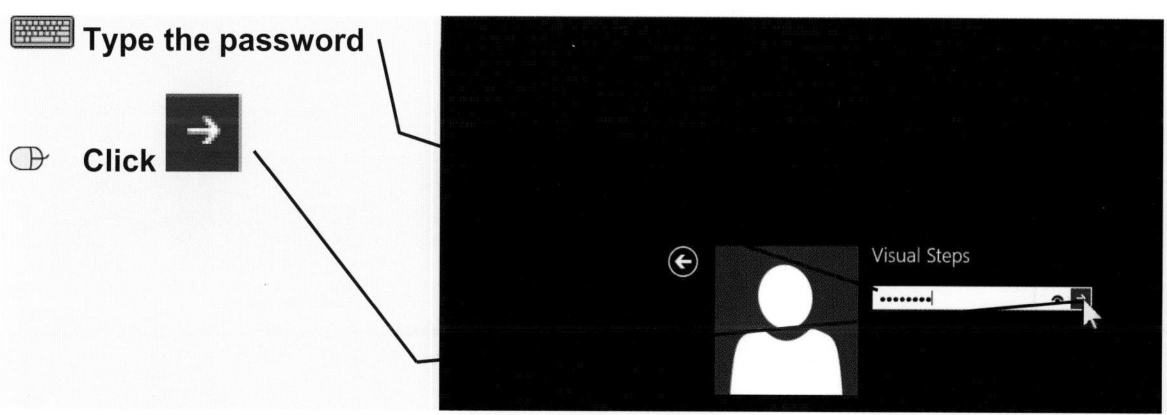


Now you will see the *Windows* Start screen:

It is possible that your screen will look a little different. For the tasks you will be performing this will not matter. They will remain pretty much the same.

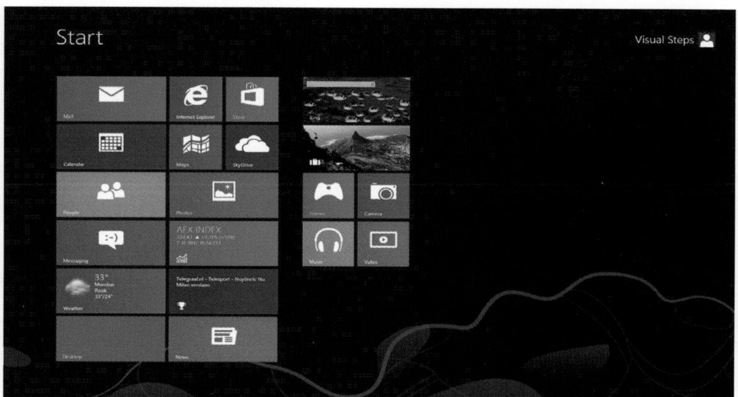

## 1.2 The Internet Explorer App

In *Windows 8* you can directly access the *Internet Explorer* app from the Start screen. This is a limited edition of the *Internet Explorer* program. You can use this app to quickly look something up on the Internet. This is how you open the app:

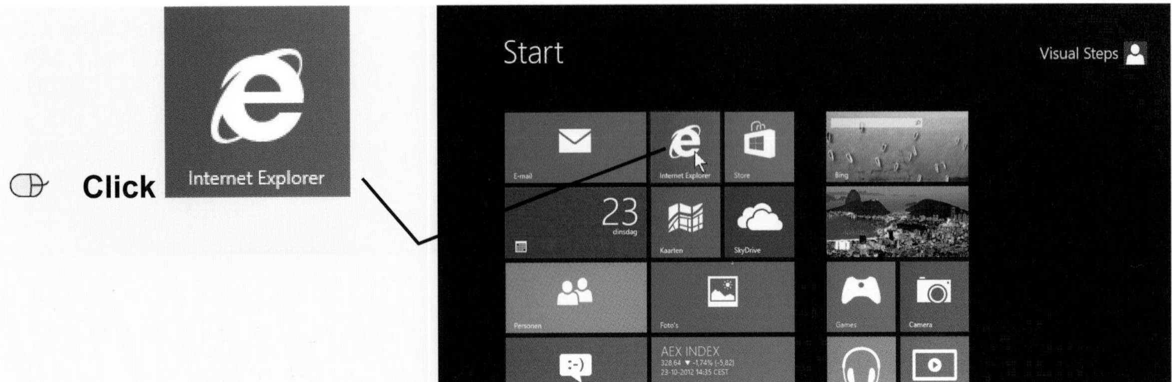


The app is opened and afterwards it will automatically connect to the Internet.

Your screen displays a *home page*:

Usually this will be a *Microsoft* page, since this is the manufacturer of *Internet Explorer*.

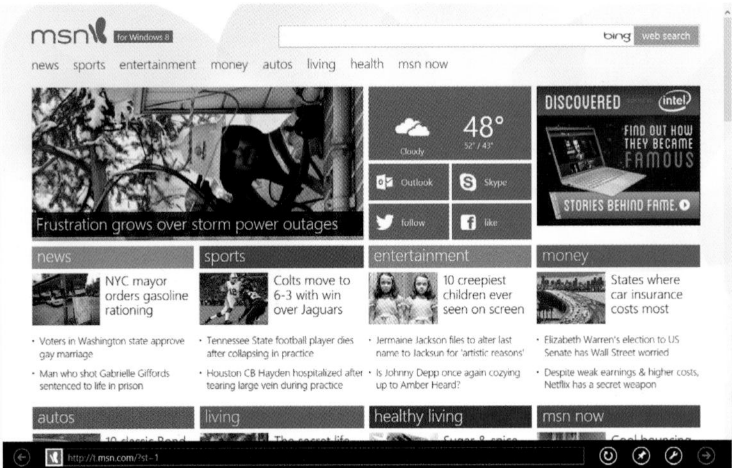

 **Please note:**

The home page displayed above may look different on your own computer. You may see a home page that has been set up by someone else, or by you.

Even if you see the same web page on your own computer, the content will be different. Many web pages on the Internet are edited on a daily basis.

### HELP! No connection yet.

If you have tried to connect to the Internet a number of times and you still are unable to establish a connection, most likely the settings on your computer are not correct. You will need to contact your ISP for assistance.

## 1.3 Typing a Web Address

Every website has its own *web address* on the World Wide Web, for example **www.visualsteps.com**. These are the addresses that start with www, you see them everywhere. You can use these addresses to find a website on any computer that is connected to the Internet.

Some websites have an extra extension next to the website's main address. This is called a sub address. The sub address is separated from the main address by a / (slash). Take a look at the website accompanying this book, for instance:

**www.visualsteps.com/internet8**

At the bottom of the window:

**Click the address bar**

The web address http://t.msn.com/?st=1 will turn blue as a sign that it is selected.

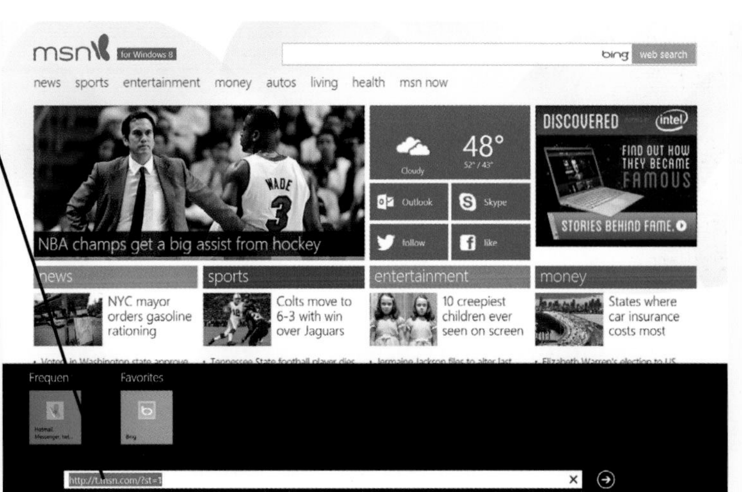

### HELP! I do not see the address bar.

If the address bar on your screen is hidden, you can display it by right-clicking an empty area on the screen.

You can type the address **www.visualsteps.com/internet8** in the address bar:

On this keyboard the / sign is located here:

It is the same key as the question mark key.

⌨ **Type:** `www.visualsteps.com/internet8`

⌨ **Press**

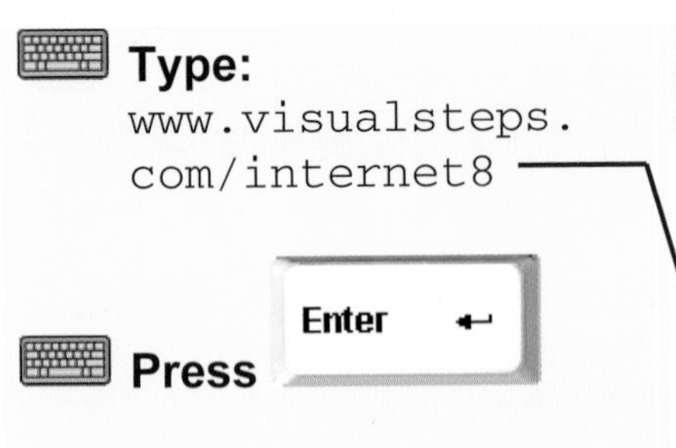


While you are typing, the program will check whether you have previously visited this page:

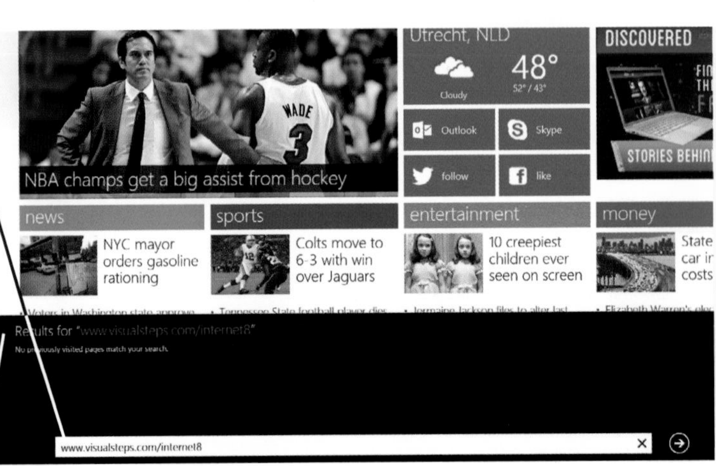


After a short while you will see the home page of the website accompanying this book:

On this website you can find additional information on the book.

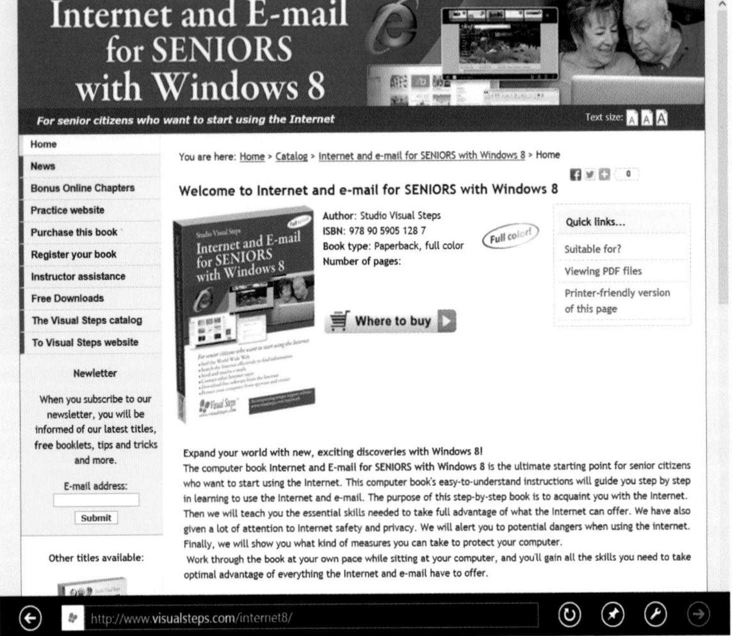

# 1.4 A Wrong Address

Once in a while a typing error is made when typing a web address. Or a particular web address may no longer exist. This is especially true because the Internet is highly dynamic and changes every day. Private individuals and companies may need to change their web addresses for a variety of reasons.

Sometimes you will see an address that starts with http://. That is additional information indicating that the address is for a website. With *Internet Explorer*, you do not need to type http://. The program automatically understands that you are looking for a website and will add it to the web address.

When typing a web address, pay close attention to the following:

- Make sure that any dots (.) or forward slashes (/) are typed in the correct places. If they are not, you will receive an error message.
- Never type spaces in a web address.

If even one dot is missing, an error message will appear. See what happens if you try to open the website of the Public Broadcasting Service with an incorrect web address:

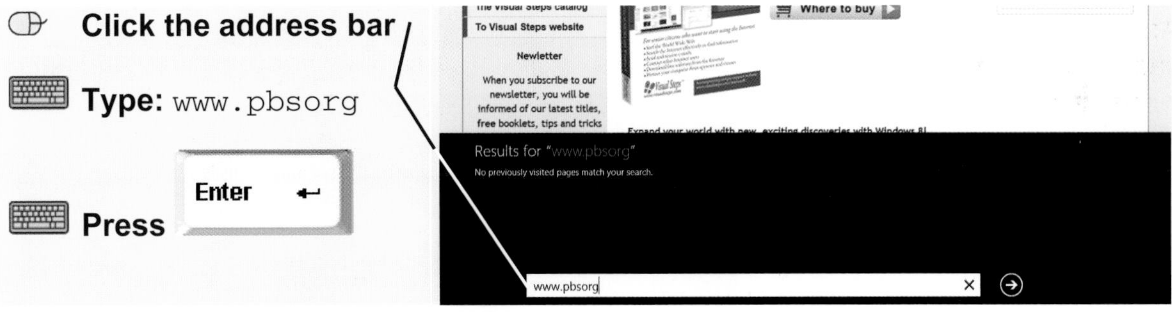


The following web page is displayed:

But this is not the web page you were looking for.

**Please note:** you may see another web page.

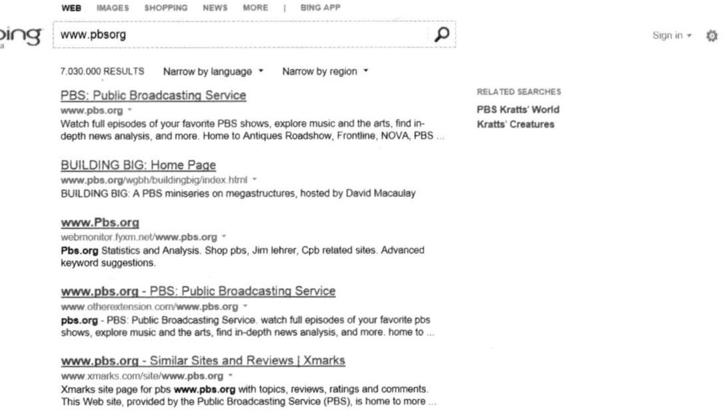

The search provider *Bing* is trying to help you. *Bing* has made these suggestions because the address you typed - www.pbsorg - was incorrect, but very similar to an address they already had stored in their database. The dot before 'org' is missing. The correct address for the Public Broadcasting Service website is:

**www.pbs.org**

Try entering the correct address:

After a short while, you see the home page for the Public Broadcasting Service.

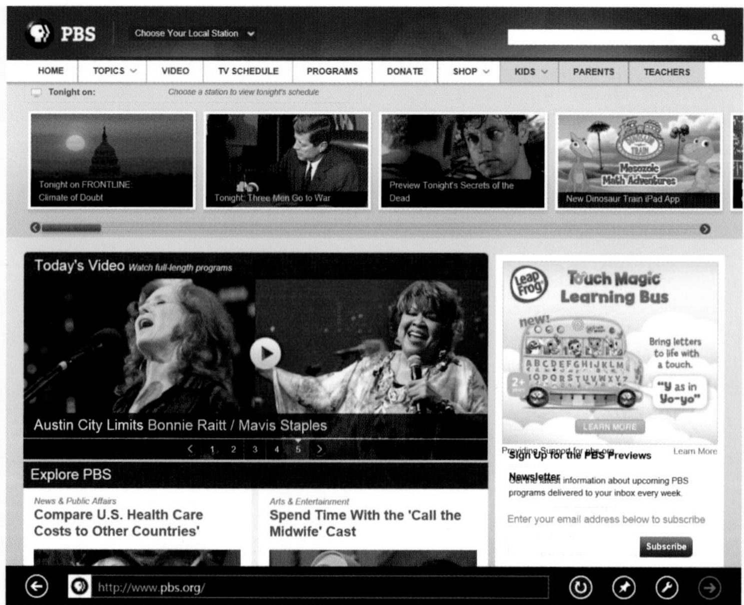


Remember, if you forget just one dot the program may not be able to find the website you want.

## Please note:

The website shown above may look different. The Internet changes all the time.

# 1.5 Refreshing a Page

Sometimes a page is not displayed on your screen as it should be. When that happens, you can tell *Internet Explorer* to reload the page: to *refresh* it or allow it to *download*. Just watch what happens:

At the bottom right of the screen:

Click

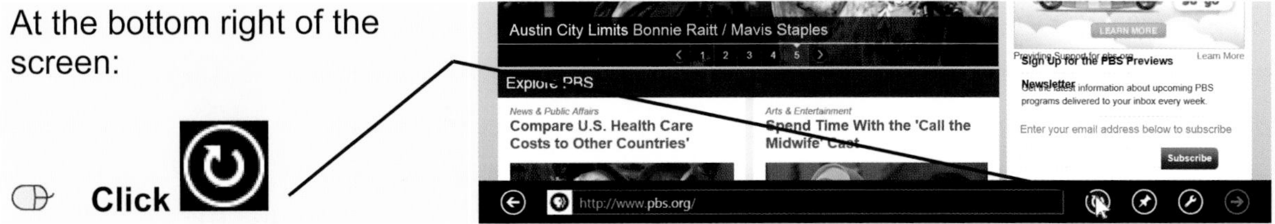


You see that the web page has been refreshed. Sometimes this happens very quickly and you will not really notice it. Everything you see on your screen needs to be sent to your computer. If you have a slow Internet connection, this may take a while. You might get the impression that nothing at all happens.

**Tip**

**The latest news**

When you view a news page, or a page with sports results, you can use the button to refresh the page and get the latest news results.

# 1.6 Forward and Back

You do not need to retype the web address of a website if you want to revisit it. *Internet Explorer* has two buttons that help you *navigate* the Internet.

Click

The web page you previously viewed will be opened.

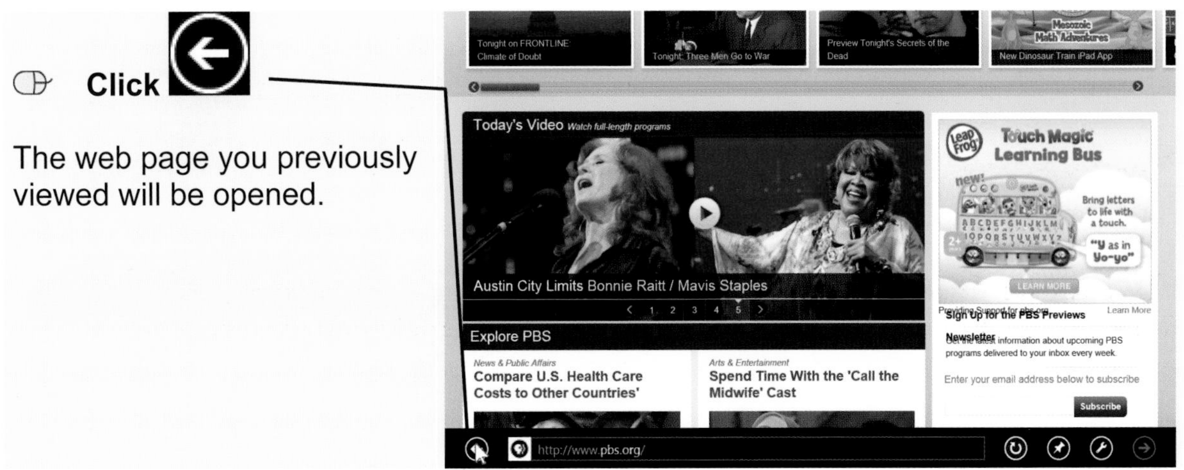

What you see now is the website where search provider *Bing* was helping you:

Perhaps you noticed how quickly this is done. *Internet Explorer* retains the websites you recently visited in its memory so that you can quickly look at them again without the need of sending the information to your computer again.

**Click** [back button] **two more times**

You will go back to the website you first visited.

Once again, the home page is displayed:

Now you can no longer browse backward. That is because this was the first website you opened.

The [back button] button is no longer active, the button is grey instead of white:

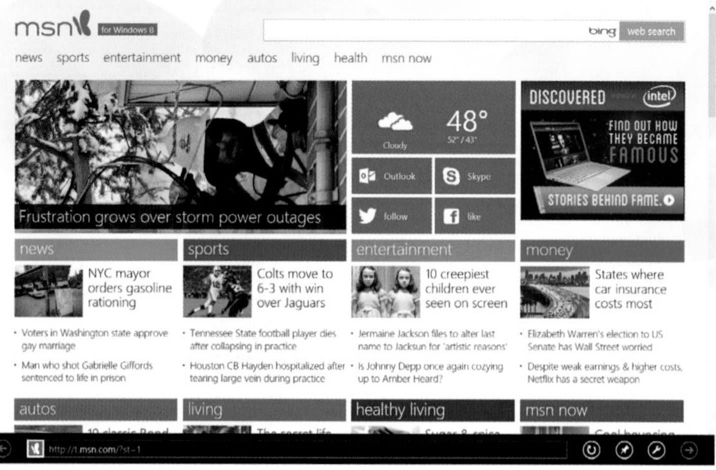

You can also leaf through the pages in the opposite direction. To do this, you use the button on the right-hand side of the screen:

Click

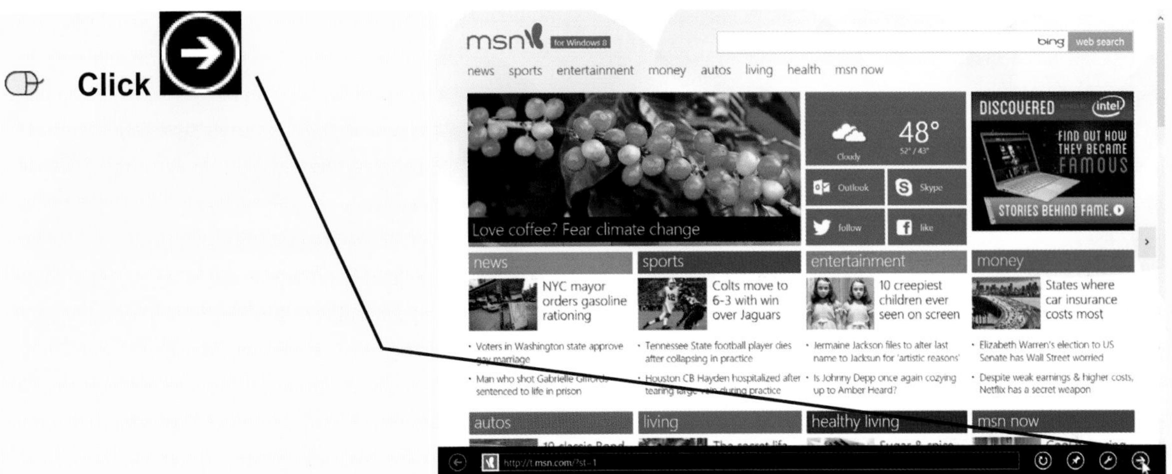


Now you see the same Visual Steps website on the screen as you did before:

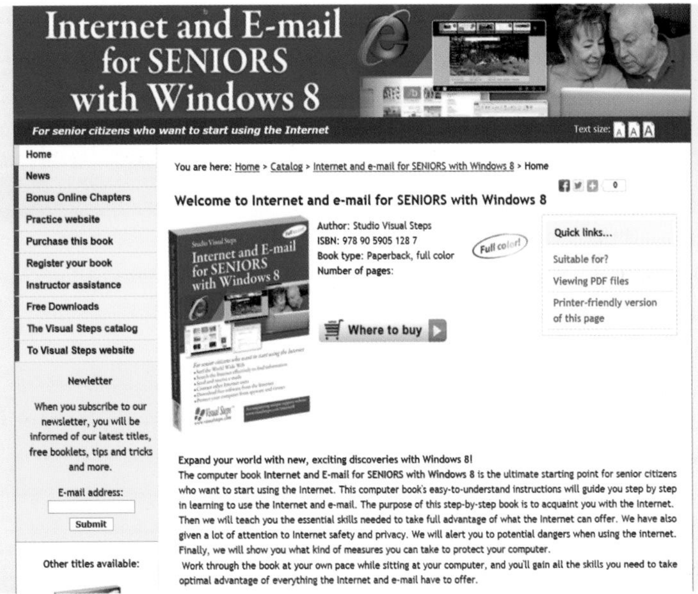


As you have seen, the buttons and can easily be used to switch back and forth between the websites you have viewed. This is called "surfing" the Internet.

## Tip

**Other buttons**

When you move the pointer to the side of the screen, you can also use < and > to go back and forward.

## 1.7 Browsing by Clicking

Almost every website will have a navigation list, a sort of *table of contents* summarizing the subjects you can find on the site. This website has one too. You can see the subjects in a column on the left-hand side. By clicking on one of the subjects, you can go to another page:

At the left-hand side of the screen:

**Place the pointer on**

**Practice website**

You see the pointer turn into a hand:

The color of the button will change too.

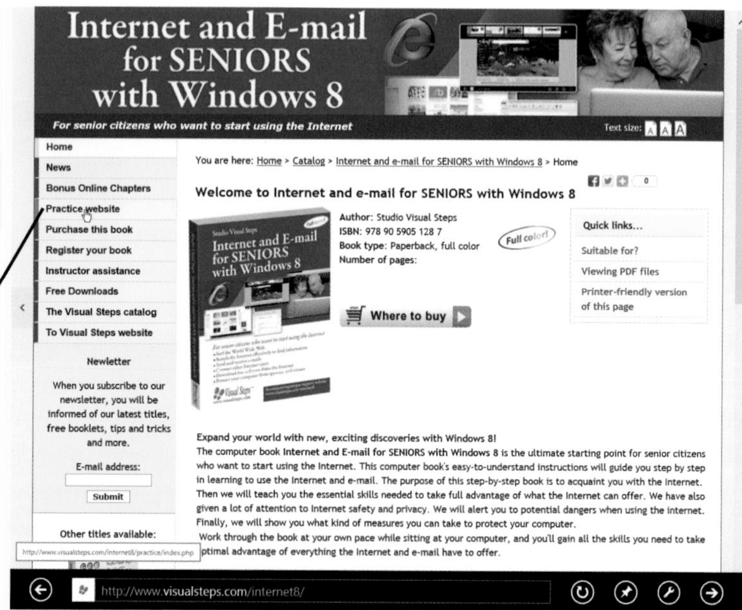


You can click anywhere on a web page where you see the little hand appear. Not only buttons, but also bits of text or images may be 'clickable'.

**Click**

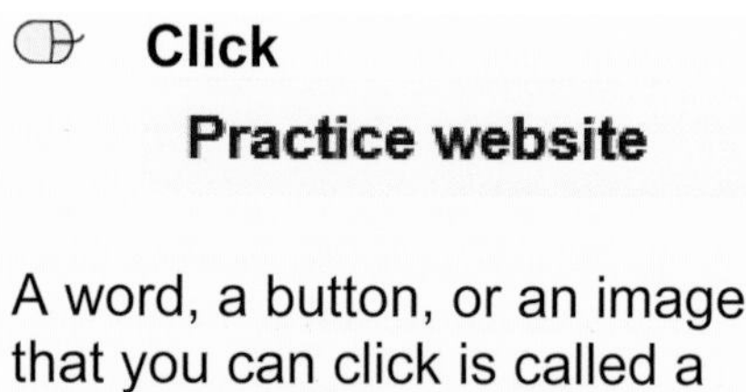


A word, a button, or an image that you can click is called a *link*. Sometimes the word *hyperlink* is used.

The practice website for this book is opened:

On this page you see various buttons that link to other pages:

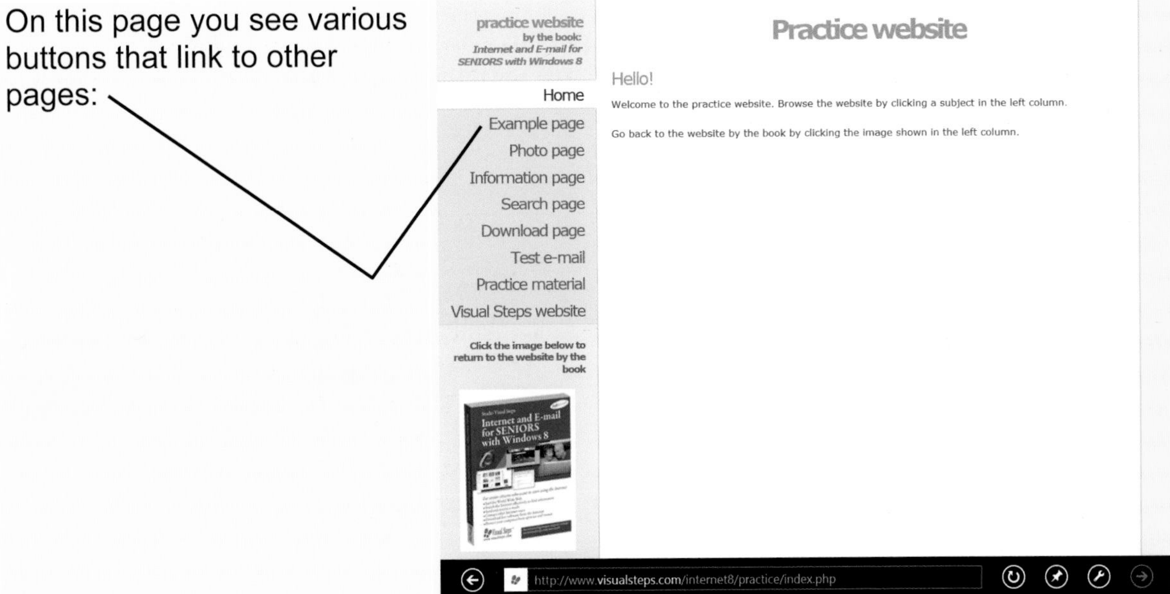


You are going to open another page:

- **Click** Example page

The new page will open:

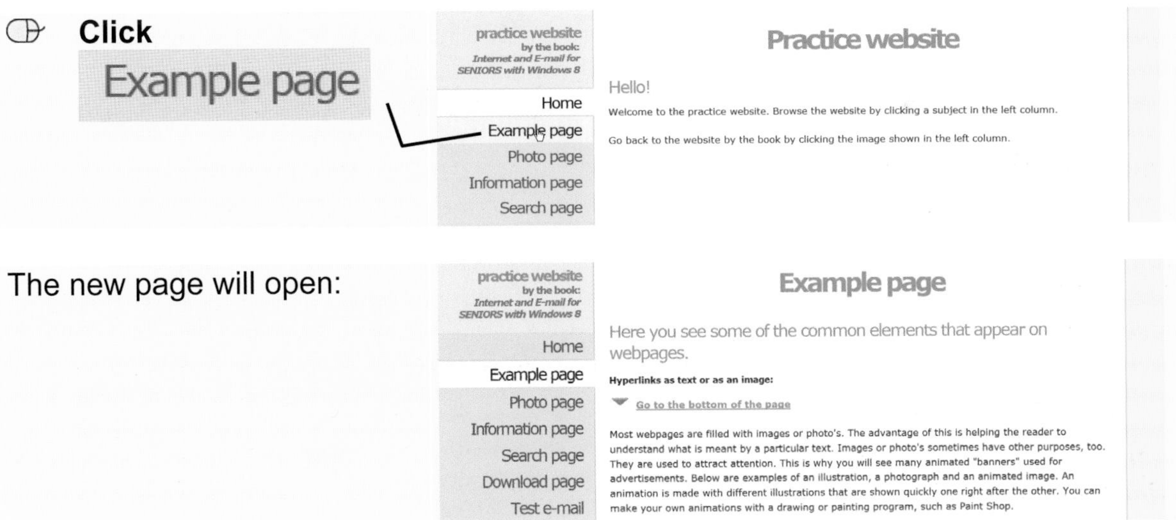


In this example, you can see that the lower part of the page is not in view. To read that part, you need to use the scroll bar on the right side of the screen. You will learn how to do that in the next section.

# 1.8 Using the Scroll Bars

In order to see the rest of the page, you must use the vertical scroll bar.
By dragging with the mouse, you can move the slidable part of the scroll bar. Give it a try:

At the right-hand side of the screen:

**Drag the scroll bar downwards**

The page slides in the opposite direction. Now you can read the bottom part of the text:

**Drag the scroll bar upwards**

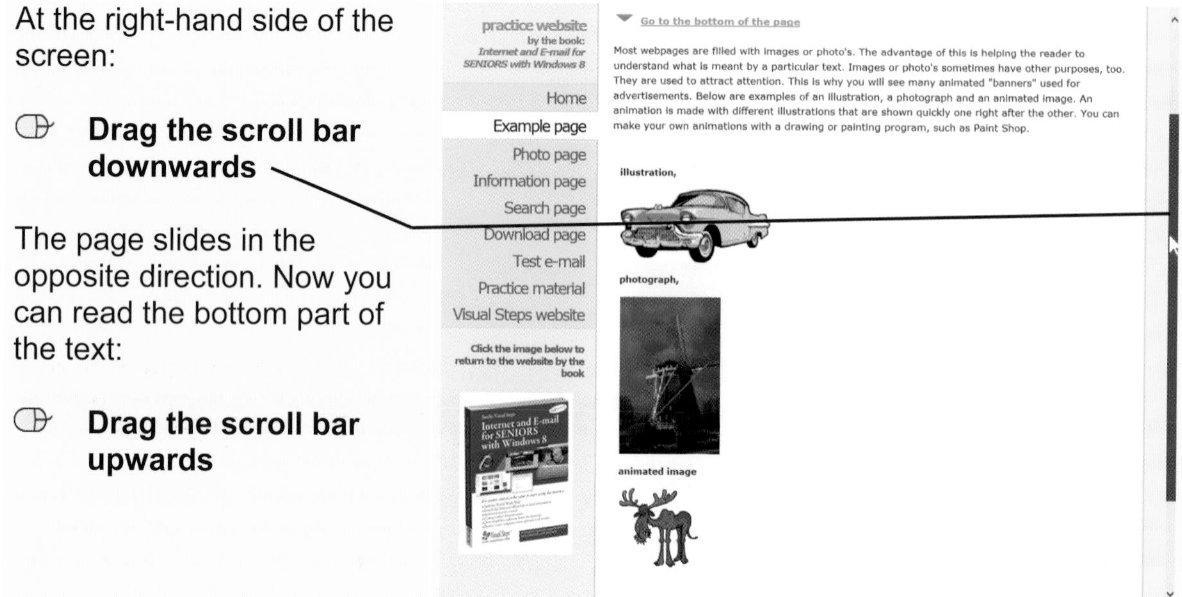


Sliding a window this way is called *scrolling* in computer language.

## Tip

**The scroll wheel**

If you have a mouse with a scroll wheel, you can easily scroll through a web page.
By turning the wheel with your finger, the contents of the window will scroll.
To scroll down, roll the wheel backwards (toward you). To scroll up, roll the wheel forwards (away from you).

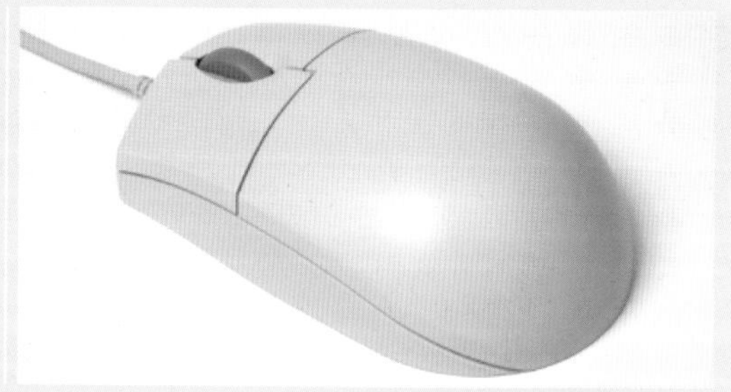

If you have a scroll wheel:

**Place the pointer on the web page**
**Turn the wheel forwards and backwards with your index finger**
**Stop turning when the scroll bar has reached the top of the bar**

A good website is made in such a way that you can easily move from one page to the next without getting lost. Most websites, for example, have a button marked *Home* or *Start* that will return you to the website's *home page*, when clicked.

**Click** Home

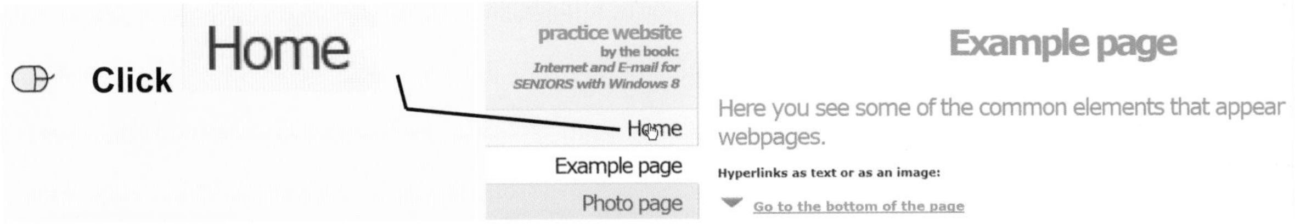


You see the opening page for the practice website for this book:

## 1.9 Browsing with Tabs

The so-called 'tabbed browsing' feature lets you open web pages on new tabs, and switch back and forth between these web pages by simply clicking the tabs. In this section you will learn how to do so. First, you will open the website of Visual Steps, the publisher of this book:

**Click the address bar**

**Type:** `www.visualsteps.com`

**Press** Enter

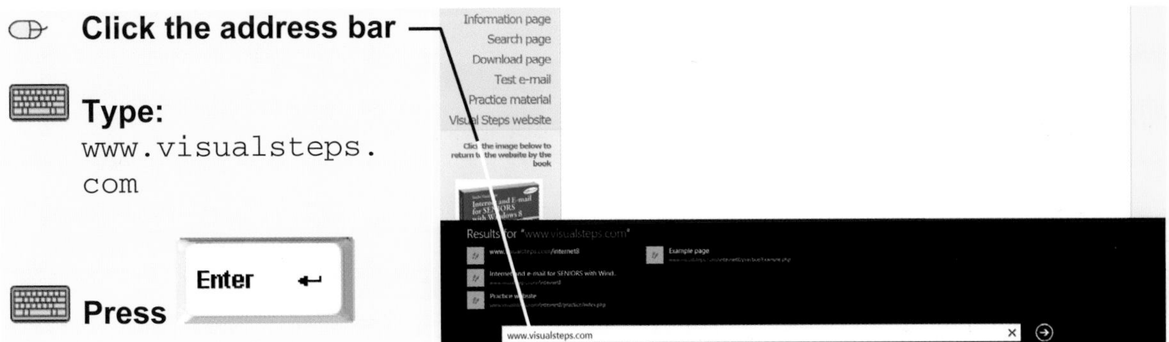


You open the tabbed menu:

**Right-click an empty area on the web page**

You will see a menu:

**Click** ⊕

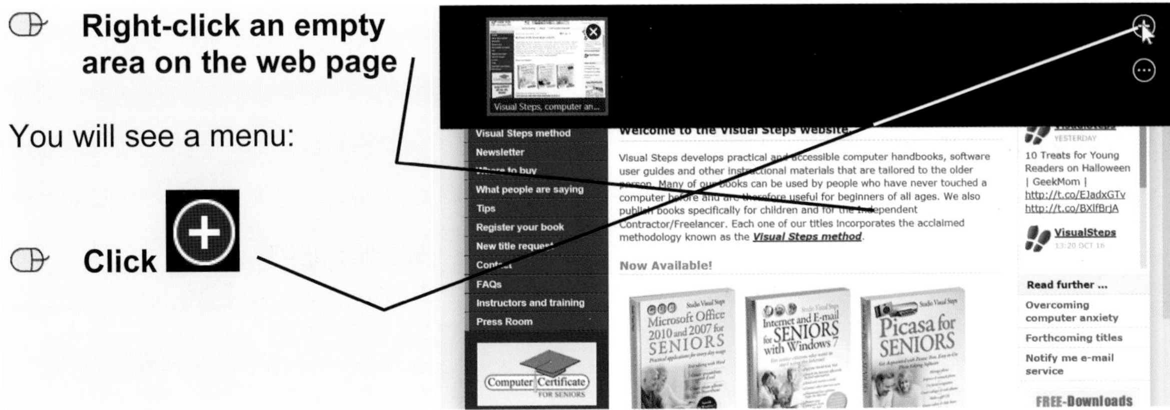

Now you will see a new, blank tab. On this tab you are going to open a website you have previously visited:

**Click a frequent web page, for example**

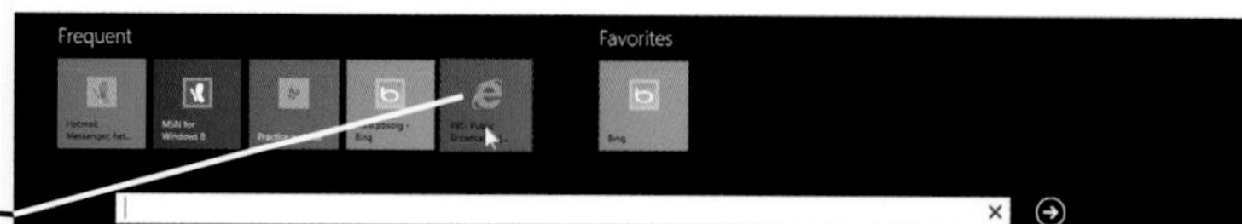


Of course, you can also type a web address in the address bar.

The PBS website will appear on this tab:

In the *Internet Explorer* app, you can not see directly which tabs you have opened. To view them, you need to open the tabbed menu:

**Right-click an empty area on the web page**

You will see both opened tabs:

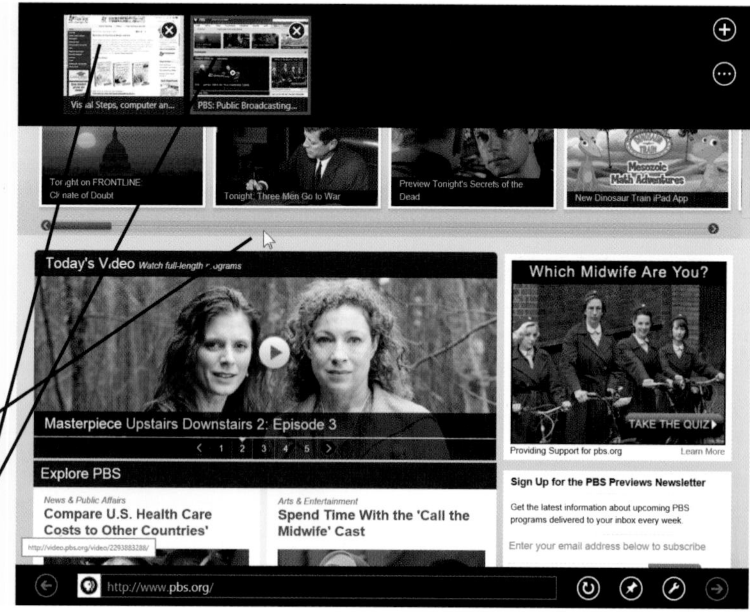


To switch to the other tab:

**Click**

To close a tab:

**Right-click an empty area on the web page**

**By** Visual Steps, computer an..., **click** ⊗

## 1.10 Switching Between Open Apps

Your computer can perform multiple tasks at once, it can multitask. For instance, you can stop surfing the net for a while, to check your e-mail with another app, or view the weather forecast. It is very easy to switch between the apps you have opened. You are going to try it. First, you need to return to the Start screen. To do this, you use the hidden button:

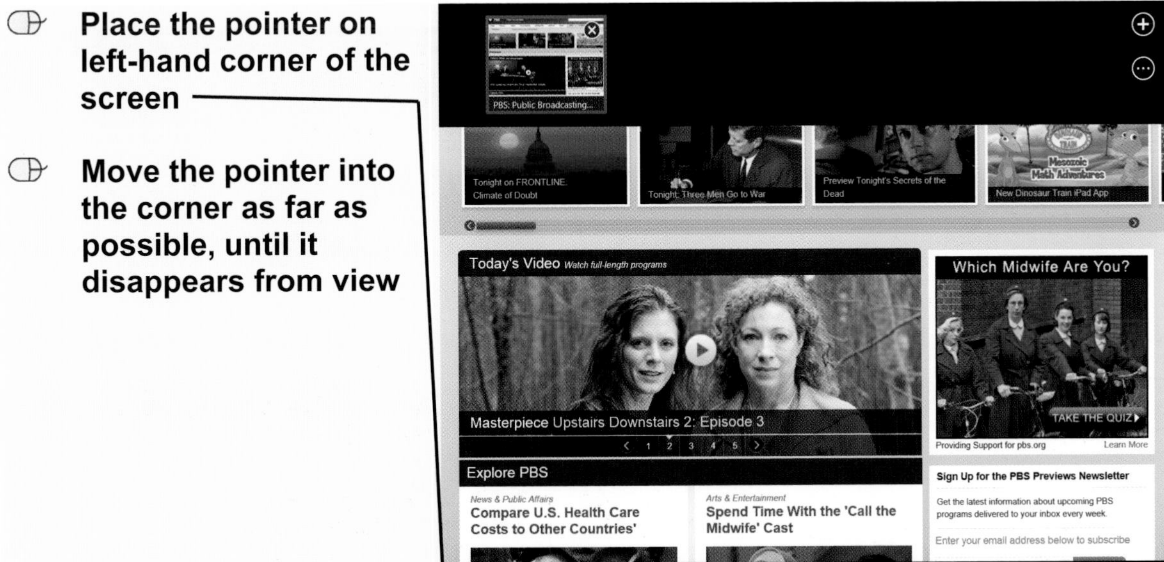


**Place the pointer on left-hand corner of the screen**

**Move the pointer into the corner as far as possible, until it disappears from view**

When you see the Start button:

Click Start

You see the Start screen. You are going to open the *News* app, an app with which you can display the news items from the sources you have selected:

Click News

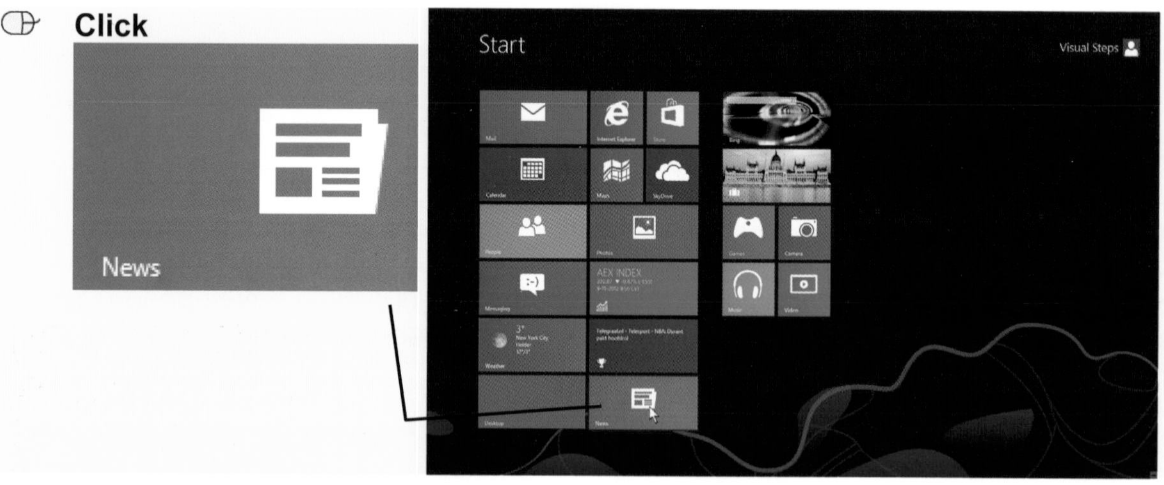


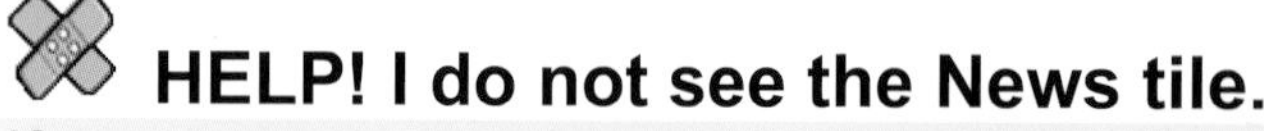

## HELP! I do not see the News tile.

If you do not see an app, you can open it from the apps screen.

**Right-click an empty area on the Start screen**

**Click**  All apps

**Click the app**

You will see a news site:

You can use the scroll bar at the bottom of the screen to view more messages:

If you click a message, the corresponding article will be opened.

On the website for this book, you can read more information about the *News* app in the *Bonus Chapter Other Useful Internet Apps*.

**Go back to the Start screen** 3

Now you open the *Weather* app:

**Click**

**Please note:** this tile can look different on your screen. Anyhow, the left side of the tile will have the name *Weather* on it.

You may see this screen:

Click **Allow**

Now you see the *Weather* app:

The *News* and *Internet Explorer* apps are still active in the background.

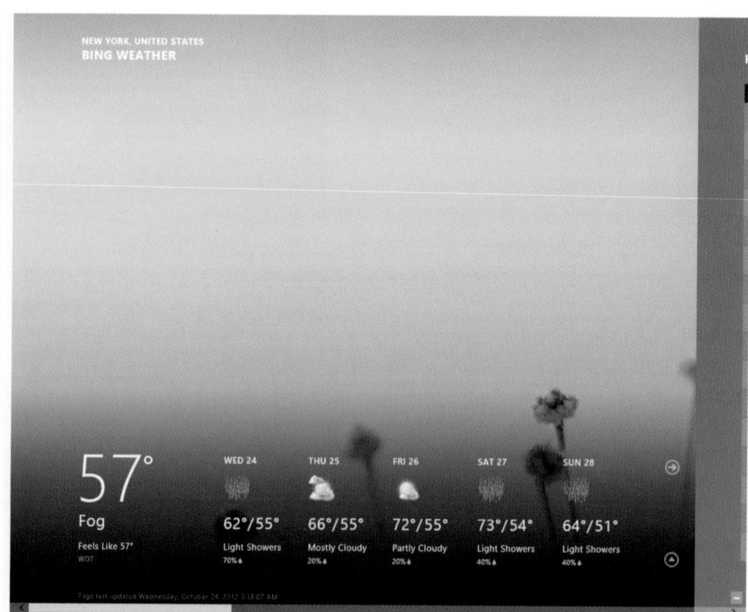


This is how you can see which apps are opened:

**Place the pointer on the upper left-hand corner**

You will see a miniature image of the app you have previously used:

**Move the pointer downwards, along the border of the screen**

A bar appears, displaying all the open apps:

This is called the switch list.

This is how you go back to the *Internet Explorer* app:

**Click**

You will see the *Internet Explorer* app again.

# 1.11 Closing Apps

The other apps will remain active in the background. This is not a problem, since they hardly use any computer capacity. In other words: you will not notice these apps being active. When you re-open an app that was already open, you can continue working where you previously left off. If you want to close the apps altogether:

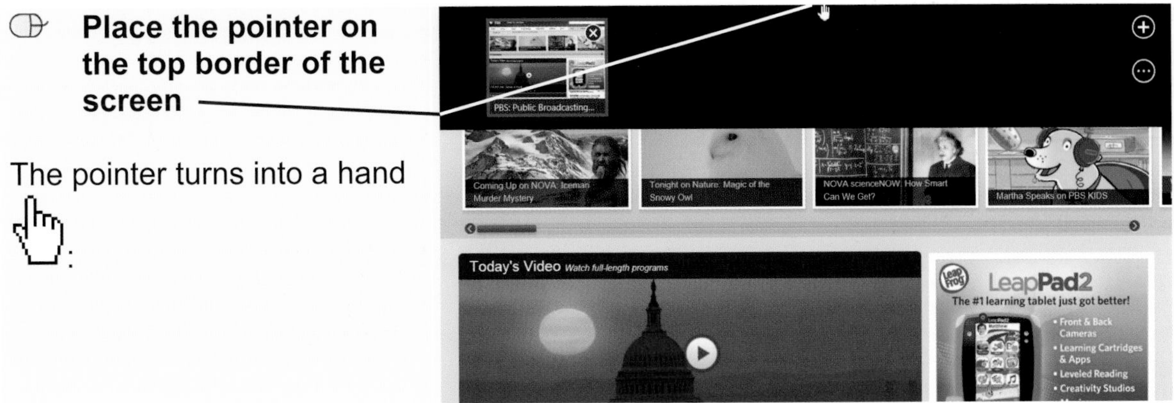


**Place the pointer on the top border of the screen**

The pointer turns into a hand:

**Drag the border of the screen downwards**

You will see that the app is diminished:

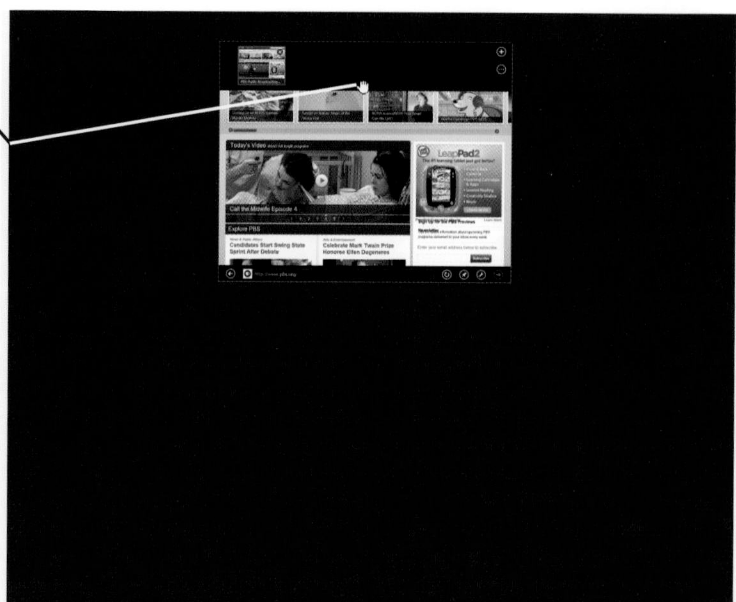

**Drag the app to the bottom of the screen**

The app will diminish even further:

**Release the mouse button**

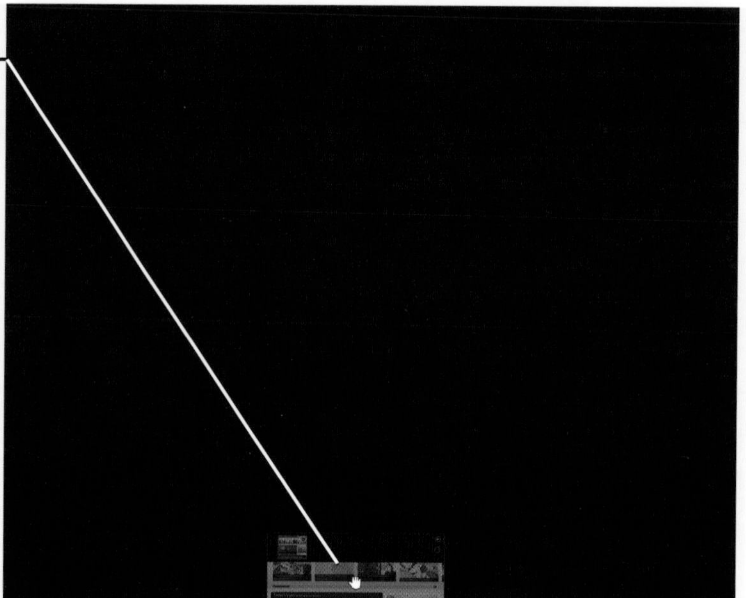

The app has been closed. You will see the Start screen again. You are going to do the same thing with the other apps:

**Open the *Weather* app with the switch list** 55

**Close the *Weather* app** 5

You can close the *News* app too:

☞ **Open the *News* app with the switch list** 👣55

☞ **Close the *News* app** 👣5

Now all apps have been closed.

In this chapter you have learned to work with the *Internet Explorer* app. There is also a more advanced version of *Internet Explorer* available which offers many more features. You can open it from the desktop. In the next chapter you will learn more about this program.

## 1.12 Exercises

The following exercises will help you master what you have just learned. Have you forgotten how to do something? Use the number beside the footsteps 1 to look it up in the appendix *How Do I Do That Again*?

## Exercise 1: Surfing

Going from one website to another is called surfing. In this exercise, you will surf to websites you previously visited.

- Open the *Internet Explorer* app. 4
- Open the web page www.visualsteps.com 1
- Open the web page www.visualsteps.com/internet8 1
- Open the web page www.pbs.org 1
- Go back to the web page www.visualsteps.com/internet8 6
- Go back to the website www.visualsteps.com 6
- Go back to the Public Broadcasting Service website. 7

## Exercise 2: Switch Between Opened Apps

While you are working with an app you can easily switch to another app. The *Internet Explorer* app is still open:

- Go back to the Start screen. 3
- Open the *News* app. 4
- Go back to the Start screen. 3
- Open the *Weather* app. 4

- Go back to the Start screen. 3
- Open the *Internet Explorer* app. 4
- Open the *Weather* app with the switch list. 55
- Close the *Weather* app. 5
- Do the same thing with the *Internet Explorer* and *News* apps. 55, 5

## 1.13 Background Information

**Dictionary**

**ActiveX** A technology for creating interactive web content, such as animations.

**Address bar** The address bar is located at the bottom of the *Internet Explorer* app screen. The bar displays the web address of the web page you are currently viewing. By typing a new web address and pressing the Enter key you can open the corresponding web page.

**ADSL** Asynchronous Digital Subscriber Line. A fast Internet connection that uses the telephone network. This type of connection is also called a broadband connection.

**App** Short for application, a program on the computer.

**Back button** With the Back button you go back to the previous web page.

**Broadband connection** A high speed Internet connection. Broadband connections are typically 256 kilobytes per second (KBps) or faster. Broadband includes DSL and cable modem service.

**Browser, Web browser** A program used to display web pages and to navigate the Internet. *Internet Explorer* is a web browser.

**Download** Retrieving a file from the Internet and storing it on your computer. For instance, a computer program, movie, or music.

**Hyperlink, Link** A hyperlink or link is a navigational element in a web page that automatically displays the referred information when the user clicks the hyperlink. A hyperlink can be text or images like buttons, icons or pictures. You can recognize a hyperlink when the pointer turns into a hand.

*- Continue on the next page -*

**Internet** A network of computer networks which operates worldwide using a common set of communications protocols. The part of the Internet that most people are familiar with is the World Wide Web (WWW). Also called web.

**Internet Explorer** App and program used to browse the Internet. The desktop version has more advanced features than the app.

**ISP** An Internet Service Provider (ISP) is a company that provides you with access to the Internet, usually for a fee. The most common ways to connect to an ISP is by using a broadband connection (cable or DSL). Many ISPs provide additional services such as e-mail accounts, virtual hosting, and space for you to create a website.

**Lock screen** The first screen you see when you turn your computer on. You unlock the screen by clicking it or pressing the spacebar. Then you enter you password to login.

**Login** By logging in, you gain entry to your user account, apps and programs, for example in *Windows*. This often requires a user name and password.

**Next button** With the Next button you can continue to the web page you have visited after the web page currently on your screen.

**Password** A string of characters that a user must enter to gain access to a resource that is password protected. Passwords help ensure that unauthorized users do not access your Internet connection or your computer.

**Refreshing** Reloading a web page.

**Scroll** Sliding along the content of a web page by using the mouse's scroll wheel.

**Start screen** The welcome screen in *Windows 8*. In this screen, the apps and programs installed to your computer are represented by a number of colored tiles.

**Surfing** Displaying one web page after the other by clicking various hyperlinks.

**Tab** Part of the *Internet Explorer* window/screen on which you can open a new website or web page.

*- Continue on the next page -*

| | |
|---|---|
| **Tabbed browsing** | The *Tabbed browsing* function lets you open multiple websites within a single *Internet Explorer* window/screen. You can open web pages on new tabs, and switch between them. |
| **Tile** | You use the tiles on the Start screen to launch your apps and programs. |
| **User name** | The name you use to log on. |
| **Web address** | The web address of a website uniquely identifies a location on the Internet. A web address is also called an URL (Uniform Resource Locator). An example of a web address is: **http://www.visualsteps.com**. |
| **Web page** | A web page is a resource of information that is suitable for the World Wide Web and can be accessed through a browser. |
| **Website** | A website is a collection of interconnected web pages, typically common to a particular domain name on the World Wide Web on the Internet. |
| **WWW** | World Wide Web - web of computers, connected to each other - containing an infinite amount of web pages. |
| **Zooming** | Enlarging or diminishing a web page. Zooming will enlarge or diminish everything on a page, including text and images. |

*Source: Windows Help and Support*

**Domain names**

A web address associated with a particular name is called a domain name. Every web address has a suffix such as **.com**.

For example: www.visualsteps**.com**

There are several variations on this suffix. In Europe, a country code is often used: The suffix **.nl** is used in the Netherlands.
Other country codes include **.be** for Belgium, **.de** for Germany, and **.uk** for the United Kingdom.
In the United States, a different system is also used. The suffix indicates the type of organization:

| | |
|---|---|
| **.com** | commercial company |
| **.edu** | educational institution |
| **.org** | non-profit organization |

**The modem**

It is easy to understand why the telephone network is used to connect computers that may be thousands of miles apart. After all, almost everyone has a telephone line nowadays. Cable TV providers have also entered the Internet market, using the cable network for Internet connections.

You need a special device to connect to the Internet through a telephone line or a cable connection: the *modem*. A modem makes it possible for your computer to communicate with your ISP's computer. There are two kinds of modems. External modems and internal modems.

The first is a separate box that is connected to your computer with a cable. This is called an *external modem.*

Another cable connects the modem to the outlet for the telephone line or the cable TV connection.

*External modem*

Almost all new computers have a built-in modem. This is called an *internal modem*. The only part of this modem visible to you is a plug for a telephone cable or for a cable connection. These may be found in the back of your desktop computer or on the side of your laptop.

*Internal modem*

In case of an ADSL connection, the modem is connected to the telephone network through a so-called splitter. A cable modem is connected to the cable network of a radio/TV network provider.

A modem can also be connected to a router that will establish a wireless connection. These days there are many modems available with a built-in router.

**How does the WWW work**
The *World Wide Web* (WWW) is one of the most recent and also one of the most popular Internet applications. The idea for such a web was first developed in 1989, by Tim Berners Lee and Robert Cailliau at CERN (the European research centre for nuclear research) in Geneva, Switzerland.

The information on the WWW is displayed in the shape of *hypermedia*. The word hypermedia is derived from hypertext. A *hypertext* is text that contains *hyperlinks*. These hyperlinks refer to the address of a different web page.

By clicking a hyperlink you execute a command to open this other web page on the web. Such a page may be located on any other computer connected to the Internet, even at the other end of the world. Words can be used as a hyperlink, but drawings and photos too. Usually, web pages do not only contain text, but also images, sounds, and animated images (*multimedia*). That is why nowadays we call it *hypermedia*. A contraction of the words *hyper*tekst and multi*media*.

How can the Internet system always find the right page? The WWW consists of millions of pages. Each page has a unique web address, called a *URL* (Uniform Resource Allocator).

An example of a URL is: **http://www.visualsteps.com**
This is the meaning of the URL:

| | |
|---|---|
| http | HyperText Transfer Protocol |
| www | World Wide Web |
| visualsteps | The domain name or brand name of the organization |
| com | This means it is a website owned by a business company |

The URL tells your provider's computer on which computer the website can be found. To enable different computers to communicate with each other, each computer receives a unique address, the *Internet Protocol Number* (IP number or IP address). In everyday life you will not use this IP number. Instead, you will use the URL, for example, **www.visualsteps.com**. When computers communicate with each other, this name will automatically be converted into the IP address, which consists of digits. You will see these digits appear sometimes, at the bottom of the *Internet Explorer* window.

# 1.14 Tips

**Tip**

**Add a website to the Start screen**

You can also add your favorite website to the Start screen, as a tile. In this way you can quickly open your favorite website.

**Open the web page www.visualsteps.com** 1

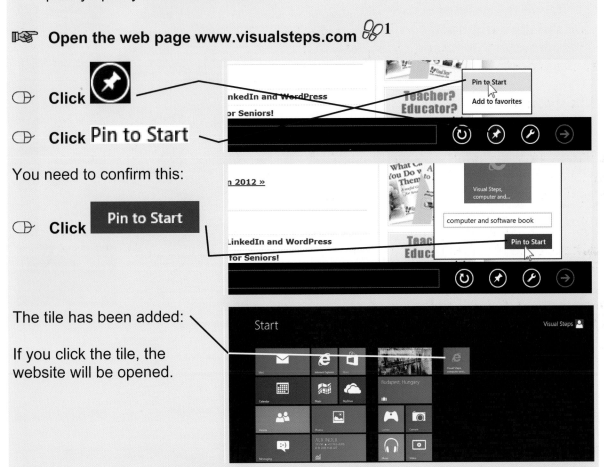

**Click**

**Click** Pin to Start

You need to confirm this:

**Click** Pin to Start

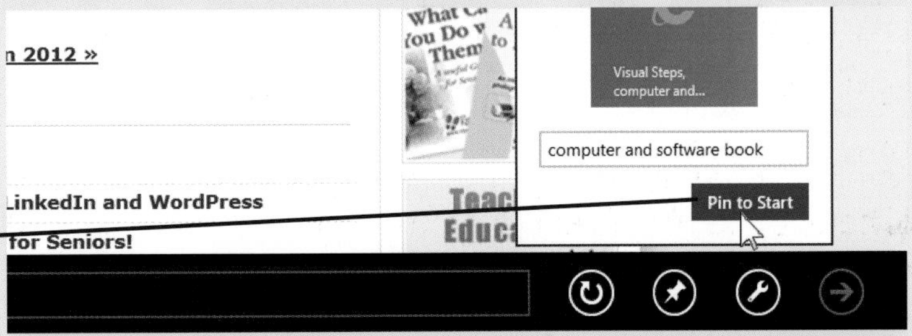

The tile has been added:

If you click the tile, the website will be opened.

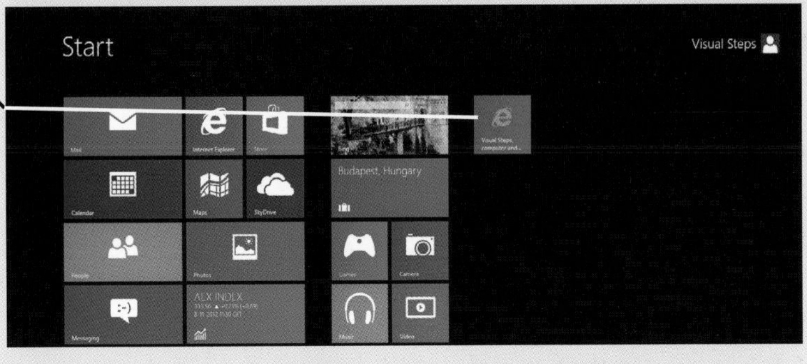

**Please note:** if you have added the website from the *Internet Explorer* app, the website will also be opened in this. If you have added the website from the *Internet Explorer* program on the desktop, as you will learn to do in the next chapter, the website will be opened in that program.

## Tip

### Zoom in on a web page

It is possible to zoom in on a web page. Zooming will enlarge or diminish a page, including the text and the images. You can zoom from 10% up to 1000%.

**Open the web page www.visualsteps.com** 1

**Move the pointer in the top-right hand corner of the screen, as far as possible**

When you see the charms bar:

**Click** 

**Click** 

By **Zoom** you will see bar on which you can regulate the zoom level:

**Click the desired zoom level**

You will see that the text and the images have become larger:

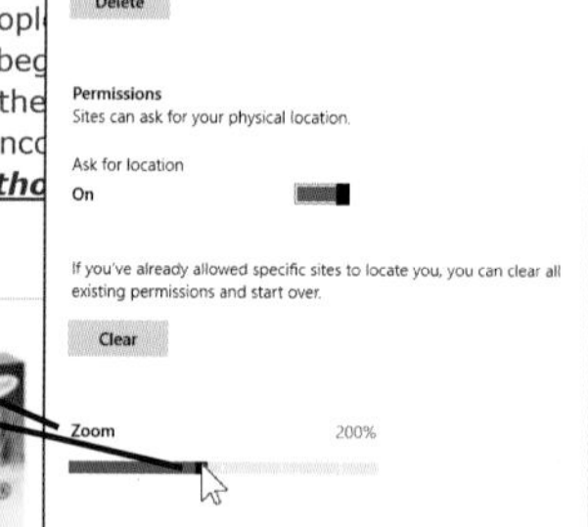


After you have set the desired zoom level:

**By** Internet Explorer Settings**, click**

**Click an empty area on the web page**

In *section 2.11 Zooming In and Out* you can read more about zooming in and out in *Internet Explorer* program.

# 2. Internet Explorer on the Desktop

In the previous chapter you have learned how to work with the *Internet Explorer* app. This app has only limited possibilities. If you open the *Internet Explorer* program on the desktop, you will have many more functions and options available. In this chapter you will learn how to use these functions. Besides surfing the Internet, you will also learn how to work with tabs, and zoom in and out on a web page.

In this chapter you will learn how to:

- open *Internet Explorer* on the desktop;
- use a web address;
- maximize and minimize a window;
- work with tabs;
- zoom in and zoom out on a web page;
- stop using the Internet.

## 2.1 Opening Internet Explorer

The *Internet Explorer* app is quite restricted in its options. The more extensive version of *Internet Explorer* on the desktop has many more options and functions to offer. In this chapter you will learn how to use these. First, you are going to check if you can open *Internet Explorer* on the desktop. This is how you do it:

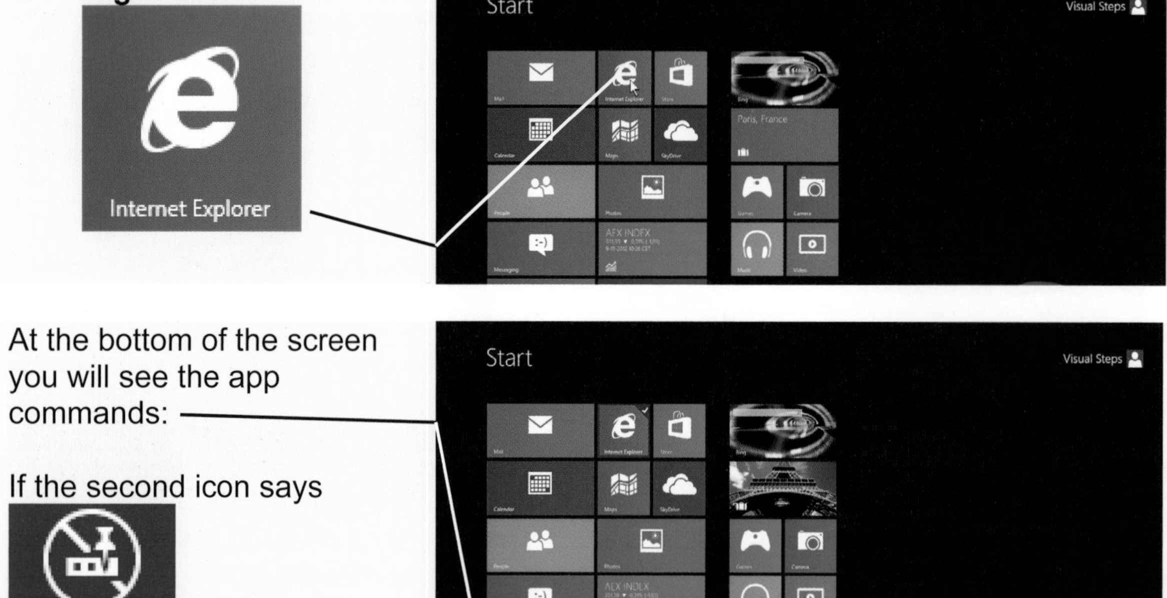

Right-click
Internet Explorer
Start
Visual Steps
At the bottom of the screen you will see the app commands:
If the second icon says
Unpin from taskbar
, you can continue on the next page.


If the second icon says Pin to taskbar, you do this:

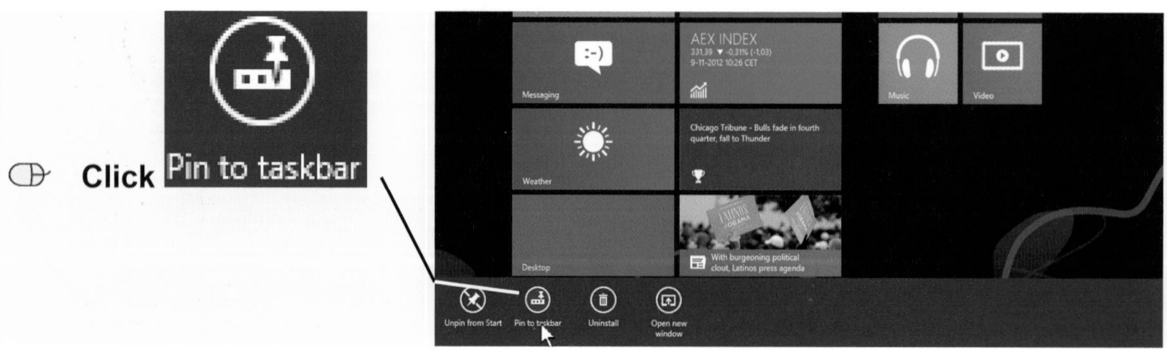

Now *Internet Explorer* has been pinned to the taskbar on the desktop. You are going to open the desktop from the Start screen and take a look at it:

**Click**

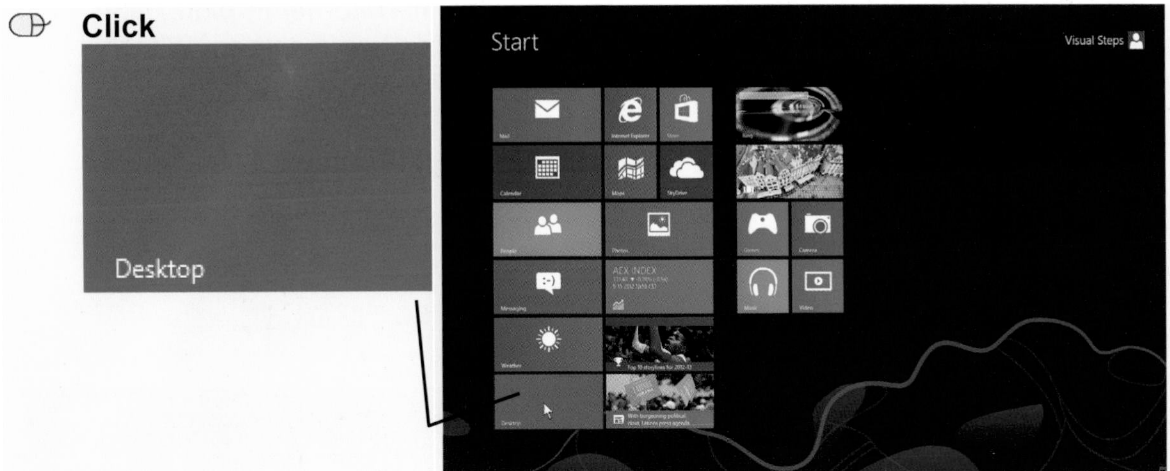


The desktop is opened. You can launch *Internet Explorer* from the button on the taskbar in the lower left of your screen:

**Click** 

If you are connected to the Internet, you will see the home page appear on the *Internet Explorer* window. Usually this is a *Microsoft* page, since this is the manufacturer of the *Internet Explorer* program:

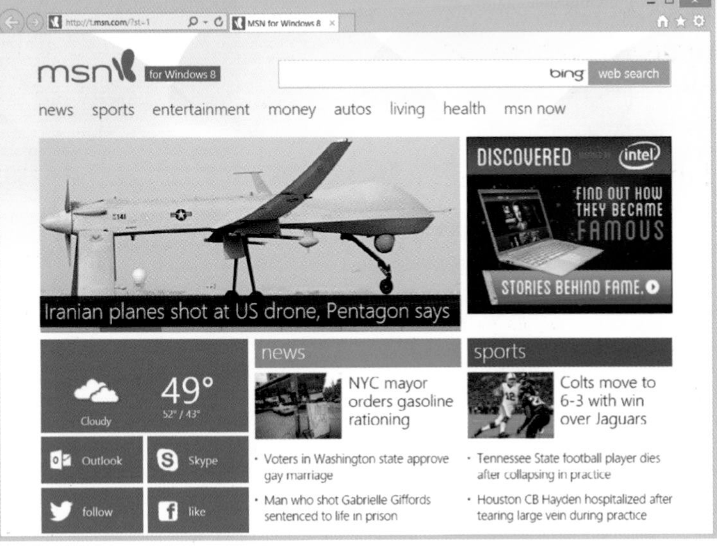

## 2.2 Typing a Web Address

In the previous chapter you have learned to work with the *Internet Explorer* app. In this app, you had to type the web address at the bottom of your screen. When *Internet Explorer* has been opened from the desktop, you need to enter the web address on the address bar at the top of the window. Try this with the website of the Visual Steps publishing company: **www.visualsteps.com**

**Click the address bar**

The web address http://t.msn.com/?st=1 will turn blue, which indicates it has been selected.

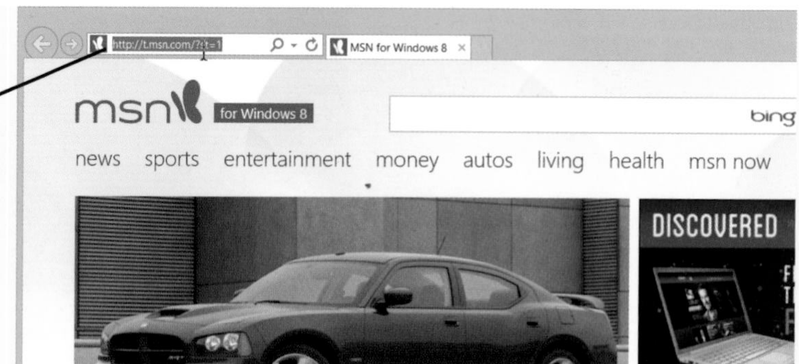


Type the web address in the address bar:

**Type:**
`www.visualsteps.com`

You will see a number of suggested sites based on the sites you have previously visited. You can read more about this feature later on in this book.

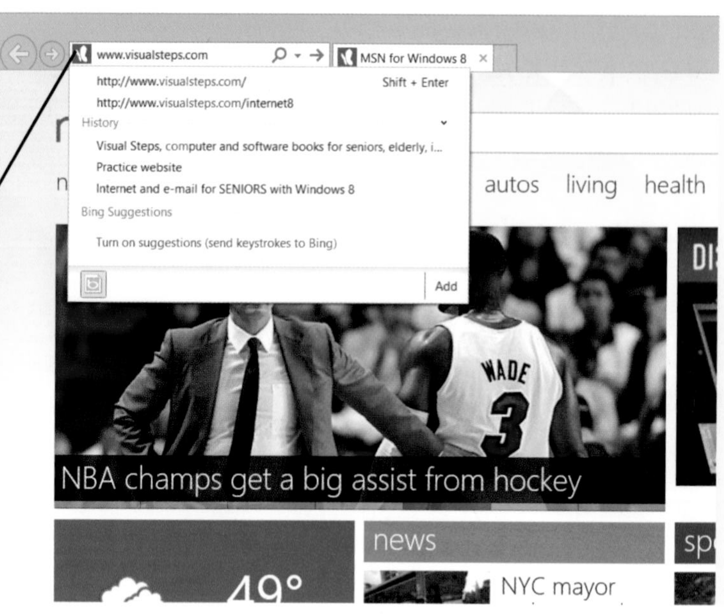


**Press**

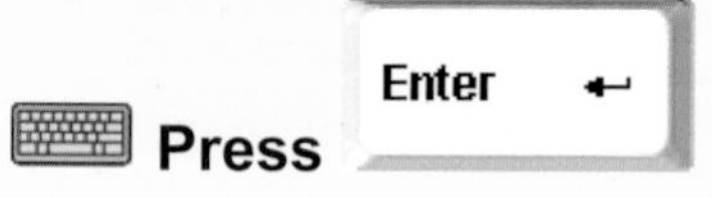

After a short while you will see again the home page of the Visual Steps website. On this page you find information on the other books published by Visual Steps, besides useful information:

This web page is regularly updated. The content of the page you see on your own window may differ from the image you see in this example.

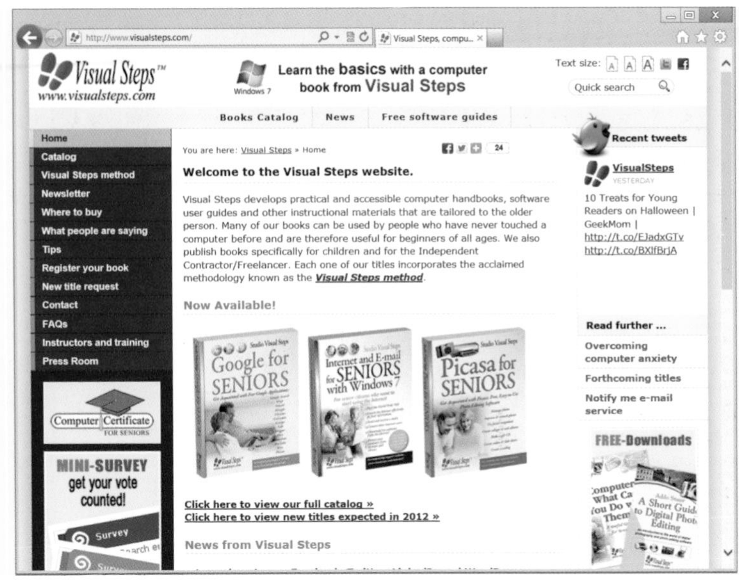


## 2.3 Maximizing the Window

You can maximize the *Internet Explorer* window, so it will fill the entire screen. This can be handy if you want to take a good look at the content of the web page. This is how you maximize a window:

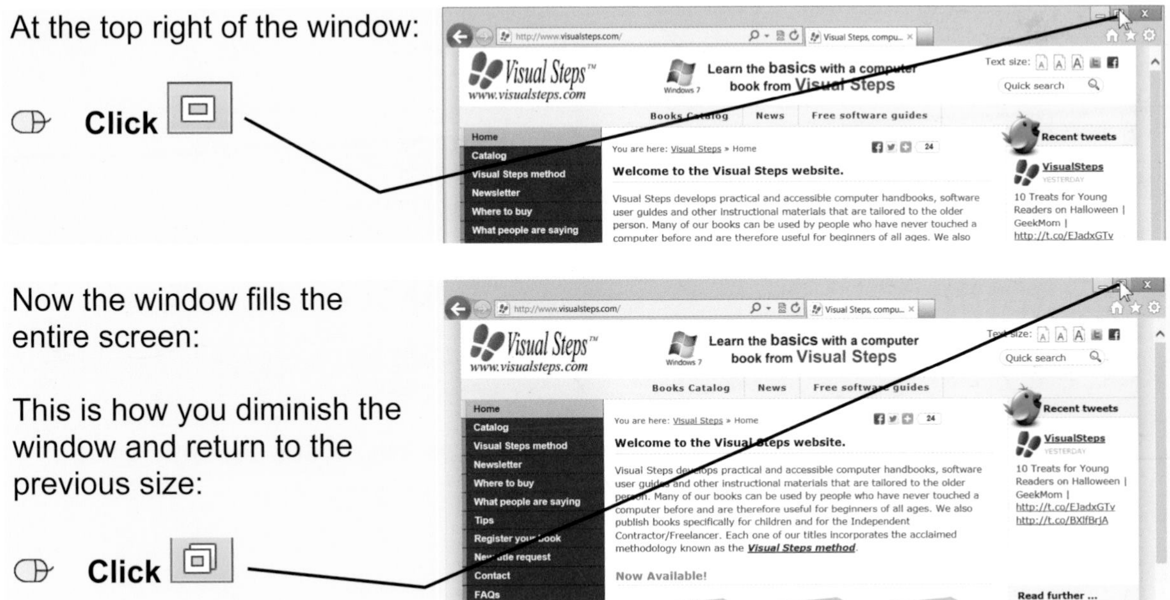

At the top right of the window:

Click

Now the window fills the entire screen:

This is how you diminish the window and return to the previous size:

Click

The window has regained its original size.

As you have already noticed, the *Internet Explorer* window looks different from the *Internet Explorer* app. For example, the address bar http://www.visualsteps.com/ is located at the top of the window. If the web page is not displayed correctly, you can let *Internet Explorer* reload the page by clicking the button.

With the buttons at the top left-hand side of the window you can easily leaf through the web pages you previously visited. This is called 'surfing' the Internet. In *Chapter 1 Surfing the Internet with the Internet Explorer App* you have learned how to leaf through web pages.

## 2.4 Browsing with Tabs

Just like in the *Internet Explorer* app, you can open more than one website in the same window. You start by opening a new, blank tab:

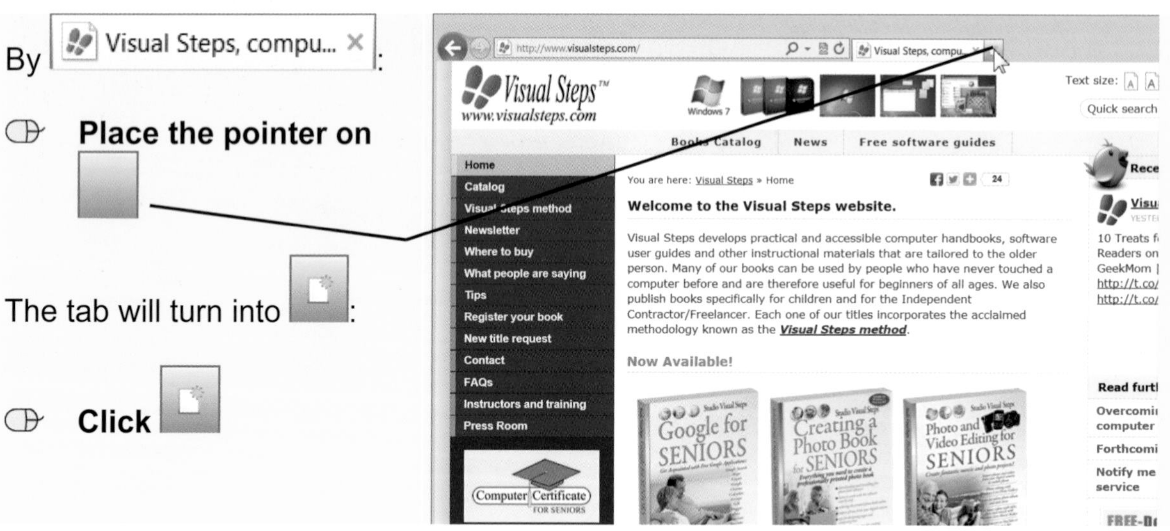

By Visual Steps, compu... :
Place the pointer on
The tab will turn into :
Click


On the new tab you see a web page with information on the most frequently visited websites. In this example you see various websites. Of course, on your own screen these may be different websites.

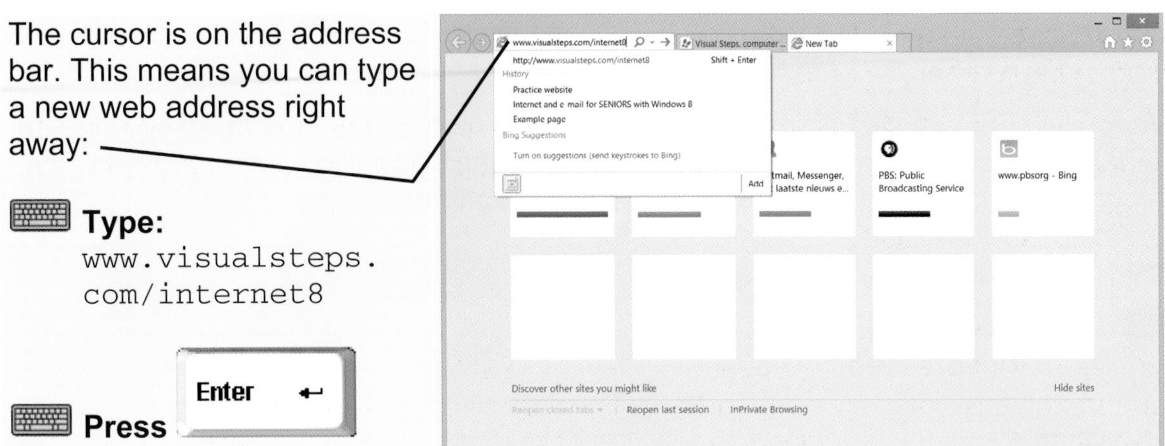


The cursor is on the address bar. This means you can type a new web address right away:

**Type:**
`www.visualsteps.com/internet8`

**Press** Enter

In *Chapter 1 Surfing the Internet with the Internet Explorer App* you have learned about hyperlinks. A hyperlink can be a clickable word, button, or an image on a web page. You are going to use such a link again.

Open the practice page:

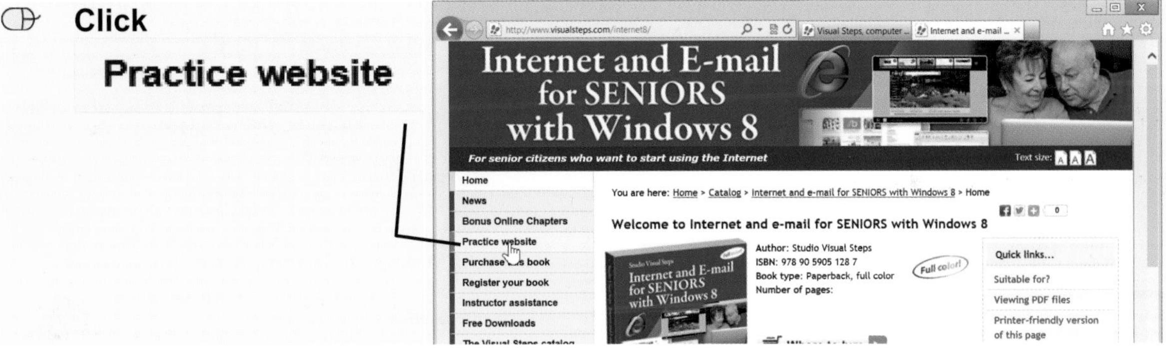


**Click** **Practice website**

The practice page opens in the same tab.

# 2.5 Opening a Link On a New Tab

When you click a hyperlink, the new web page will replace the previous web page on the tab you were viewing. *Internet Explorer* offers the possibility of directly opening a link on a new tab. Just try to open one of the links on this web page:

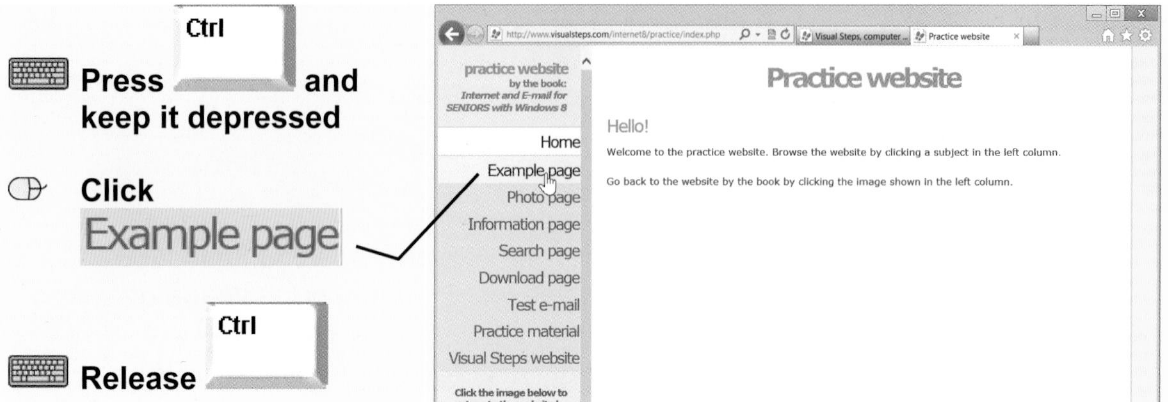


**Press** Ctrl **and keep it depressed**

**Click** Example page

**Release** Ctrl

The example page will be opened on a new tab. This tab is still hidden behind the second tab with the practice page. You open the third tab by clicking it:

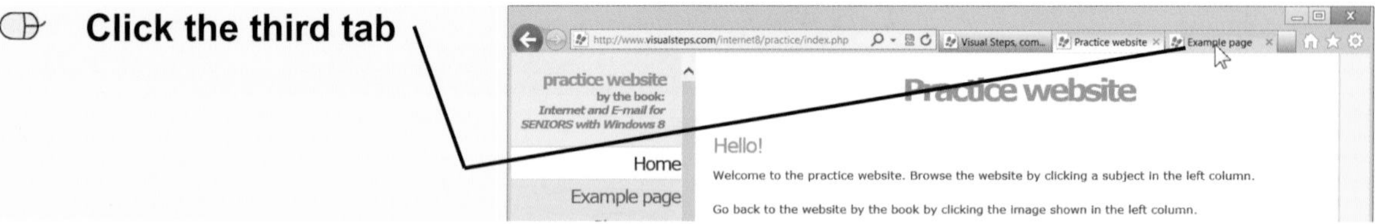


**Click the third tab**

You can see what is on the example page:

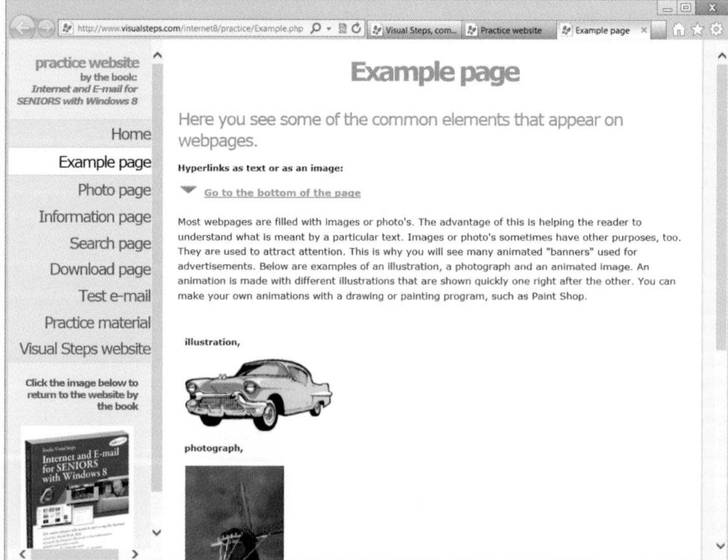

# 2.6 A Second Window

Until now you have viewed all the web pages on different tabs within a single window in *Internet Explorer*. But a website may also have been created in such a way that a new window is opened when you click a hyperlink. You cannot control this, because this has been programmed into the hyperlink, and it happens all by itself. The example page contains such a hyperlink too. Just try this:

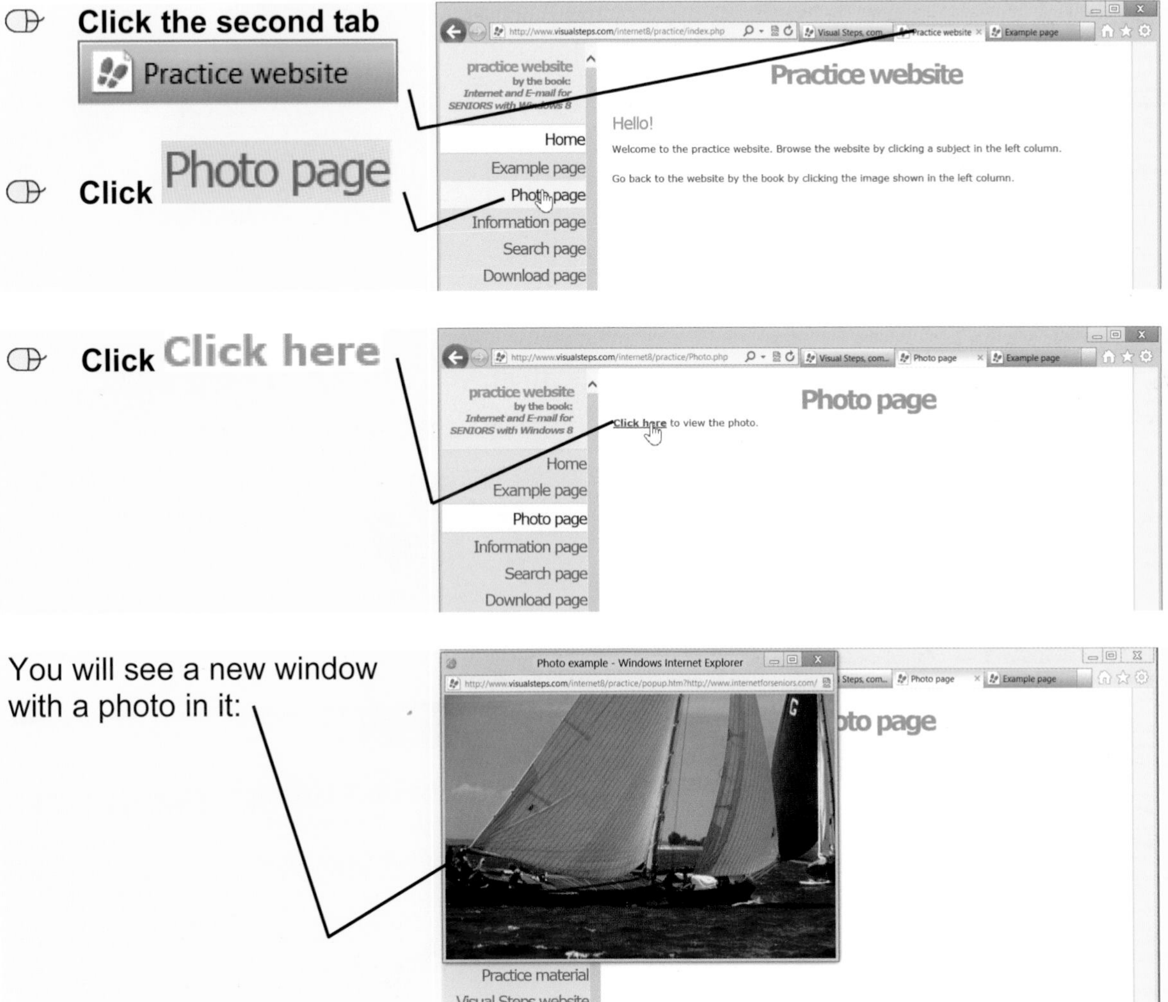


**Click the second tab**

**Click** Photo page

**Click** Click here

You will see a new window with a photo in it:

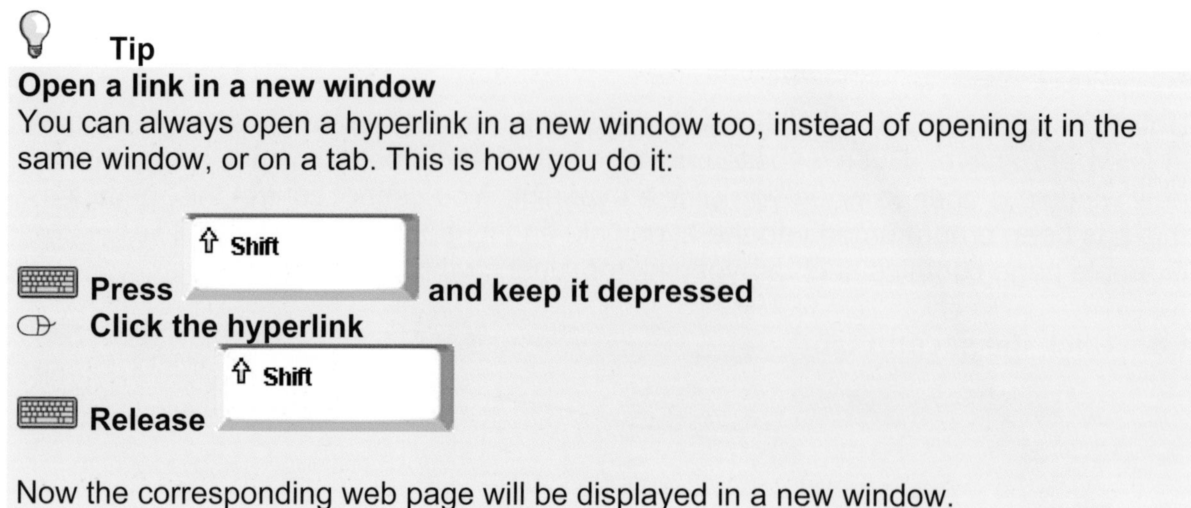

### Tip

**Open a link in a new window**

You can always open a hyperlink in a new window too, instead of opening it in the same window, or on a tab. This is how you do it:

**Press** ⇧ **Shift** **and keep it depressed**

**Click the hyperlink**

**Release** ⇧ **Shift**

Now the corresponding web page will be displayed in a new window.

## 2.7 Minimizing a Window

If you want to hang on to this web page for a while, you can diminish this new window. Diminishing a window is called *minimizing*.

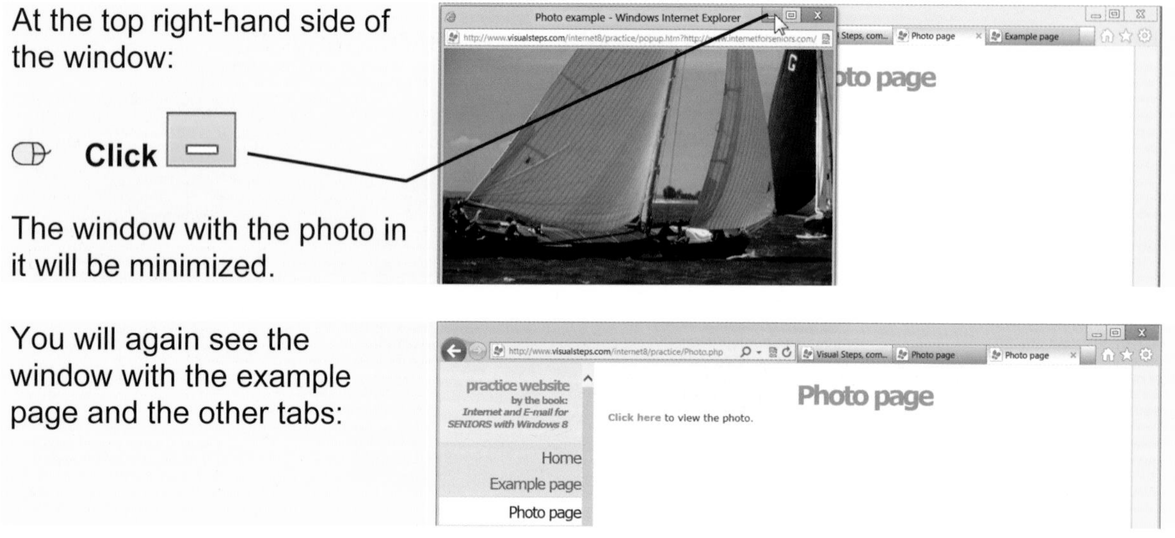


At the top right-hand side of the window:

**Click**

The window with the photo in it will be minimized.

You will again see the window with the example page and the other tabs:

You can minimize this window as well:

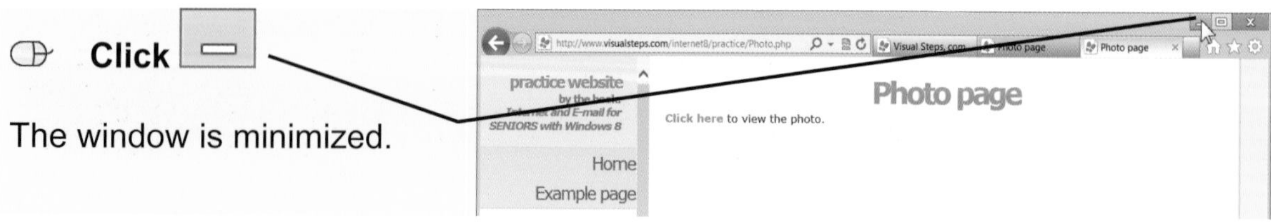


**Click**

The window is minimized.

Now you have minimized two windows. The window with the photo and the window with the practice page and the other tabs.

Both windows have been minimized:

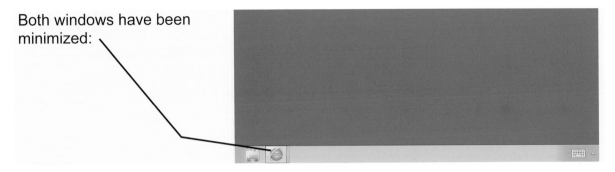

On the taskbar, down below, you will always see the buttons of the windows that are currently in use. In the example above you will find the minimized windows beneath the  button.

## 2.8 Opening a Minimized Window

With the buttons on the taskbar you can restore a minimized window:

On the taskbar:

**Place the pointer on**

You will see a miniature image of the windows appear above the taskbar:

**Click**

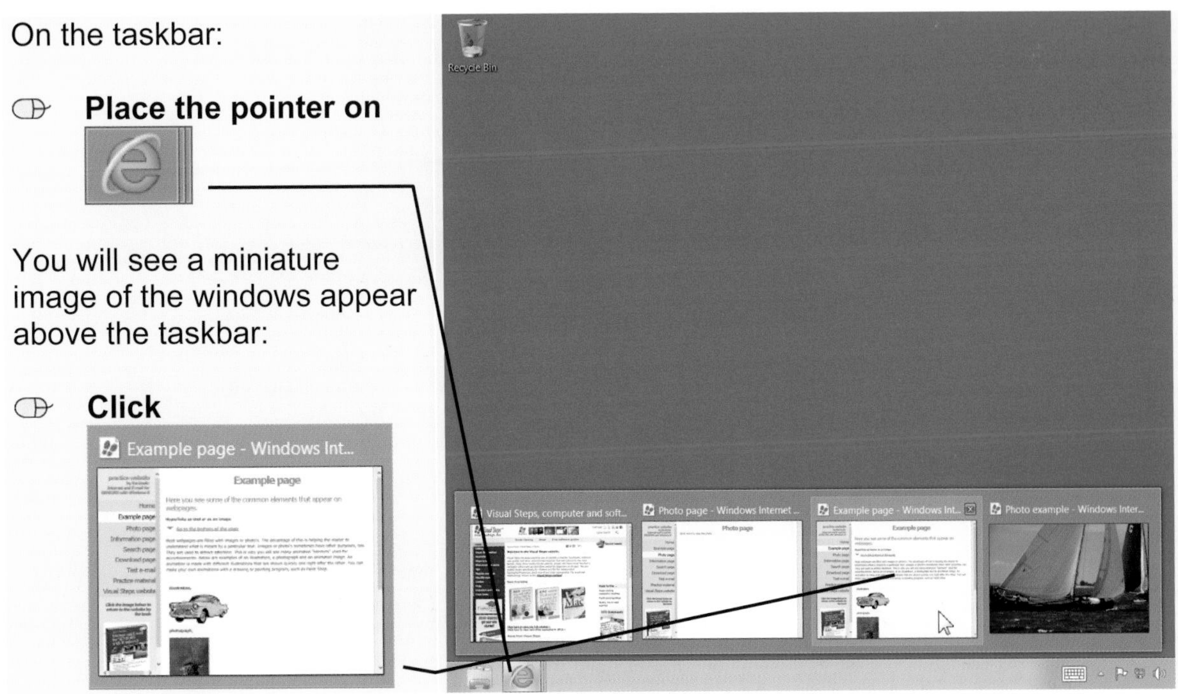

Now you will see the window with the example page again. In the same way, you can open the window with the photo in it:

**Place the pointer on**

The miniature images of the window will appear above the taskbar:

**Click**

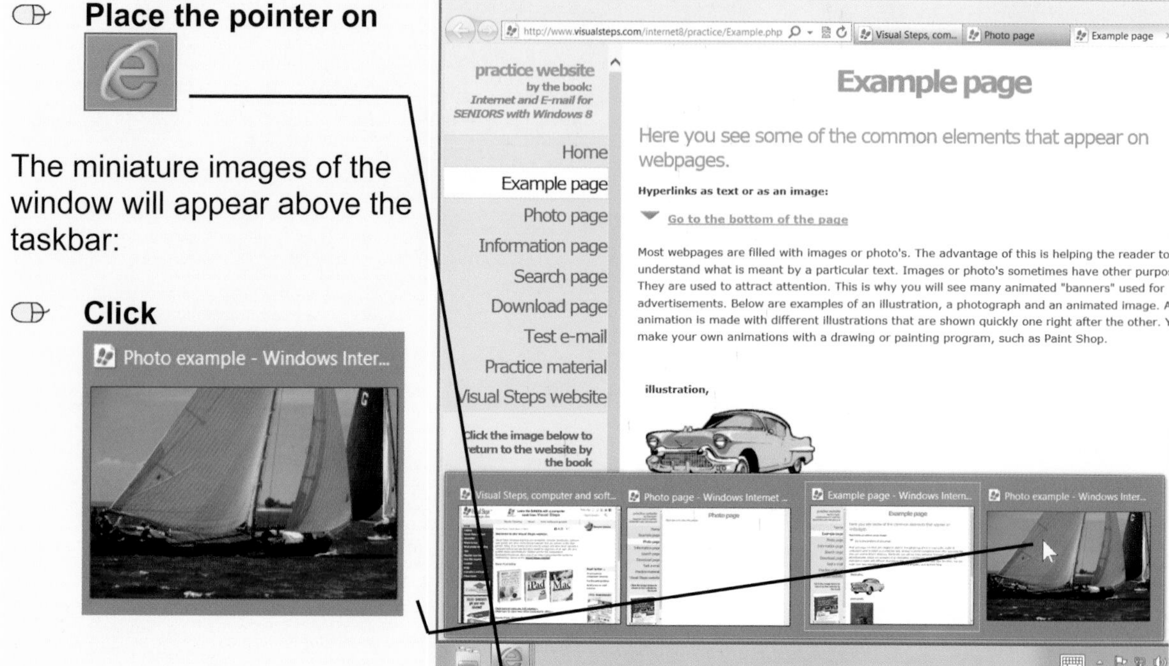


The window with the photo will be displayed on top of the other window:

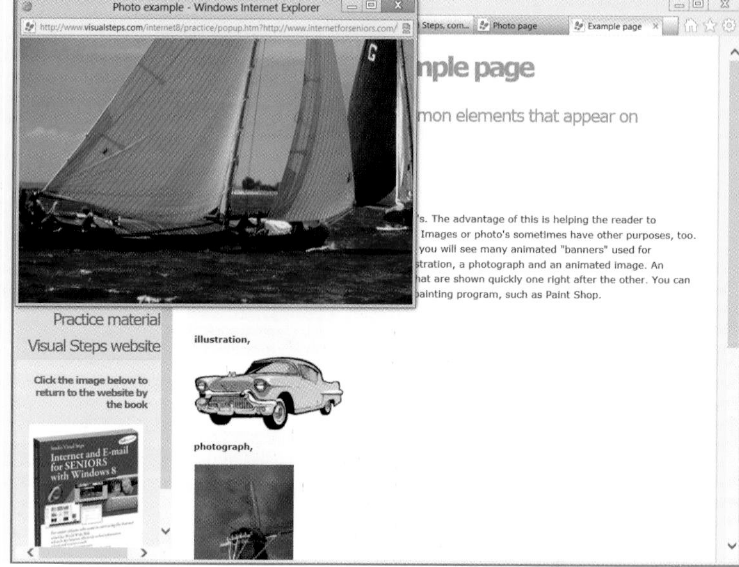

## 2.9 Closing Windows

If you have opened multiple windows, you can always close the windows you no longer need. In this case you can close the window with the photo:

In the photo window:

Click X

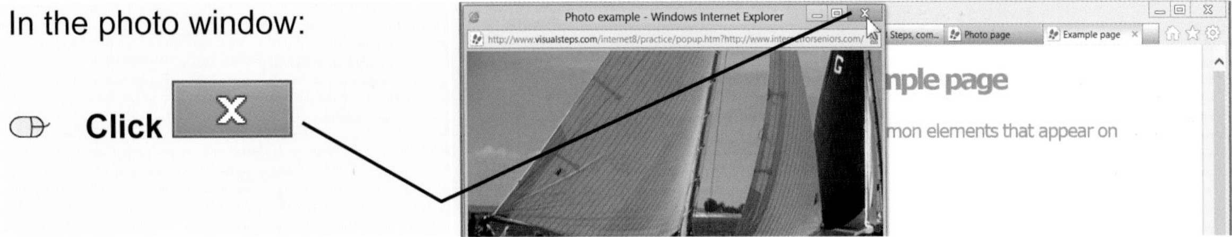


The window is closed.

## 2.10 Closing Tabs

You can close a tab that is no longer in use. Just try to do this with the first tab:

**Click the first tab**

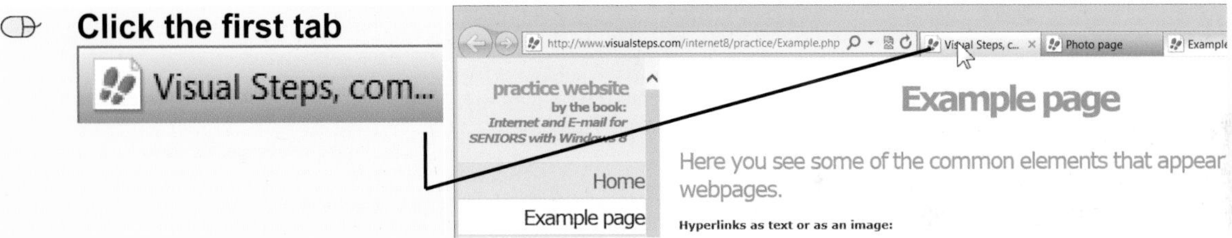


You will see the Visual Steps web page again. On the active tab you will see a small button ✕ with which you can close this tab.

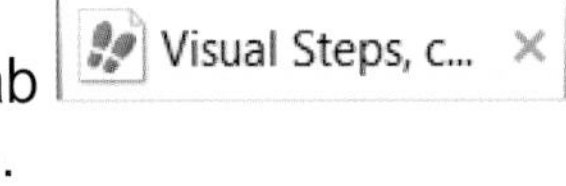


Click ✕

The first tab has disappeared. Now there are two tabs left:

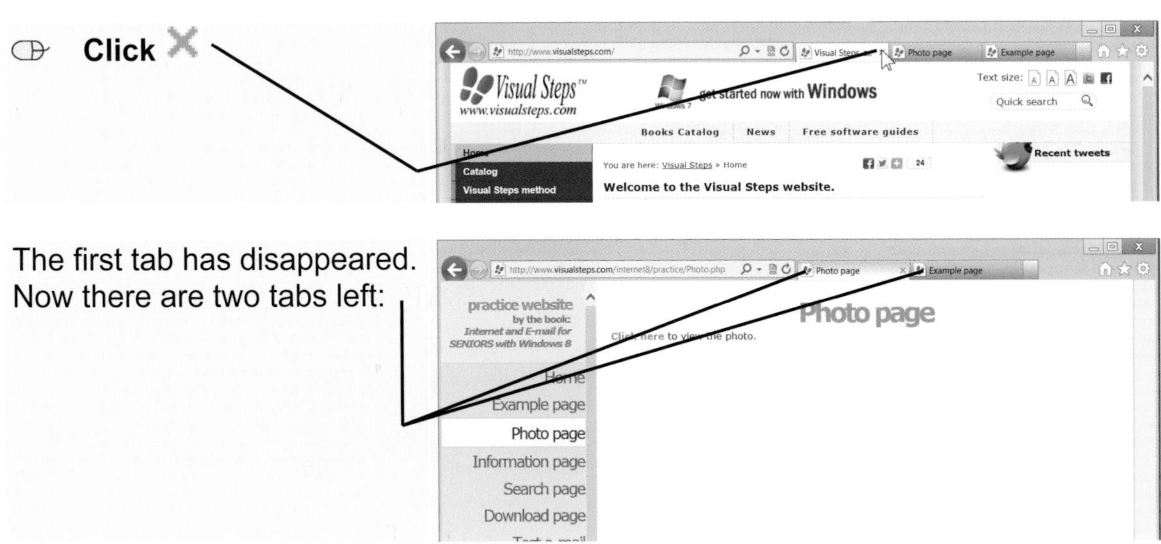

## 2.11 Zooming In and Out

The images and text on a web page can be very tiny sometimes. By zooming in on a section of the page you can get to see more details, or make the text clearer. You can zoom in from 10% up to 1000%. Try this on the example page:

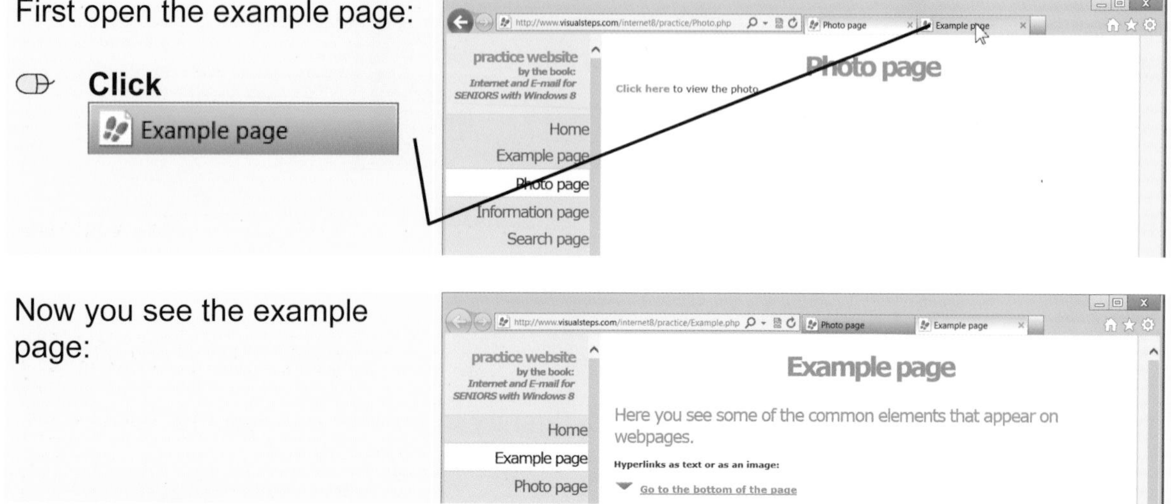

First open the example page:

- Click Example page

Now you see the example page:

By zooming in you enlarge the text and the objects on your screen. You zoom in as follows:

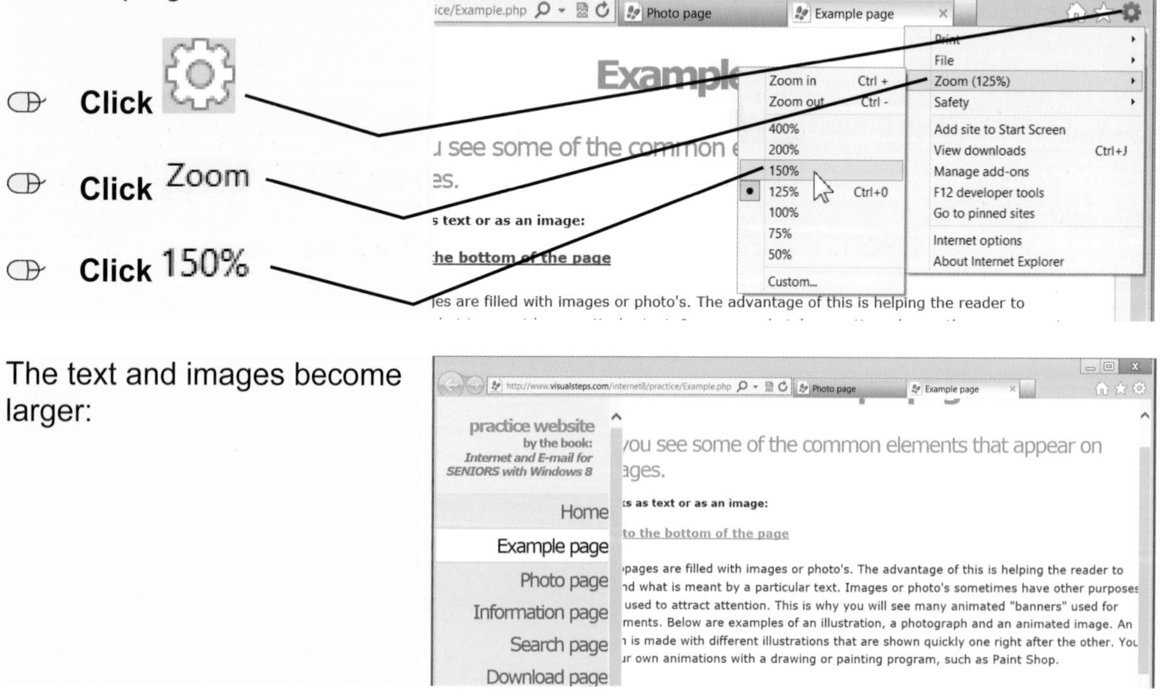

At the top right of the window:

- Click
- Click Zoom
- Click 150%

The text and images become larger:

You can zoom in even further:

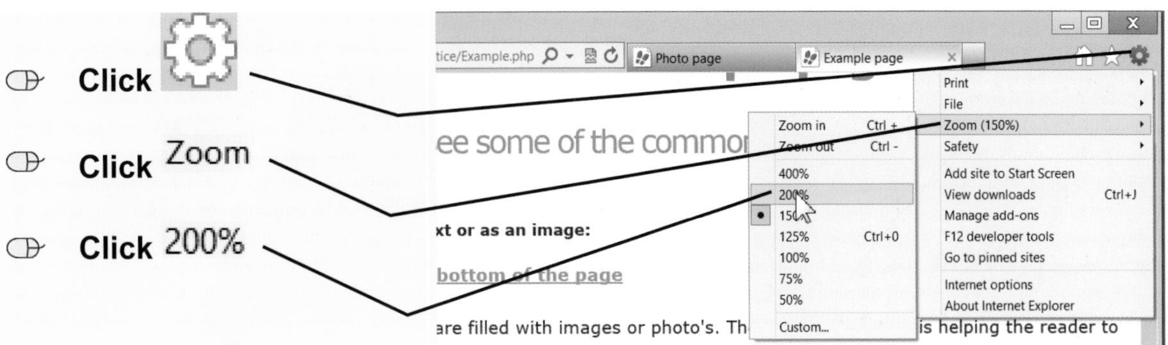


The zoom level has now been increased to 200%. With a zoom level of 75% you will be able to see most of the web page.

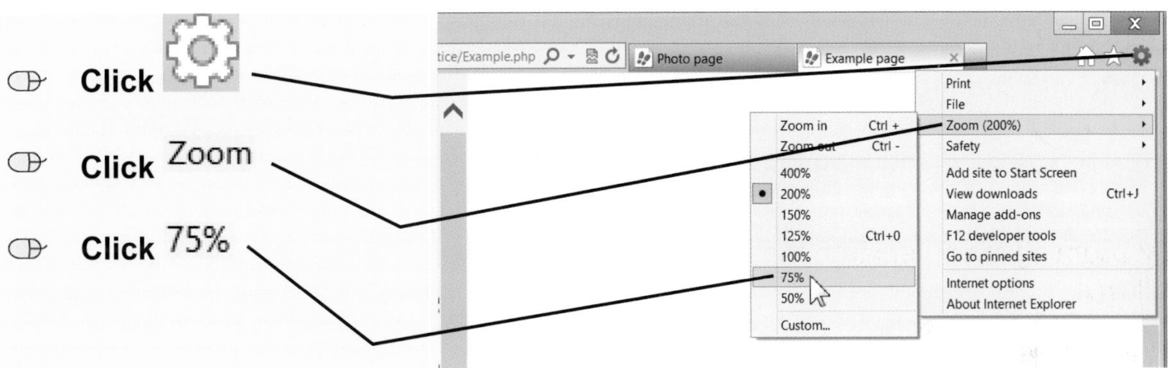


## Tip

**Watch the size of the scroll bar**

By the size of the scroll bar you can tell if the web page is much larger. If the scroll box is small, you will only be seeing part of the entire web page. If the scroll bar is large, you will be looking at the entire page, more or less.

This goes for the scroll bar in both the horizontal and the vertical bars.

If there is no scroll bar at all, you will be looking at the full web page.

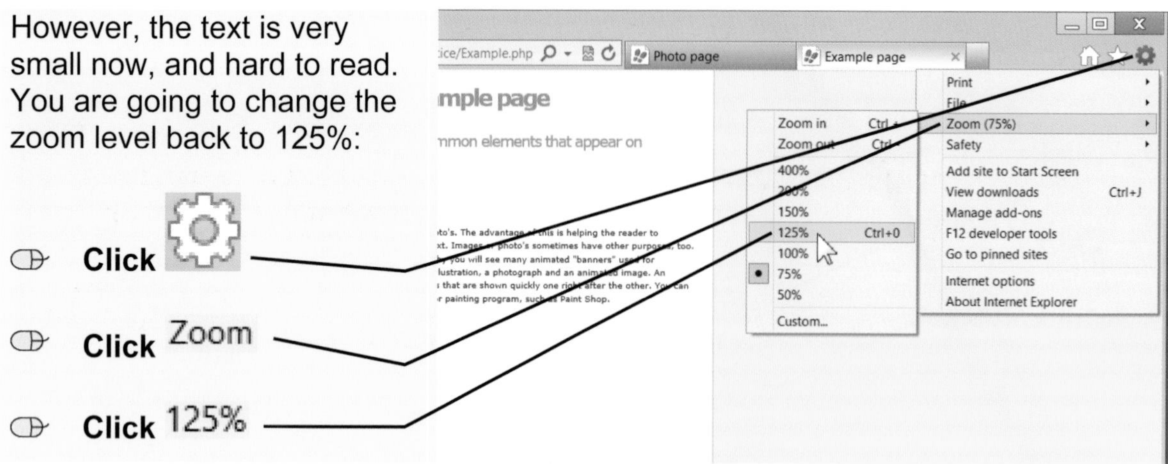

However, the text is very small now, and hard to read. You are going to change the zoom level back to 125%:

- Click
- Click Zoom
- Click 125%

Now the web page is displayed in its normal size again.

## Tip

**Zoom with the mouse**
If you have a mouse with a scroll wheel, you can zoom in and out by keeping the Ctrl key depressed and turning the scroll wheel.

This is what you do to close the *Internet Explorer* window:

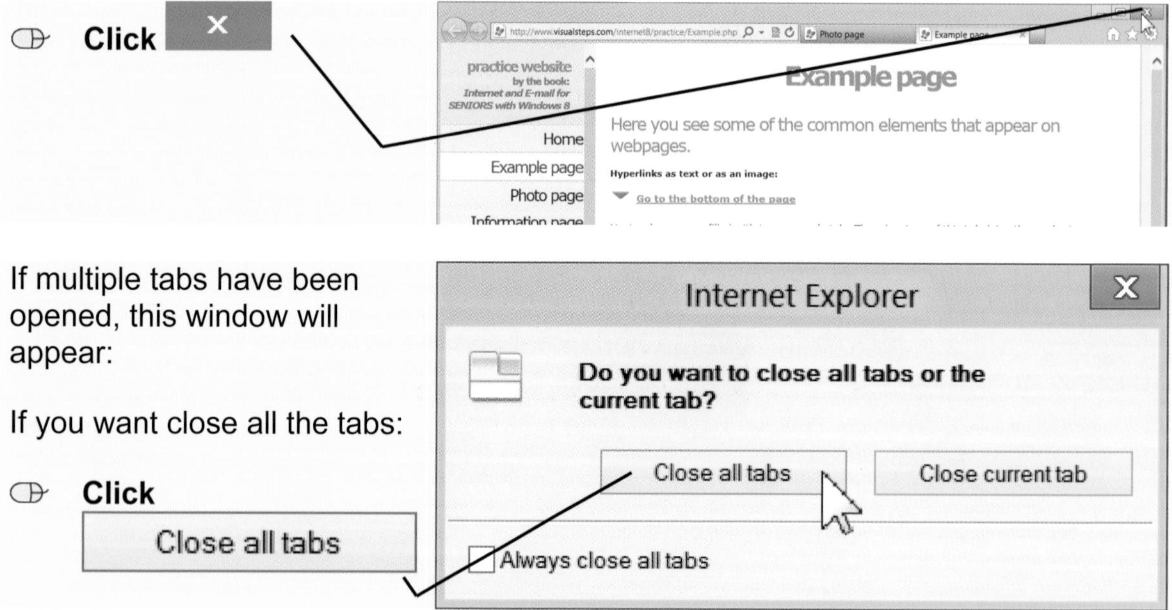


- Click

If multiple tabs have been opened, this window will appear:

If you want close all the tabs:

- Click Close all tabs

In this chapter you have learned how to work with the *Internet Explorer* program on the desktop. The following exercises will allow you to repeat and practice the operations.

## 2.12 Exercises

In the flowing exercises you can repeat the operations you have learned in this chapter. Have you forgotten how to do something? Use the number beside the footsteps to look it up in the appendix *How Do I Do That Again?*

## Exercise 1: Surfing

- Open *Internet Explorer* on the desktop. 9
- Open the web page www.pbs.org 1
- Open the web page www.visualsteps.com/internet8 1
- Return to www.pbs.nl 6
- Refresh the web page. 10
- Go on to visit www.visualsteps.com/internet8 7
- Click **Practice website** and then click Example page.
- Scroll to the bottom of the example page. 11
- Return to the Public Broadcasting Service website. 6
- Close *Internet Explorer*. 12

## Exercise 2: Tabs and Windows

In this exercise you will repeat working with tabs and windows.

- Open *Internet Explorer* on the desktop. [9]
- Open the web page www.visualsteps.com [1]
- Open a new tab. [13]
- Open the web page www.visualsteps.com/internet8 on a new tab. [1]
- Click **Practice website**.
- Open the Example page link on a new tab. [14]
- Click Photo page and then **Click here**.
- Minimize the window with the photo. [15]
- Switch to the first tab. [53]
- Minimize the *Internet Explorer* window. [15]
- Open the window with the photo from the taskbar. [16]
- Close the window with the photo. [12]
- Open the *Internet Explorer* window from the taskbar. [16]
- Close the second tab. [17]
- Close *Internet Explorer*. [12]

# 2.13 Background Information

**Dictionary**

| | |
|---|---|
| **Desktop** | The work surface on a computer screen, comparable to an actual desktop. When you open a program it will appear on the desktop. |
| **Dragging** | Moving an item on the screen by selecting it and keeping the left mouse button depressed while moving the mouse. |
| **Maximize** | Enlarging a window, so it will fill the entire screen. |
| **Minimize** | Diminishing a window. You will only see the program button on the taskbar. |
| **Scroll bars** | Whenever a document, web page, or an image is larger than the window, scroll bars will appear at the edges of the window. You can use the horizontal or vertical scroll bar to display the section of the web page you want to see. |
| **Window** | A square box or frame on the screen that displays programs and other content. |

*Source: Windows Help and Support*

## 2.14 Tips

### Tip

**Add a website to the Start screen**

You can also add your favorite website from *Internet Explorer* on the desktop to the Start screen, as a tile. In this way you can quickly open your favorite website.

**Open the web page www.visualsteps.com** 1

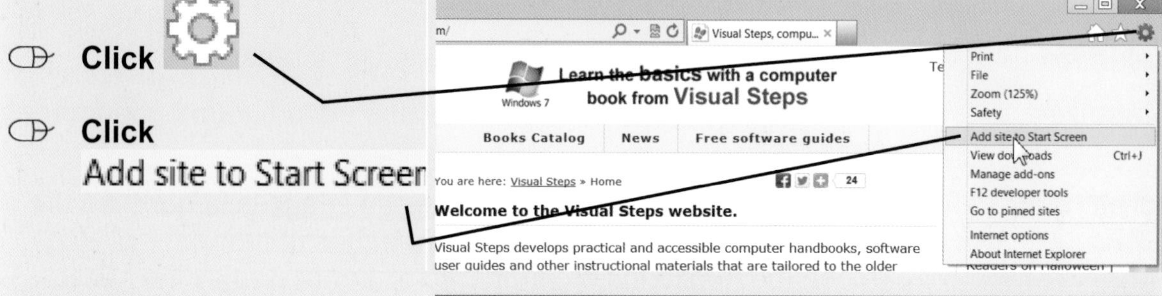


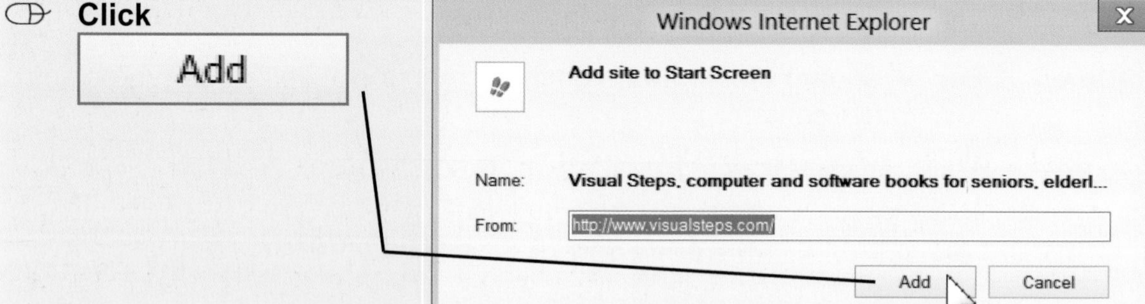


**Close the window that will be opened** 12

The tile has been added:

If you click it, the website will be opened.

**Please note:** if you have added the website from the *Internet Explorer* app, the website will be opened in that app. If you have added the website from the *Internet Explorer* program on the desktop, the website will be opened in that program.

## Tip

**Open frequently visited websites from the taskbar**

In the *Internet Explorer* desktop program you can open a website you often visit directly from the taskbar. This is how you do it:

**Right-click** 

You will see a miniature window with various tasks:

**Click the website, for example** Visual Steps, computer and sc

The website will be opened.

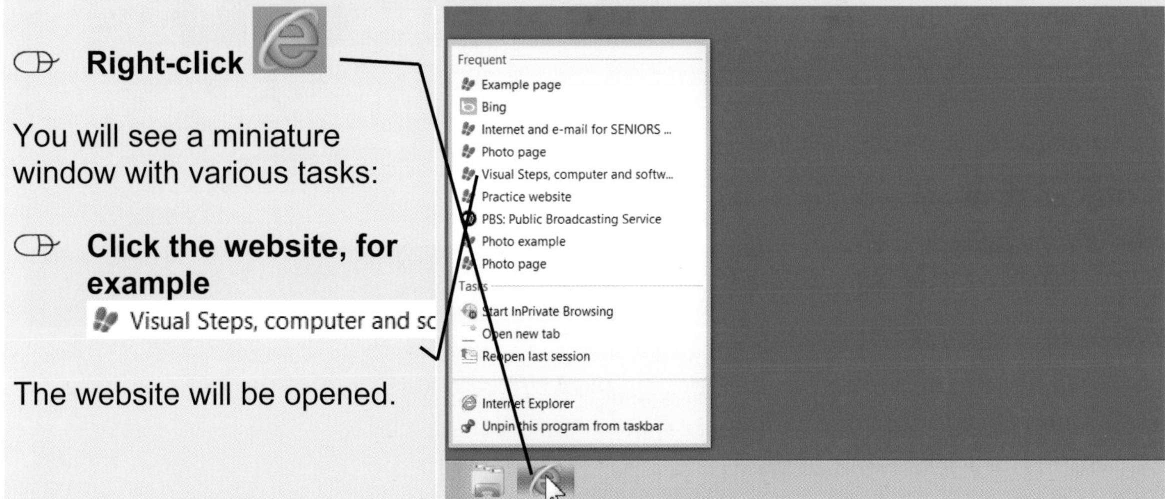


In the window you will find even more options:

Internet Explorer: open a new *Internet Explorer* window.

Open new tab: open a new tab.

Reopen last session: open *Internet Explorer* with the web page(s) you were viewing during the most recent session.

Start InPrivate Browsing: visit websites without storing them in your computer's memory.

## Tip

**Message bar**

While surfing the Internet, you may see a message bar appear in *Internet Explorer*. This message appears below the window, in the *Internet Explorer* desktop program:

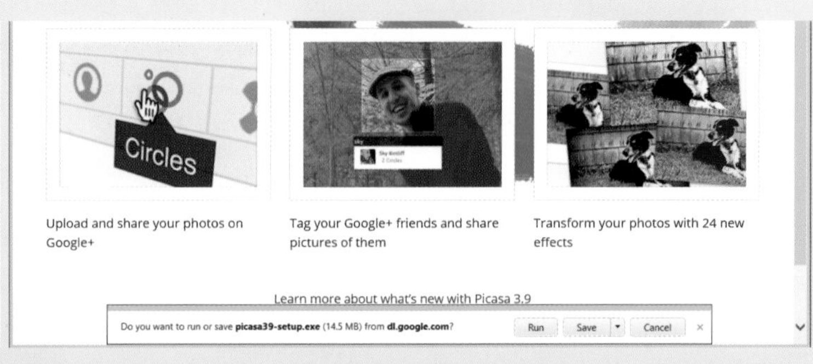


In the *Internet Explorer* app this message bar has a different color:

These messages and information bars display options for downloads, blocked pop-up windows (window that suddenly appear like this, will often contain advertisements) and various other activities.
Among others, you will see such a message bar in the following situations:

- If a website tries to download a file top your computer.
- If a website tries to open a pop-up window.
- If a website tries to install an ActiveX component to your computer, or tries to activate an ActiveX component that is not safe (ActiveX is a technology used for creating interactive web content, such as animations, or credit card transactions).
- If your security settings are lower than recommended.

The message bar in *Internet Explorer* will let you select the command you want to execute, for example, Run or Save.

If necessary, ask an experienced computer user what to do if you are not sure, and click Cancel if this message suddenly appears. For instance, when you have no intention of downloading something.

In *Chapter 6 Downloading and Printing* you will learn more about downloading and saving files and programs.

## Tip

**InPrivate navigation**

If you do not want others to know which websites you visit, you can use the *InPrivate navigation* option. This option makes sure your computer does not store any information on the websites you visit. This is how you use InPrivate navigation:

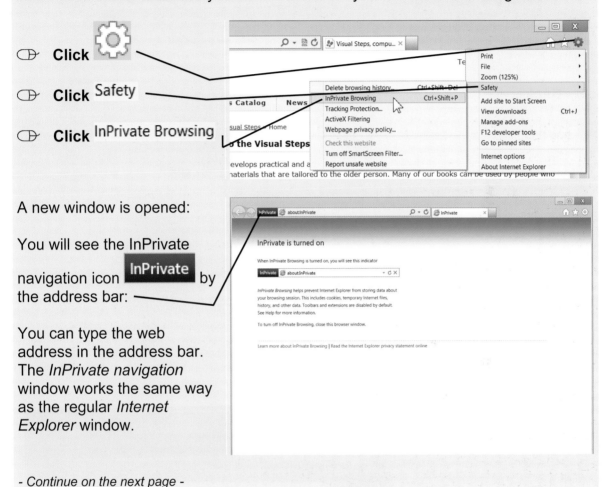

- **Click** ⚙
- **Click** Safety
- **Click** InPrivate Browsing

A new window is opened:

You will see the InPrivate navigation icon InPrivate by the address bar:

You can type the web address in the address bar. The *InPrivate navigation* window works the same way as the regular *Internet Explorer* window.

*- Continue on the next page -*

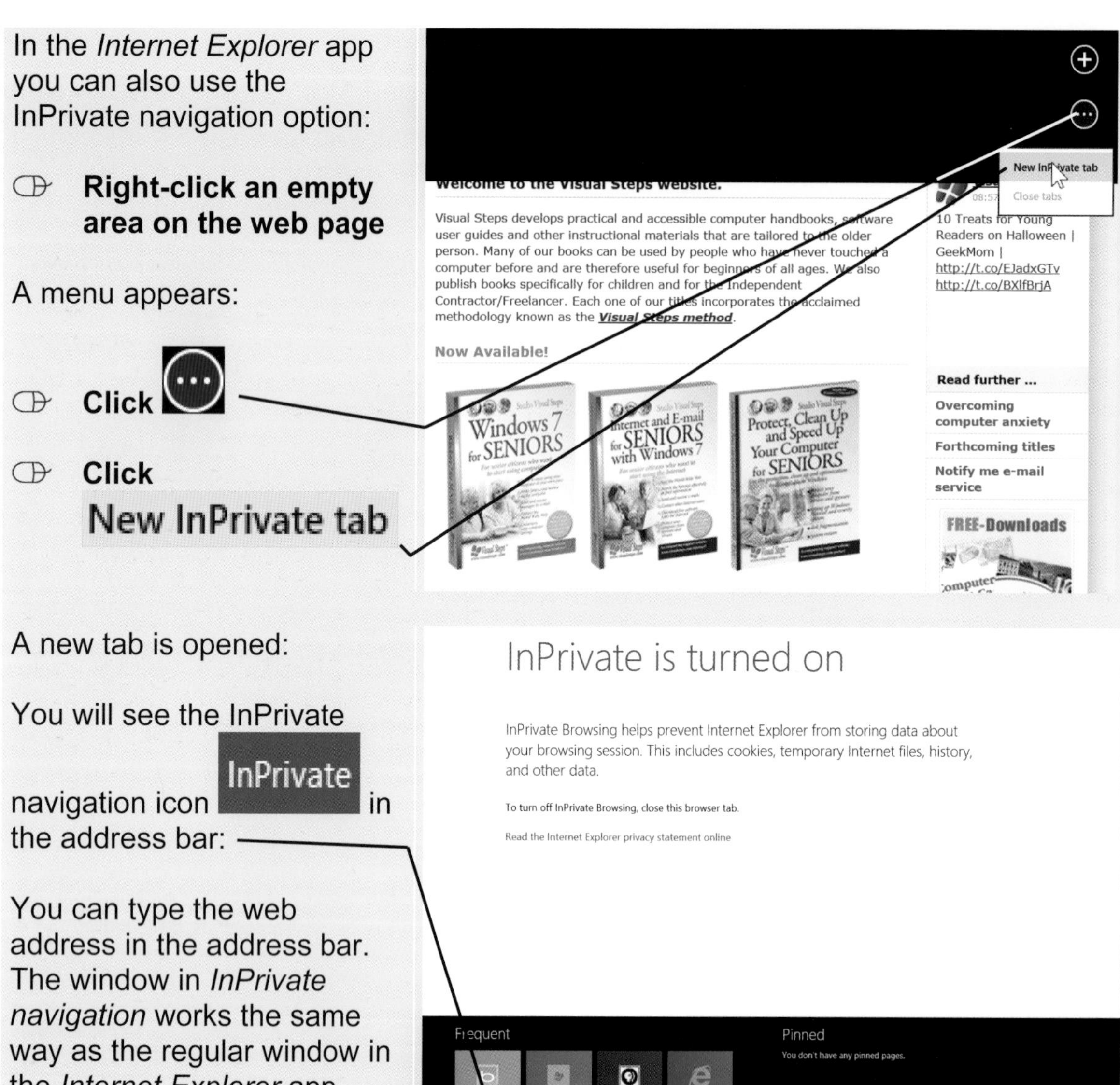


In the *Internet Explorer* app you can also use the InPrivate navigation option:

**Right-click an empty area on the web page**

A menu appears:

**Click** (...)

**Click** New InPrivate tab

A new tab is opened:

You will see the InPrivate navigation icon InPrivate in the address bar:

You can type the web address in the address bar. The window in *InPrivate navigation* works the same way as the regular window in the *Internet Explorer* app.

# 3. Navigating the Internet

Surfing the Internet is a fun and enjoyable activity. By clicking on various hyperlinks, you can visit many interesting websites and personal home pages. By *website* we mean an extensive system of web pages for a company or organization. A personal *home page* may consist of only a few web pages. It usually belongs to an individual, or contains only a little commercial information about a company.

The World Wide Web is infinitely large and every day thousands of websites are added. After surfing for a while, you will no doubt want to revisit an interesting website from time to time. However, all those hyperlinks make it easy to lose your way.

Fortunately, *Internet Explorer* has several built-in options to help you get to where you want to go. In this chapter, you will learn how to use these convenient features, allowing you to 'navigate' straight to your target: back to the web pages you visited earlier.

In this chapter you will learn how to:

- save a web address;
- open a favorite;
- open website by typing part of a web address;
- organize your favorites;
- use the Favorites bar;
- set the home page;
- use the *History*.

# 3.1 Saving a Web Address

Once you have found an interesting website, you can save its address. From then on, you can quickly reopen this website anytime without having to remember the web address or retyping it. Saved websites are called favorites in *Internet Explorer*.

**Open *Internet Explorer* on the desktop** 9

**Please note:**

You can only save a web address when the associated website is displayed in the *Internet Explorer* window.

**Open the web page www.visualsteps.com** 1

At the top right of the window:

Click

You will see the Favorites Center. Here you can save your favorite websites:

Click Add to favorites

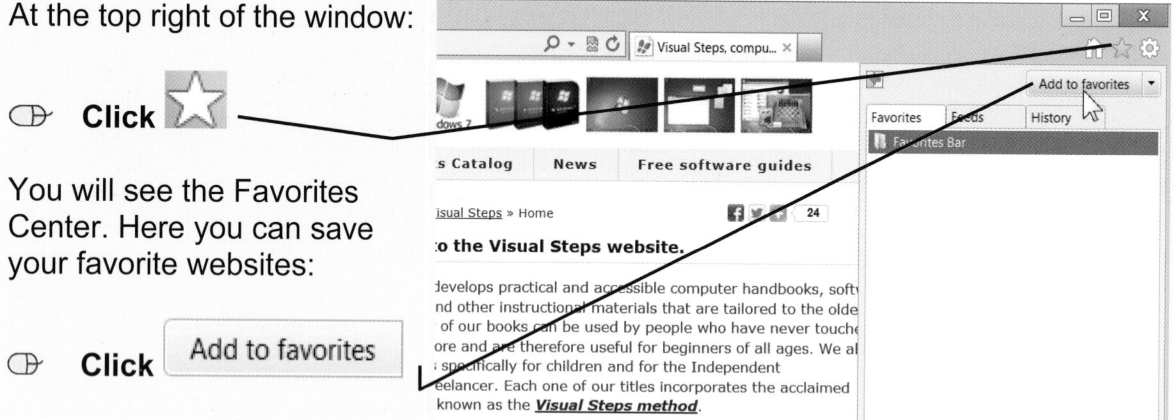


Now you see a small window on top of the web page in which the name of the website has already been inserted:

You can also change the name if you like. For now that is not necessary.

Click Add

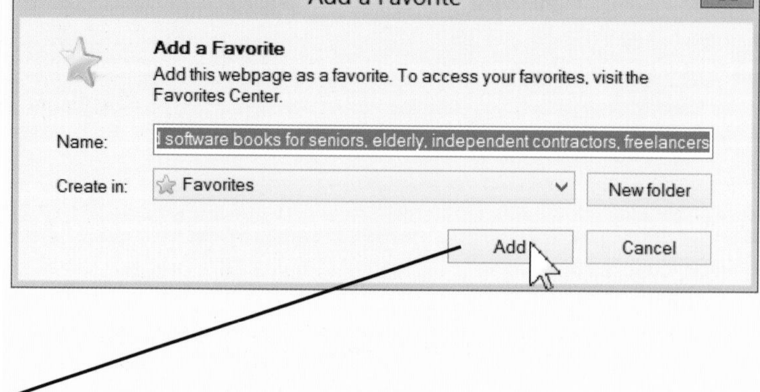

Later, you will learn how to quickly reopen this favorite website. To see how a favorite works, you will first need to go to a different website. For example, you could visit the website of *SeniorNet*, a computer organization for seniors.

**Open the web page www.seniornet.org** [1]

You see the *SeniorNet* home page:

## 3.2 Opening a Favorite

You can quickly open your favorite websites using the Favorites Center:

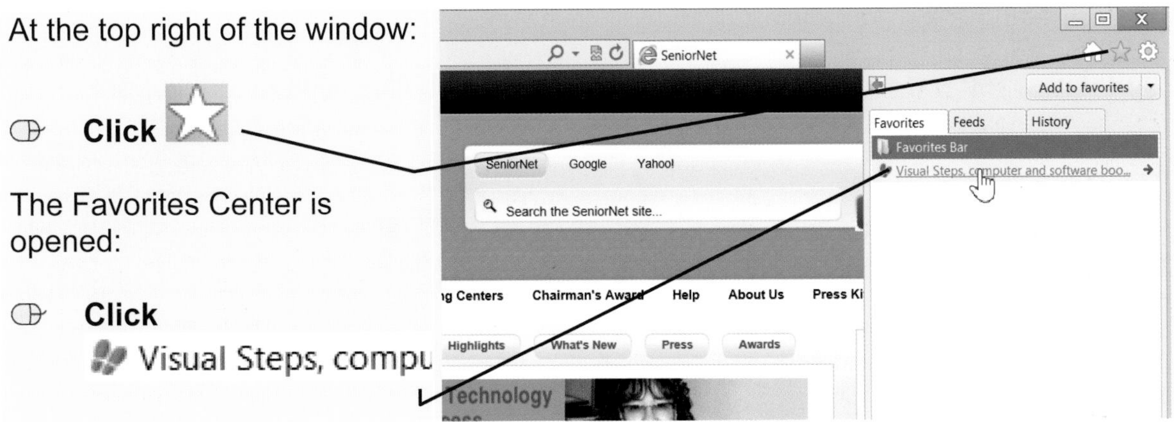


At the top right of the window:

Click ☆

The Favorites Center is opened:

Click Visual Steps, compu

*Internet Explorer* immediately jumps to the Visual Steps website:

*Internet Explorer* remembers your favorites even after you have closed the program. This allows you to create an entire collection of websites that you can visit again later.

## 3.3 Organizing Your Favorites

You can save all your favorite websites in one long list in the Favorites Center, but in the long term this is not very practical. It is better to organize your favorites in separate folders. You can save websites according to subject, for example.
You can also use folders to separate your own favorites from those of other users on the same computer.

To practice, you are going to create a folder for the websites related to this book.

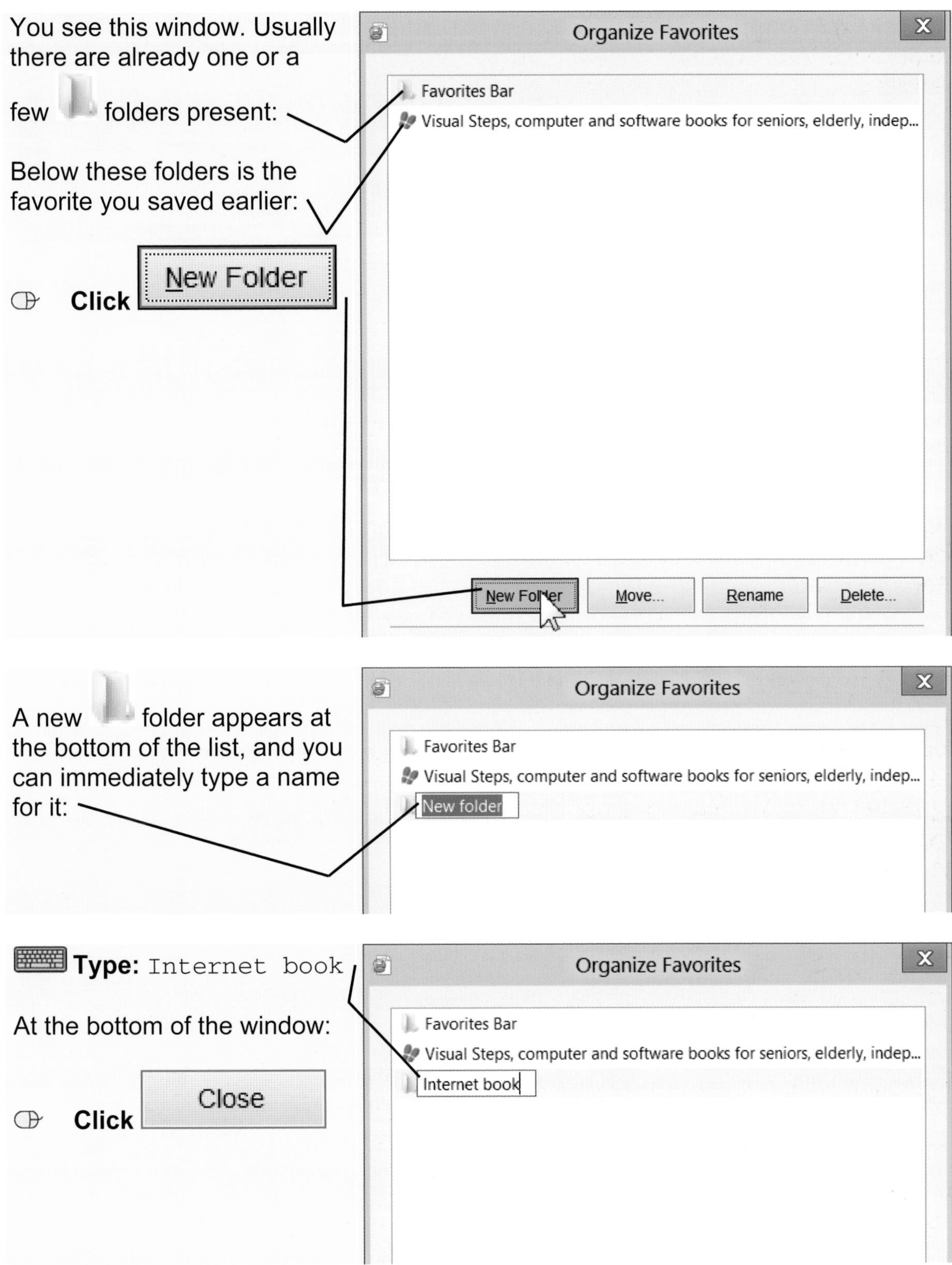


You see this window. Usually there are already one or a few folders present:

Below these folders is the favorite you saved earlier:

Click New Folder

A new folder appears at the bottom of the list, and you can immediately type a name for it:

**Type:** `Internet book`

At the bottom of the window:

**Click** Close

Now the folder has been created. You can check this right away in the Favorites Center:

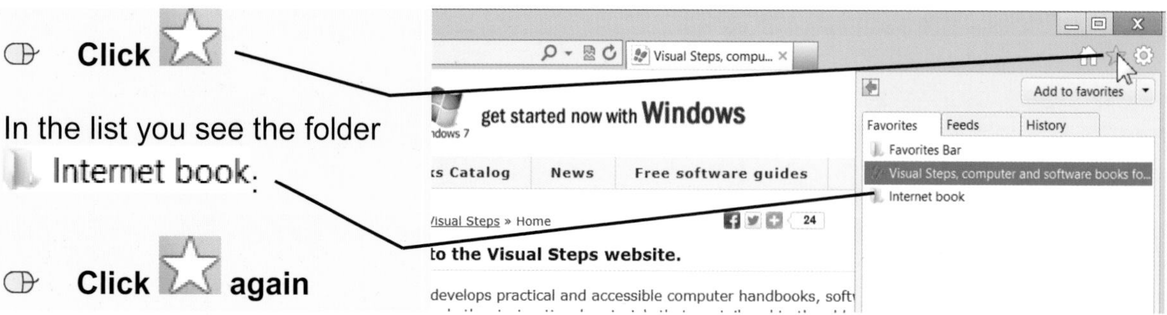


**Click** ☆

In the list you see the folder Internet book:

**Click** ☆ **again**

You have seen that the folder has been created. A little later on, you will read how you can save all the websites related to this book in this new folder.

# 3.4 Typing Part of a Web Address

*Internet Explorer* has quite a handy feature on the address bar. By clicking the ▼ button on the address bar, you can see a list of the web addresses you have recently entered (typed).
This list can become very long, which makes is difficult to find an address. Just see what happens when you type part of a web address:

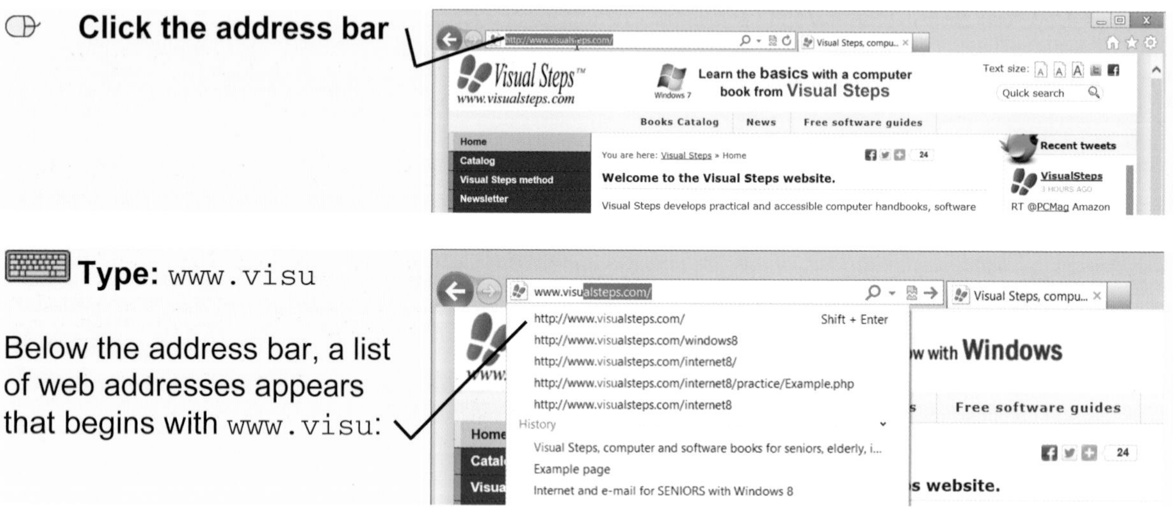


**Click the address bar**

**Type:** `www.visu`

Below the address bar, a list of web addresses appears that begins with `www.visu`:

Now you just need to click the desired web address in the list:

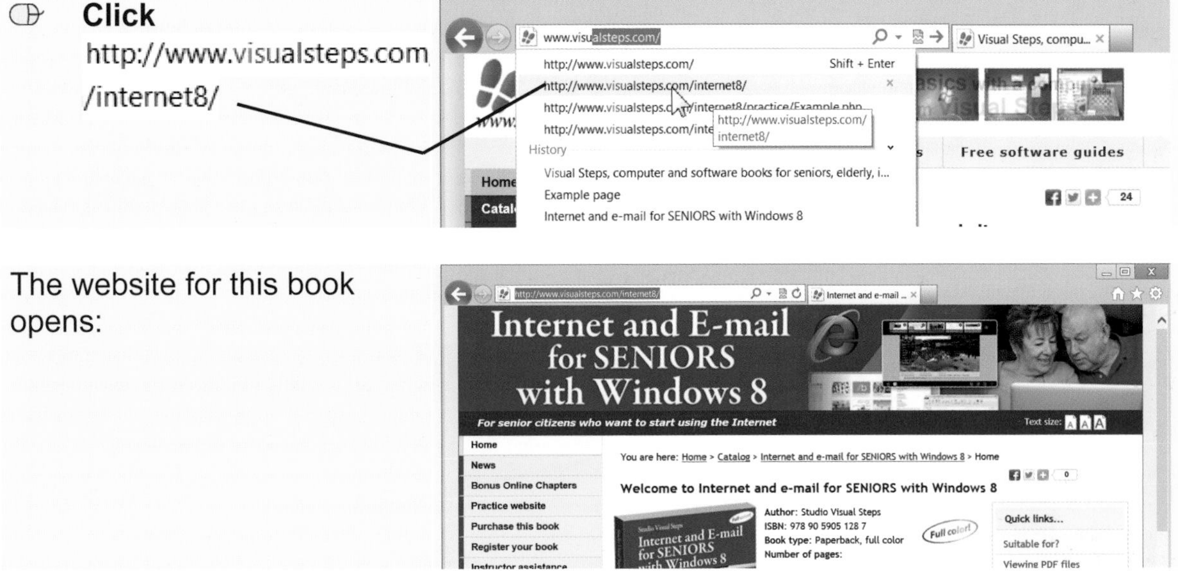


Click
http://www.visualsteps.com
/internet8/

The website for this book opens:

## 3.5 Saving a Web Address in a Folder

It is pretty easy to save a website in the new folder in the Favorites Center.

**Please note:**

You can only save a web address when the associated website is displayed in the *Internet Explorer* window.

In this case, you now see the website for this book in the window. You can save this website in the new *Internet Book* folder.

Click

Click Add to favorites

You see this window:

The name of the website has already been filled in:

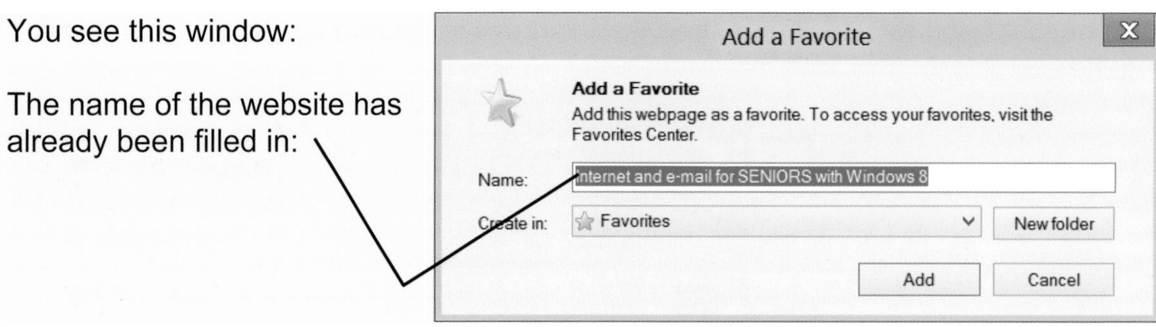


Now you open the folder where you want to save this favorite:

- **By** Create in:**, click**

- **Click** Internet book

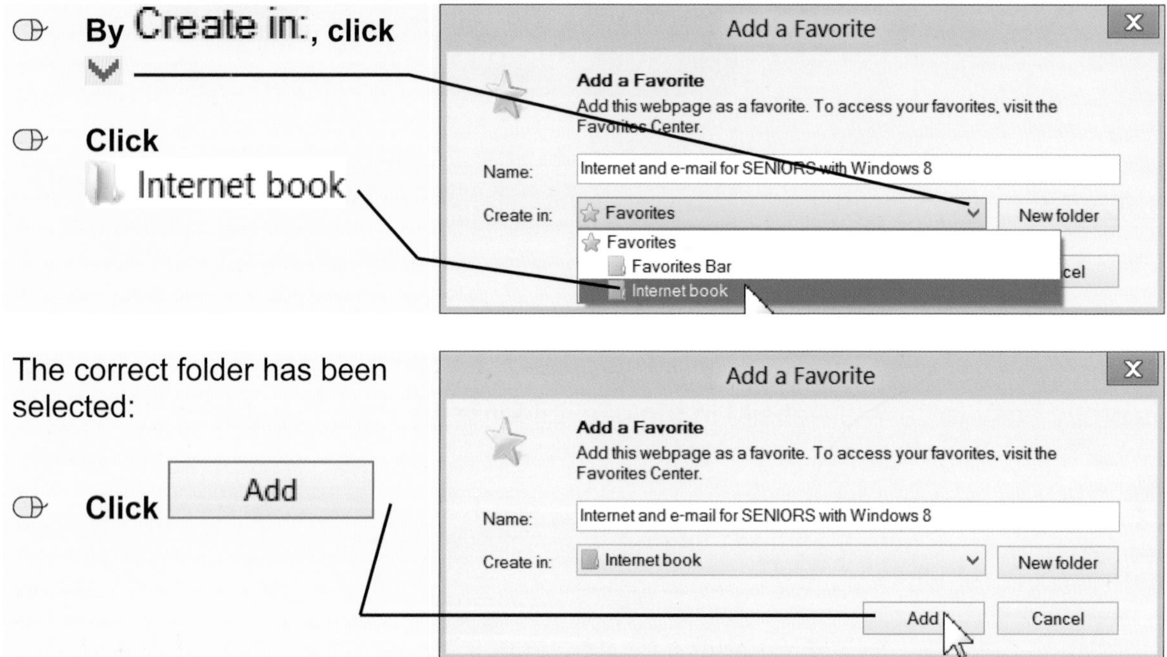


The correct folder has been selected:

- **Click** Add

Later on, you will check if the website has been saved in the folder. First you open another website, for example the CNN website:

**Open the web page www.cnn.com** [1]

You see the CNN website:

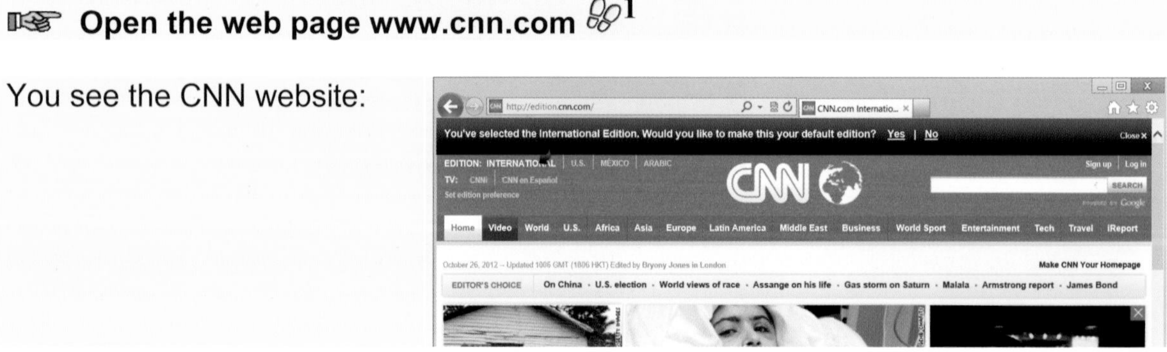

Now you can open the Favorites Center to see if the favorite has been stored in the right folder:

**Click** ☆

**Click** Internet book

You will see the stored favorite:

**Click** Internet and e-mail for SEN

You see the website for this book again:

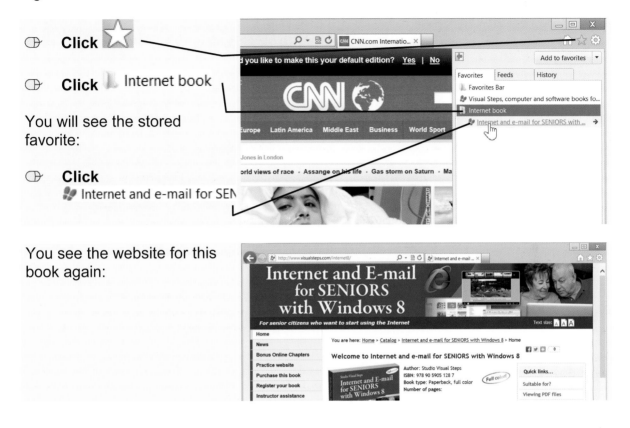

## 3.6 The Favorites Bar

You can also add a favorite website to the *Favorites* bar at the top of the *Internet Explorer* window. This way, you can jump to your favorite website with just one click. First, the *Favorites* bar needs to be displayed. This is how you do it:

**Right-click next to**

You will see a menu. To display the *Favorites* bar:

**Click** Favorites bar

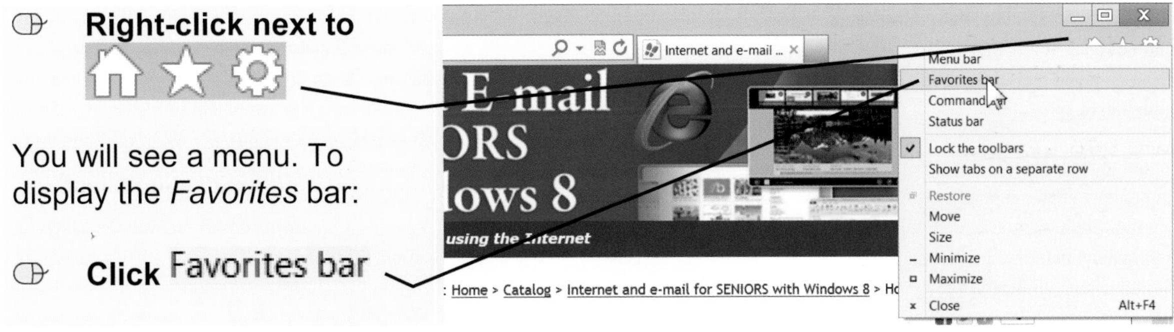

The *Favorites* bar has been added at the top of the window:

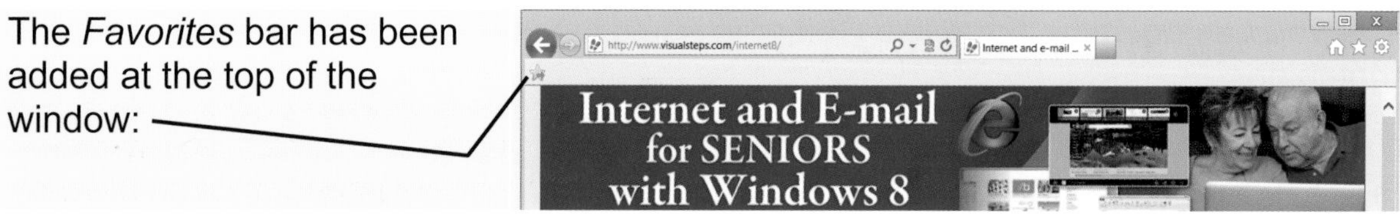


Now you are going to add a website to this toolbar:

**Open the web page www.pbs.org** [1]

You can make this a favorite website. This is how you do it:

**Click**

You will see that the pbs Public Broadcasting S... website has been added to the *Favorites* bar. You can easily open such a favorite website from this toolbar. You are going to check this out. First, you return to the previous web page:

**Go back to the previous web page** [6]

On the *Favorites* bar:

**Click** pbs Public Broadcasting

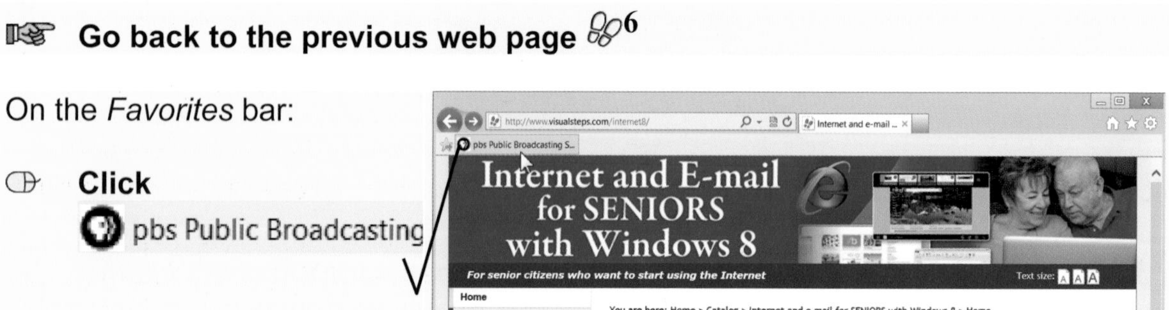


Now you see the PBS website again. As you see, this is a simple way of displaying your favorites, and quickly visiting these favorite websites. If you add any new favorites in this way, they will be displayed in the toolbar too. For now you can just close the toolbar, if you want.

**Right-click next to**

**Click** Favorites bar

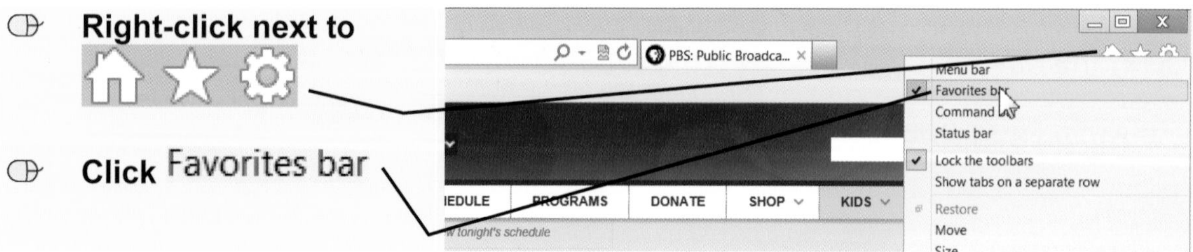


The *Favorites* bar has disappeared again.

# 3.7 Changing the Home Page

When opened, *Internet Explorer* displays a particular web page, called the *home page*. You can change this setting and make this your favorite page, for example the website of Visual Steps.

**Please note:**

You can set a page as your home page when it is displayed in the *Internet Explorer* window.

**Open the web page www.visualsteps.com**

Use the *Internet options* window to set the home page. This is how you open this window:

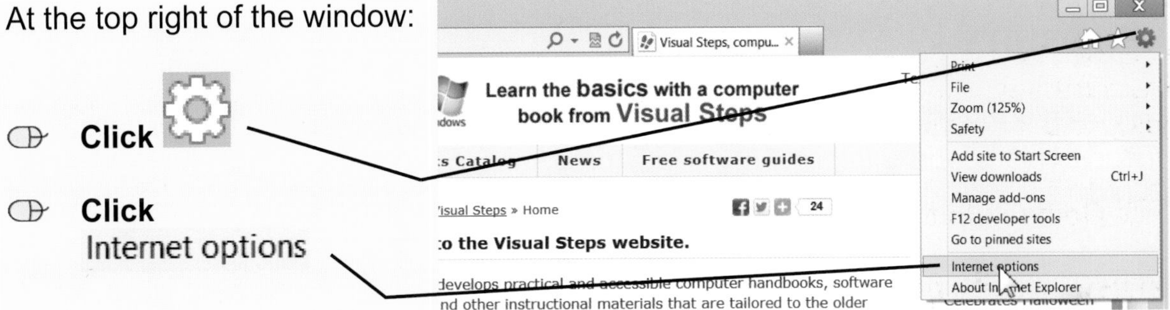


You want to use the website currently displayed in *Internet Explorer* as a home page:

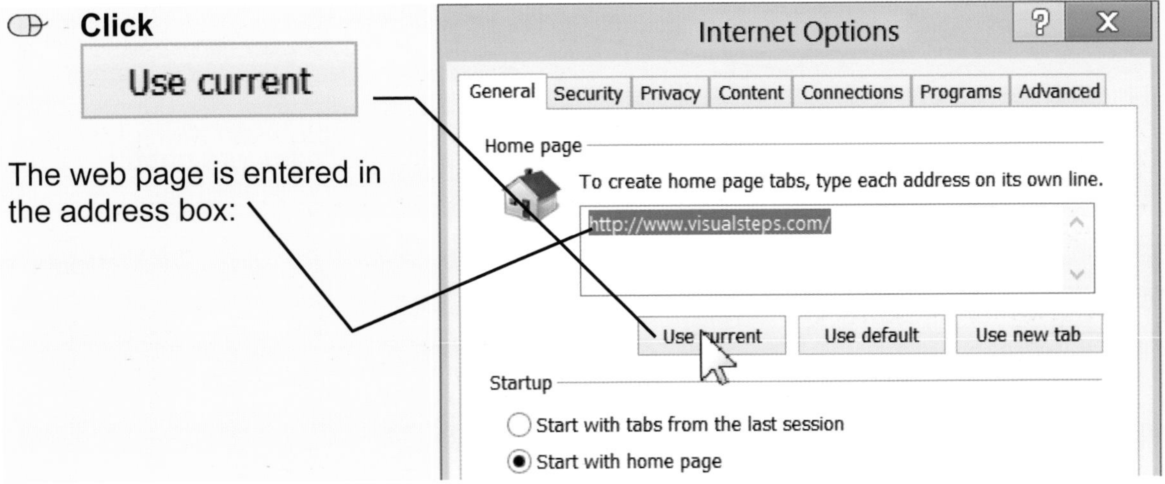

At the bottom of the window:

Click Apply

Click OK

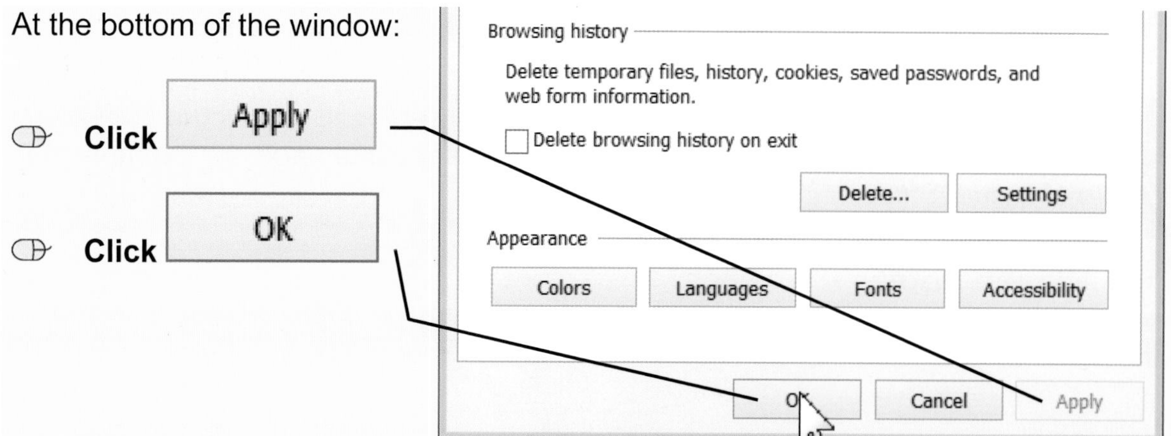


The Visual Steps website has been stored as the home page. From now on, this home page will also be displayed in the *Internet Explorer* app, when you open it.

## 3.8 History

Besides the favorites, the Favorites Center also has a section with a button called *History.* This is where *Internet Explorer* stores links to the websites you have recently visited.

Click

Click the History tab

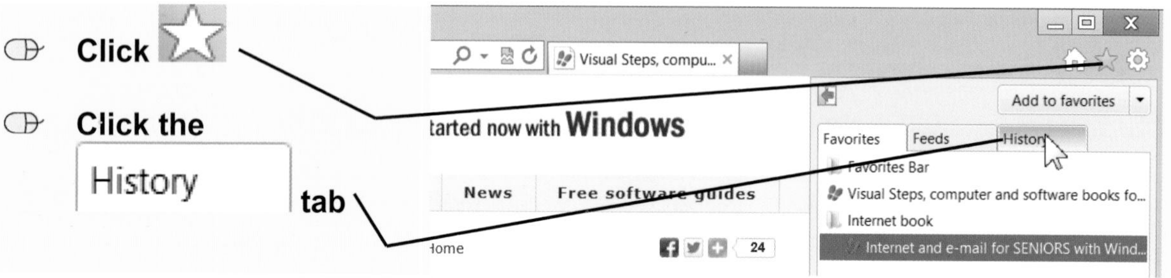


The *History* is presented as a chronological list, where the websites are neatly organized under today, previous days, or previous weeks.

Click Today

In Today, you see the folders for the websites you have visited, arranged in alphabetical order:

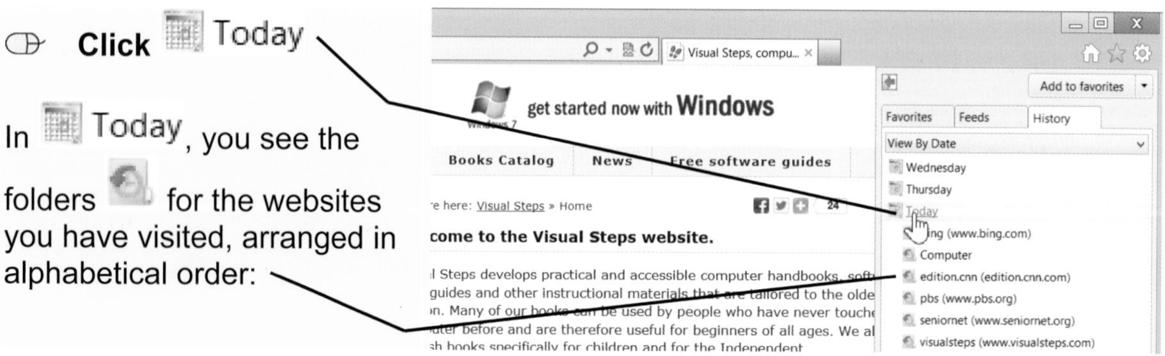

When you open one of these folders, you can see the specific web pages you have visited on that website. By clicking one of these hyperlinks, the corresponding web page will be opened. Take a look:

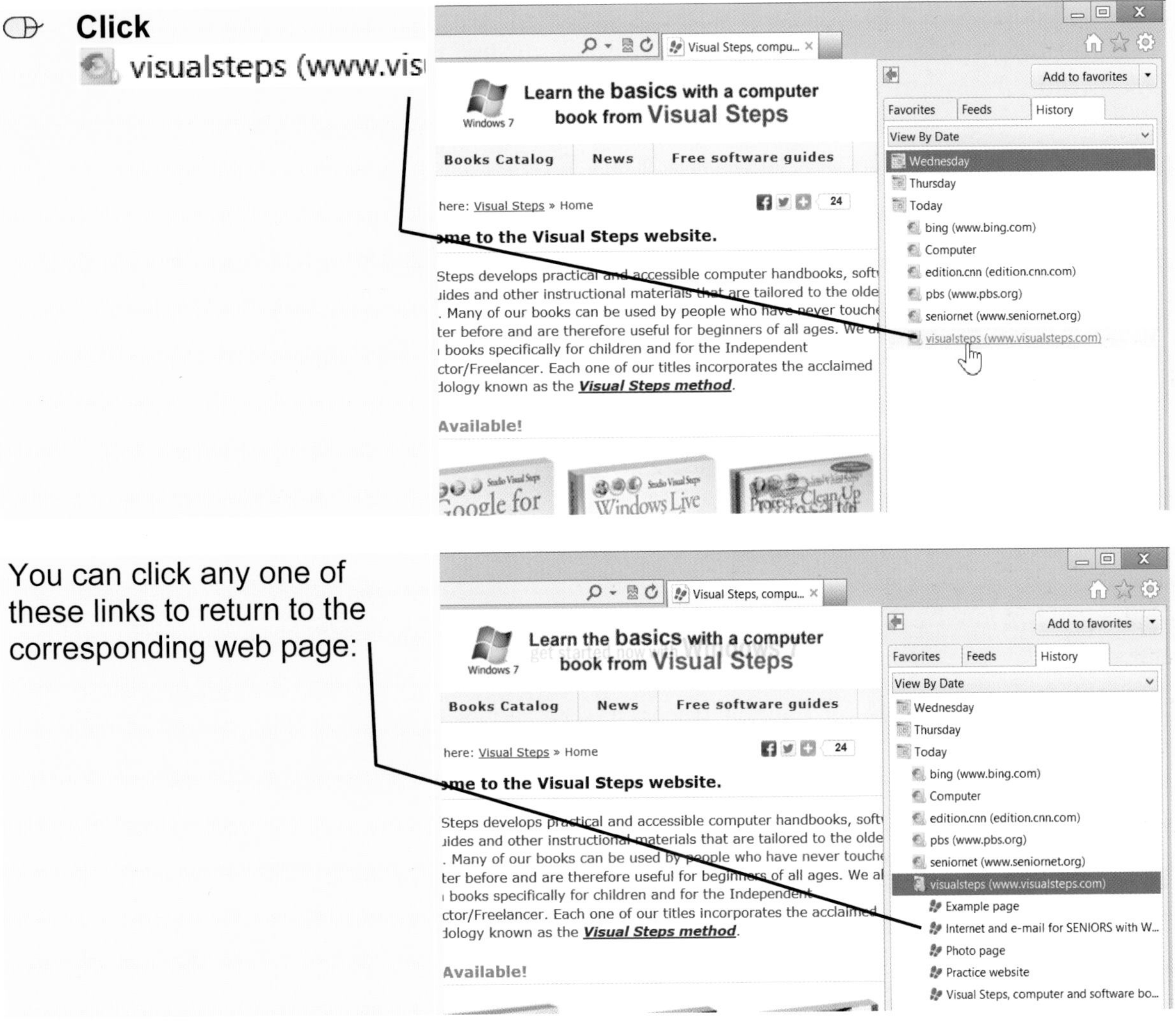


**Click** visualsteps (www.visi

You can click any one of these links to return to the corresponding web page:

Returning to a website in this way is only useful if you remember when you last visited it. If you are on the Internet daily, however, and you surf to many websites, this method is not as useful. In that case, it is a lot easier to store these web addresses as favorites, like you have practiced before.

**Close *Internet Explorer*** 12

Now you have learned several ways to navigate the Internet effectively and to find your way back and forth between websites.

You can practice these techniques in the following exercises.

## 3.9 Exercises

The following exercises will help you master what you have just learned. Have you forgotten how to perform a particular action? Use the number beside the footsteps to look it up in the appendix *How Do I Do That Again?*

## Exercise 1: The SeniorNet Favorite

In this exercise, you will open the websites for SeniorNet and CNN and add them to your favorites.

- Open *Internet Explorer* on the desktop. 9
- Use the list under the address bar to open: www.seniornet.org 18
- Make the address for SeniorNet a favorite. 19
- Use the *History* tab to open: www.cnn.com 20
- Make the address for CNN a favorite. 19
- Open the SeniorNet favorite. 21
- Open the CNN favorite. 21

## Exercise 2: A New Favorite

In this exercise, you will open the National Geographic website and add it to your favorites in the folder related to this book.

- Open the web page www.nationalgeographic.com 1
- Save the address as a favorite in the Internet book folder. 22
- Open the favorite. 23
- Close *Internet Explorer*. 12

# 3.10 Background Information

**Glossary**

| | |
|---|---|
| **Favorites** | *Internet Explorer* favorites are links (bookmarks) to websites that you have added. By adding a website to your favorites list, you can go to that site by simply clicking its name, instead of having to type its address in the address bar. |
| **Favorites Center** | The *Internet Explorer* area where you can view and organize your favorites. |
| **History** | The section of the Favorites Center that displays the websites you recently visited. By default, the *History* listing is sorted by date. |
| **Home page** | The web page that is displayed each time you open *Internet Explorer* or click the button. |
| **Shortcut** | A shortcut is a link to a website, file or program, represented by an icon. Double-clicking a shortcut will open the file or program. |

*Source: Windows Help and Support*

**HTML**
Web pages are created (written) in a special programming language. This language is called *HTML* or *HyperText Markup Language*. *Internet Explorer* translates this language into a visible and readable page.
Each HTML page looks the same, in its most elementary shape.

```
<HTML>
        <HEAD>
                <TITLE> Internet for Seniors </TITLE>
        </head>
        <BODY>
                <p>This will be the text.</p>
        </body>
</HTML>
```

On your screen you will not see any HTML codes in your *Internet Explorer* window, but just the following text:

**Internet for Seniors**
This will be the text.

Web programmers who work with these HTML codes cannot make any typing errors, otherwise *Internet Explorer* will not be able to correctly display the web page. Fortunately we do no longer need to struggle to understand these often incomprehensible codes. Software companies such as *Microsoft* have created special programs that enable us to create web pages without knowing anything about HTML. Such programs are called *editors*.

An editor works the same way as a text editor. You type your text, add pictures and make sure the page looks pretty. The editor converts all your work into HTML codes. It does not get any easier.

## 3.11 Tips

**Tip**

**Organizing favorites**

You might want to remove, rename or move some of your favorites from time to time. This is how you do it:

- **Click** ☆
- **By** Add to favorites**, click** ▾
- **Click** Organize favorites...

You see this window where you can Delete..., Move... or Rename the favorite:

With the New Folder button you create a new folder for a group of favorites:

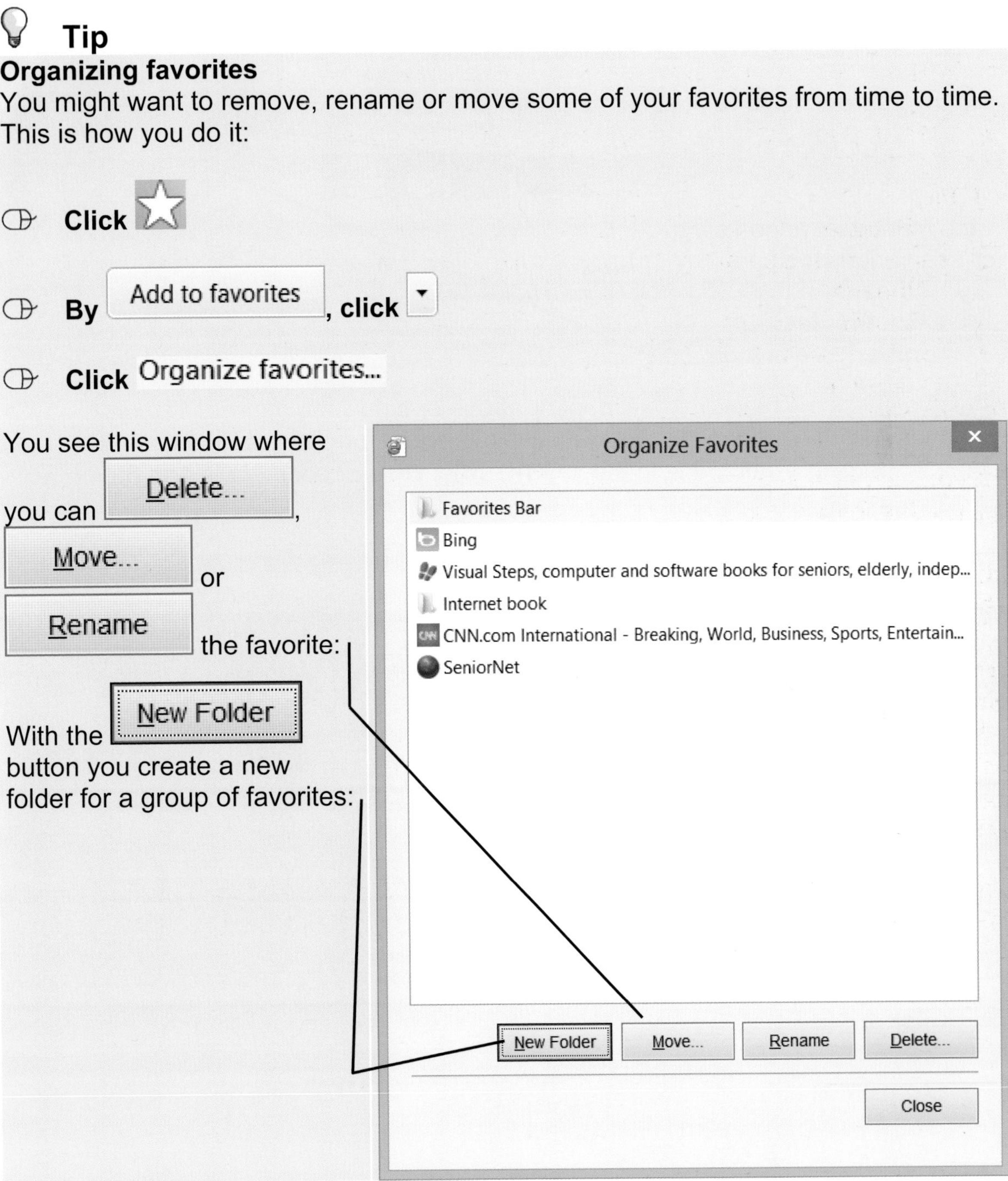

## Tip

**Display the toolbars**

You have learned how to work with the *Favorites* bar. But you can display more toolbars in *Internet Explorer*. This is how you do it:

**Right-click next to**

In the menu that appears you will see various toolbars:

**Click the desired toolbar**

When you click a toolbar, this will appear above or below the *Internet Explorer* window. The toolbars provide quick access to several functions and options. For example, printing a web page in the Command bar, or zooming in and out on a web page on the Status bar.

## Tip

**Multiple home pages**

You can set up multiple home pages on different tabs. These will open each time you open *Internet Explorer* on the desktop:

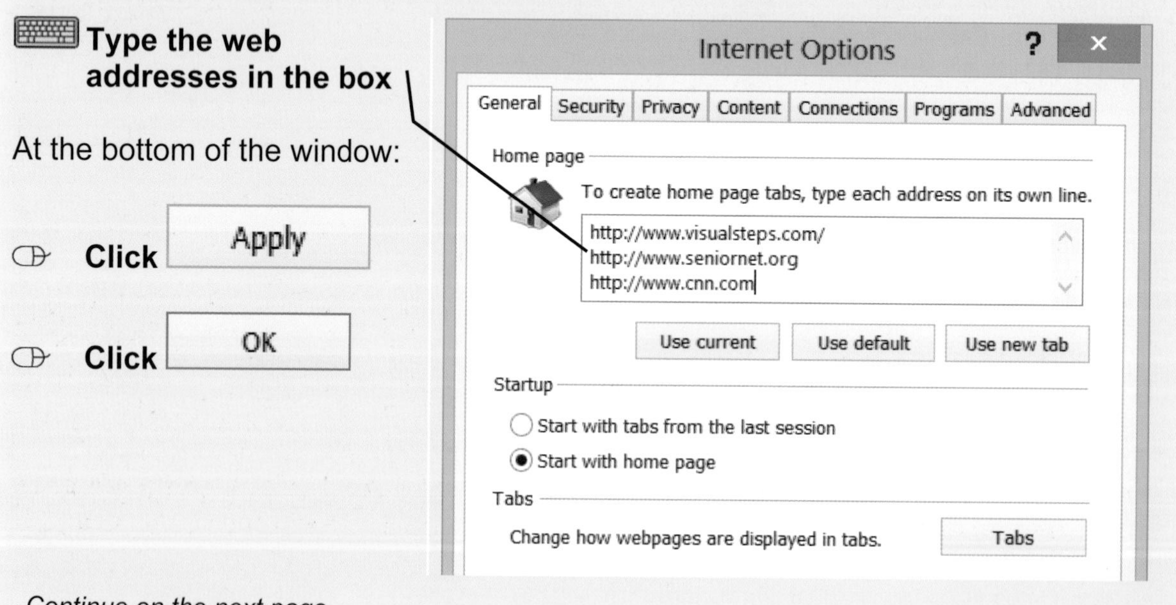


**Type the web addresses in the box**

At the bottom of the window:

**Click** Apply

**Click** OK

- *Continue on the next page* -

If you open *Internet Explorer* on the desktop or click the [home] button, the home pages will be opened on different tabs:

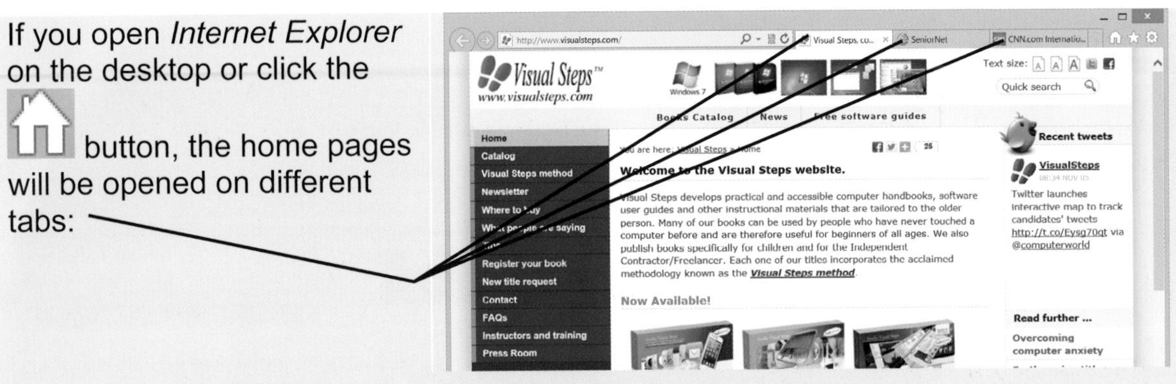


In the *Internet Explorer* app, these home pages will be opened on the different tabs as well. You can show the tabs by right-clicking an empty area on the web page.

## Tip

**Add favorites with the Internet Explorer app**

In the *Internet Explorer* app you can save favorite web addresses too:

- **Click** [pin button]

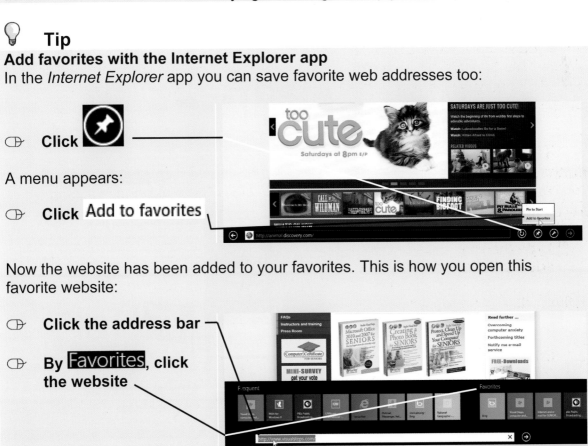

A menu appears:

- **Click** Add to favorites

Now the website has been added to your favorites. This is how you open this favorite website:

- **Click the address bar**
- **By** Favorites**, click the website**

*Internet Explorer* remembers all your favorites, even after you have closed the app. In this way you can collect a whole group of favorite websites, which you can visit whenever you feel like it.

## Tip

**Keep the Favorites Center on the screen**

If you want to keep displaying the Favorites Center while working:

**Click** ☆

**Click** (pin icon)

Now the Favorites Center has been locked on the left side of the screen.

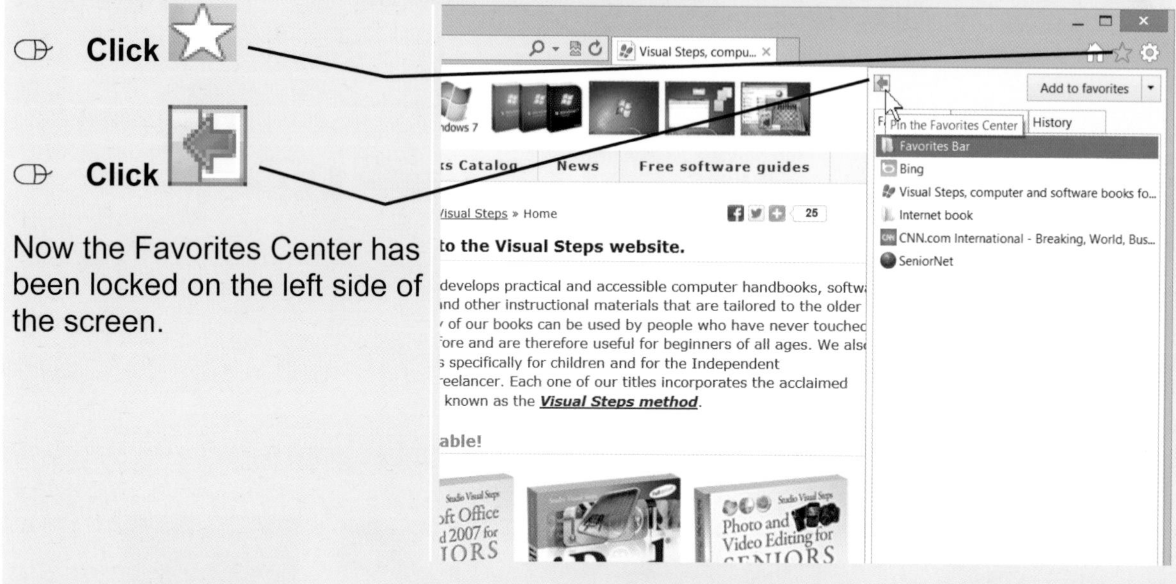


To close the Favorites Center again:

**Click** X

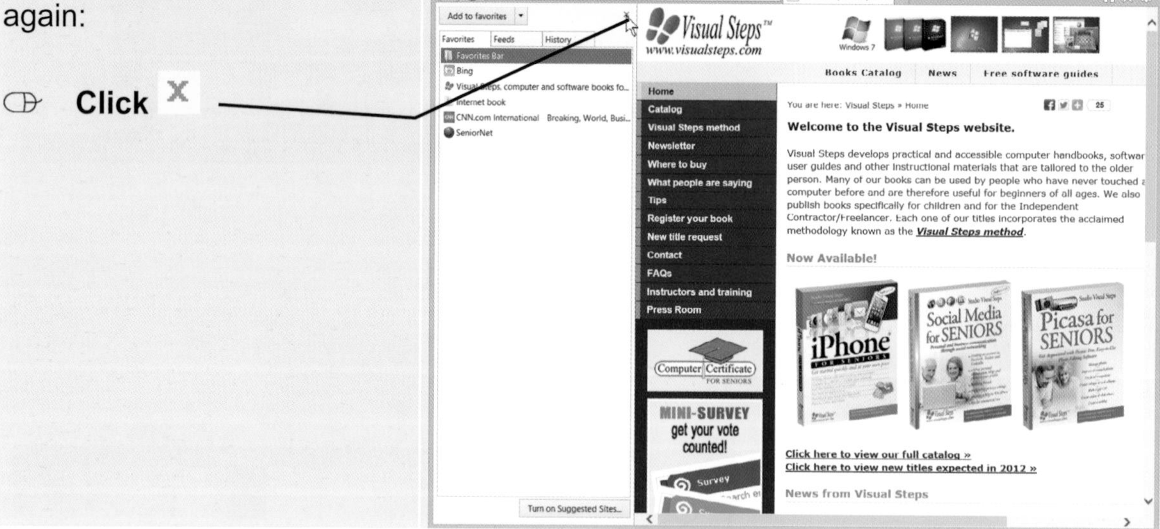

## Tip

**Subscribe to the Visual Steps Newsletter**

By subscribing to the free Visual Steps Newsletter you will keep informed of our new books, receive free tips and tricks, special offers, and you can download computer booklets and guides for free. The Newsletter is sent about once or twice a month, through e-mail.

**Open the web page www.visualsteps.com** 1

On the left-hand side of the website:

**Click** Newsletter

You see this window:

**Type your e-mail address**

**Click** Submit

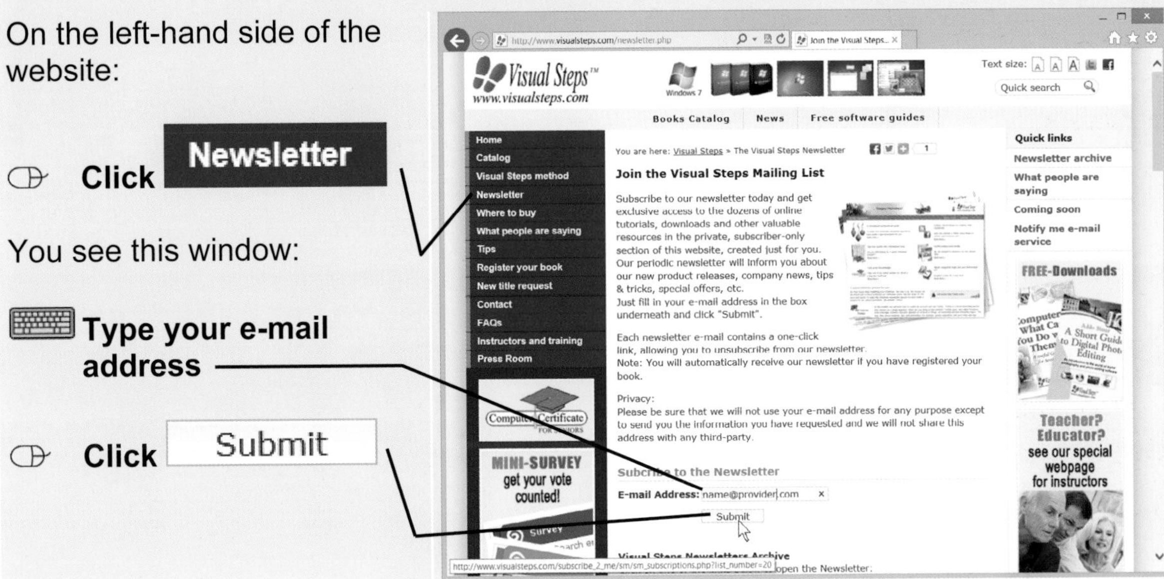

## Tip

**Save a web page**

You can save an entire web page, including text and images, on your computer's hard disk. Later on you can open this web page in *Internet Explorer* again, and read it in your own time. This is how you save a web page:

**Press** Alt

**Click** File

**Click** Save as...

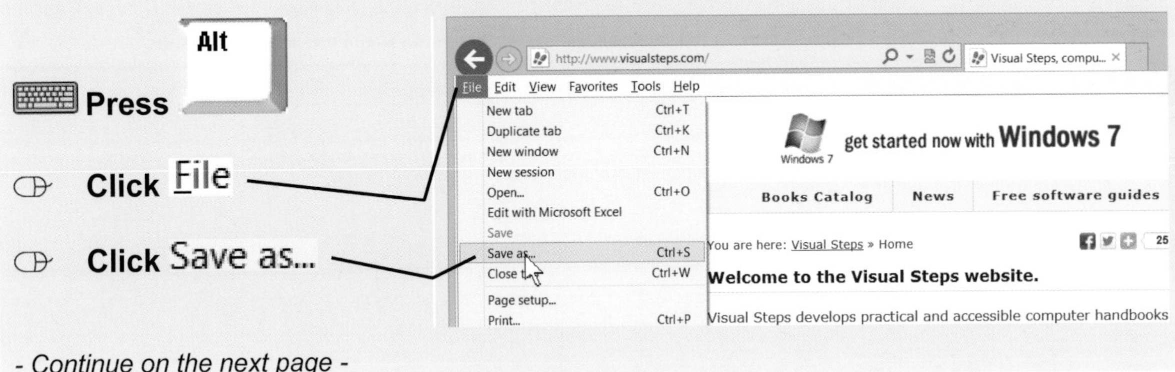

*- Continue on the next page -*

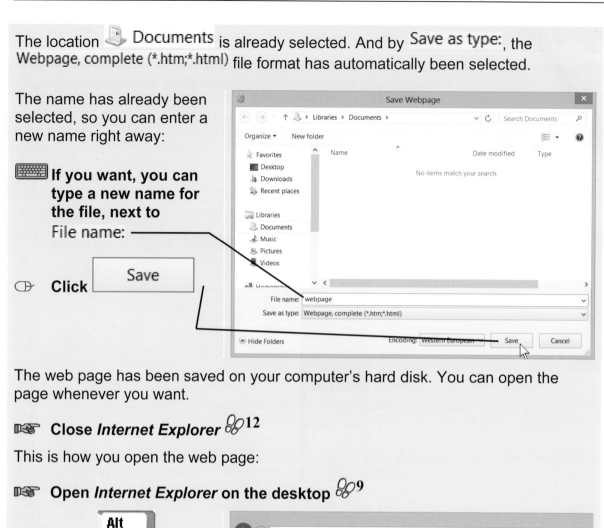

The location Documents is already selected. And by Save as type:, the Webpage, complete (*.htm;*.html) file format has automatically been selected.

The name has already been selected, so you can enter a new name right away:

**If you want, you can type a new name for the file, next to** File name:

**Click** Save

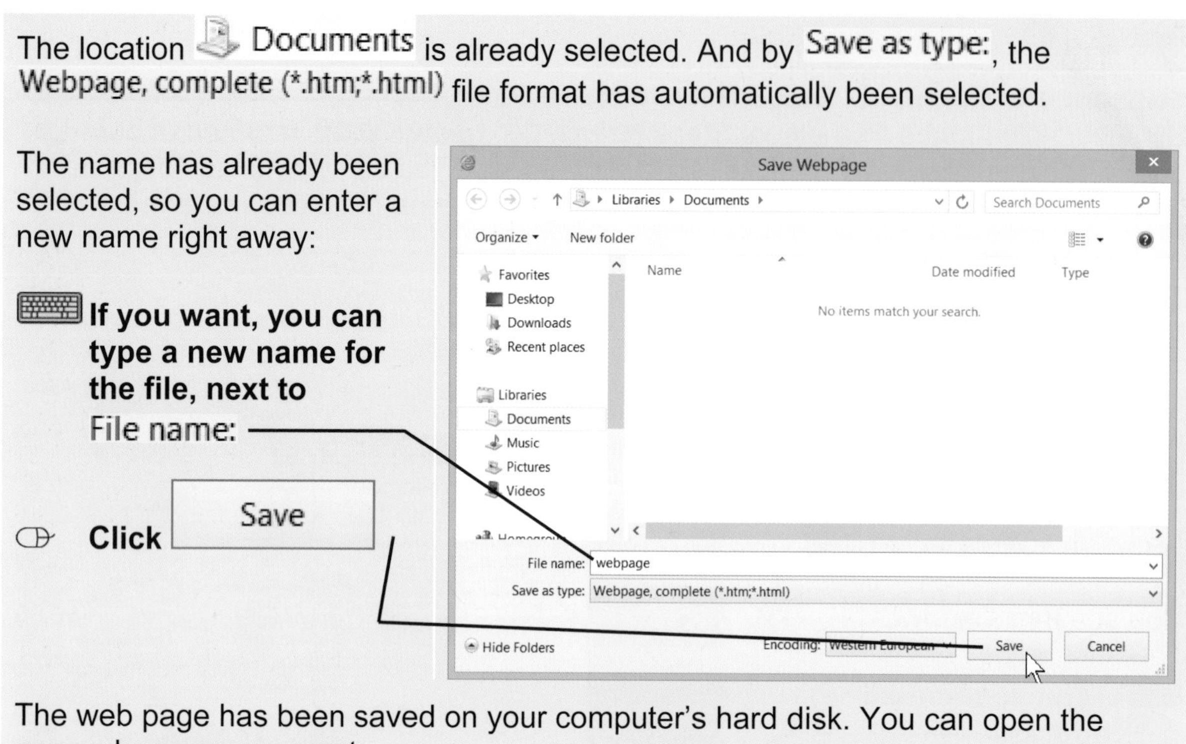


The web page has been saved on your computer's hard disk. You can open the page whenever you want.

**Close *Internet Explorer*** 12

This is how you open the web page:

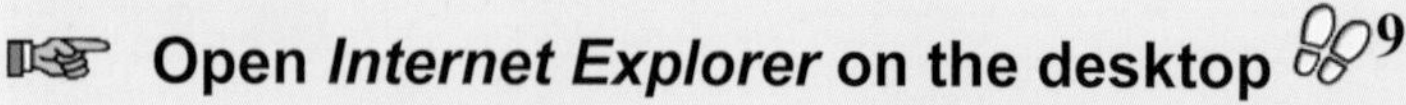

**Open *Internet Explorer* on the desktop** 9

**Press** Alt

**Click** File

**Click** Open...

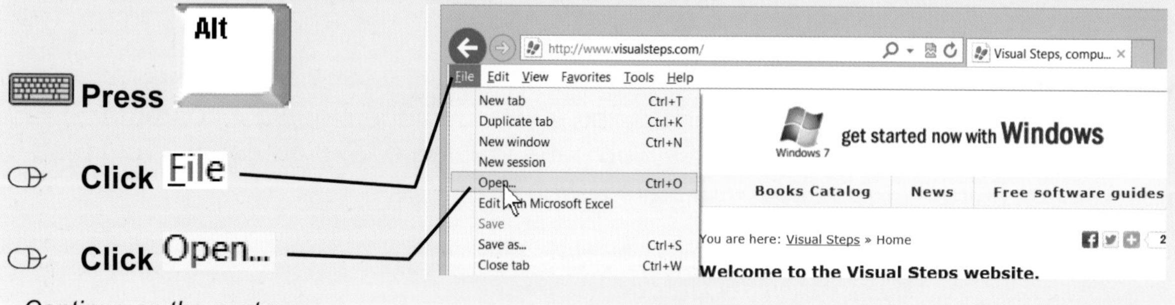


*- Continue on the next page -*

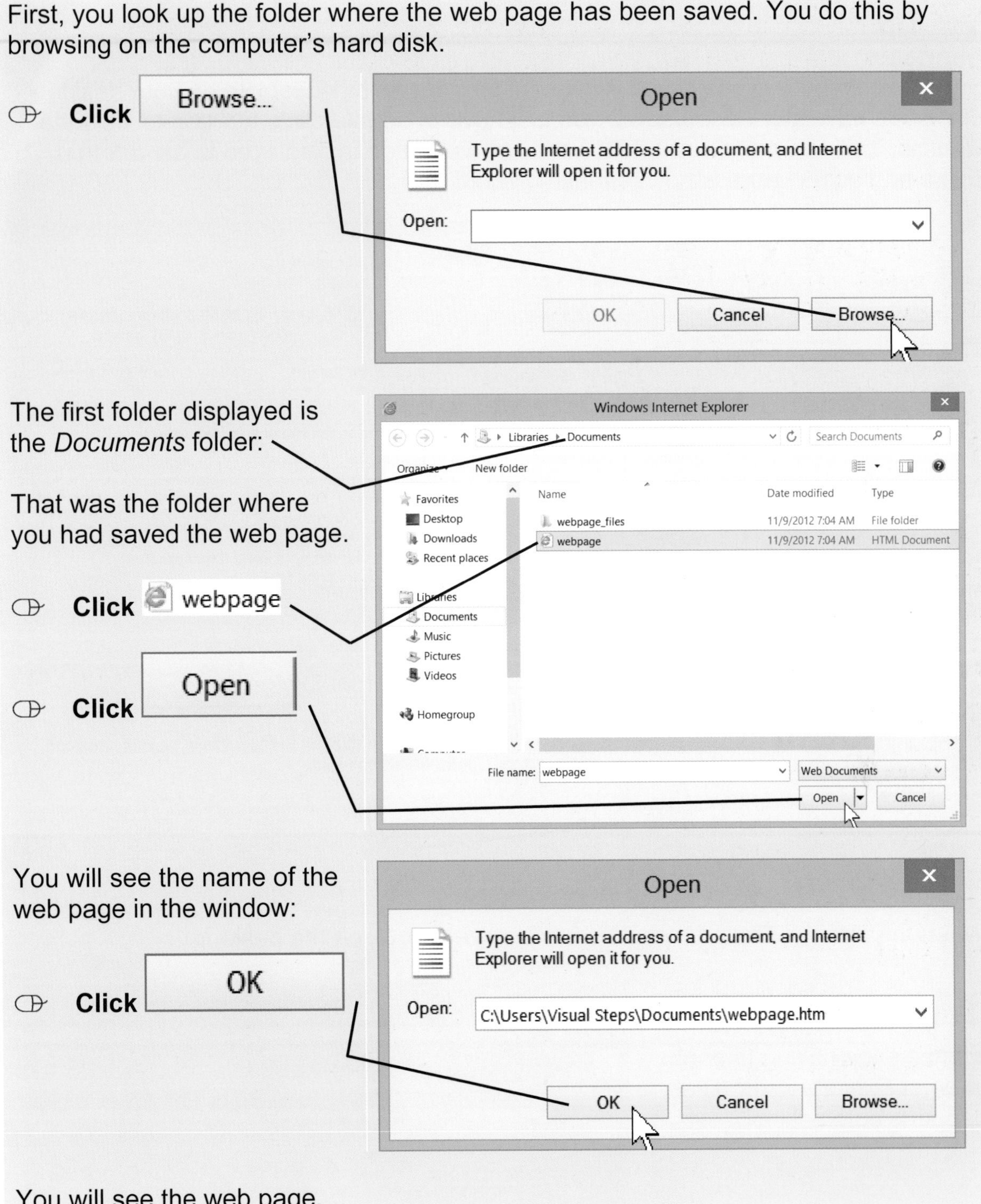


First, you look up the folder where the web page has been saved. You do this by browsing on the computer's hard disk.

- **Click** Browse...

The first folder displayed is the *Documents* folder:

That was the folder where you had saved the web page.

- **Click** webpage
- **Click** Open

You will see the name of the web page in the window:

- **Click** OK

You will see the web page.

## Tip

**Shortcuts**

You can also put an icon called a *shortcut* for your favorite website on your desktop. Once you have started *Windows*, you just have to double-click this icon to view the website. You can make a shortcut when the web page is displayed in the *Internet Explorer* window. Here is how to make a shortcut:

**Press** Alt

The menu bar appears:

**Click** File

**Click** Send

**Click** Shortcut to Desktop

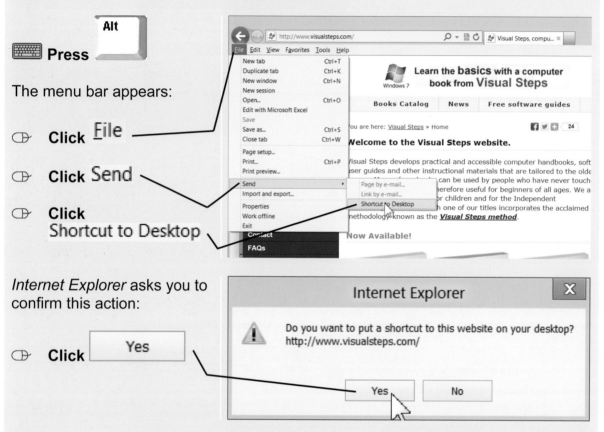

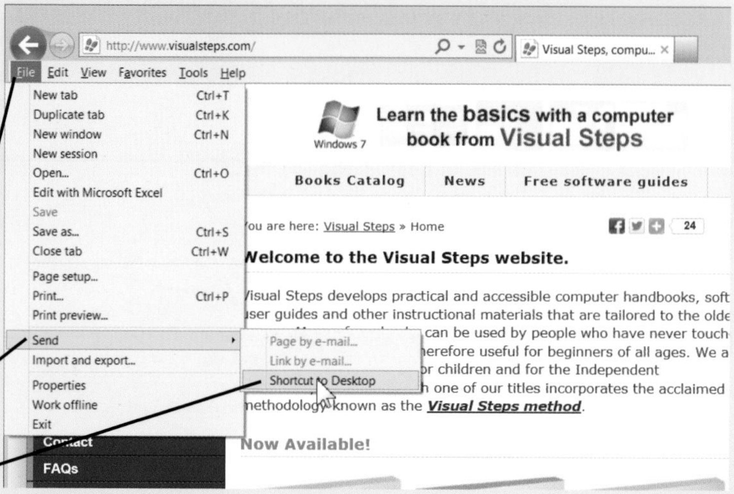

*Internet Explorer* asks you to confirm this action:

**Click** Yes

When the *Internet Explorer* window is minimized, you see the desktop:

By double-clicking this icon, you can open the website without even having to open *Internet Explorer* itself. That happens automatically.

# 4. Searching for Information

The World Wide Web is sometimes compared to a very large library, full of information regarding all sorts of subjects, but without a librarian to keep an eye on things. All the books in this enormous library are mixed up and not arranged in any clear order. This comparison is quite accurate. Indeed, there is no coordinating organization that manages and arranges all the information available on the Internet. Anyone can publish his own information on the Internet. This information will immediately be accessible to others, too. This does not make things easier, if you want to find something on the net.

A large number of companies are trying to help the Internet users by arranging this huge mountain of information, and making it accessible to the public. This is done in several ways. A search engine is a computer program that continuously searches the web pages on the Internet and collects the keywords for those pages in a gigantic index. You can use the website of such a search engine to look for web pages that are included in this index. For example, the *Google* search engine which you surely know.

*Windows 8* has a simple app that helps you look for information on the Internet. This app is called *Bing*. This is the search engine manufactured by *Microsoft*. You will learn more about this app in this chapter.

Another way or arranging the information on the Internet are directories. Here, a company has already selected a large number of web pages and arranged them according to their subject or category. For instance, all the pages regarding a certain country.

In this chapter you will learn various methods for searching and finding information.

In this chapter you will learn how to:

- use the *Bing* app;
- search with the address bar;
- search for information, images, and videos;
- set up *Google* as your default search engine;
- use the advanced search options in *Google*;
- search within a web page;
- use directories.

## 4.1 Searching with the Bing App

In *Windows 8* you can access the *Bing* app. With this app you can easily and quickly find information on the Internet. This is how you open the app:

**Click**

**Please note:** the image depicted on the tile changes daily. Anyhow, the left side of the tile will have the name *Bing* on it.

### HELP! I do not see the Bing tile.

If you do not see an app, you can open it from the apps screen.

**Right-click an empty area on the Start screen**

**Click** 

**Click the app**

Now you can use the *Bing* search engine made by *Microsoft*. At the top of the screen you see the search box. Here you can type your keyword:

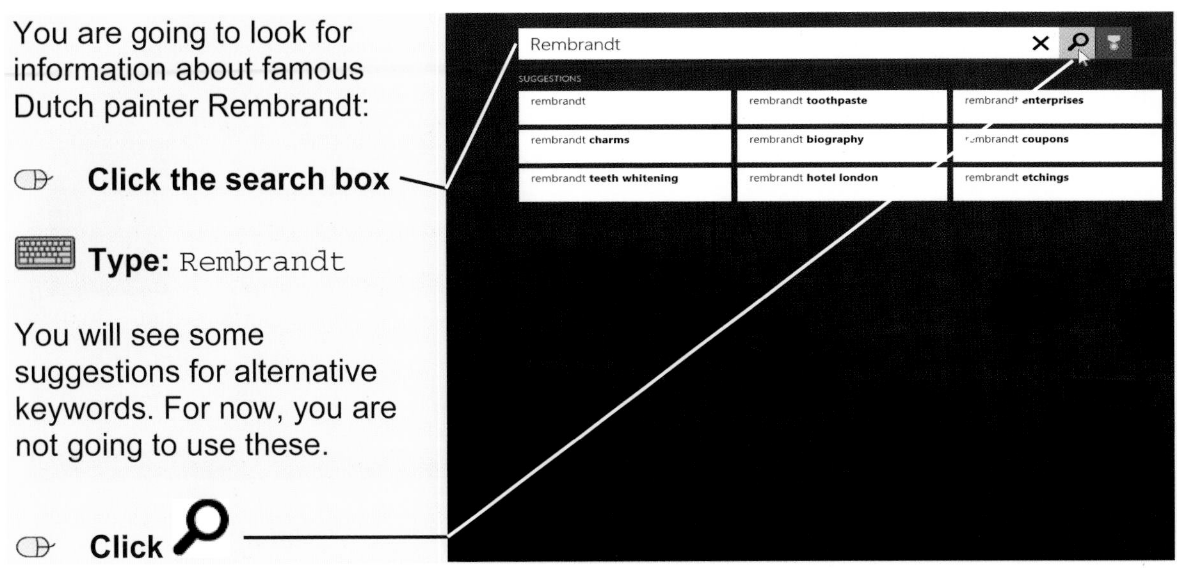


You are going to look for information about famous Dutch painter Rembrandt:

**Click the search box**

**Type:** `Rembrandt`

You will see some suggestions for alternative keywords. For now, you are not going to use these.

**Click**

After a few seconds you will see the search result. There are results on a single page, but you can view even more results by dragging across the page, from right to left.

Open one of the search results:

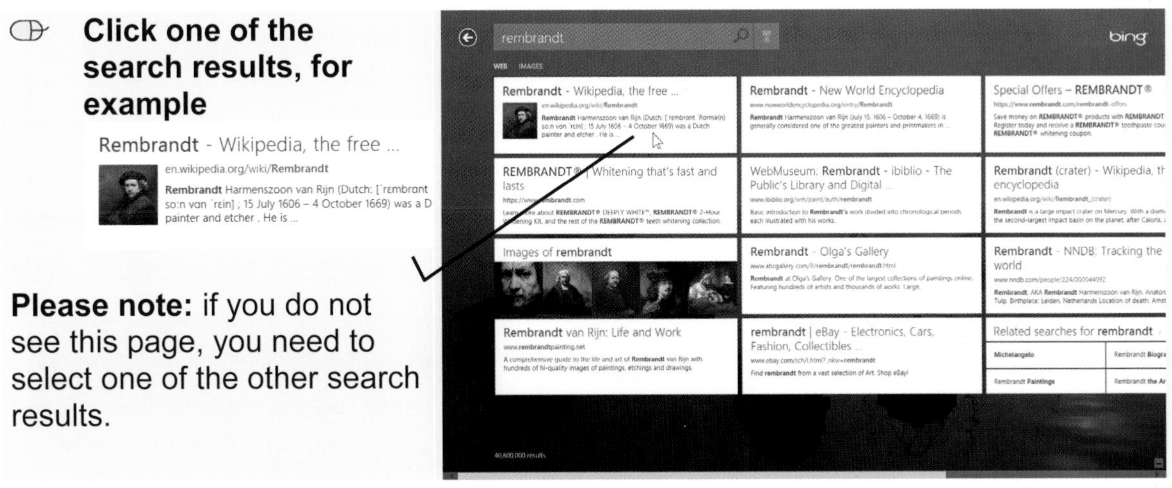


**Click one of the search results, for example**

Rembrandt - Wikipedia, the free ...
en.wikipedia.org/wiki/Rembrandt
**Rembrandt** Harmenszoon van Rijn (Dutch: [ˈrɛmbrɑnt ˈɦɑrmə(n)soːn vɑn ˈrɛin]; 15 July 1606 – 4 October 1669) was a D painter and etcher . He is ...

**Please note:** if you do not see this page, you need to select one of the other search results.

Now the *Internet Explorer* is opened. You see a web page with information on Rembrandt:

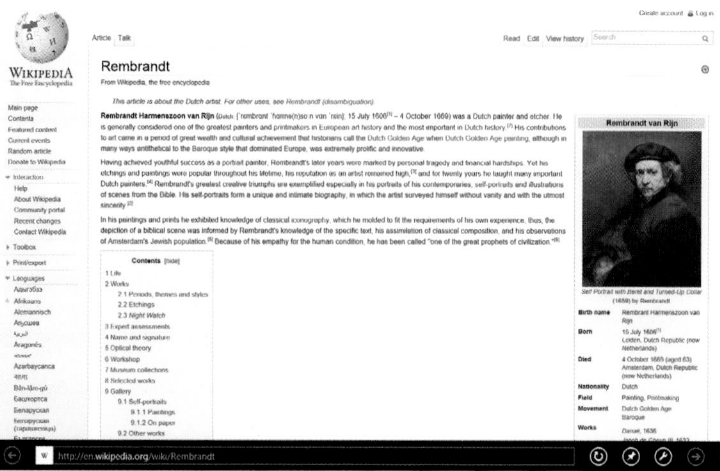

Go back to the *Bing* app. With this app you can also search for images:

**Open the *Bing* app with the switch list** 55

Again, you will see the search results. To limit the search results and only view the images that have something to do with Rembrandt:

**Click** IMAGES

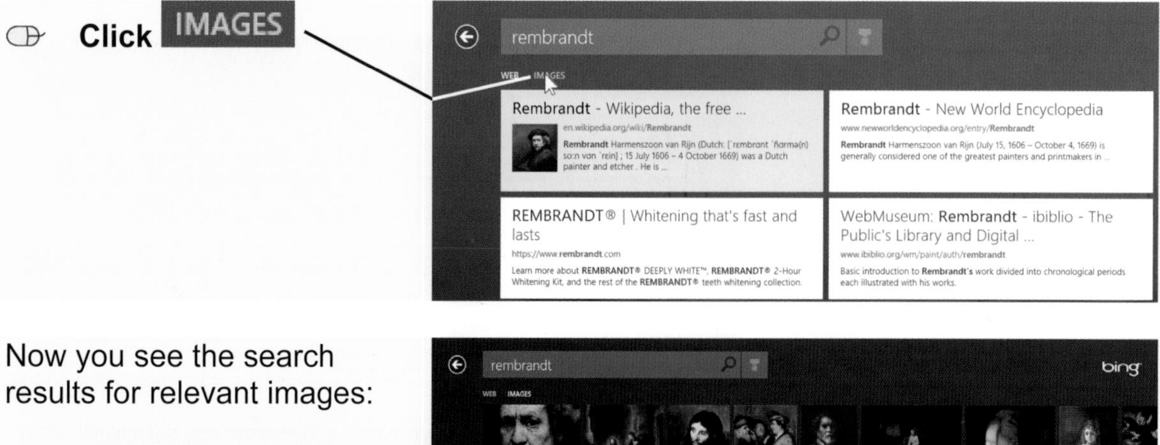


Now you see the search results for relevant images:

**Click one of the images**

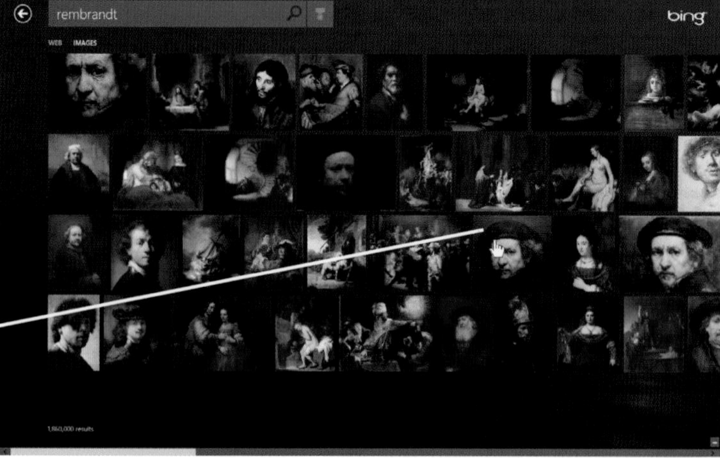

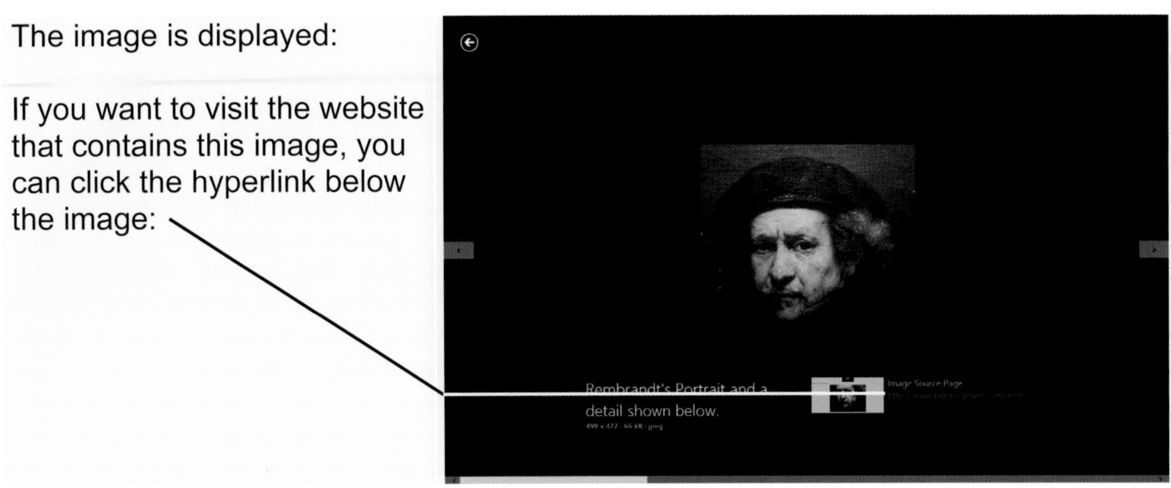


The image is displayed:

If you want to visit the website that contains this image, you can click the hyperlink below the image:

*Internet Explorer* offers many more options for looking up information on the Internet. You will learn to use these options in the next section. You can close the apps.

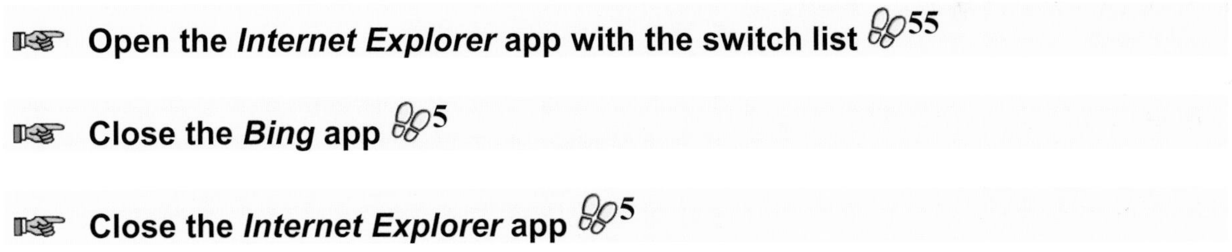

**Open the *Internet Explorer* app with the switch list** 55

**Close the *Bing* app** 5

**Close the *Internet Explorer* app** 5

## 4.2 Searching With the Address Bar

*Internet Explorer* offers direct access to *Microsoft's Bing* search engine, through the address bar. You can type your keyword in this bar. You are going to search for information on Rembrandt the painter, once more:

**Open *Internet Explorer* on the desktop** 9

**Click the address bar**

**Type:** `Rembrandt`

**Press** Enter

## Tip

**Search with the address bar in the Internet Explorer app**
You can also search using the address bar in the *Internet Explorer* app.

After a few seconds you see the search results of the *Bing* search engine:

At the top of the window you see various search options. For example, you can also search for images or news regarding a certain topic.

Usually, sponsored links are displayed at the upper side of the search results:

Bing also shows related searches:

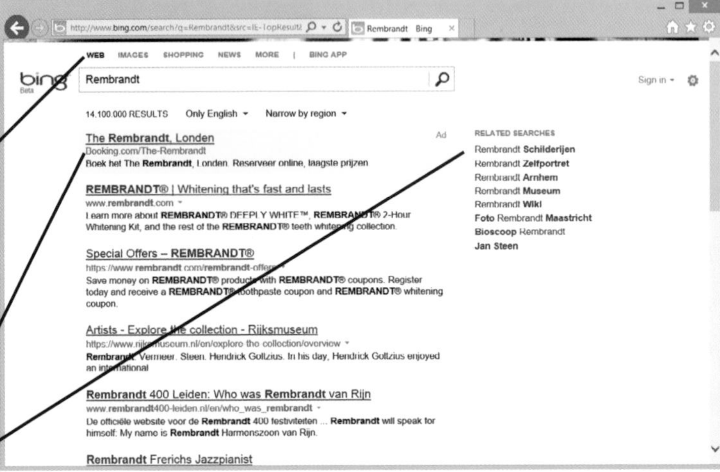


**Drag the scroll bar downwards**

You will see more search results:

**Drag the scroll bar upwards**

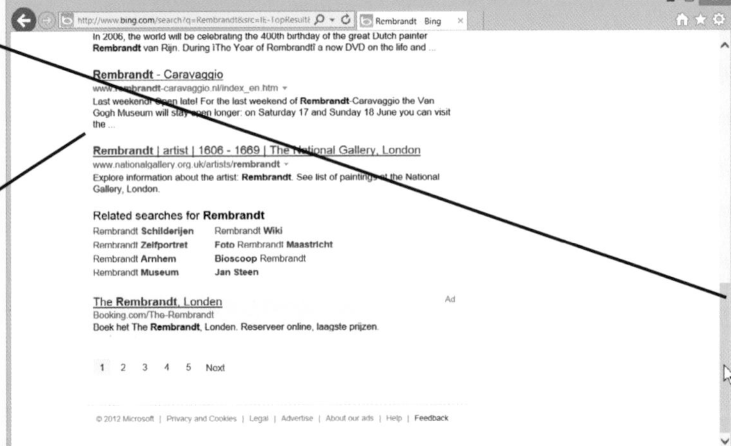


**Click one of the search results, for example** Artists - Explore the c

**Please note:** if you do not see this page, then just select one of the other search results.

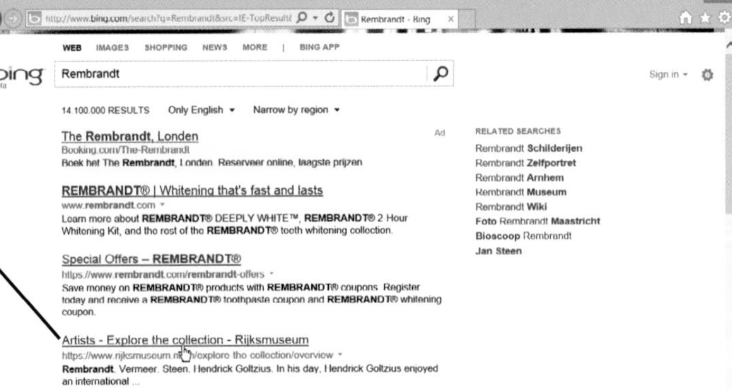

In this example you see a web page with information on Rembrandt:

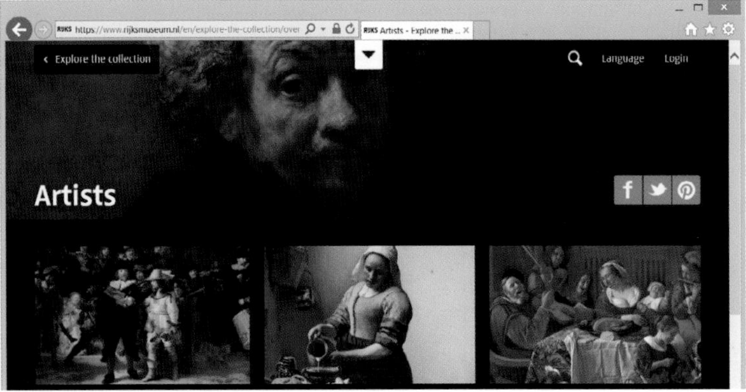


## 4.3 Setting Up the Default Search Engine

*Bing* is the default search engine in *Internet Explorer*. This is quite understandable, since *Bing* has been manufactured by *Microsoft*, just like *Internet Explorer*. With a few mouse clicks you can change the default search engine and choose another one, for instance, the much-used *Google* engine:

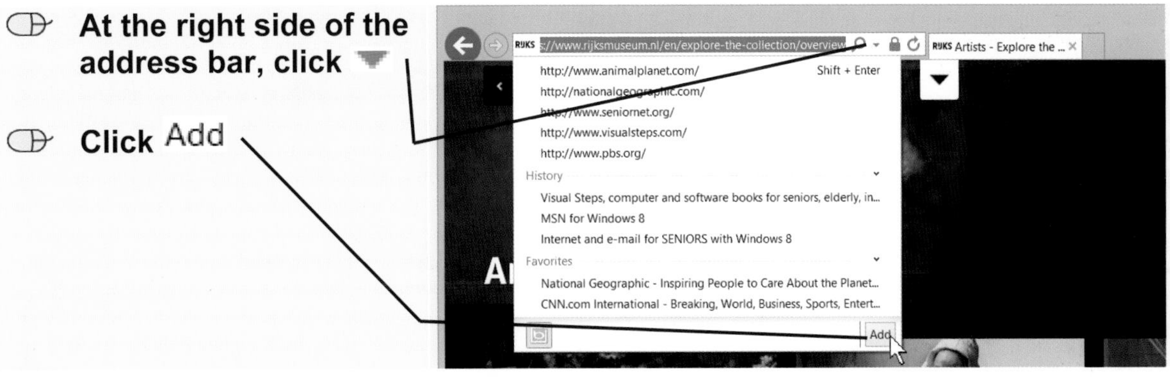


**At the right side of the address bar, click** ▼

**Click** Add

On this web page you can search for the search engine you want to add to *Internet Explorer*.

At the top right of the search box:

**Type:** `Google`

**Press** Enter

**By** Google Search, **click** Add to Internet Explorer

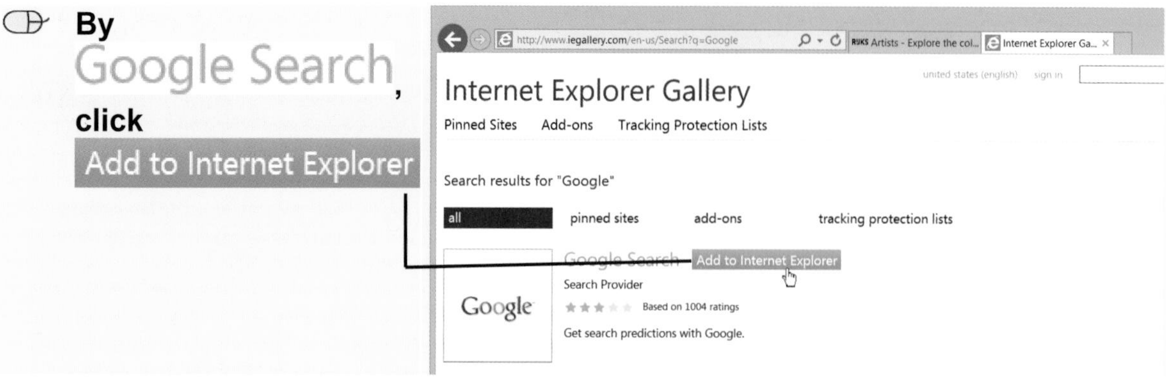


You will see this window:

**Click** Add to Internet Explo

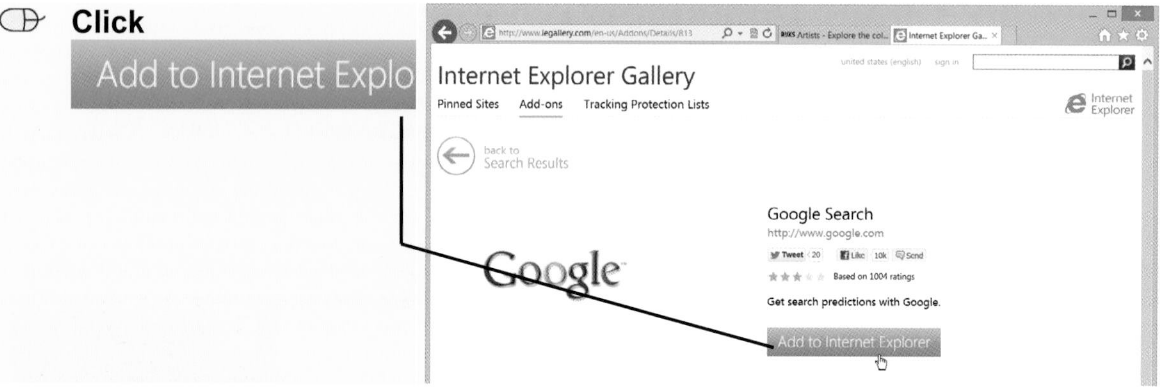


The *Add Search Provider* window appears:

Here you can set up *Google* as your default search engine:

**Check the box** ☑ **by** Make this my default searcl

**Click** Add

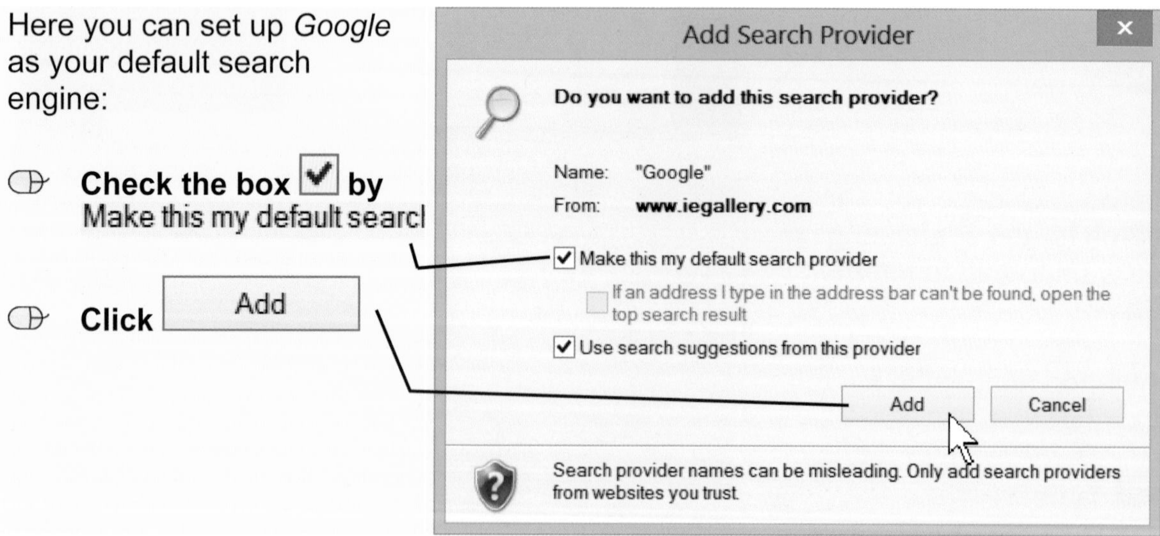

Now *Google* has been set as your default search engine. This is how you check it:

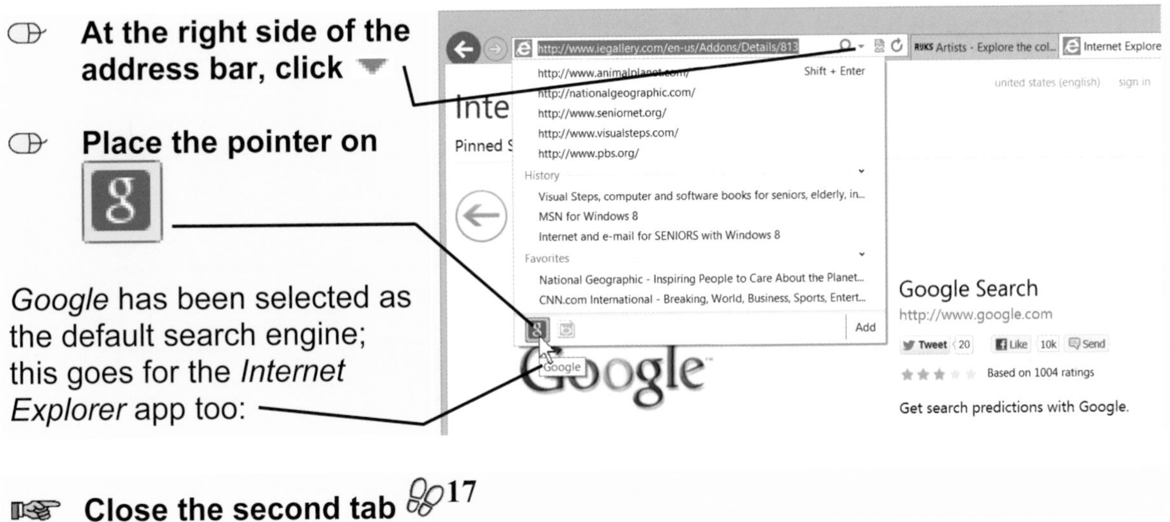


**At the right side of the address bar, click**

**Place the pointer on**

*Google* has been selected as the default search engine; this goes for the *Internet Explorer* app too:

**Close the second tab** 17

## 4.4 Searching with Google

*Google* works practically the same way as *Bing*. Because you have now set up *Google* as the default search engine, you can also use the address bar to start searching with *Google*. Just try and find some information on Vincent van Gogh, for example:

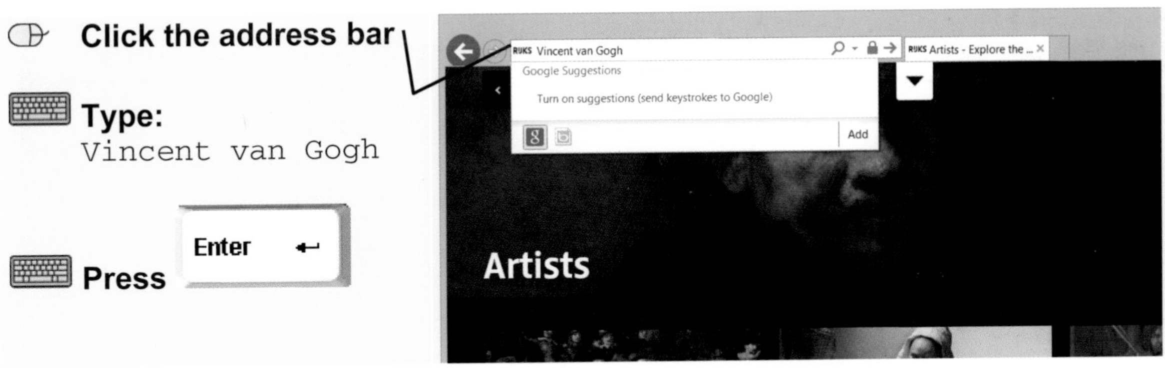


**Click the address bar**

**Type:**
`Vincent van Gogh`

**Press** Enter

**Tip**

**Google.com**
Of course, you can also open the www.google.com web page first, and start searching from there.

On this *Google* page you can see that about twenty million hits (search results) have been found:

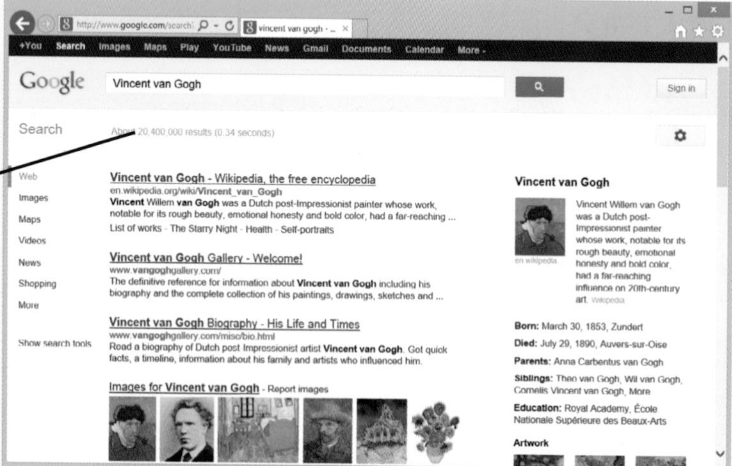


**Drag the scroll bar downwards**

At the bottom of the page you will see a row of numbers, with the word **Next**:

If you click **Next** you will see the next ten search results.

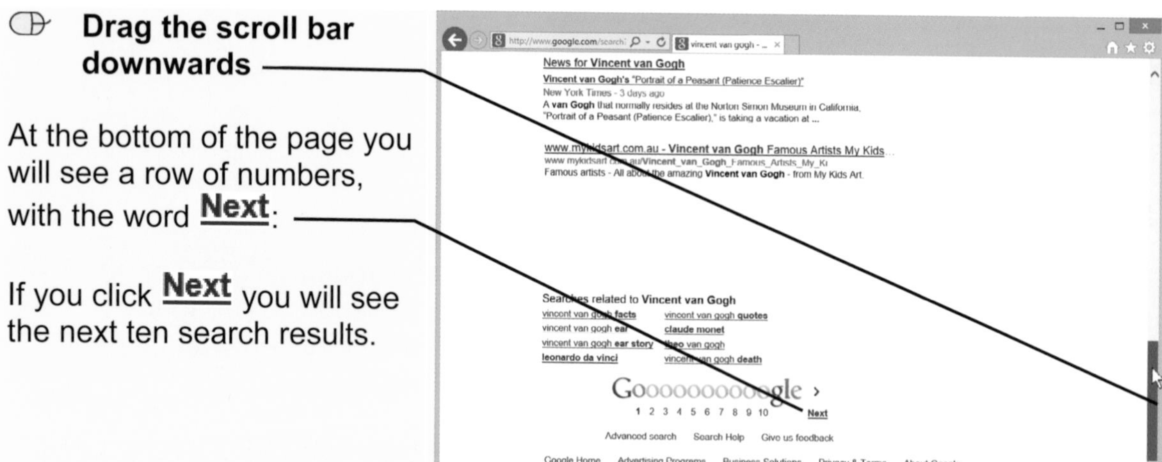

# 4.5 Specific Searching

It is impossible to leaf through all of these search results, and very difficult to find exactly what you wanted to know about Vincent van Gogh. If you want to search for more specific terms, you can search within the current search results.

Maybe you would like to know which museum you could visit, to look at one of his famous sunflower paintings. Just try this:

**Drag the scroll bar upwards**

**Click next to the word** Gogh **in the search box**

**Press the space bar**

**Type:** `visit museum sunflowers`

**Click**

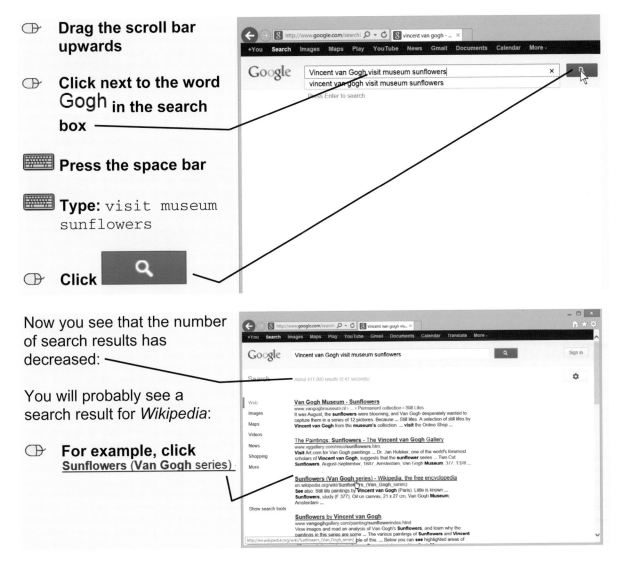

Now you see that the number of search results has decreased:

You will probably see a search result for *Wikipedia*:

**For example, click** Sunflowers (Van Gogh series)

## Please note:

The Internet is subject to constant changes. That is why the search results described in this book may have changed after this book was written. If you do not see the search result from the example above, just use one of the other search results.

You will see the *Wikipedia* page for Vincent van Gogh. This page also contains information regarding the museums that exhibit his paintings:

Now you can go back again:

Click

The web page with the *Google* search results is displayed again.

**Wikipedia**
*Wikipedia* is a free encyclopedia, accessible to everyone on the Internet, and written by many volunteers. Every blue word in the text is a hyperlink to a new article regarding that word. *Wikipedia* has quickly become the largest reference book on the Internet. The *Wikipedia* website is regularly updated with new information. Qualified users are allowed to update pages whenever they want. That is why the window above may look different from the window on your screen.

## 4.6 Advanced Searching

A more specific search within the initial search results will usually get you what you were looking for. However, if you know exactly what you are looking for, you can give the *Advanced search* option in *Google* a try:

**If necessary, drag the scroll bar downwards**

**Click** Advanced search

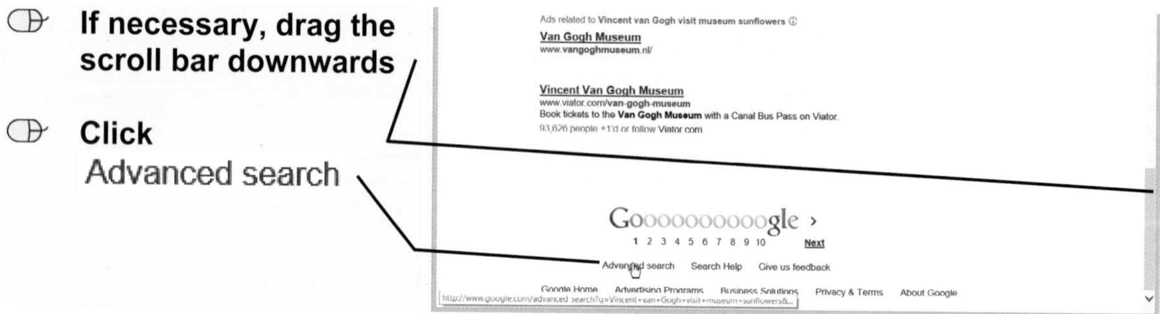

The *Advanced search* window will be opened:

The most recently used keywords have already been entered in one of the search boxes:

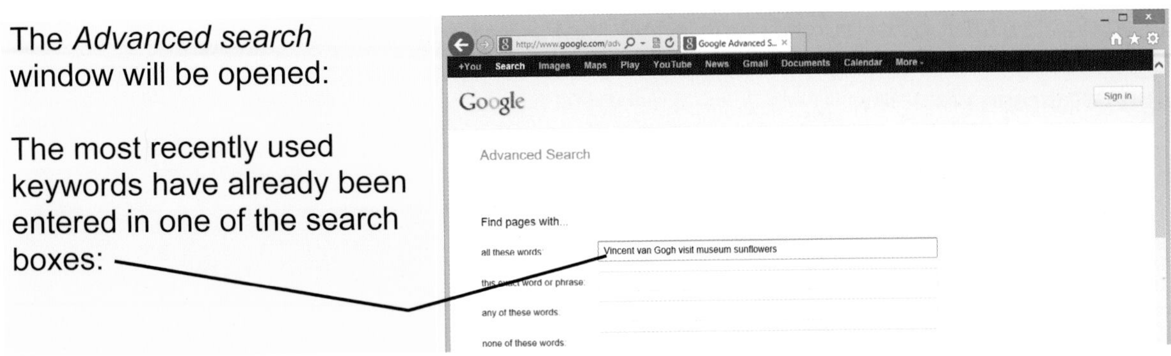


You are going to search all over again, so you can delete these keywords:

**Click the search box three times**

The words have been selected. Now you can delete them:

**Press** Delete

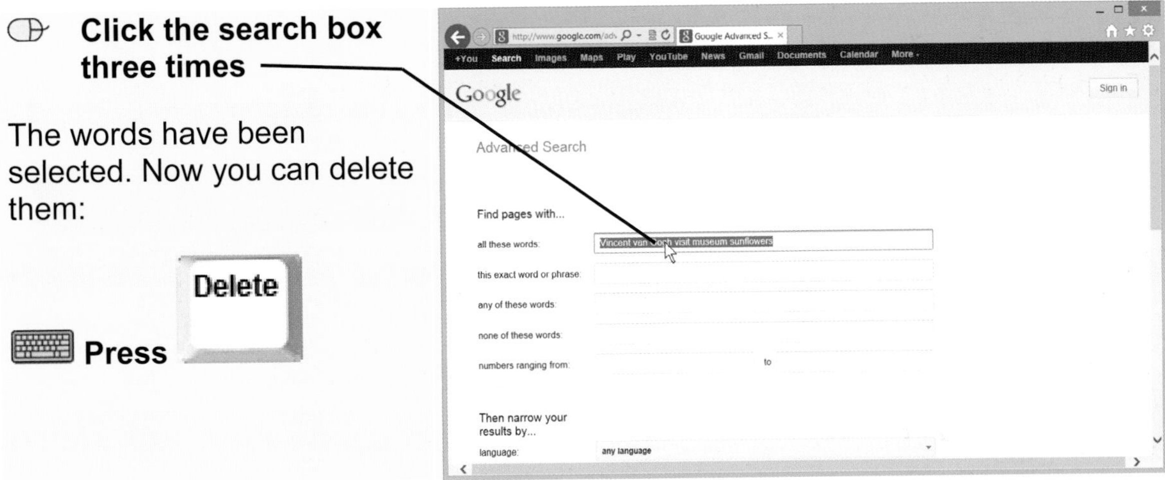


For example, you would like to know whether the Rijksmuseum in Amsterdam is open on weekends, and exactly what are the opening hours. First you fill in the name and location of the museum. The search box behind all these words: will make sure the web pages containing both words will be found. Although these words do not need to be entered in any specific order:

**By** all these words:, **type:** `Rijksmuseum Amsterdam`

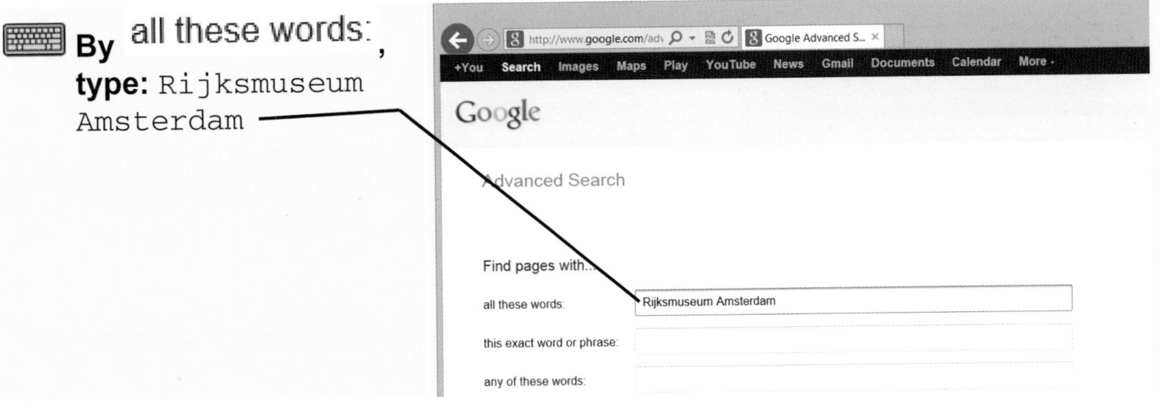

In the next search box you can type additional keywords, for instance, part of a sentence, or a specific combination of words. Most search engines call this an 'exact word or phrase'.

**By** this exact word or phrase:, **type:** `opening hours`

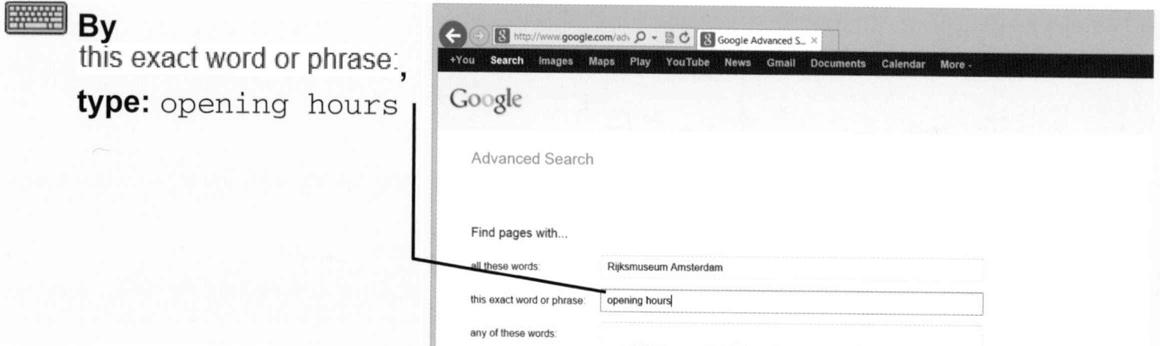


You can also type several words, of which at least one has to be found:

**By** any of these words:, **type:** `Saturday Sunday`

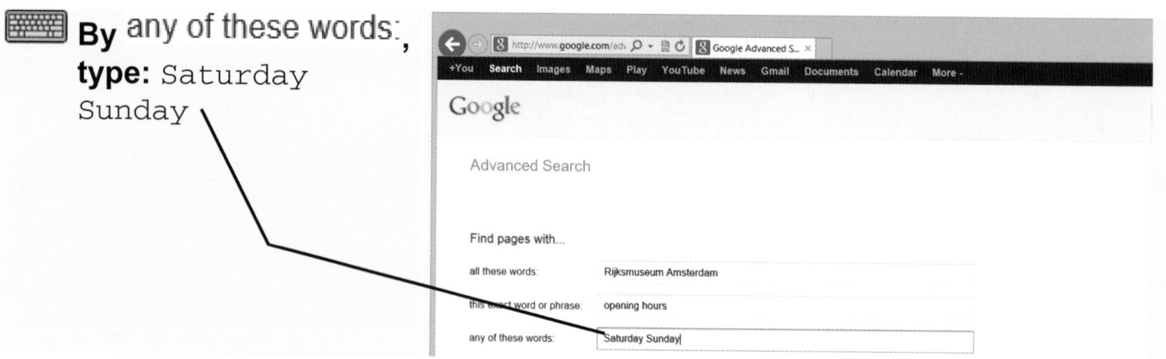


You can enter even more conditions, but for now this will not be necessary. Start the search:

**Drag the scroll bar downwards**

**Click** **Advanced Search**

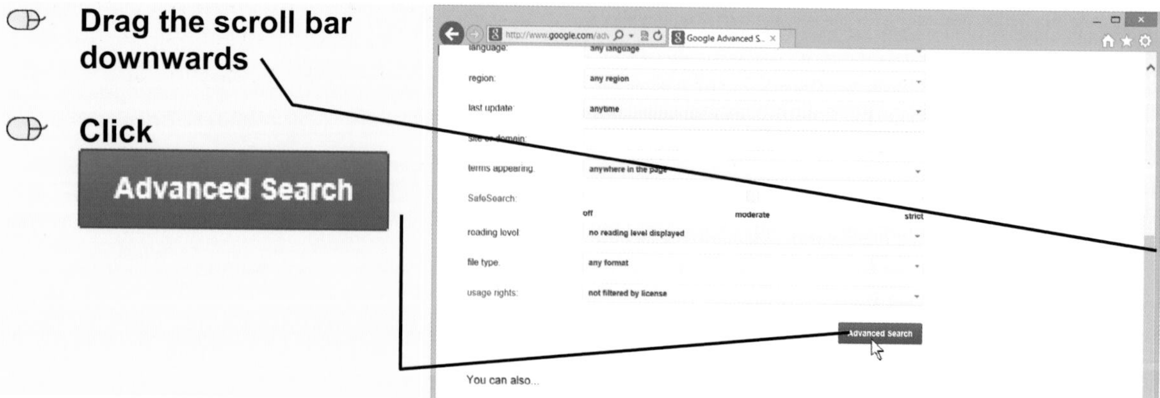


The search results will be displayed.

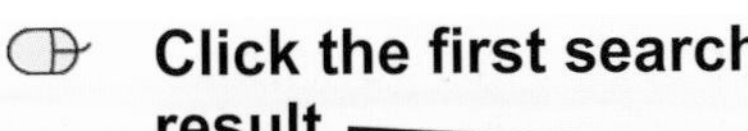

**Click the first search result**

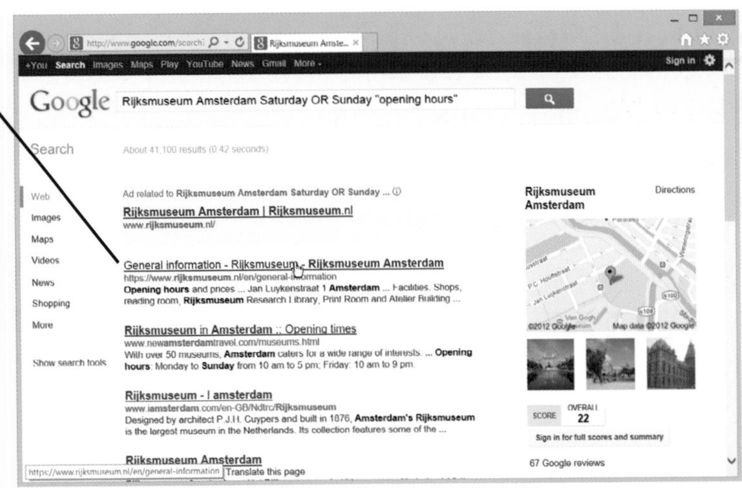


**Please note:** do not click the advertisement above the result.

In this example, the first search result will lead you to the Rijksmuseum website, right away.

The correct page of the Rijksmuseum website is displayed. That is to say, the page containing the information on the opening hours:

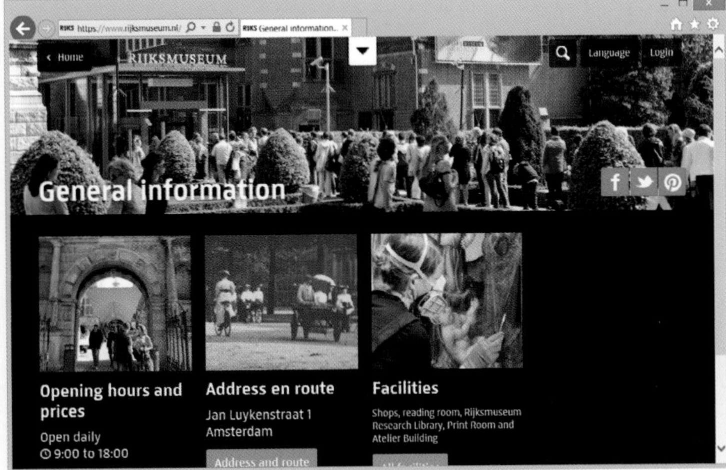


## Please note:

Since the Internet is continuously changing, it may be possible that the first search result on your screen does not lead you to the website of the Rijksmuseum. If this is the case, then just select the website that seems most suitable to your search.

In the next section you are going to search for images.

## 4.7 Searching for Images

It is possible to limit the search to the images that have to do with Vincent van Gogh:

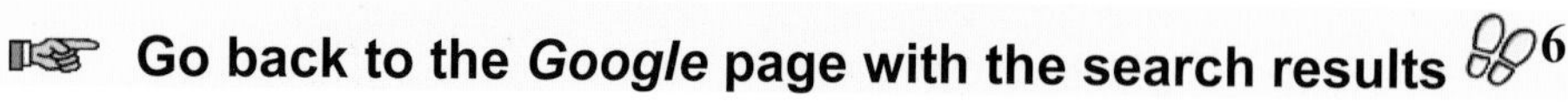

**Go back to the *Google* page with the search results** 6

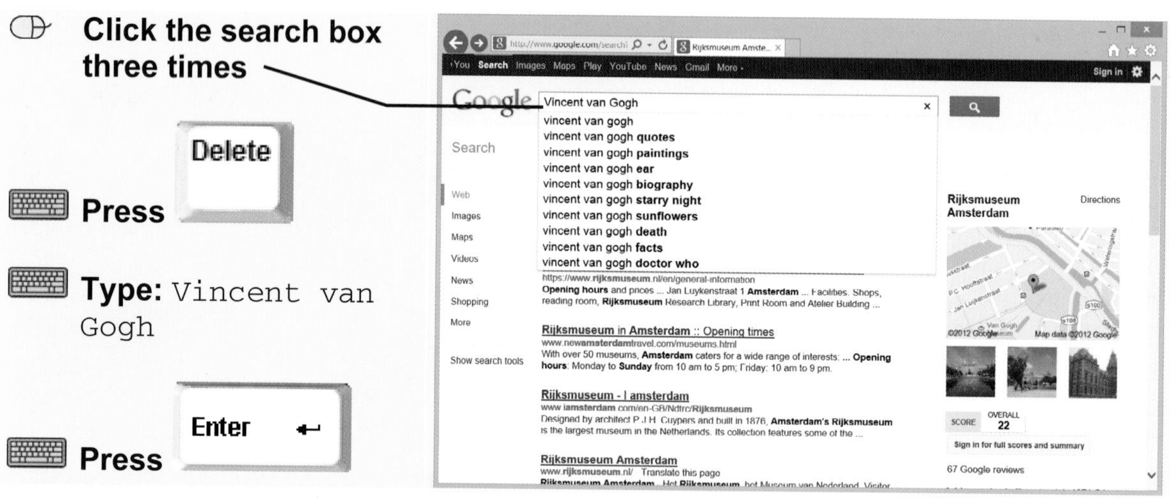

**Click the search box three times**

**Press** Delete

**Type:** `Vincent van Gogh`

**Press** Enter



You will see the search results for the keyword 'Vincent van Gogh'. To go to the image results:

**Click** Images

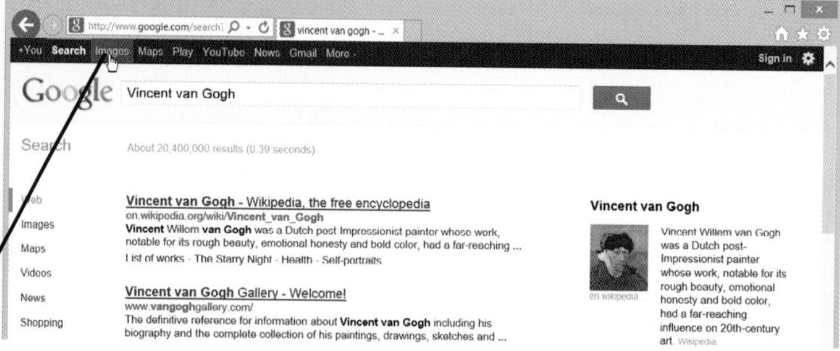



Now you see the search results for images of paintings by Vincent van Gogh:

**Click one of the images**

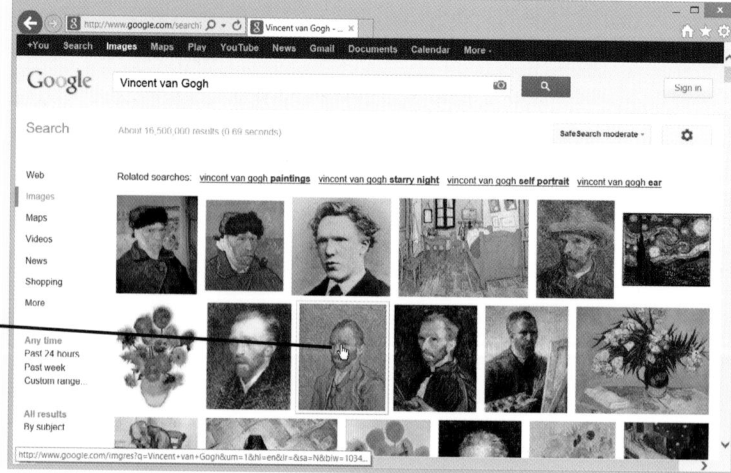

On this page you see an example of the website where the image has been found.

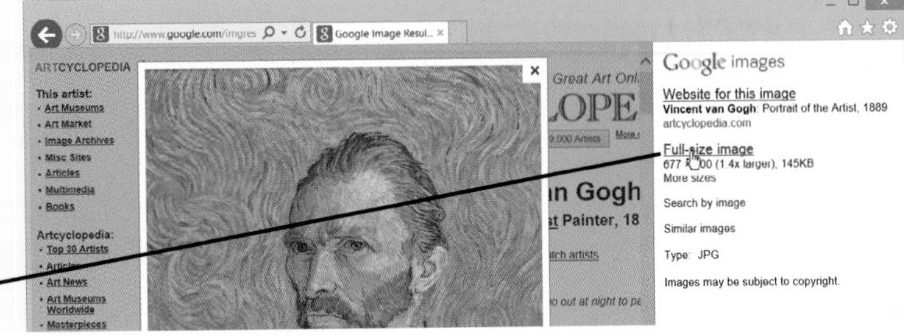


Click Full-size image

The image will be opened:

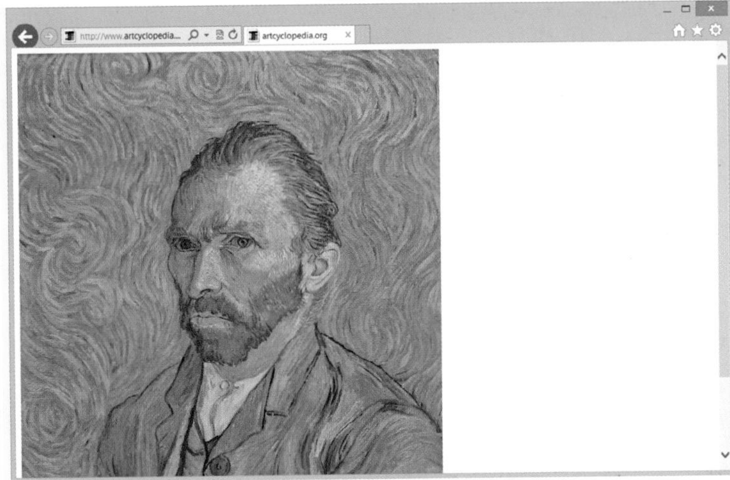

Go back to the previous page 6

If you want to visit the website where this image has been found, you can use the hyperlink that is displayed here:

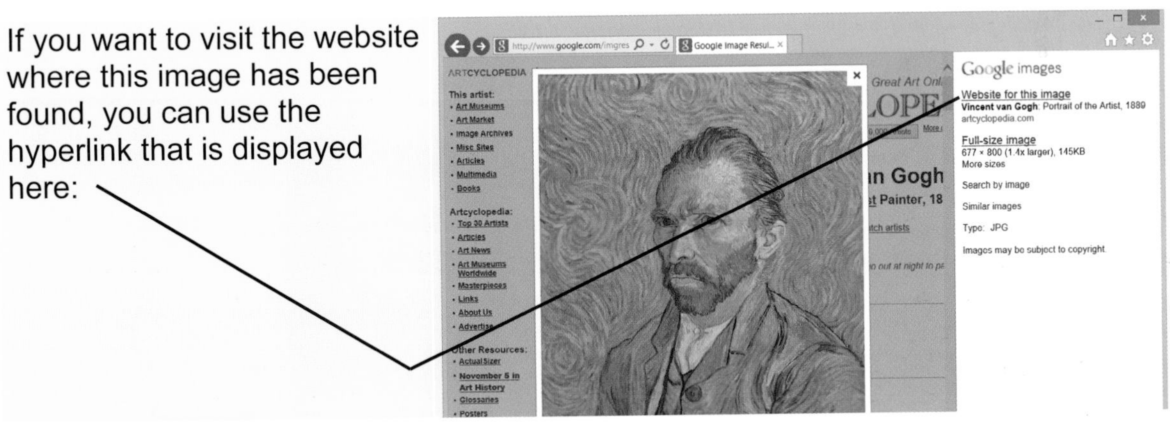


Go back to the previous page 6

## 4.8 Searching for Videos

Besides for looking for images, you can also use *Google* to search for videos.

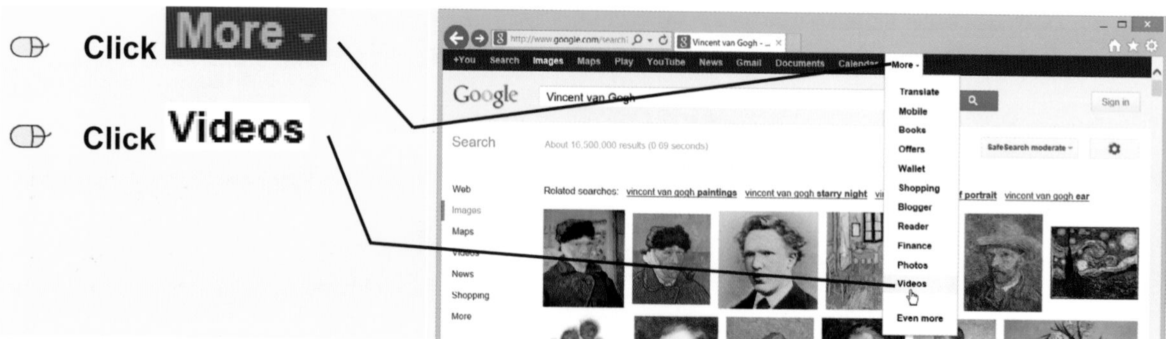

- **Click** **More**
- **Click** **Videos**

On this page you will see a list of videos that have something to do with Vincent van Gogh. This is how you watch a video:

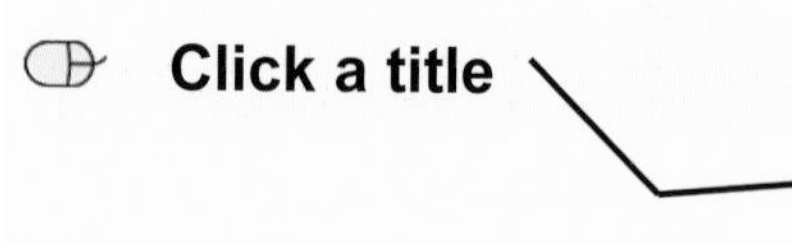

- **Click a title**

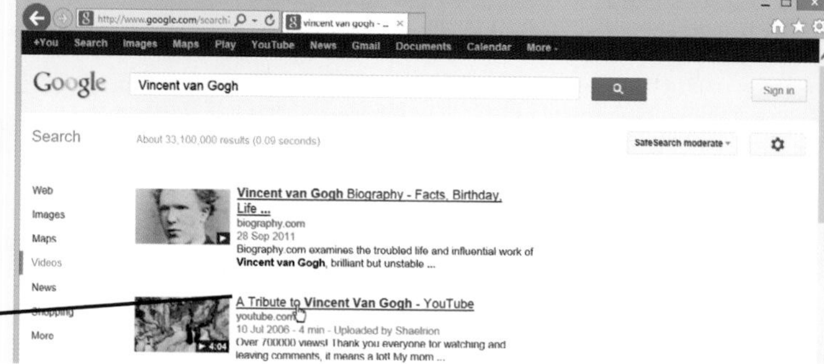

The video will be played in the window:

In this example, it is a video that is published on *YouTube*. This is a popular website for viewing and sharing videos. In the *Tip* at the back of this chapter you can read more about *YouTube*.

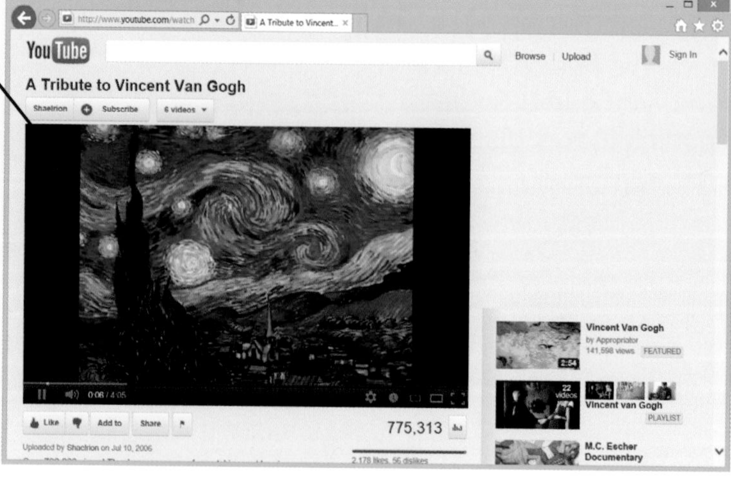

## 4.9 Searching Within a Page

Sometimes a web page contains so much text that you cannot find your keyword right away. In such a case you can search the text in the window for a certain word or a sentence. This is how you do it:

**Open the web page www.visualsteps.com/internet8** 1

**Click** **Practice website**

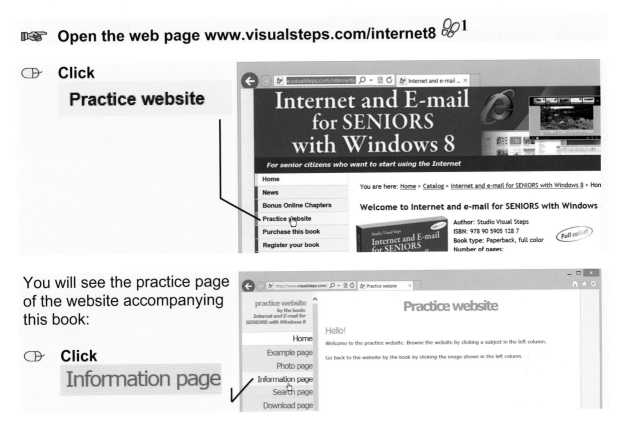

You will see the practice page of the website accompanying this book:

**Click** Information page

In a separate window you will see a text with a description of the Anne Frank house:

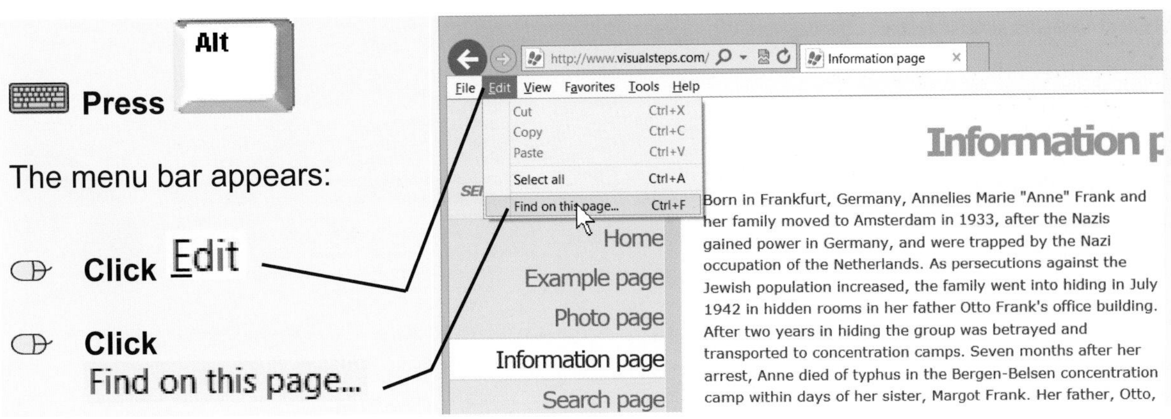

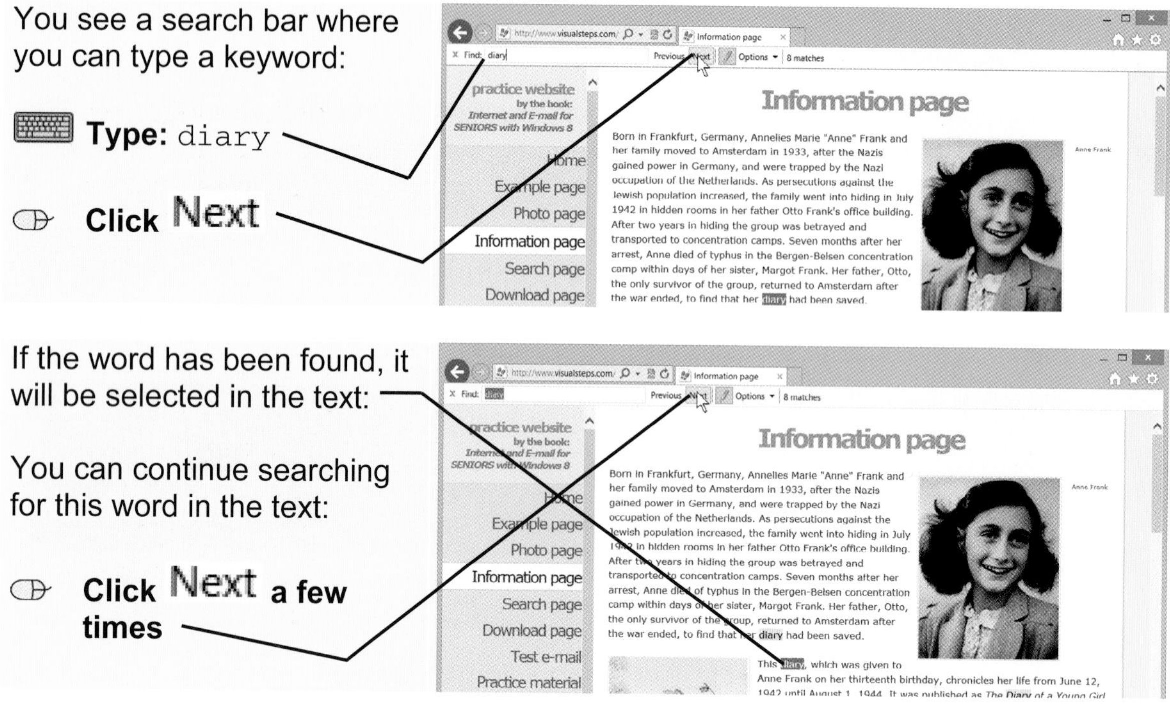

You see a search bar where you can type a keyword:

Type: `diary`

Click Next

If the word has been found, it will be selected in the text:

You can continue searching for this word in the text:

Click Next a few times

If the word does not occur in the text more often, you will see the first search result again. You can stop searching by closing the search bar:

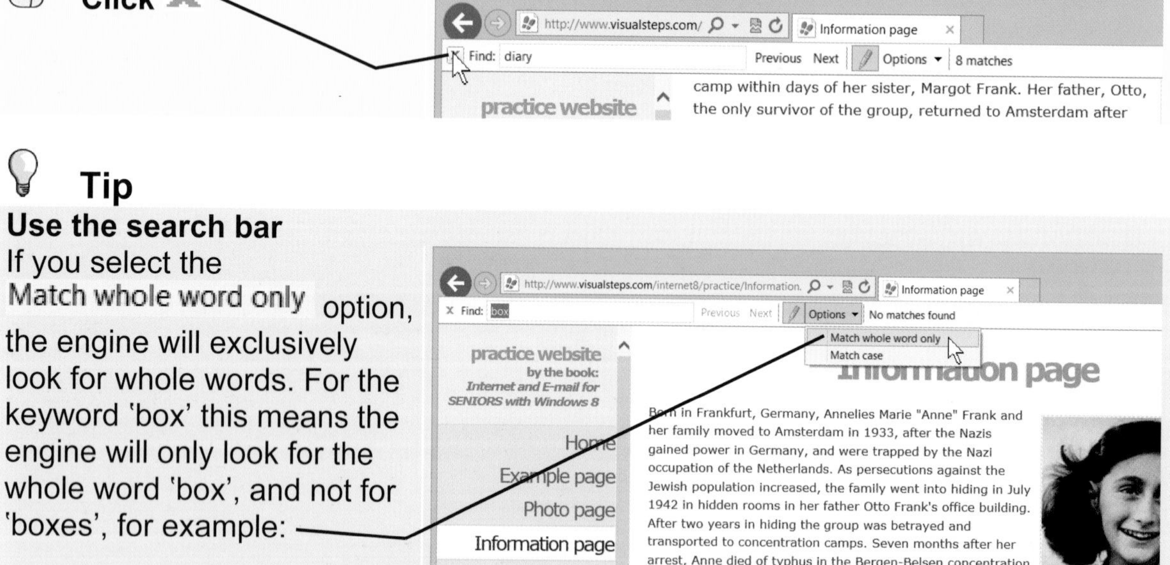

Click X

## Tip

**Use the search bar**

If you select the Match whole word only option, the engine will exclusively look for whole words. For the keyword 'box' this means the engine will only look for the whole word 'box', and not for 'boxes', for example:

If you select the Match case option, the engine will take into account in what case the words are typed. In this example, 'box' would be found, but 'Box' not. With these options you can search for items in a very effective way.

# 4.10 Directories

A directory is a website containing a large number of web addresses categorized by subject. This categorizing is done by a large editorial staff who work on the directory by organizing, evaluating and checking websites. This results in a useful summary. A good example of such a directory is the Open Directory Project. You are going to take a look at it:

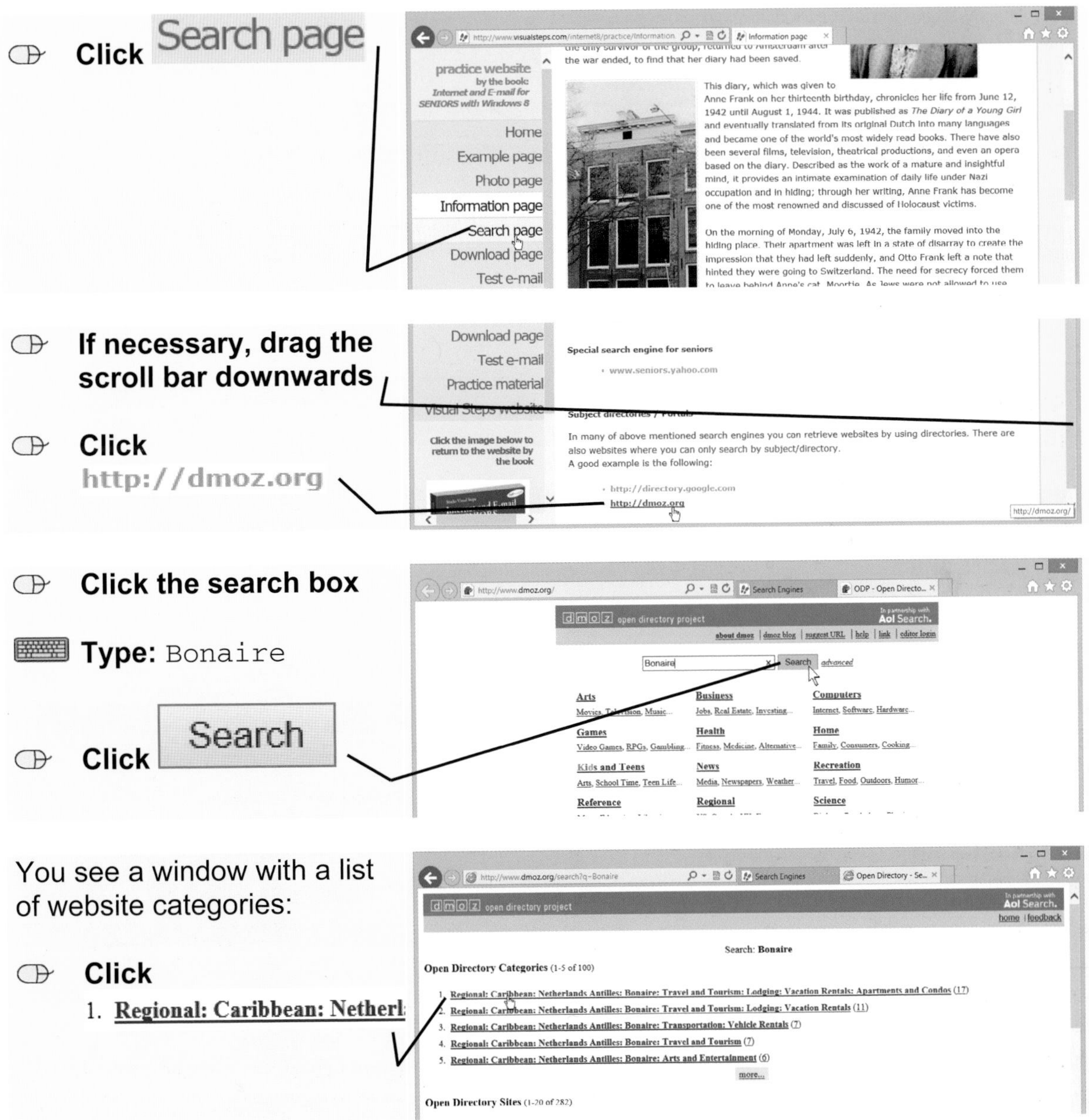


**Click** Search page

**If necessary, drag the scroll bar downwards**

**Click** http://dmoz.org

**Click the search box**

**Type:** Bonaire

**Click** Search

You see a window with a list of website categories:

**Click** 1. Regional: Caribbean: Netherl

All pages will be searched for the word Bonaire.

You will see a sub category:

- Click **Travel and Tourism** *(41)*

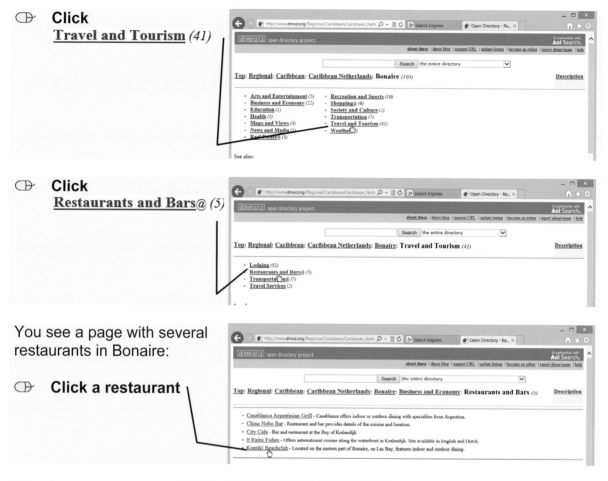

- Click **Restaurants and Bars@** *(5)*

You see a page with several restaurants in Bonaire:

- **Click a restaurant**

The page is opened. You see the website of a restaurant on Bonaire:

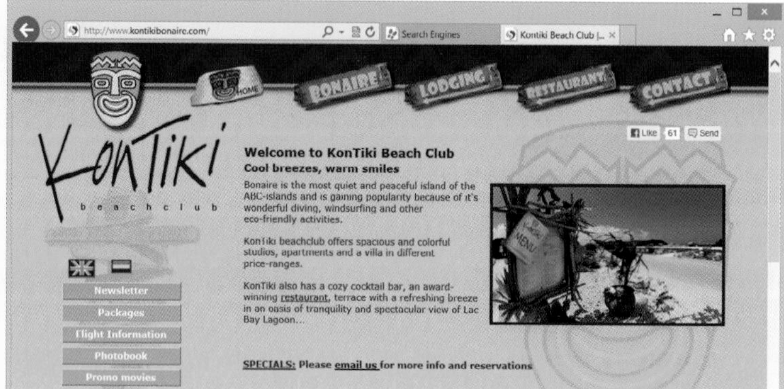


- **Close *Internet Explorer*** 12

In this chapter you have learned how to search for information on the Internet in various ways. You can repeat these search operations and practice searching the Internet in the following exercises.

# 4.11 Exercises

Have you forgotten how to perform a particular action? Use the number beside the footsteps to look it up in the appendix *How Do I Do That Again?*

## Exercise 1: Searching with the Instant Search Box

In this exercise, you will practice searching for information.

☞ Open *Internet Explorer* on the desktop. 9

☞ Use the address bar to search for the word *bridge*. 25

☞ Take a look at the websites that were found. 26

☞ Use the address bar to search for the word *holiday*. 25

☞ Take a look at the websites that were found. 26

## Exercise 2: Searching with a Directory

In this exercise, you will practice searching using the *Open Directory Project*.

☞ Open *dmoz.org* from the browser *History*. 20

☞ Search for *Ford*.

☞ Choose the category called *Recreation: Autos: Makes and Models: Ford*.

☞ Choose the category called *Explorer*.

☞ Take a look at a the websites that was found. 26

☞ Close *Internet Explorer*. 12

# 4.12 Background Information

**Dictionary**

| | |
|---|---|
| **Advanced search** | A separate search page in *Google* where you can enter very exact words or phrases for the search engine to find. |
| **Bing** | Search engine made by *Microsoft*. |
| **Case sensitive** | Words can differ in meaning based on the differing use of uppercase and lowercase letters. The case may filter words with a certain significance. For example, the case sensitive keyword 'Holiday' may result in finding people who are called Holiday, while 'holiday' will result in vacation websites being found. Searches performed by *Google* and *Bing* are not case sensitive. |
| **Default search engine** | Search provider that is used by default by *Internet Explorer*. |
| **Directory** | A collection of links to other websites, listed by category and sub-category. This categorizing is done by a large editorial staff who work on the directory by organizing, evaluating and checking websites. This results in a useful summary. The *Open Directory Project* is a good example. |
| **Exact phrase** | Search terms that are treated as a unit. An option offered by *Google Advanced search*. |
| **Google** | A popular search engine. |
| **Keyword** | The word for which you search. |
| **Search box** | Also called instant search box. Box that can be used to start a search on the Internet. |
| **Search engine** | A program that is constantly busy indexing web pages. *Google* and *Bing* are search engines. You can use the search engine's web page to search for all the web pages that contain your search terms. |
| **Wikipedia** | A multilingual, web-based, free content encyclopedia project. *Wikipedia* is written collaboratively by volunteers, its articles can be edited by anyone with access to the website. |

*Source: Windows Help and Support*

**How does a search engine work?**
Search engines such as *Bing* en *Google* are programs that are busy indexing web pages on the basis of keywords around the clock.

Search engines differ in the method they use to do this. That is why the results from different search engines are often different. Some search engines index as many words as possible on a web page. Others only use search terms found in the titles of web pages.
There are also search engines that primarily use keywords on web pages. These hidden keywords are put in by the web page designer. Sometimes this feature is abused, and particular keywords are intentionally used because these words are frequently typed into searches. This can be the reason why you sometimes see web pages in your search results that have very little to do with your search term.

Search engines work like a kind of robot and are therefore fairly limited and a bit 'stupid'. No editing or selection is performed on the pages. This limitation becomes particularly evident when you search for words that have multiple meanings. An editor would be able to separate the web pages based upon their content.
Although all the well-known search engine companies have a department where editing does take place, and hundreds of websites have been organized by subject or category.

However, usually a website has to be submitted to a search engine in order to be included in its index. Websites that have not been submitted cannot be found by the search engine. That may be the reason why you cannot find a particular website you were looking for.

## 4.13 Tips

 **Tip**

**Using search engines**

Here are some handy tips to improve your seach results:

- First, get a lot of practice using a particular search engine such as *Google* and thoroughly investigate all its search options. Which specific search options are you going to use? How does the search engine handle multiple keywords? You can find all of this information in the search engine's help pages.
- Once you have some experience, give other search engines a try. You will discover through experience which search engines you like best.
- Always begin with the most specific search possible. For example, if you want to find information about the *Epson Stylus Photo 1400* printer, then you should use this whole phrase (*Epson Stylus Photo 1400)* as your search phrase. If you do not get enough results, then try *Epson Stylus*. As a last resort, type just the word *Epson*.

 **Tip**

**Google search tips**

In this tip you will find additional tips for searching with *Google*:

- Keep it simple: if you are looking for information on the city of Barcelona, try *Barcelona.* But remember: this will get you millions of search results.
- Use multiple keywords: if you are looking for a hotel in Barcelona, you will get better results with *hotel Barcelona* than with either *hotel* or *Barcelona*.
- *Google* only returns pages that include all of your keywords. To restrict a search further, just include more words.
- *Google* searches are not case sensitive. All letters will be interpreted as lower case letters. For example, searches for *Rembrandt Van Rijn* and *rembrandt van rijn* will return the same results.
- To find pages that include either of two search terms, add an uppercase OR between the terms. For example, here is how to search for a hotel in either Barcelona or Rome: *hotel Barcelona OR Rome*.
- When you place the tilde sign (~) immediately in front of your search term, *Google* will also search for synonyms of your search term. For example, a search for *~milk* will also produce results for *dairy*.

 **Tip**

**Using special symbols**

You can also use various symbols in your search, such as +, -, ", *

If you type: +Jackson +Browne
The search engine will search for web pages containing both *Jackson* and *Browne*.

If you type: Jackson -Browne
The search engine will search for web pages containing *Jackson* but not *Browne*.

If you type quotation marks around the words: "Jackson Browne"
The search engine will search for web pages containing the phrase *Jackson Browne*.

If you type a star * next to a word, for example: Brown*
This means that any symbol(s) at all can come at the end of the word, and the search engine will find Brown, Browning, Brownies, Brownbag, etcetera.
For example, if you search for Jackson Brown*, then you might find sites for the singer Jackson Browne, but also for the author H. Jackson Brown.

 **Tip**

**Obvious names for websites**

You do not always have to use a search engine to find a particular web address. You can also have a guess and try to enter some obvious names.
Brand names and companies are generally easy to find. Usually, if you follow the brand name by .com, you will find the correct address.

For example, if you want to visit the website of the car manufacturer *Ford*, you can type www.ford.com in the address bar. And the clothes store Macy's uses www.macys.com as a web address.

## Tip

**Searching in Google Maps**

Except for being a well-known search engine, *Google* is also a company that offers all types of services. A handy service of *Google's* is the possibility of looking up addressed in *Google Maps*.

**Open the web page www.google.com** 1

**Click Maps at the top of the window**

You see *Google Maps*:

**Type your address in the box**

**Click**

The address you are looking for will immediately appear on the map. The map itself has an option for zooming in or out:

**Drag upwards**

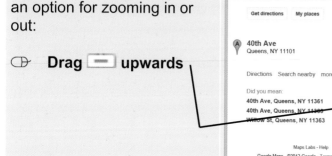

*- Continue on the next page -*

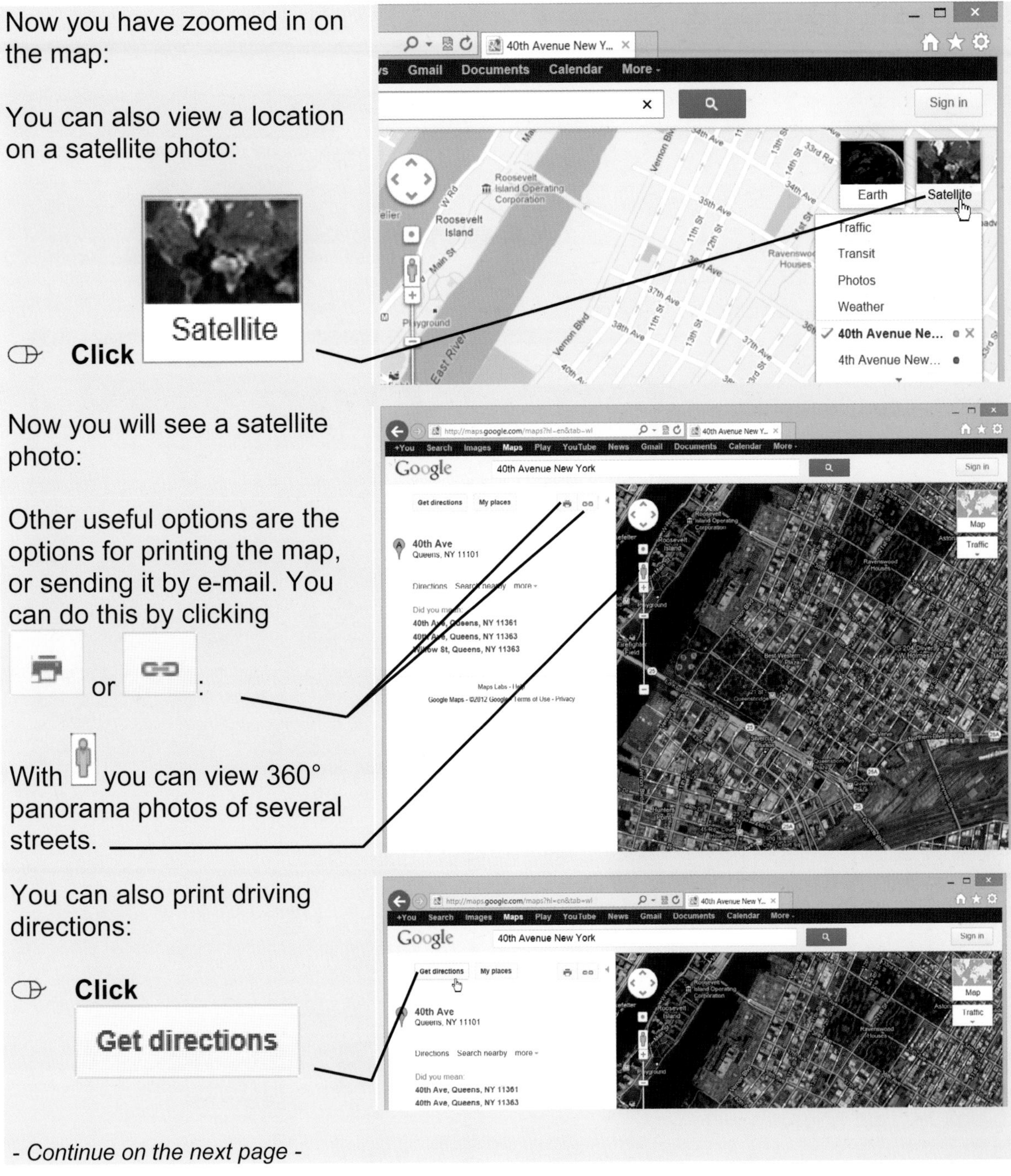


Now you have zoomed in on the map:

You can also view a location on a satellite photo:

- Click **Satellite**

Now you will see a satellite photo:

Other useful options are the options for printing the map, or sending it by e-mail. You can do this by clicking [print icon] or [link icon]:

With [person icon] you can view 360° panorama photos of several streets.

You can also print driving directions:

- Click **Get directions**

*- Continue on the next page -*

**Type the address**

**Click** GET DIRECTIONS

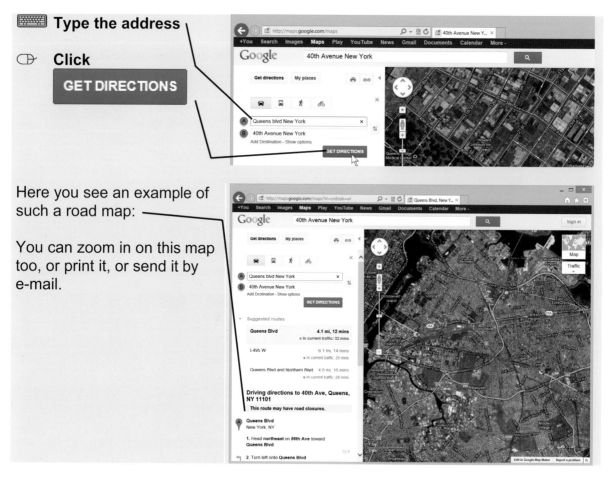

Here you see an example of such a road map:

You can zoom in on this map too, or print it, or send it by e-mail.

## Tip

**Display the menu bar all the time**

If you want to see the menu bar at all times, this is what you need to do in *Internet Explorer*:

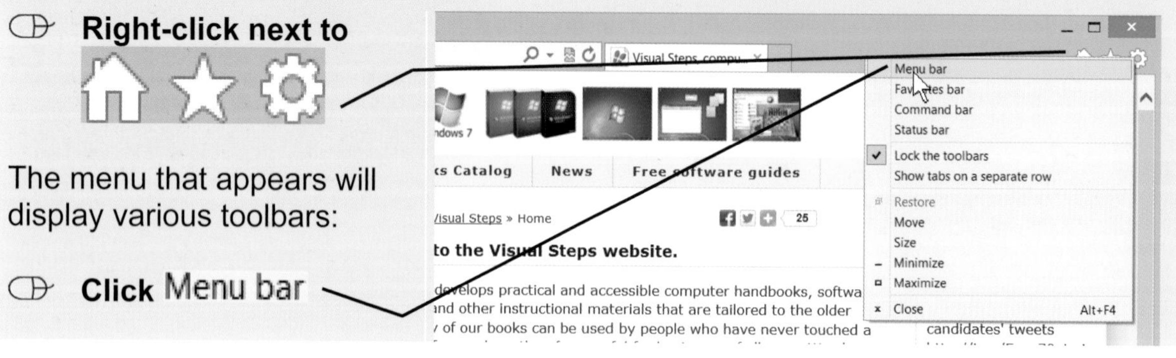


**Right-click next to**

The menu that appears will display various toolbars:

**Click** Menu bar

## Tip

**Searching in YouTube**

*YouTube* is a free and extremely popular source of video files. Users can upload their own videos, view them and share them. Each video is awarded a rating, and you will be able to see how many times the video has been watched. You can search for a video on this website by entering a keyword.

**Open the web page www.youtube.com** [1]

**Type the keyword in the search box**

**Press** Enter

You will see the videos that have been found:

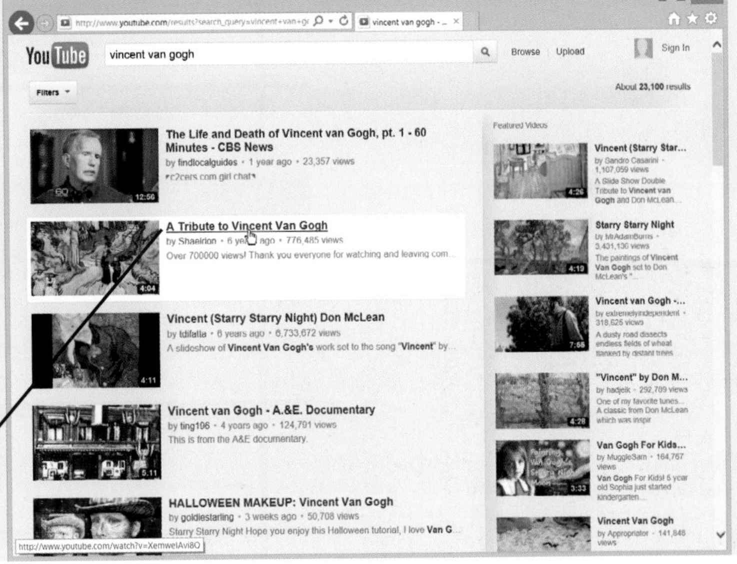


If there is a large number of results found, you can use the Filters button to decrease the number shown.

To open a video:

**Click the desired video**

The video will be played.

## Tip

**Safe searches with the Bing app**

In the *Bing* app you can apply the search filter. This is how you do it:

- **Move the pointer in the top right-hand corner of the screen, until you see the charms bar**

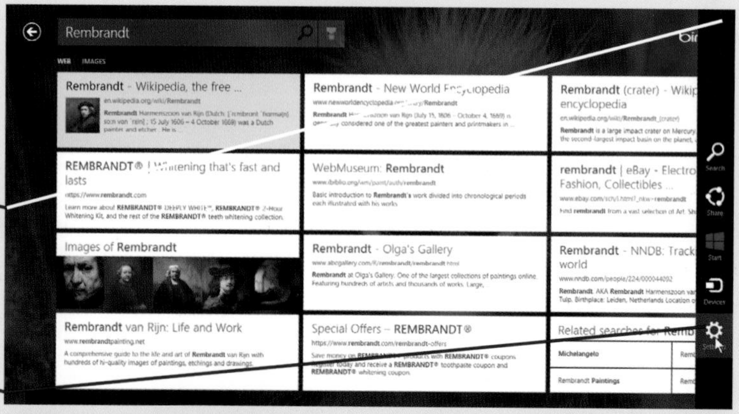

- **Click** Settings

The *Settings* menu appears:

- **Click** SafeSearch

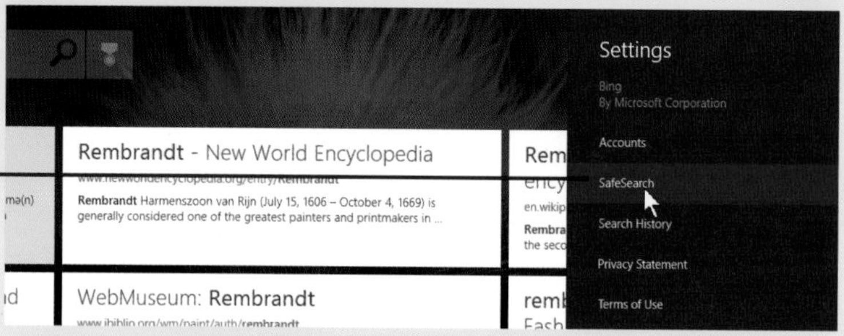

At the right side of the screen you can click a radio button for the option you would like to use while filtering the content of the websites:

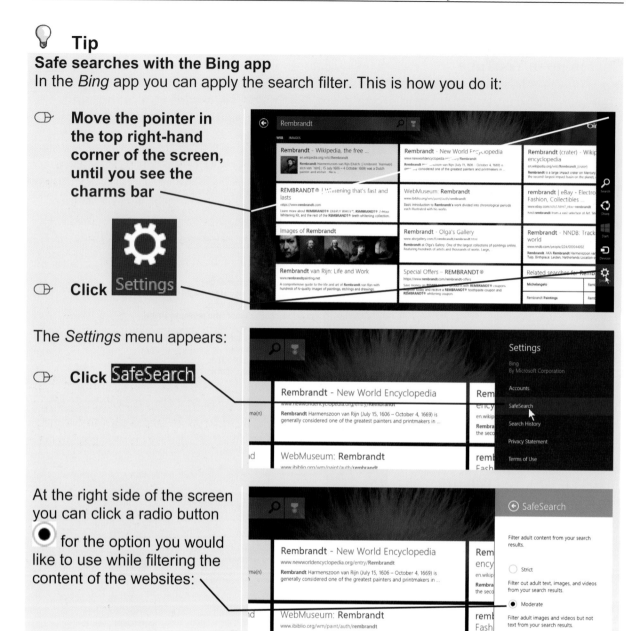

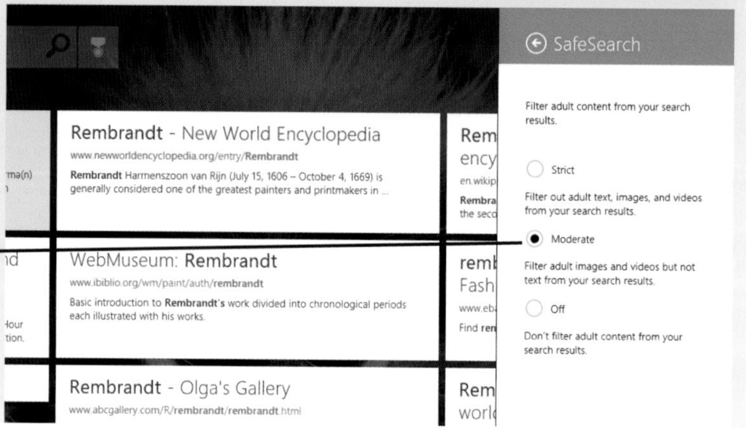

# 5. Working with Mail

One of the most useful features of the Internet is the electronic mail function: e-mail. With e-mail you do not use a pen, paper, an envelope or a stamp. You simply type your e-mail message on the computer and send it away at once, through the Internet. If you want to send an e-mail message to someone, this person needs to have an e-mail address too. It does not matter where this person lives. Sending an e-mail to Australia will be just as quick as sending an e-mail within Europe, for instance. Sending an e-mail will not cost you extra, except for the regular fee you pay to an Internet service provider.

*Mail* is a simple app that lets you send and receive electronic mail, quickly and easily. In this chapter you will learn how to use this app. You will discover how easy it is to use e-mail. You no longer need to buy stamps, or walk to the mailbox.

First, you need to have an e-mail address ending with *hotmail.com*, which means you can send and receive e-mail messages. If you do not yet have such an address, you will learn how to create one in this chapter. This e-mail address is also relevant if you want to use some of the other apps on the *Windows 8* computer. You can read more about this subject later on in this book.

If you have a subscription with an Internet service provider, you might have yet another e-mail address. If you want, you can also set this address up in the *Mail app*. In the *Tips* at the back of this chapter you can read how to do this.
Your Internet service provider, or *Microsoft*, in case you use *Hotmail*, will take care of your e-mail traffic. You can compare this to the services provided by a post office.

In this chapter you will learn how to:

- open and configure *Mail*;
- compose an e-mail message;
- send, receive and open e-mail messages;
- delete e-mail messages;
- reply to an e-mail;
- send, open and save an attachment;
- change the signature;
- search for e-mail messages;
- use an e-mail address on a website.

# 5.1 Opening and Setting Up the Mail App

With the *Mail* app you can send and receive e-mail messages. In order to be able to use this app, you will need to have a *Microsoft* account. This is a combination of an e-mail address ending with *hotmail.com* and a password. With your *Microsoft* account you can send and receive e-mail messages and you will have access to all sorts of services in *Windows 8*, such as the ability to download apps for free or for a small fee. If you do not yet have a *Microsoft* account, you can create one in the *Mail* app.

### HELP! I already have a Microsoft account.

If you already have an e-mail address that ends with *hotmail.com* you can open the *Mail* app as described on this and the next page and then proceed further with the steps on page 138.

### HELP! I already have a different e-mail address.

Maybe you already have a different e-mail address, provided by your Internet service provider, such as AOL, Yahoo! or XS4ALL. You can also use such an e-mail address in *Mail*, but only after you have signed in with your *Microsoft* account first. This is why, in this chapter, you will first create a *Microsoft* account with which you will be able to execute all the steps in this book. If you want, you can set up your Internet service provider's e-mail address in the *Mail* app afterwards. In the *Tip* at the back of this chapter you can read how to do this.

This is how you open the *Mail app*:

**Click**

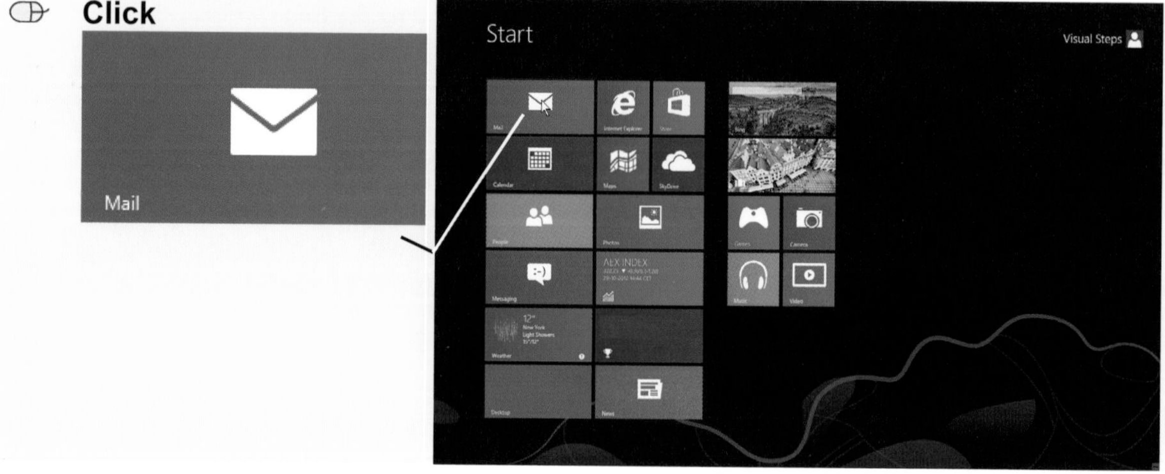

You will see a login screen. If you do not yet have a *Microsoft* account, you need to follow these steps:

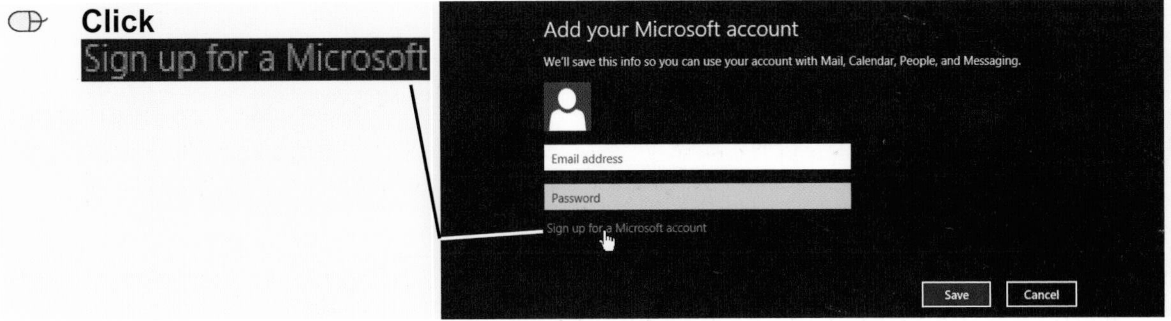


The *Internet Explorer* app is opened. You are going to enter your personal data in the screen that is displayed. Start with your name. Your name will also be used as the sender's name in the e-mails you send to others.

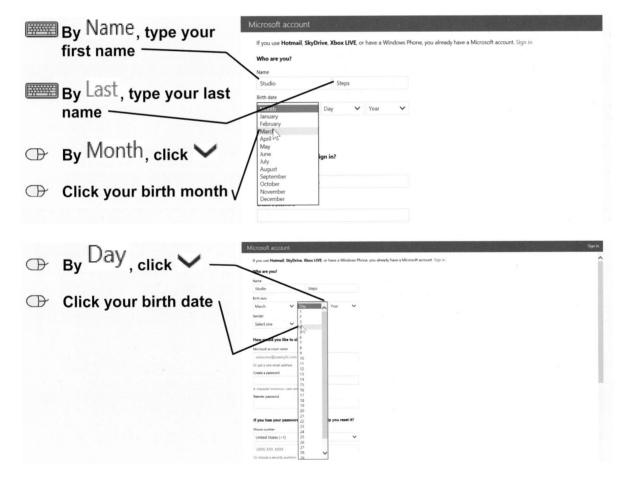

**By** Name**, type your first name**

**By** Last**, type your last name**

**By** Month**, click**

**Click your birth month**

**By** Day**, click**

**Click your birth date**

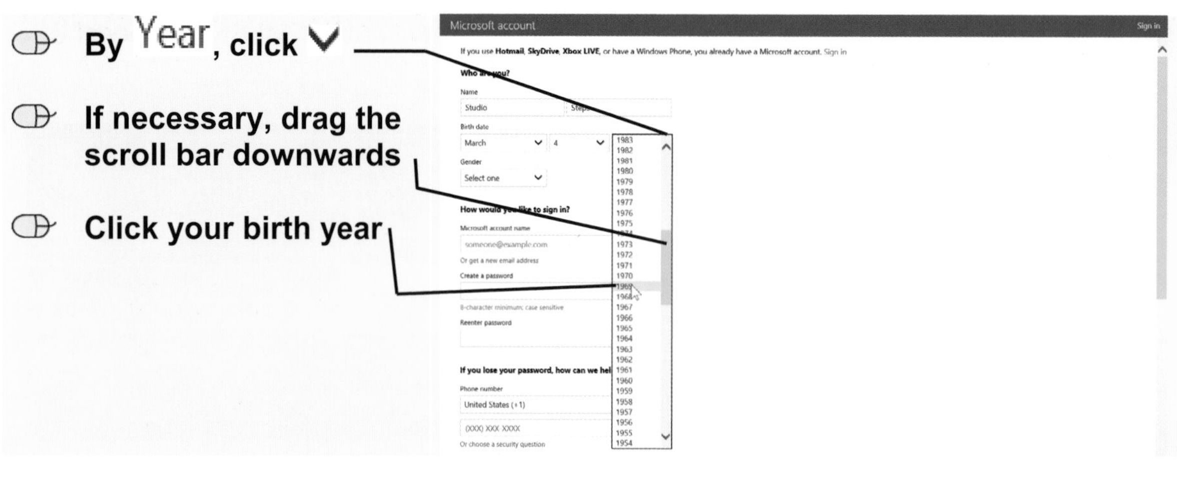

By Year, click ∨

If necessary, drag the scroll bar downwards

Click your birth year

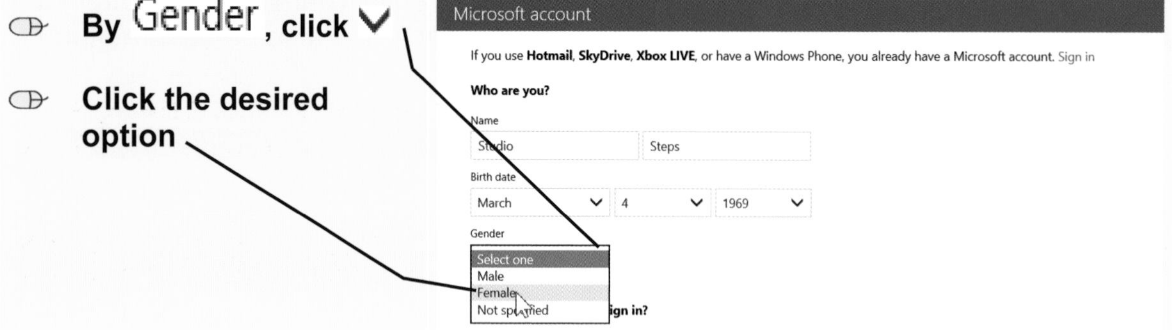


By Gender, click ∨

Click the desired option

Now you are going to choose a new e-mail address:

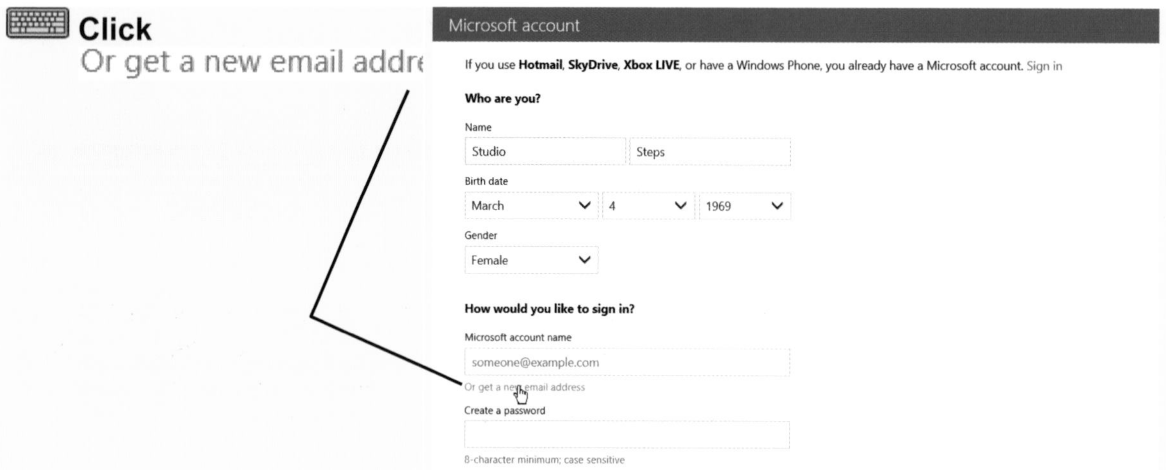


Click Or get a new email addre

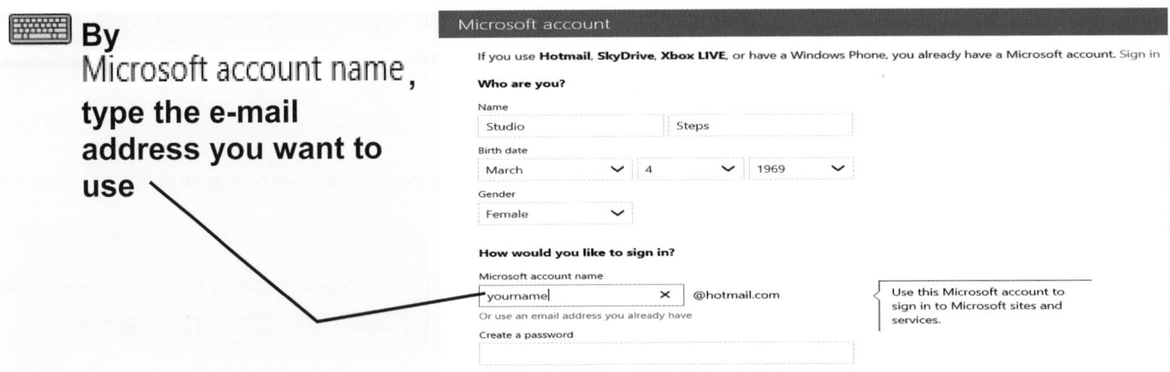


**By** Microsoft account name, **type the e-mail address you want to use**

## HELP! The e-mail address is already in use.

If you see a message that this e-mail address is already in use, you need to choose a different e-mail address.

Now you need to choose a password. A password is a combination of characters only known to you. In this way you can access your e-mail messages. Make sure you remember your password.

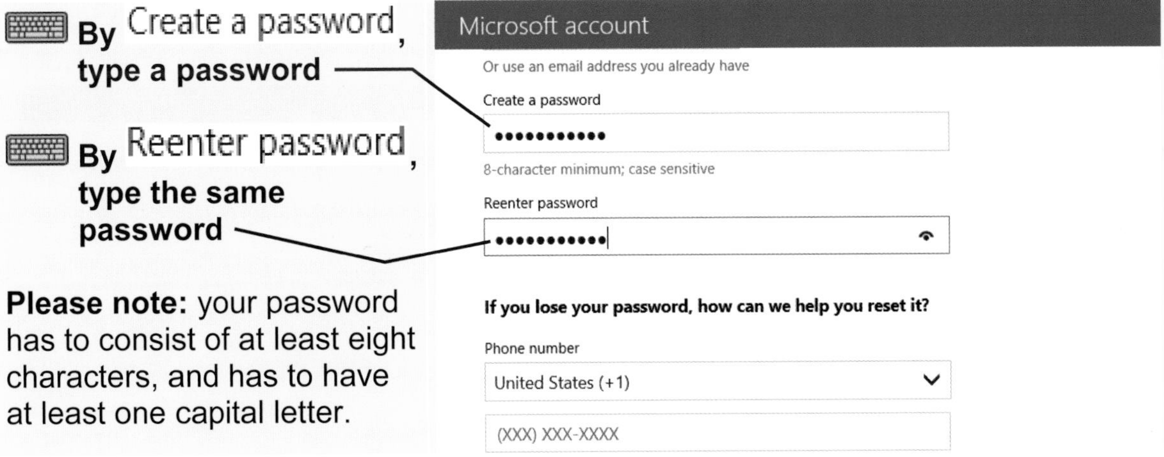


**By** Create a password, **type a password**

**By** Reenter password, **type the same password**

**Please note:** your password has to consist of at least eight characters, and has to have at least one capital letter.

In case you forget your password, you can also enter a phone number, an alternative e-mail address, and a security question. You will need to select two of these options. In this example we have chosen to enter a phone number and a security question. You can also select the option to use an alternative email address.

- **By** Phone number**, type your phone number**

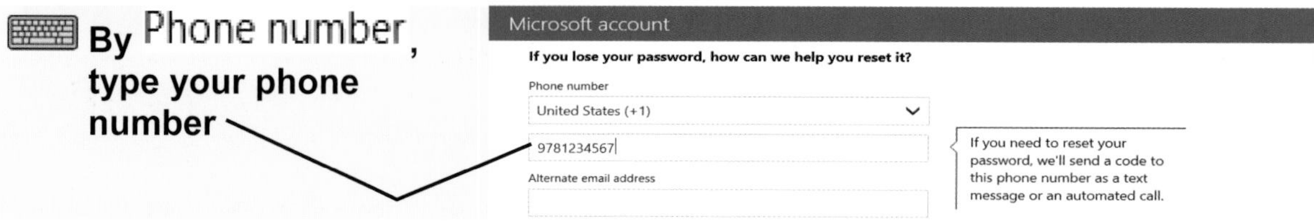


You are going to select and answer a security question:

- **Drag the scroll bar downwards**
- **Click** Or choose a security qu

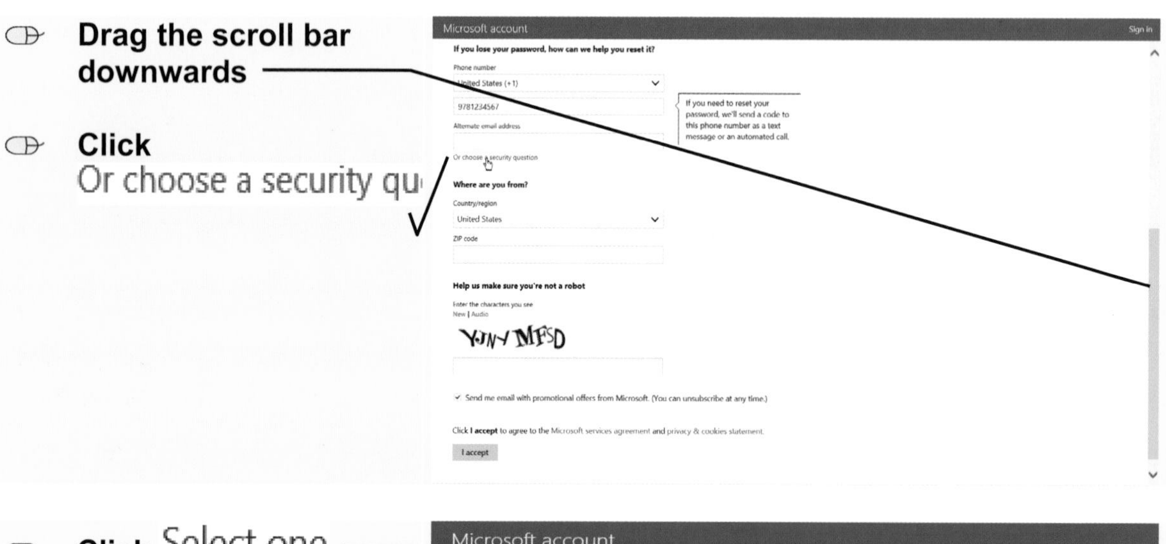


- **Click** Select one
- **Click a question**
- **By** Answer**, type your answer**
- **By** ZIP code**, type your postal code**

You will see underneath a few letters or numbers that must be typed:

- **Type the characters**

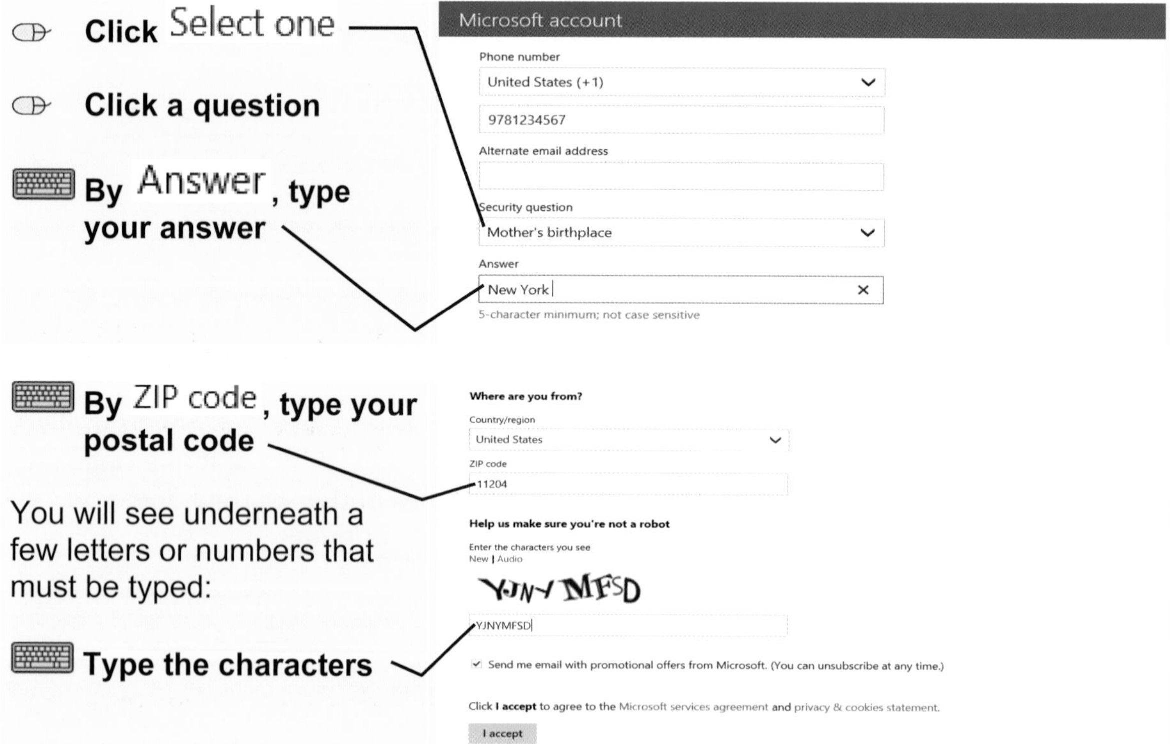

## HELP! I cannot properly read the characters.

If you are unable to read the characters, you can display a new set of characters by clicking New.

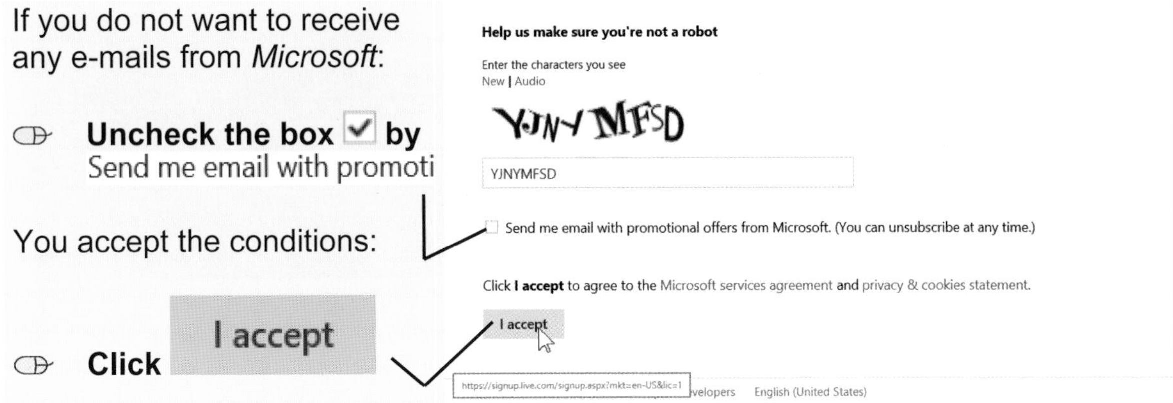


The *Internet Explorer* app will be opened and you will see a message concerning the use of HTTPS. This is a secure method for using your e-mail service. In *Chapter 7 Security and Privacy* you can read more about security and https.

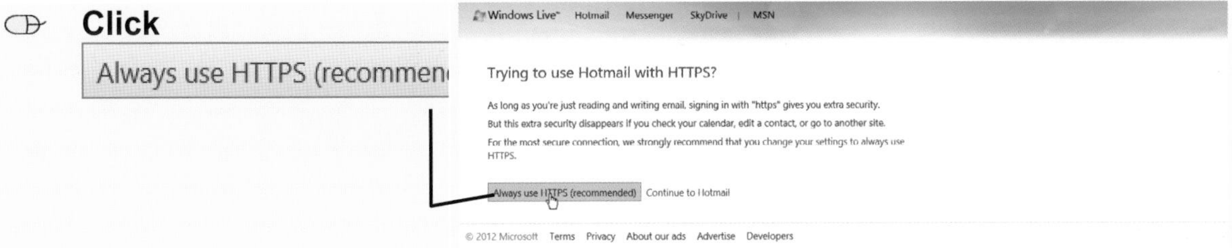


Maybe you see the following message:

Your *Microsoft* account has been created. Now you can start using the *Mail app*.

**Close the *Internet Explorer* app** 12

**Open the *Mail app* with the switch list** 55

You will see the login window. Now you can enter the data for your *Microsoft* account:

**Type your e-mail address**

**Type your password**

**Click** Save

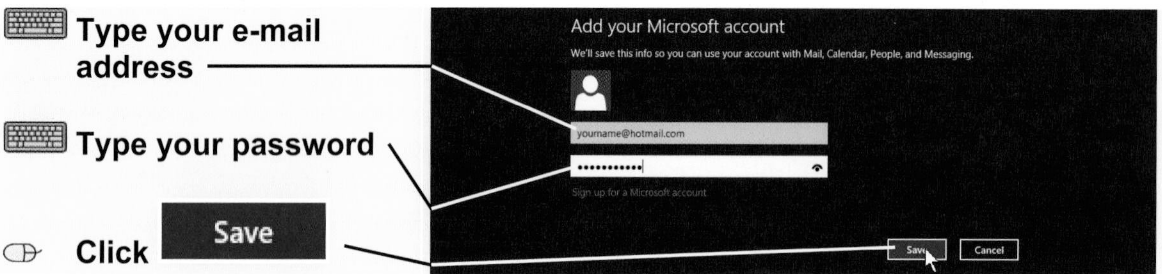


Afterwards you will see the home screen of the *Mail app*:

To the left you see the folder pane:

In the middle you see the message pane. This pane contains the e-mail messages. In this example the pane contains a message from the *Hotmail*-team:

The right pane is the reading pane. Here you can view the content of the message you have selected:

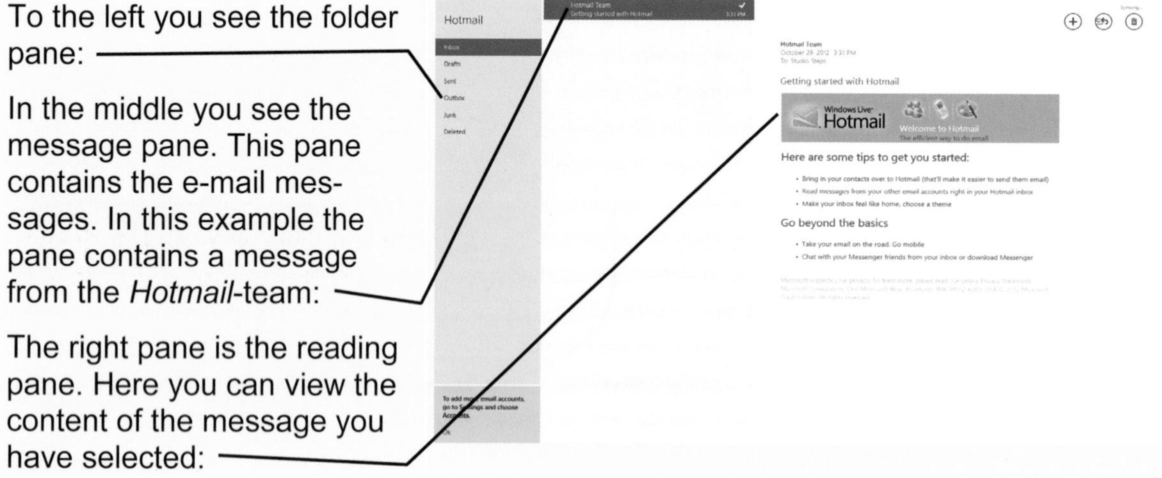

## Tip

**Different e-mail address**

If you have subscribed to the service of an Internet provider, you probably received an e-mail address from your provider too. If you want, you can also set up an e-mail account in the *Mail app* for this other e-mail address. You can use this e-mail address and send and receive e-mail messages in the same way as you use your *Microsoft* account. In the *Tips* at the back of this chapter you can read how to set up an extra account in the *Mail app*.

# 5.2 The E-mail Address

You are going to practice using the app by sending a message to yourself. In this way you can learn how to send an e-mail. Furthermore, you will receive the message right away, since you are the recipient, and this way you will also learn how to receive a message. This is how to create a new e-mail message:

At the top right-hand corner of the screen:

Click

Now you see a screen where you can write a new e-mail message:

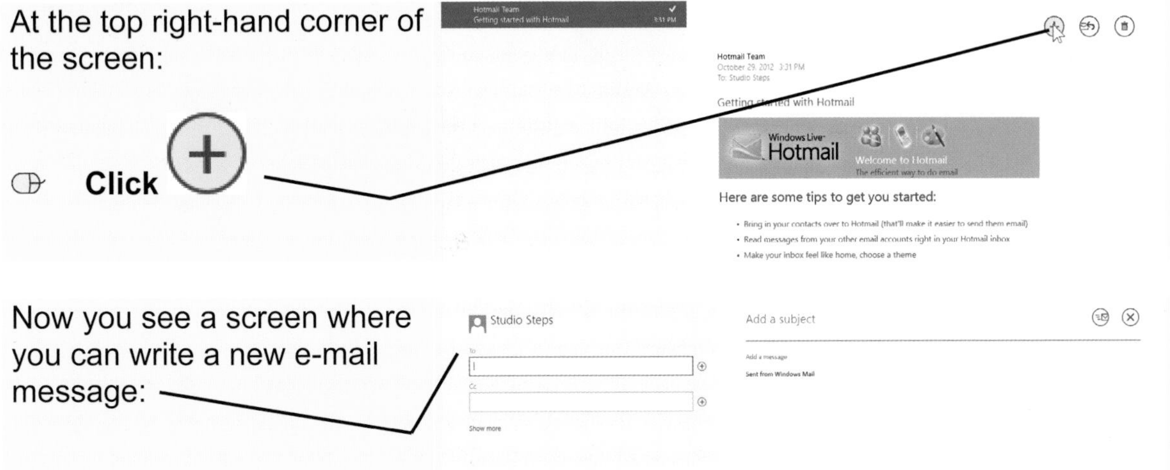


First, the 'letter' needs to have an address, the e-mail address. Every e-mail address is made up of a number of words, with the well-known apetail @ somewhere in the middle. This is what an e-mail address looks like:

**yourname@provider.com**

In front of the @ sign (also called the at-sign), the person's name is entered. Usually, the name of the Internet provider who has supplied you with the e-mail address, is mentioned behind the @ sign. For example, hotmail.com, or yahoo.com.

## Please note:

E-mail addresses cannot contain blank spaces. That is why names or words are sometimes separated by a full stop. These full stops are very important. If you forget to insert such a full stop in the e-mail address, the message will never be delivered. A mailman will understand what the sender means if the address is not completely correct, but a computer will not know what to do.

## 5.3 Creating an E-mail Message

The best way to test your e-mail app is by sending an e-mail to your own address.

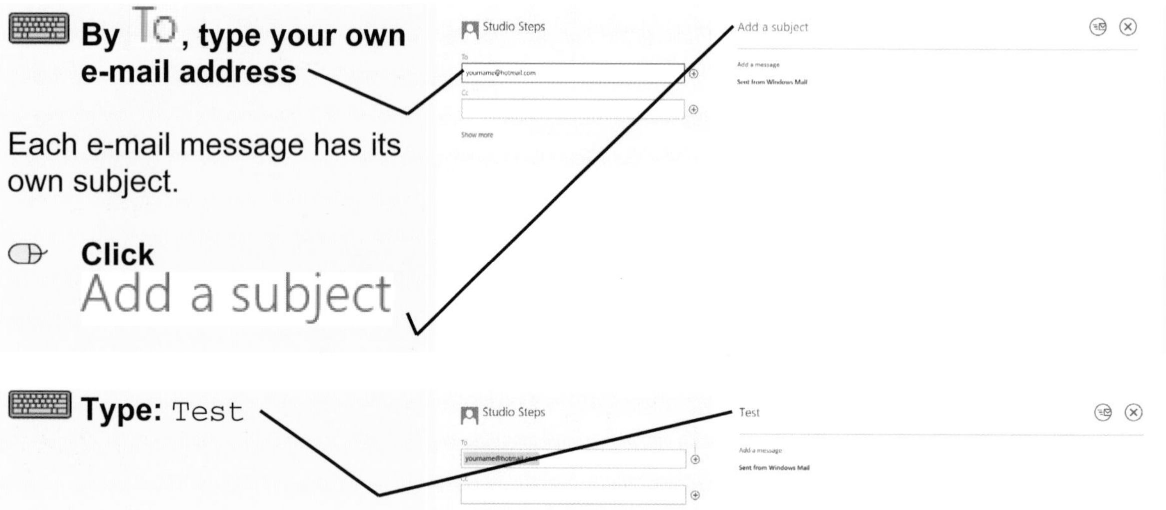

**By To, type your own e-mail address**

Each e-mail message has its own subject.

**Click** Add a subject

**Type:** `Test`

**Tip**

**Adding multiple e-mail addresses**

You can send an e-mail to multiple recipients. If you want to send an e-mail message to more than one person, you can just type the next person's e-mail address behind the previous one.

**Tip**

**People app**

With the *People* app you can edit and store contact persons information. You can read more about this about in the *Online Bonus Chapter Other Internet apps*.

Now you can enter the text of your message:

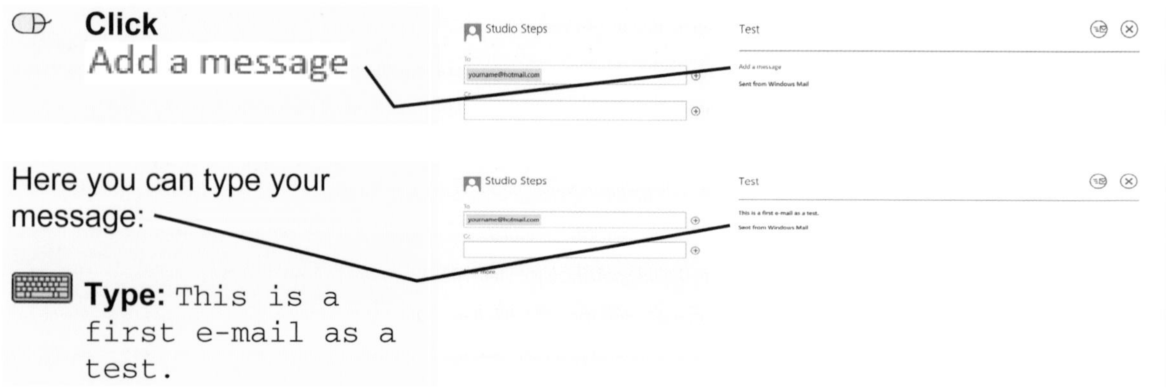

**Click** Add a message

Here you can type your message:

**Type:** `This is a first e-mail as a test.`

# 5.4 Sending and Receiving the E-mail Message

After you have finished writing the e-mail message, you can send it:

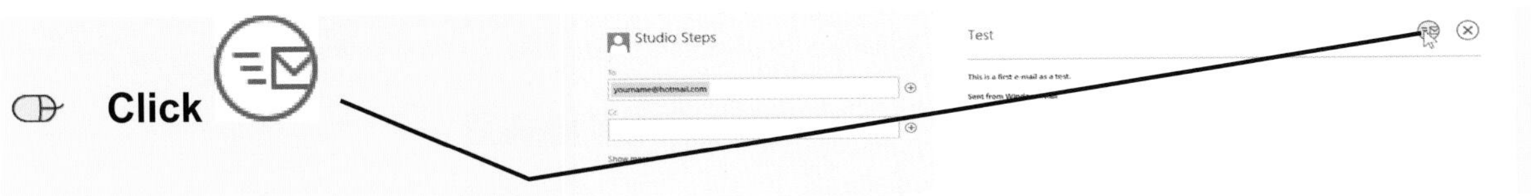


The message has been sent. Now you are going to check if you have received a message.

At the top left of the screen:

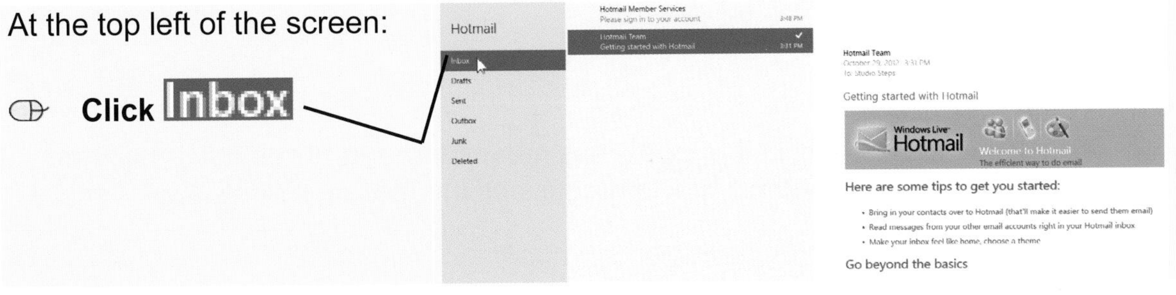


## Tip

**Received messages are displayed on the Start screen**
The tile of the *Mail* app is a so-called *Live* tile. When an e-mail message is received, you will also see this on the Start screen:

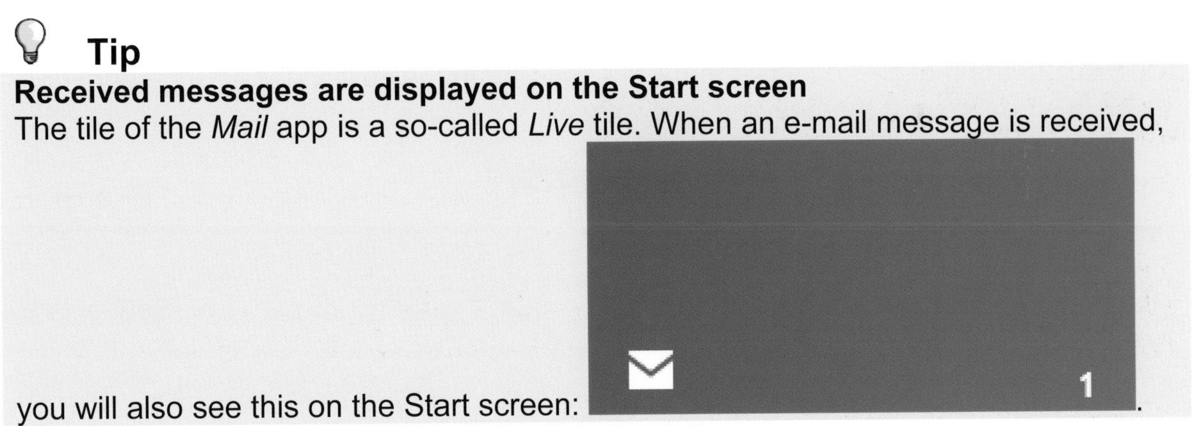


Now you will be connected to your Internet service provider. Next, the system will check whether you have received any mail. If that is the case, these e-mail messages will be retrieved on your computer.

If everything went well, your test message has been sent to you right away.

# 5.5 Reading an E-mail Message

All the e-mail messages you receive are saved in a separate folder called the *Inbox*. The name of the *Inbox* tells you if there are any new messages. If a new message has been received, the mailbox will look like this: **Inbox 1**.

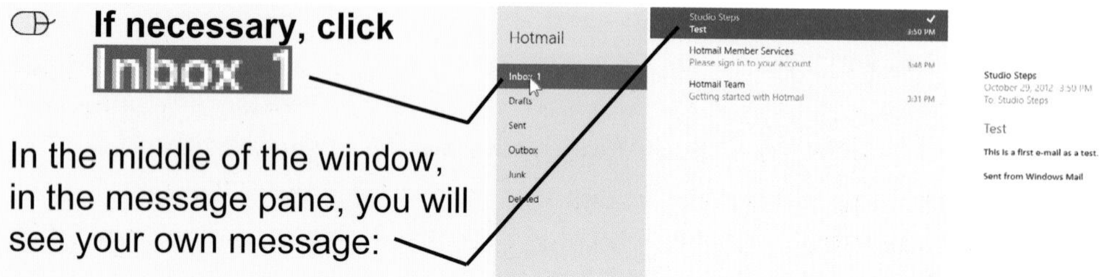


**If necessary, click Inbox 1**

In the middle of the window, in the message pane, you will see your own message:

## HELP! No mail.

If you do not see a message in the *Inbox*, this means the e-mail has not yet arrived. Some Internet providers need a while to process all the messages. Wait a few more minutes, and try again:

**Click Inbox**

You will see the message appear in the message pane. The sender and the subject are displayed too, and the delivery time as well.

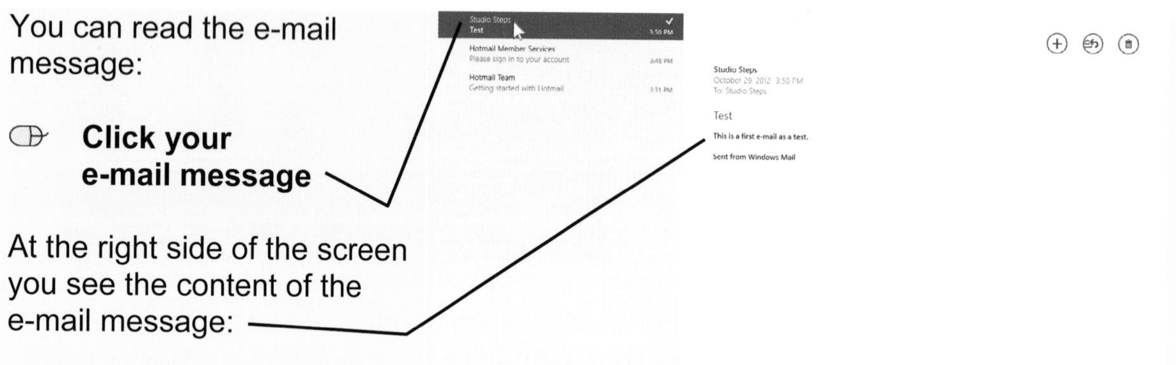


You can read the e-mail message:

**Click your e-mail message**

At the right side of the screen you see the content of the e-mail message:

As soon as you have clicked the e-mail message (the upper item), the conversation is shown. This means the previous message you have send is also shown:

Now you have created, sent, and received your very first e-mail message.

 **Please note:**

In this screen you will also see the message from Hotmail Members Services. In the *Tip* at the back of this chapter you can read more about this.

## 5.6 The Folders

*Mail* uses a system of folders to arrange your e-mail messages. Apart from the *Inbox* there are five more folders. The *Outbox* stores the messages that have not yet been sent, for example, because you are not connected to the Internet for a while.
*Mail* saves all the messages you have sent, in a separate folder called *Sent*.
Messages that resemble unwanted, commercial and promotional e-mail are moved to the *Junk* folder by the *Mail* app.
You can also delete sent and received messages from these folders. Messages that have been deleted are stored in the *Deleted* folder. Finally, there is a folder for messages that have not been finished yet. They are stored in the *Drafts* folder.

The Sent folder contains copies of the e-mail messages you have sent. This folder will also contain the message you sent to yourself.

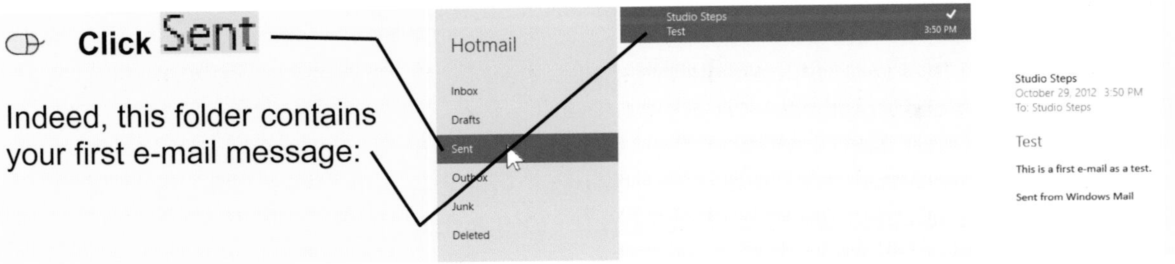


As a test, you can delete this e-mail message.

## 5.7 Deleting E-mail Messages

For many users, the *Inbox* and *Sent* folders make useful archives too. All your correspondence has already been neatly arranged in these folders, and you can easily retrieve e-mail messages. You can store a large number of e-mail messages in these folders. In practice you will regularly delete all superfluous messages, in order to keep your folders ‘tidy’.

Before you can delete a message, you need to select it first:

**If necessary, click the message**

Now the message has turned dark green, to indicate it has been selected:

Now you can tell the *Mail* app to delete the message:

Click 

Now the Sent folder is empty:

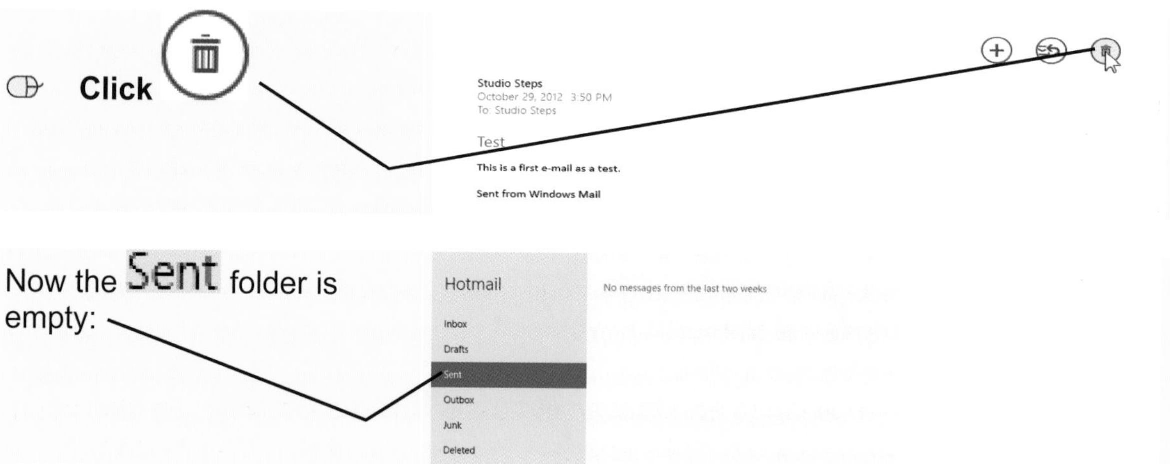


When you delete an e-mail message in this way, it will not be permanently deleted. *Mail* saves all the messages you have deleted in the *Deleted* folder. This is an extra safety measure. This way, you can always restore a message, if you have accidentally deleted it.

In the following steps you will learn how to permanently delete an e-mail message:

**Click Deleted**

You see your test message:

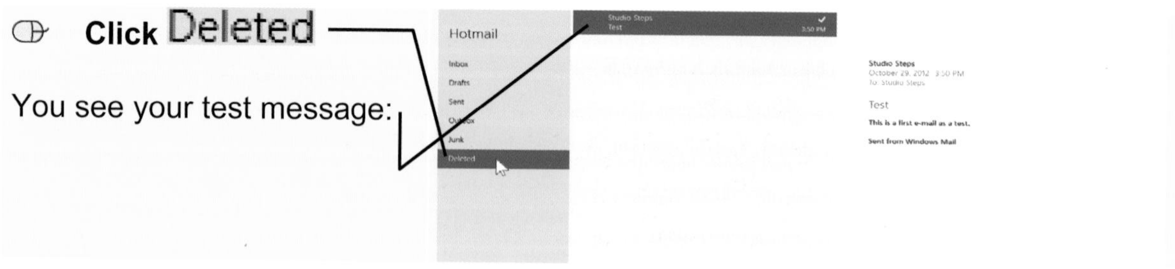

You can delete a message in the *Deleted* folder in the same way as you just did:

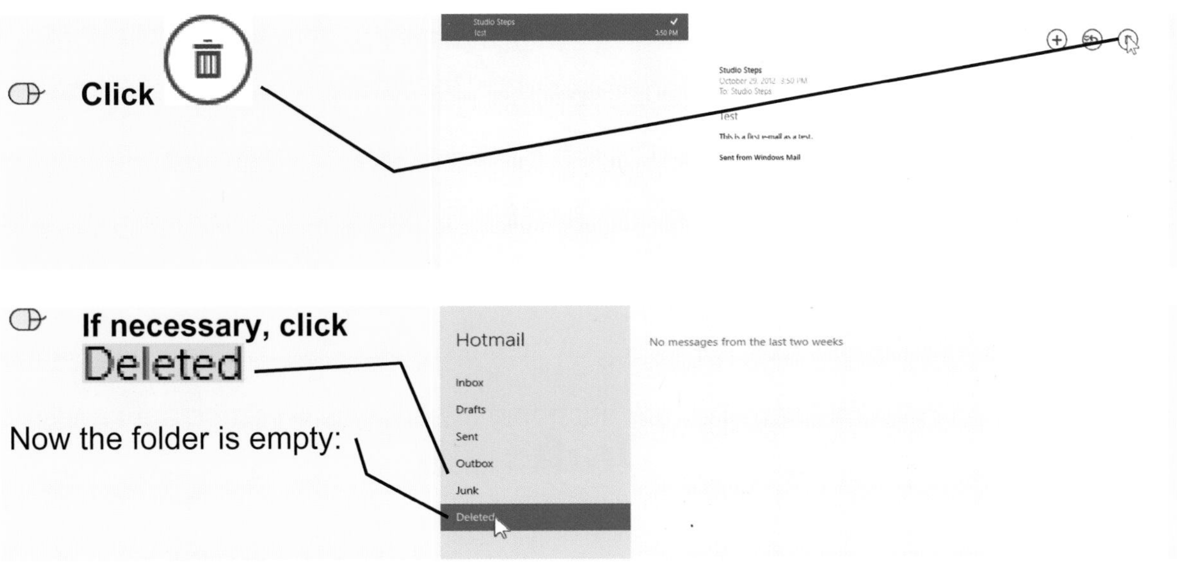


## 5.8 A Second Test Message

To practice receiving, replying to and forwarding e-mail messages, you can also send a test message to a special e-mail address. You will receive an automated reply in return.

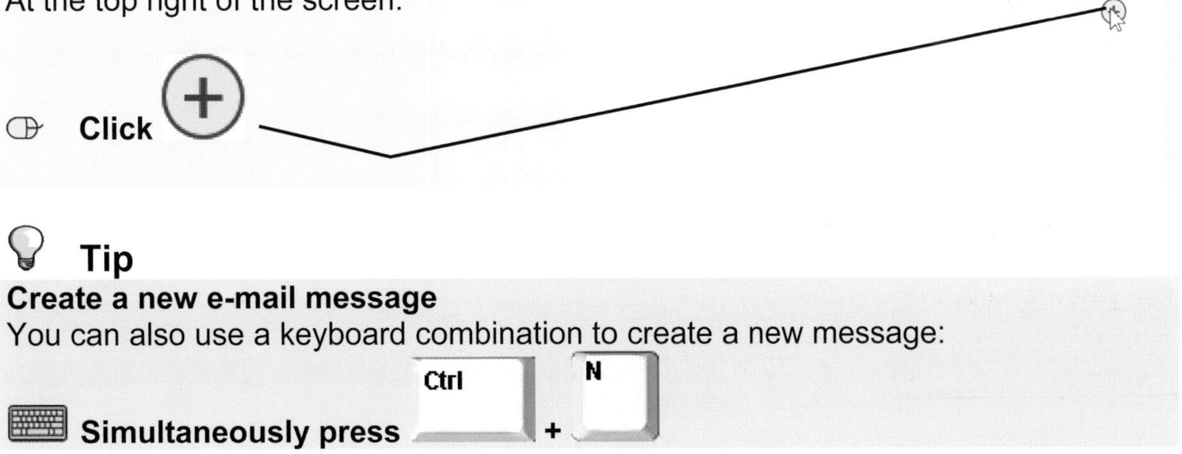


**Tip**

**Create a new e-mail message**
You can also use a keyboard combination to create a new message:

**Simultaneously press** Ctrl + N

The e-mail address for the test message is: **test@visualsteps.com**

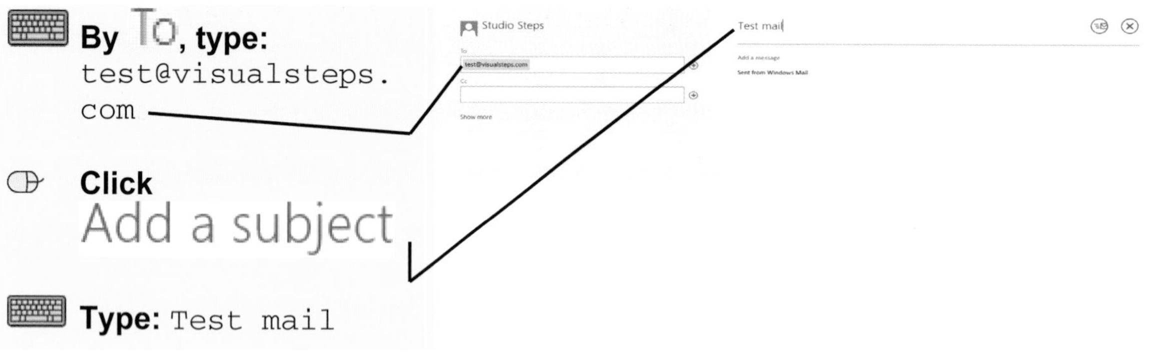


**By** To**, type:** `test@visualsteps.com`

**Click** Add a subject

**Type:** `Test mail`

The test message is completed. You are not going to send this message right away, but first you are going to store it in the **Drafts** folder.

## 5.9 The Drafts Folder

It might occur that you do not want to send a message right away, for example, because you still need to think about its content. In that case you can save such a message in the **Drafts** folder. This is how you do it:

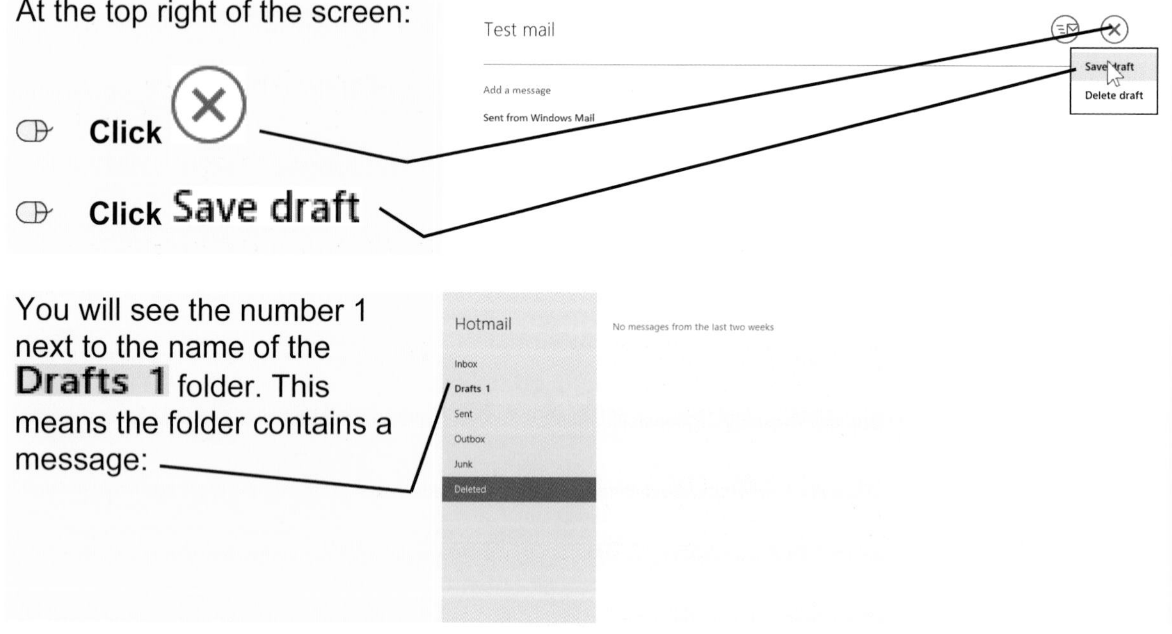


At the top right of the screen:

**Click** ⊗

**Click** Save draft

You will see the number 1 next to the name of the **Drafts 1** folder. This means the folder contains a message:

You can leave the message stored in this folder, even if you close the *Mail* app and turn off your computer. You can open a message in the *Drafts* folder any time you like, and continue writing the message. You are going to do this at right away:

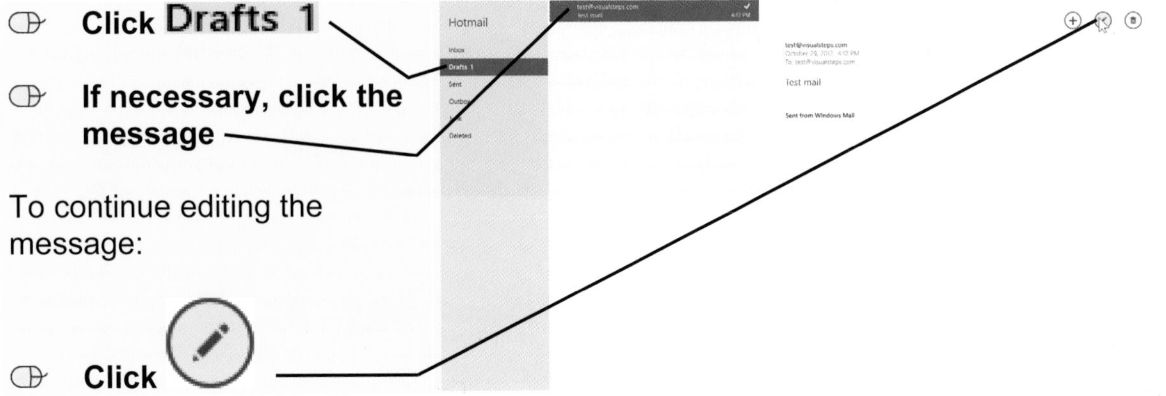


**Click** Drafts 1

**If necessary, click the message**

To continue editing the message:

**Click**

The message has been opened. You can send it:

**Click**

Your message has been sent, and *Mail* will immediately check if there is any incoming mail. Usually it takes a while before you receive a reply to your test mail. Just wait a minute, until you see the number 1 appear in the Inbox title.

If you have received the reply to your test mail message, you will see a message in the *Inbox*:

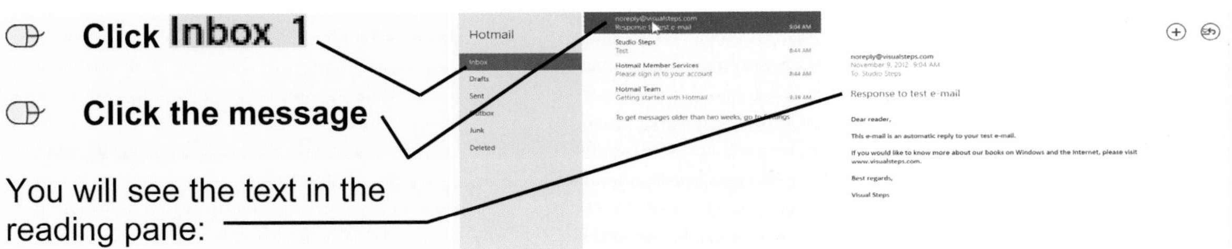


**Click** Inbox 1

**Click the message**

You will see the text in the reading pane:

## HELP! I do not see the message in the Inbox.

Possibly, the message has been moved to the Junk folder:

You can open the *Junk* folder:

**Click** Junk

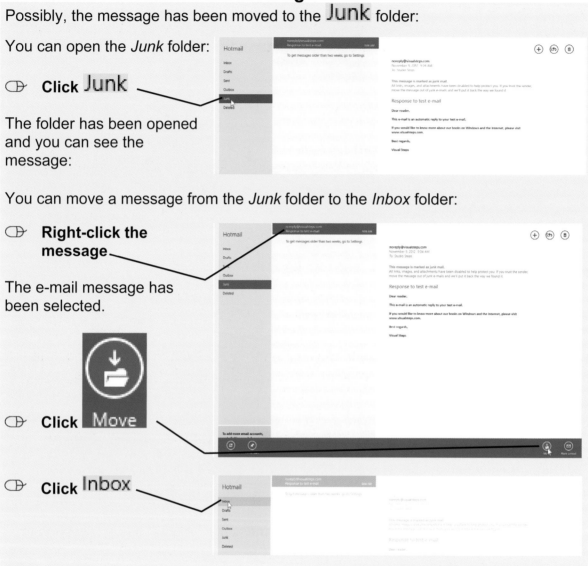

The folder has been opened and you can see the message:

You can move a message from the *Junk* folder to the *Inbox* folder:

**Right-click the message**

The e-mail message has been selected.

**Click** Move

**Click** Inbox

Now the reply to your test e-mail has been moved to the *Inbox* folder.

## Please note:

Unfortunately, *Mail* cannot tell the difference between an innocent, harmless e-mail message and unwanted, commercial or promotional e-mails (also called *spam*). E-mail messages sent by your friends and family may also end up in the Junk folder. That is why you need to check this folder on a regular basis, to be sure you do not miss any important messages.

 Tip

**Read more about the junk filter**

In *Chapter 7 Security and Privacy* you can read more about the junk filter, and how to adjust the settings according to your wishes.

## 5.10 Replying To an E-mail

If you have received an e-mail message and you want to reply to this message, you do not need to type the recipient's address all over again. *Mail* offers various options for replying to an e-mail. After you have clicked [reply icon], you will see the following buttons for these options:

**Reply**

A reply message is created, where the correct e-mail address has already been entered. The original message is sent along.

**Reply all**

You can send an e-mail message to multiple addresses. With this button you create a new e-mail message that is sent to all the recipients listed in the original e-mail message. The original message is sent along.

**Forward**

The original e-mail is turned into a new e-mail message, which you can send to someone else.

In most cases you will such want to reply to a message. Try it:

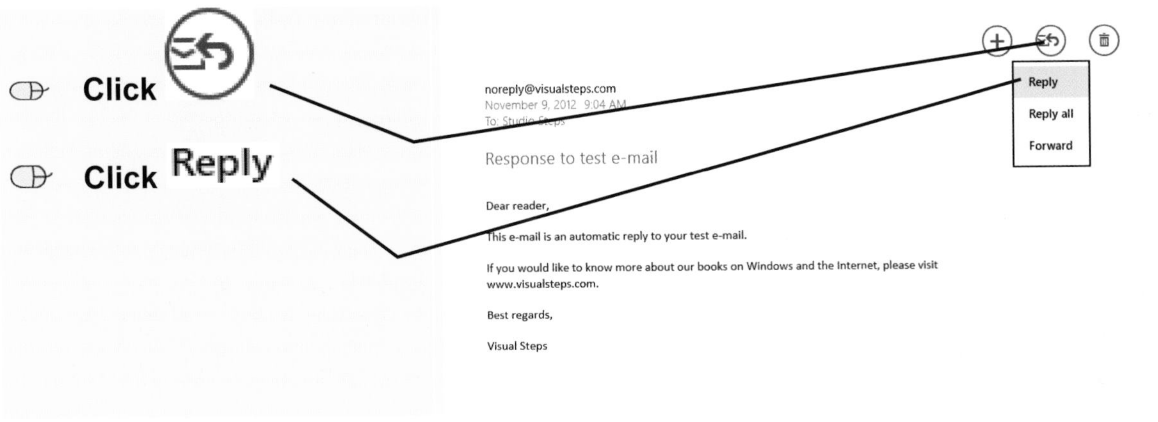

Now you see this screen:

The e-mail address has been copied and entered in the right box:

The subject has been copied and is now preceded by *'Re'*. This stands for *Regarding*:

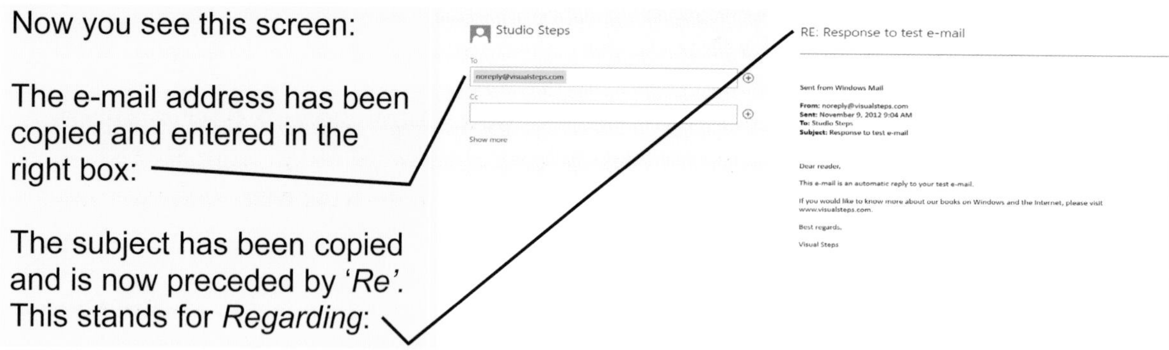


The text of the original message is automatically inserted into the reply. In itself this can be quite useful. The person who receives your reply will immediately see what the original message was all about. The downside is that this message will become longer and longer, as the correspondence lasts.

You can type your reply at the top of the message:

**Type:** `This is my reply.`

**Press** Enter

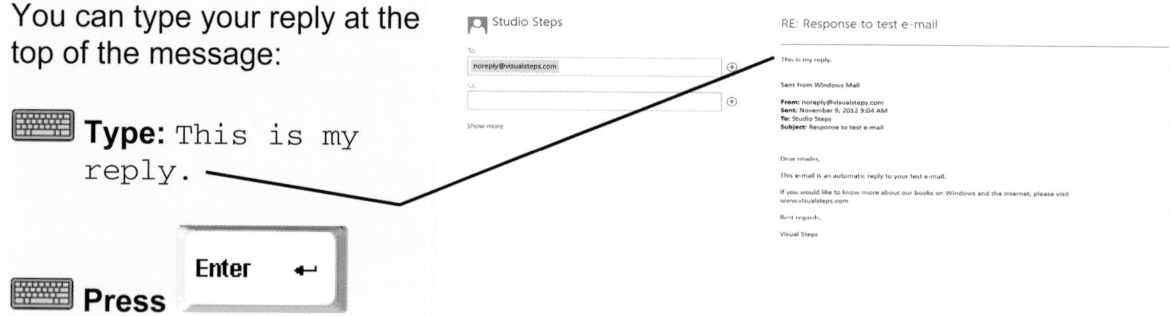


## Please note:

When you send a test e-mail to the test@visualsteps.com address, you will only receive a reply once a week. In this case, the reply is automatically sent by the computer of the Internet service provider hosting this test address. The restriction of just one message a week is in place to prevent two computers from endlessly sending each other automated messages back and forth.

You can send this message, but you will not receive a reply.

**Send your e-mail** 28

# 5.11 Including an Attachment

A very handy feature of an e-mail program is the possibility of sending all kinds of items along with your e-mail message. For example, you can add a photo or a document to your message. An item that is sent along with an e-mail message is called an *attachment*.

You are going to practice sending an attachment by sending an e-mail to yourself.

**Create a new e-mail message** 29

**By** To**, type your own e-mail address**

**Click** Add a subject

**Type:** `Test with attachment`

**Click** Add a message

**Type:** `Here is a nice picture!`

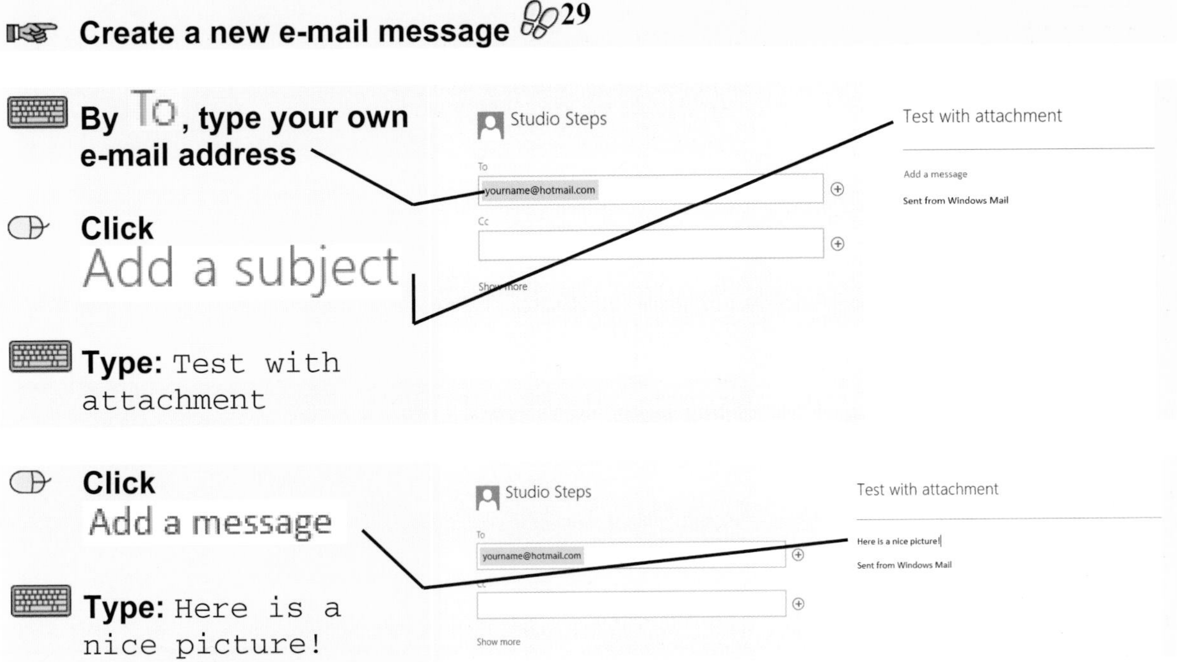


Now you can add the attachment. In this example we have used a photo. You can select your own picture:

**Right-click an empty area on the screen**

You see the app commands:

**Click** Attachments

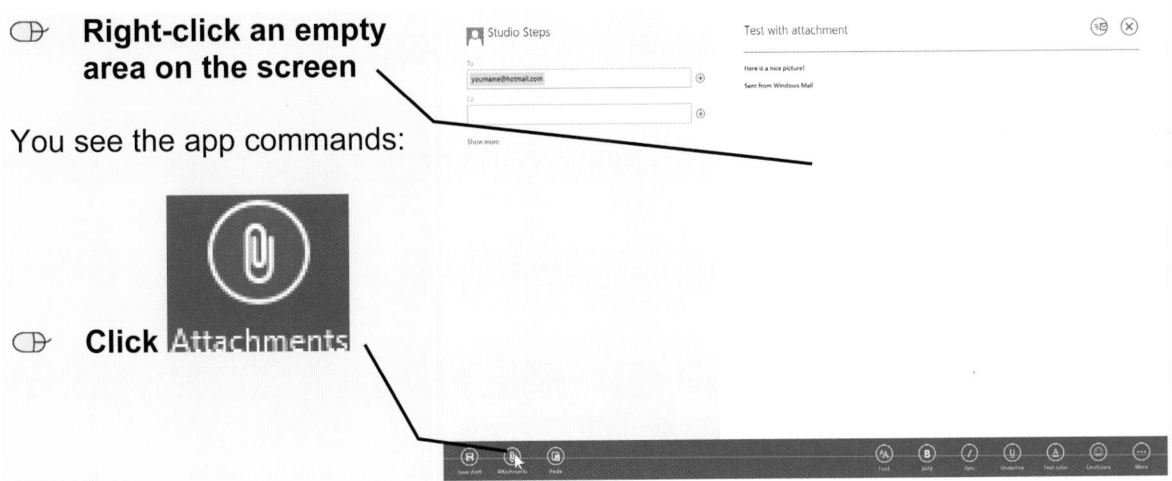

Now you see a screen in which you can select the type of attachment, for example, a picture:

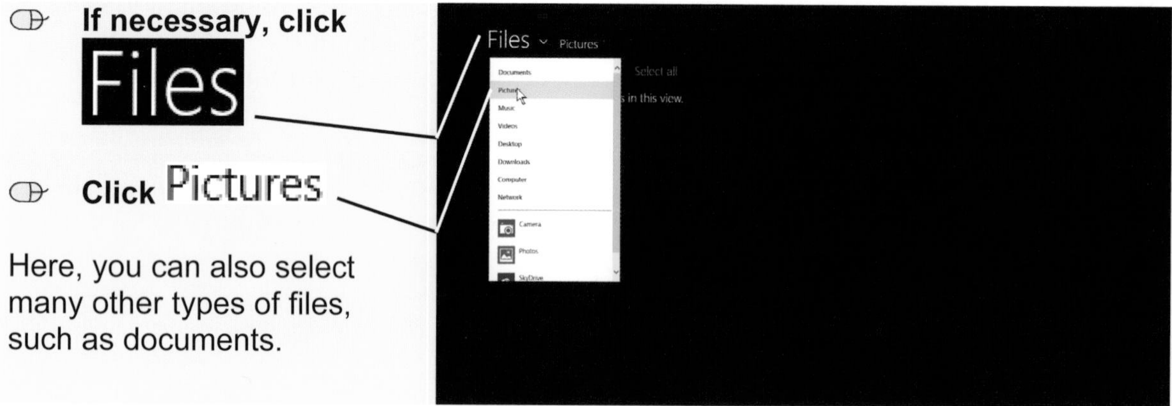

- If necessary, click **Files**
- Click **Pictures**

Here, you can also select many other types of files, such as documents.

The content of the *Pictures* folder will be displayed. You can select any picture you want. In this example, a picture has already been stored on the computer. If you do not (yet) have any pictures stored on your computer, just read through this paragraph, and the next few paragraphs.

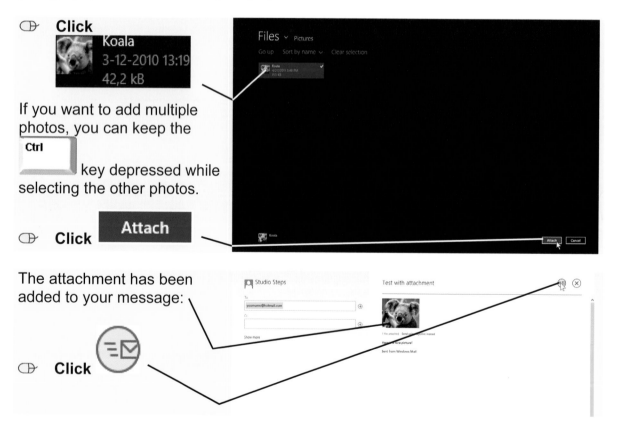

- Click **Koala 3-12-2010 13:19 42,2 kB**

If you want to add multiple photos, you can keep the **Ctrl** key depressed while selecting the other photos.

- Click **Attach**

The attachment has been added to your message:

- Click

The e-mail message with the picture is sent.

# 5.12 Opening an Attachment

If you have received the e-mail with the attachment you can open it:

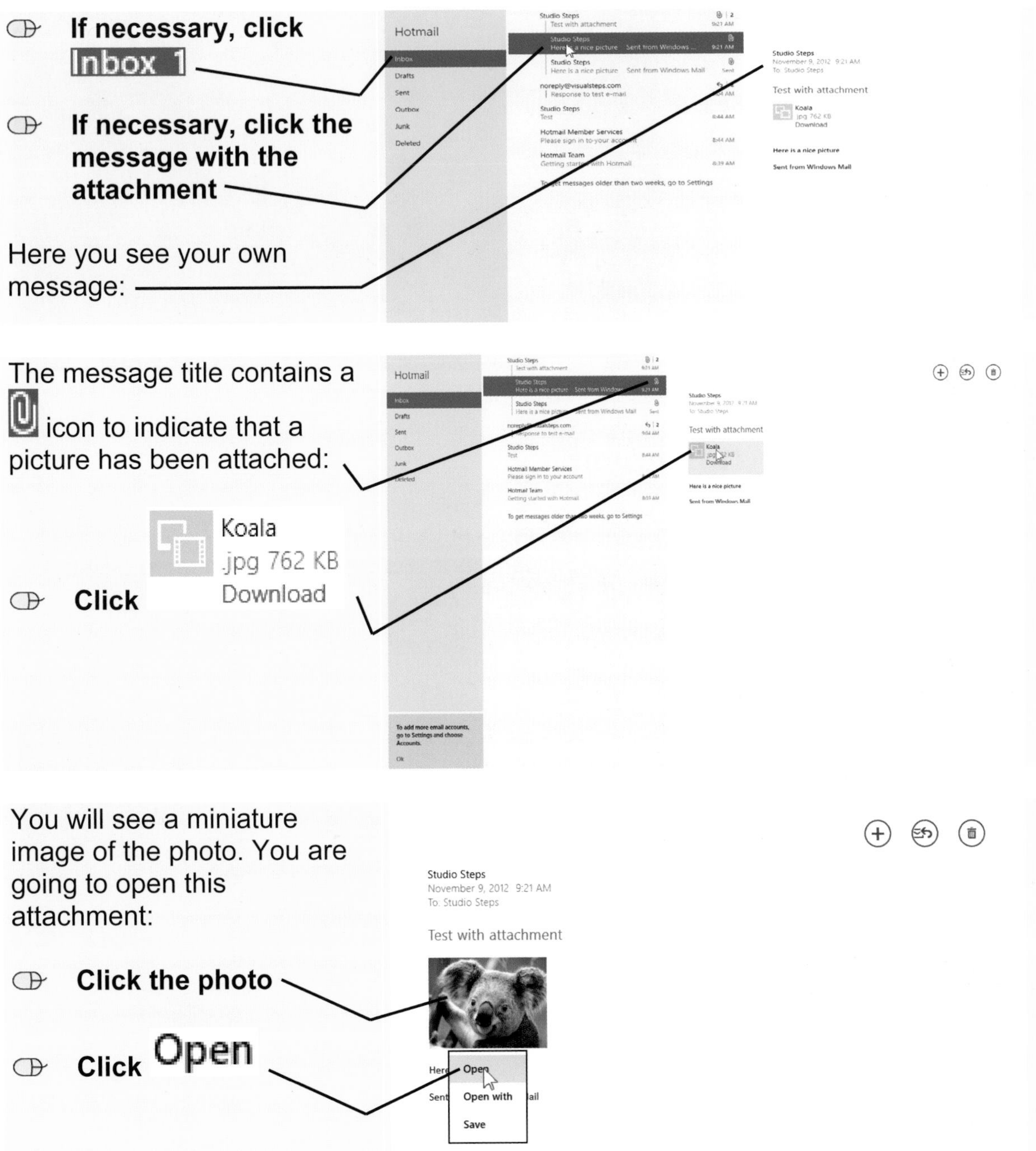

If necessary, click
Inbox 1
If necessary, click the message with the attachment
Here you see your own message:
Hotmail
Inbox
Drafts
Sent
Outbox
Junk
Deleted
Studio Steps
Test with attachment
Koala
.jpg 762 KB
Download
The message title contains a
icon to indicate that a picture has been attached:
Click
Koala
.jpg 762 KB
Download
You will see a miniature image of the photo. You are going to open this attachment:
Click the photo
Click Open
Studio Steps
November 9, 2012 9:21 AM
To: Studio Steps
Test with attachment
Open
Open with
Save


In this example, the photo is displayed in the *Photos* app. This is also the default setting in *Windows 8*. This app is included in the *Windows 8* operating system. You can use the app for viewing, sharing, and printing digital photos.

But if your computer is set to open a different program or app for viewing photos, the photo will be displayed in the other program.

After you have looked at the photo, you can close the app or the program:

☞ **Close the app** 5

Or, if a different program is opened:

☞ **Close the program** 12

## 5.13 Saving an Attachment

You can store an attachment that is sent along with an e-mail on your computer's hard disk. Afterwards you can use this attachment yourself, for instance, in a photo editing program. And you can also forward an e-mail with an attachment to somebody else.

☞ **Open the *Mail* app with the switch list** 55

You are going to save the attachment in a folder on your computer:

**Click the photo**

**Click** Save

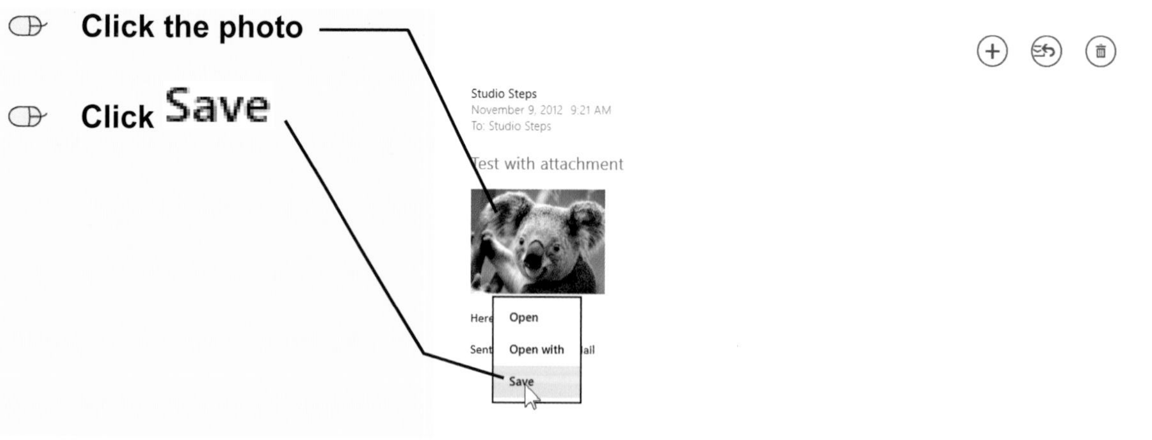

You will see the window with the locations for saving your files:

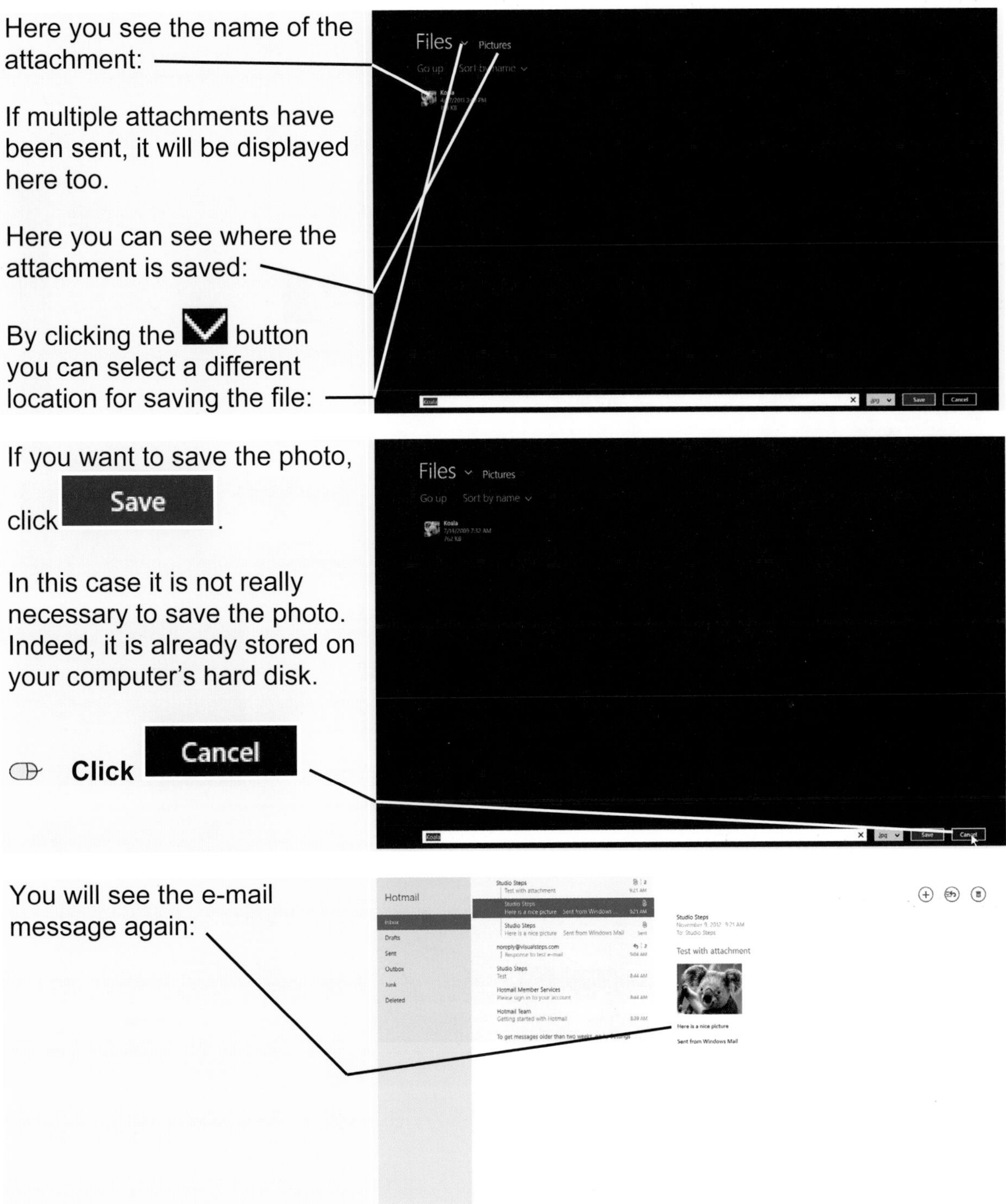


Here you see the name of the attachment:

If multiple attachments have been sent, it will be displayed here too.

Here you can see where the attachment is saved:

By clicking the button you can select a different location for saving the file:

If you want to save the photo, click **Save**.

In this case it is not really necessary to save the photo. Indeed, it is already stored on your computer's hard disk.

Click **Cancel**

You will see the e-mail message again:

At the bottom of the message you will see a default signature. You are going to change this signature in the next section.

# 5.14 Your Signature

By default, every e-mail you send includes the text *Sent from Windows Mail*. This text is called the default signature. You can replace this text by another standard salutation, or by your name and address. This is how you adjust your e-mail signature:

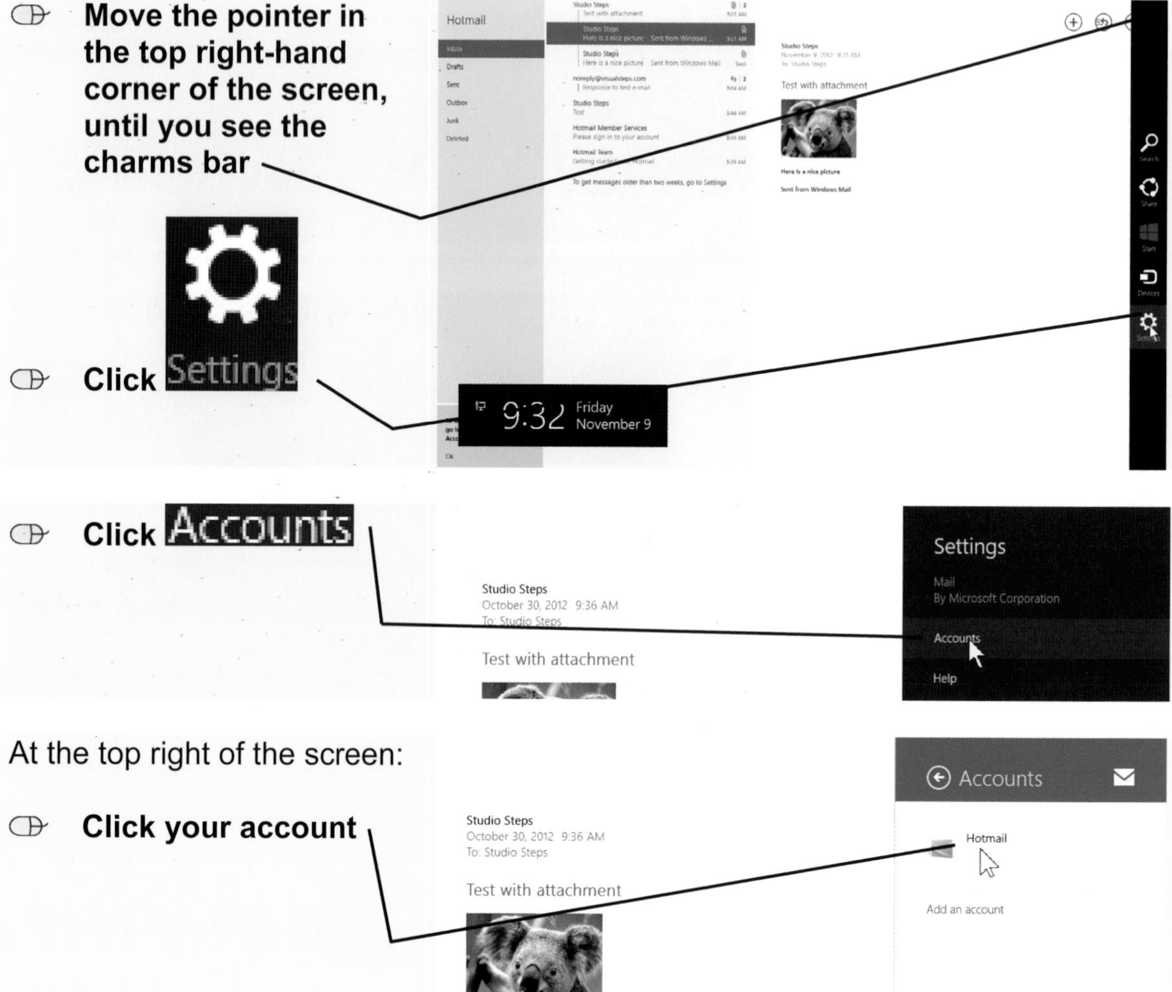

By Use an email signature you will see that the signature option is enabled (turned on):

You see the signature in the text box:

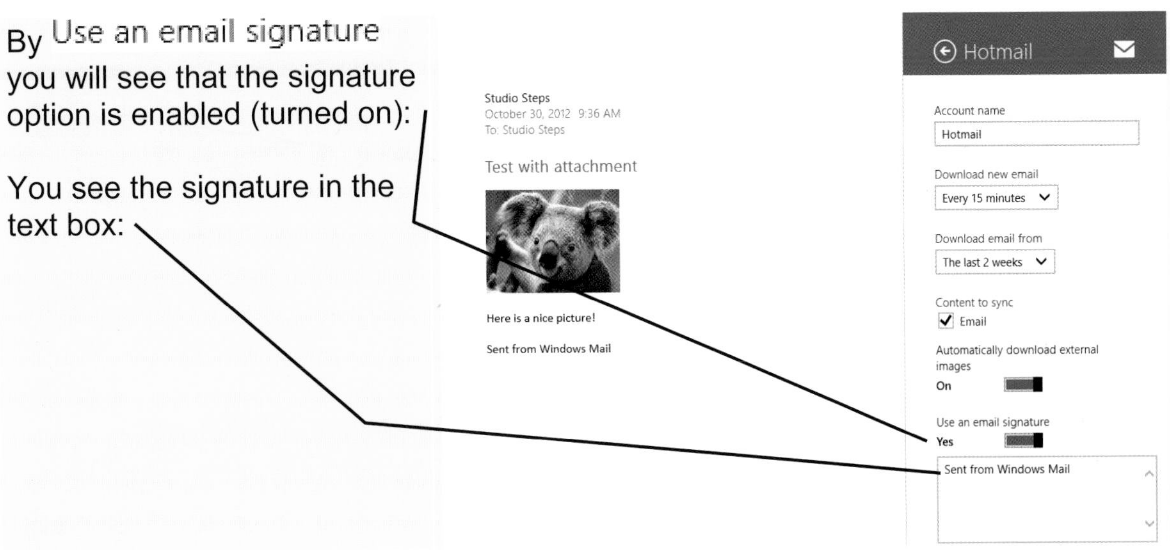


You are going to change the signature. In this example you will just write 'With kind regards', and your name:

☞ **Delete the text in the box by** Use an email signature 24

⌨ **Type:** `With kind regards, your name`

🖱 **Click the reading pane**

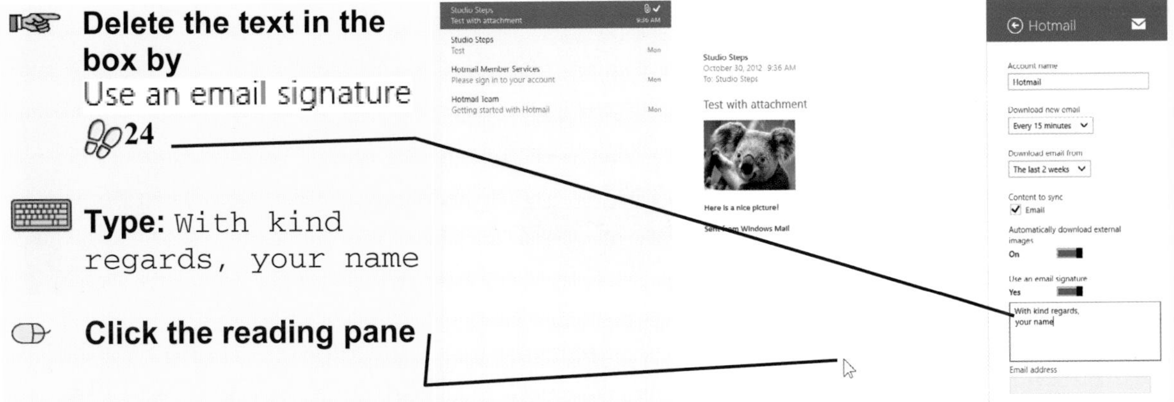


Now the signature will automatically be added to every e-mail message you send. You are going to see this for yourself:

☞ **Create a new e-mail message** 29

Here you see that the new signature has been added:

You do not need to save this message.

## 5.15 Searching Your E-mails

*Windows 8* has an extensive search function with which you can search your collection of messages for certain topics. This is how you open this search option:

Move the pointer in the top right-hand corner of the screen, until you see the charms bar
Click Search
Hotmail
9:36 Friday November 9


You can search for each part of an e-mail message. For example, you can search for a sender, a recipient, the subject, or you can search through the actual text of the message. If you know what the content of a message was, you can enter a keyword and let the program search for this word. For example, the word 'books' . This word is written in the test mail you received.

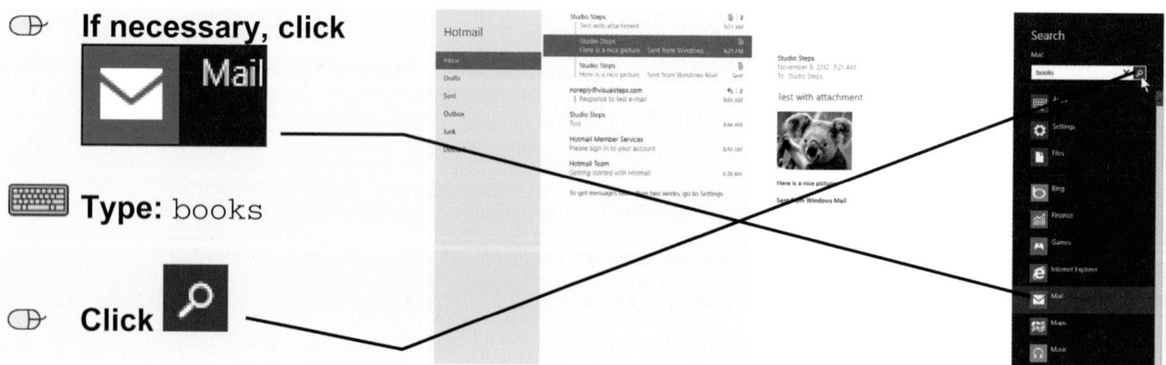

In the message pane you will see the e-mail message containing the word 'books':

This is how you view the message:

If necessary, click the message

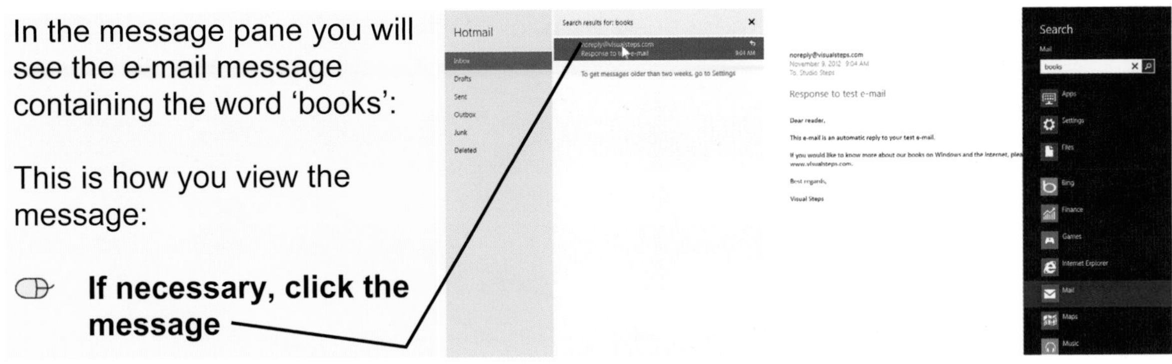


You can read the message. The search function will immediately disappear.

**Close the *Mail* app** 5

## 5.16 Using an E-mail Address On a Website

Many websites contain links to e-mail addresses, which let you contact a specific person, company, or organization. The *Mail* app on your own computer is set to open with a new message. Just try it:

**Open *Internet Explorer* on the desktop** 9

**Open the web page www.visualsteps.com/internet8/practice** 1

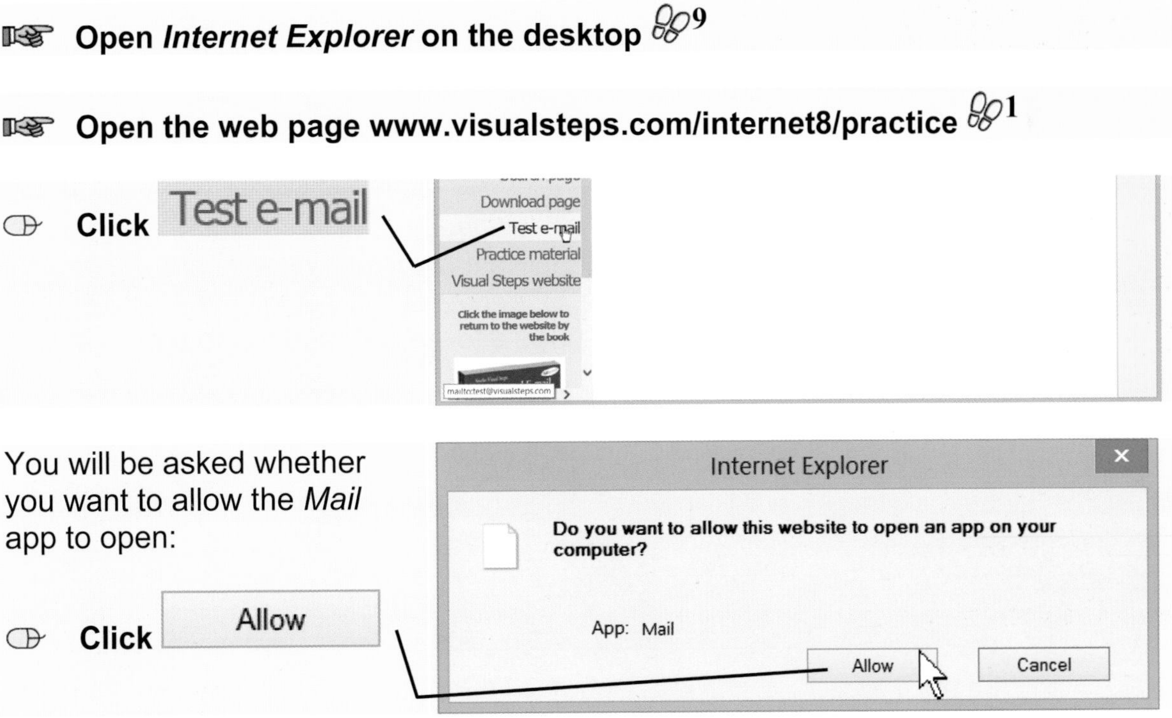

Click Test e-mail



You will be asked whether you want to allow the *Mail* app to open:

Click Allow

The *Mail* app is opened. A new message has been created:

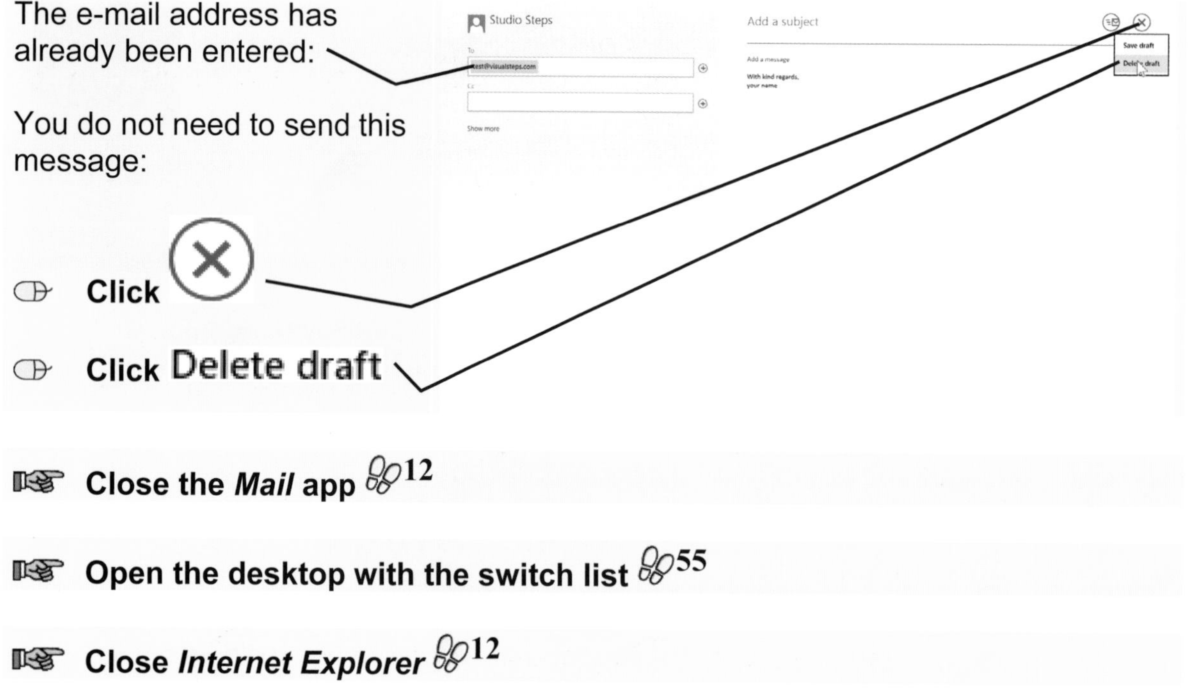


The e-mail address has already been entered:

You do not need to send this message:

- **Click** ⊗

- **Click** Delete draft

**Close the *Mail* app** 12

**Open the desktop with the switch list** 55

**Close *Internet Explorer*** 12

In the following exercises you can practice sending and receiving e-mail messages a bit more.

## Tip

**More about e-mail**

In this chapter you have become acquainted with the *Mail* app. For some of you the options covered may seem too limited. For more advanced email options, *Microsoft* offers an additional service with its internet application called *Outlook.com.* You can read more about this application in the *Bonus Chapter Outlook.com*.

The *Windows Live Mail* program is another good alternative offering more advanced email features.

## 5.17 Exercises

Have you forgotten how to do something? Use the number beside the footsteps to look it up in the appendix *How Do I Do That Again?*

## Exercise 1: Creating an E-mail Message

In this exercise you are going to create a new e-mail message.

- Open the *Mail* app. 4
- Create a new e-mail message, address it to yourself and add the subject *practice*. 29
- Send the message. 28
- Check whether you have received the message in the *Inbox*. 30
- Read your e-mail message. 31

## Exercise 2: Deleting an E-mail Message

- Delete the mail you received in the previous exercise. 32

## Exercise 3: An E-mail Message in the Drafts Folder

- Create a new e-mail message. 29
- Save this message as a draft. 33
- Check whether your e-mail message has been saved in the *Drafts* folder. 34
- Delete your new e-mail from the *Drafts* folder. 32

## Exercise 4: Sending With Attachment

In this exercise you are going to repeat creating a new e-mail message with an attachment.

- Create a new e-mail message, address it to yourself and add the subject *practice with attachment*. 29
- Add a photo as an attachment. 35
- Send your message. 28

## Exercise 5: Viewing the Attachment

- Check the *Inbox* and see if you have received the e-mail with the attachment. 30
- Open the e-mail message with the attachment. 31
- View the attachment. 36
- Close the app or the window containing the photo. 5, 12
- Close the *Mail* app. 5

# 5.18 Background Information

**Dictionary**

**Attachment** A file that can be linked to an e-mail message and sent along with it. This can be a document, picture, or another type of file. Messages that contain attachments can be recognized by their paperclip icon in the message pane, next to the message title.

**Deleted folder** Deleted e-mails are moved to the *Deleted* folder. In order to permanently delete these items from your computer you will need to delete the messages in this folder also.

**Drafts** E-mail message that are written and saved first, instead of being sent right away, are stored in the *Drafts* folder.

**E-mail** Short for *electronic mail*. These are messages you send through the Internet.

**E-mail account** The server name, user name, password, and the e-mail address used by the *Mail* app to connect to an e-mail service. You can set up your e-mail account by using the information supplied to you by your Internet service provider.

**Emoticons** Sequences of keyboard characters that symbolize facial expressions. For example, :-) looks like a smiling face when you look at it sideways.

**Folder list** List of folders in the *Mail* app. It contains among others, the *Inbox* with all of your received mail and *Deleted* folder with the mails you have deleted.

**Hotmail** A free e-mail service provided by *Microsoft*.

**IMAP** A method used by computers to send and receive e-mail messages. This method will give you access to your e-mail without having to download the messages to your computer.

**Inbox** The *Inbox* is the folder in which all incoming e-mail messages are collected.

*- Continue on the next page -*

| | |
|---|---|
| **Junk folder** | *Mail* filters all messages that resemble unwanted, commercial e-mail, and moves them to the *Junk* folder. |
| **Log in** | Sign in with your computer, Internet service or e-mail service. |
| **Message pane** | A list of messages stored in the folders of the *Mail* app. |
| **Microsoft account** | A *Microsoft* account consists of an e-mail address and a password, and you can use it to sign in with various services from *Microsoft*. |
| **Password** | The letters, numbers and/or other characters needed by the user to login to their account and gain access to their email messages in the *Mail* app. |
| **POP3** | Post Office Protocol. A standard method used by computers to send and receive e-mail messages. POP3 messages are stored on an e-mail server, until you download them to your computer. Then they are deleted from the server. |
| **Search box** | *Windows 8* has a search box with which you can easily look up specific e-mail messages on your computer. |
| **Sent folder** | In the *Sent* folder, a copy of each sent message is stored, in case you may need it later on. |
| **Signature** | A text that you enter beforehand, such as your name and address, and that you can add to your e-mail messages. |
| **SMTP server** | SMTP servers (Simple Mail Transfer Protocol) take care of sending your e-mail messages to the Internet. The SMTP server processes outgoing e-mail and is used alongside a POP3 or IMAP server for the incoming e-mail. |
| **Spam** | Unsolicited, commercial e-mail, also called *junk* or *unwanted e-mail*. |

*Source: Windows Help and Support*

**Microsoft account**

Your *Microsoft* account consists of an e-mail address and a password, which you can use to sign in with various services, such as *Hotmail*, the *Store*, and *Windows* itself.

Where *Hotmail* is concerned, you can use the e-mail address that goes with the *Microsoft* account for sending and receiving e-mail. And you will also need a *Microsoft* account if you want to download and install apps, since this account grants you access to the *Store*. You can read more about this subject in *Chapter 6 Downloading and Printing* and the online *Bonus Chapter Downloading Apps*.

You can also use such a *Microsoft* account to sign in with the *Windows* operating system itself. If you want to sign in with *Windows* with this account, you need to use your e-mail address and password. You can also use these on other computers and tablets, and *Windows* will then display the same settings on all these computers.

**Icons**

Several icons are used in the *Mail* app. Below we have explained the meaning of these icons:

 a message to which you have replied.

 the message contains an attachment.

 a message you have forwarded.

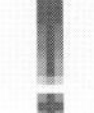 a message flagged as 'important' by the sender.

**How does e-mail work?**

All e-mail messaged are delivered to a so-called *mail server*. This is a computer owned by the e-mail provider and specially designated for processing electronic mail. After you have written and sent an e-mail message, this message will be sent on through your e-mail provider's mail server, and through a number of intermediate stops, until it reaches the mail server of the recipient's e-mail provider, where it will be stored.

It works both ways: your own e-mail is stored on your Internet provider's mail server, until you retrieve it with the *Mail* app.

The e-mail message only arrives at the recipient's computer when he retrieves his e-mail from his e-mail provider. Some people check their mailbox every day, others just once a week. This means your e-mail messages may already have been stored on the recipient's mail server for a week, before he or she actually retrieves and reads them.

**Netiquette**
The word *netiquette* is a contraction of *internet* and *etiquette*. It stands for a set of rules that people are urged to follow when they use e-mail services.

In order to communicate in an effective way, it is best to follow these rules:

- Think before you send. Writing and sending e-mail messages is terribly easy. Make sure you have thought about what to write beforehand, and avoid writing e-mails while you are angry. Once you have sent the message you cannot take it back.
- Use a brief, clear description of the subject. This will provide people who receive lots of e-mail messages with a quick overview of the main topics, and enable them to select the most important e-mails first.
- Avoid using only CAPITALS. Many people think that sentences that use nothing but capital letters are 'loud', rude, and offensive.
- Be careful with sensitive and confidential information. The recipient may well share his computer with other people. In such a case, anyone will be able to forward your mails, on purpose or by accident.

**The smaller the attachment, the faster send and received**
This is the rule on the Internet: the smaller the message is, the faster it will be sent from A to B. The same goes for attachments. In this case 'small' refers to the file size.

This is something you or the recipient of the message need to account for, especially if you have a slow Internet connection. Nowadays most people in Europe, Australia, and North America use a fast Internet connection, but there are some countries where this kind of connection is not available.

When you send an attachment, you will always be able to see the file name and the size, in kB or MB. This is a measure, just like meters and grams, feet, and gallons.

One kilobyte equals (approximately) a thousand bytes.
20 kilobytes equal 20.000 bytes. Kilobyte is abbreviated to kB.
One megabyte equals (approximately) a thousand kilobytes.
This means that a megabyte equals (approximately ) one million (a thousand times thousand) bytes. The abbreviation for megabyte is MB.

*- Continue on the next page -*

The speed with which something is sent or received depends on a number of factors, among others, the speed of your modem, the type of Internet connection, and the degree of traffic on the Internet. An e-mail message that consists of only text, will be sent within less than a second. A picture (unedited), taken with a modern digital photo camera (for example, 10 megapixels), is usually much larger. Sending such a photo will take up a lot more time. This can be especially hard on recipients who do not have a fast Internet connection, retrieving such a large file may cause them serious problems.

You can send all sorts of files along with an e-mail message, audio files and video files too. But be careful. Especially the video files can be extremely large.
But if you have a fast broadband connection, such as ADSL or cable, sending large files will not pose a problem.
**Please note:** some Internet providers set a limit to the amount of data you can send along with an e-mail. If the limit is exceeded, the message will not arrive. Usually you will receive a warning message when this happens.

**Open an attachment**

By clicking the attachment, you will automatically open an app or a program with which you can view the attached file. Which program will be opened, depends on the settings on your computer.
If the attachment is a text document, in most cases *Microsoft Word* will be opened, or *WordPad* if *Word* has not been installed to your computer.
If the attachment is a photo, the default setting in *Windows 8* is to open the *Photos* app. If you have installed a photo editing program on your computer, this default setting is sometimes adapted and this editing program will be opened instead.
If you receive an attachment that can only be opened with a program that is not installed on your computer, you will not be able to open the attachment. For some file types it is possible to download a so-called *viewer*. With such a viewer you can view the file, but you cannot edit it. For example, on www.microsoft.com you can download free viewers for *PowerPoint* files (extension: PPS or PPT) and *Excel* files (XLS).
If the attachment is a computer program (for instance, an .EXE file), access to this file will be blocked most likely by your antivirus program. You will see this on your screen and if you want you can unblock the files. But be cautious, especially with any files containing the extension .exe. These files could contain viruses. It is always best to download files or programs directly from the manufacturer's website or from the CD or DVD included in the program's packaging.

## 5.19 Tips

### Tip

**Setting up multiple e-mail accounts**

In the *Mail* app you can add multiple e-mail accounts. This is how you do it:

- **Move the pointer in the top right-hand corner of the screen, until you see the charms bar**

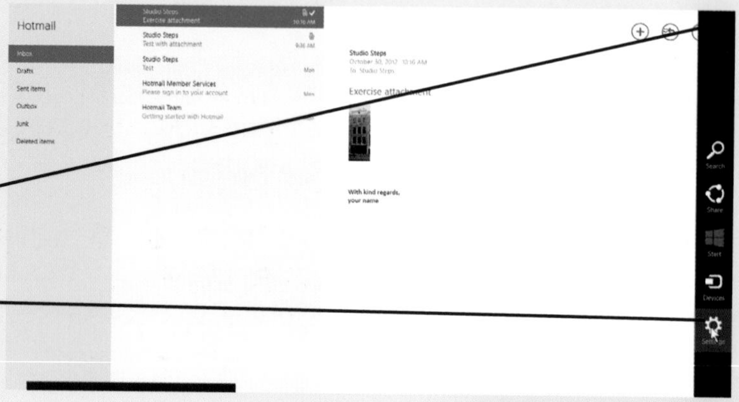

- **Click** Settings

- **Click** Accounts

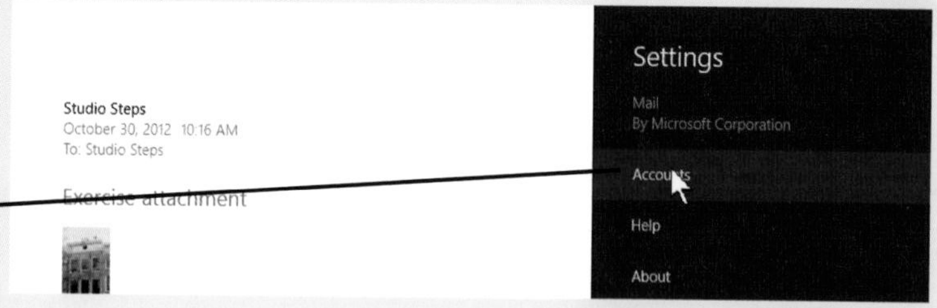

- **Click** Add an account

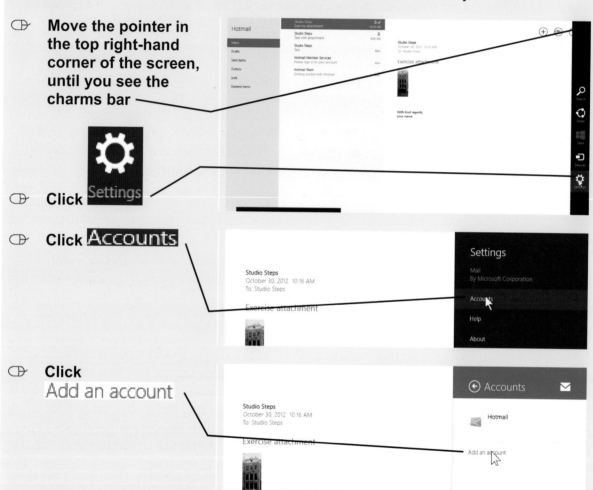

In this example we will add an e-mail address that has been supplied by an Internet provider. While we were writing this book, it was only possible to add e-mail addresses of Internet providers who had IMAP servers at their disposal. Many Internet providers only use POP3 servers.

*- Continue on the next page -*

These are the differences between IMAP and POP:

- IMAP stands for *Internet Message Access Protocol*. This means you manage your e-mail messages on the mail server. The messages you have read will remain stored on the mail server, until you delete them. IMAP is useful if you want to manage your e-mail from more than one computer. Your mailbox will look exactly the same on each computer. If you create folders to organize your messages, you will also find these folders on the other computer(s) you use. If you want to use IMAP, you will need to set up your e-mail account as an IMAP on all computers involved.
- POP stands for *Post Office Protocol*, the traditional way of managing e-mail messages. When you retrieve your e-mail messages, they will be deleted from the server right away.

It is not yet clear whether *Windows 8* will support POP3 in future. Many Internet providers are expected to expand their service and include IMAP servers as well. If necessary, contact your Internet provider for additional information.

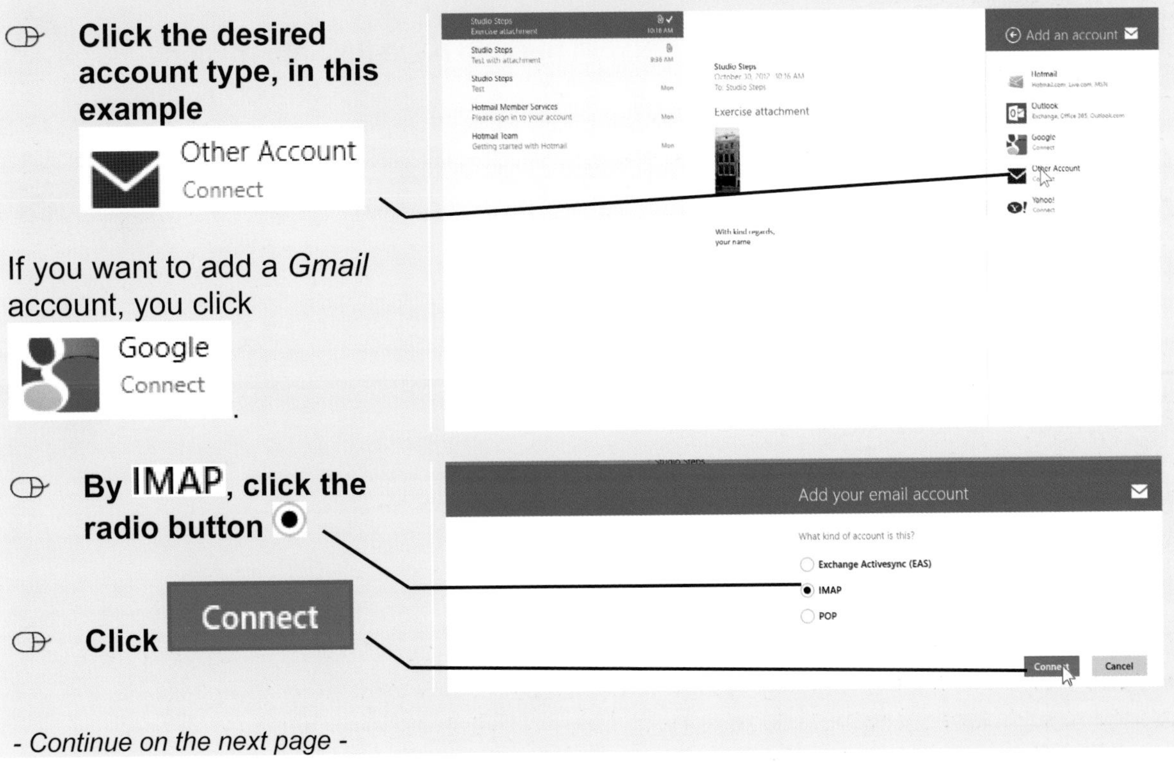


**Click the desired account type, in this example** Other Account Connect

If you want to add a *Gmail* account, you click Google Connect.

**By** IMAP**, click the radio button** ●

**Click** Connect

*- Continue on the next page -*

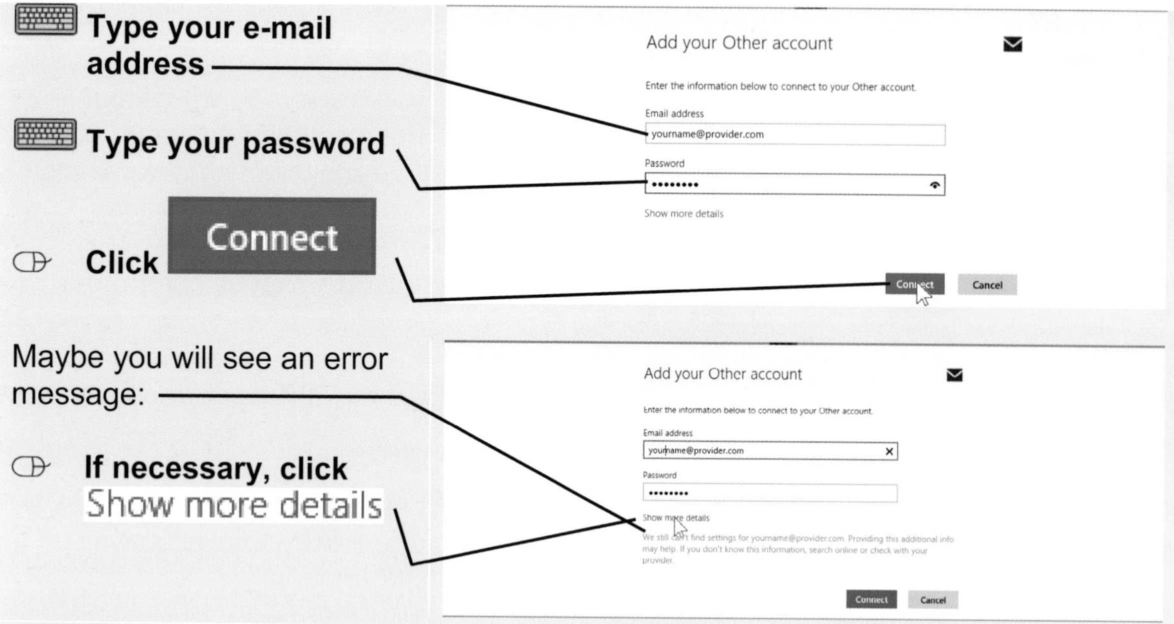


**Type your e-mail address**

**Type your password**

**Click** Connect

Maybe you will see an error message:

**If necessary, click** Show more details

When you set up an e-mail account, you will need to have this information:

- your e-mail address;
- the corresponding password;
- the name of the IMAP server of your Internet provider;
- the name of the SMTP server of your Internet provider.

**Help! I do not have this information.**
Your Internet provider has supplied you with this information. If you do not have it, or cannot find it, contact your Internet provider.

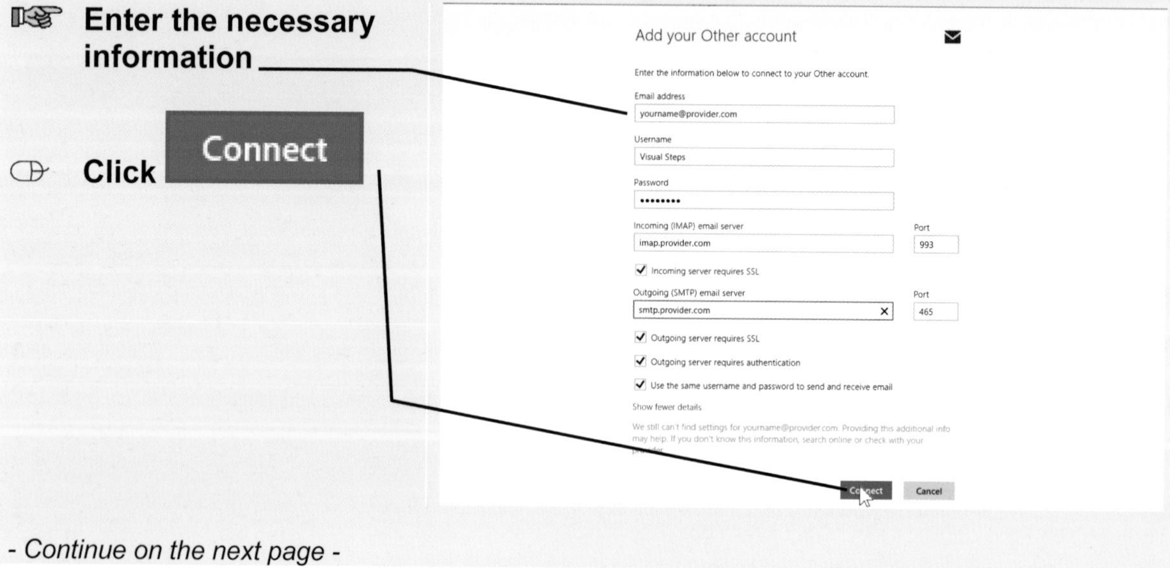


**Enter the necessary information**

**Click** Connect

- *Continue on the next page* -

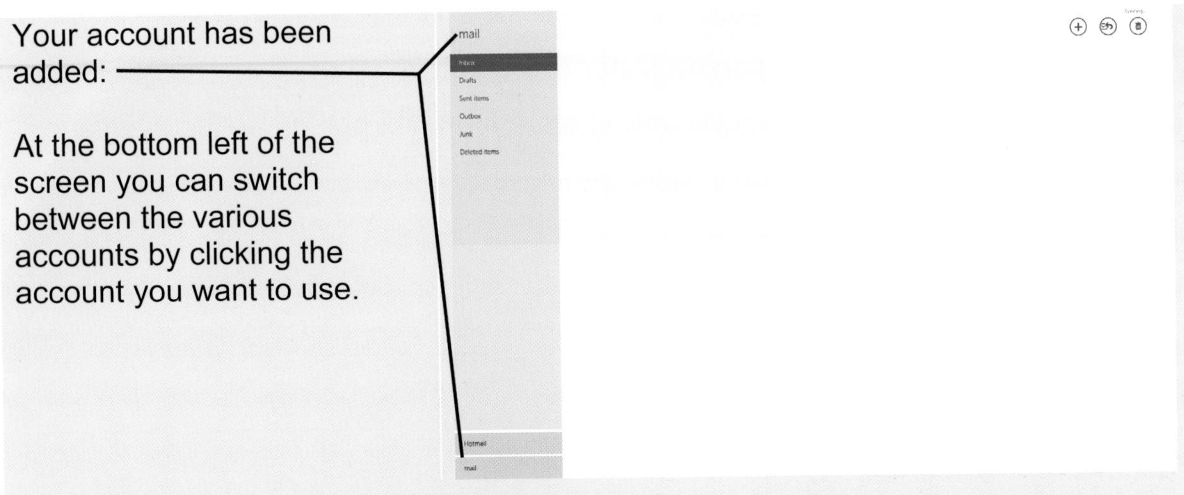


Your account has been added:

At the bottom left of the screen you can switch between the various accounts by clicking the account you want to use.

Your e-mail will be sent form the account selected by you. If you want to send messages from the other e-mail address, read the next *Tip*.

## Tip

**Set a different account while sending e-mail**

If you want to send an e-mail message from the other e-mail account, then you do this:

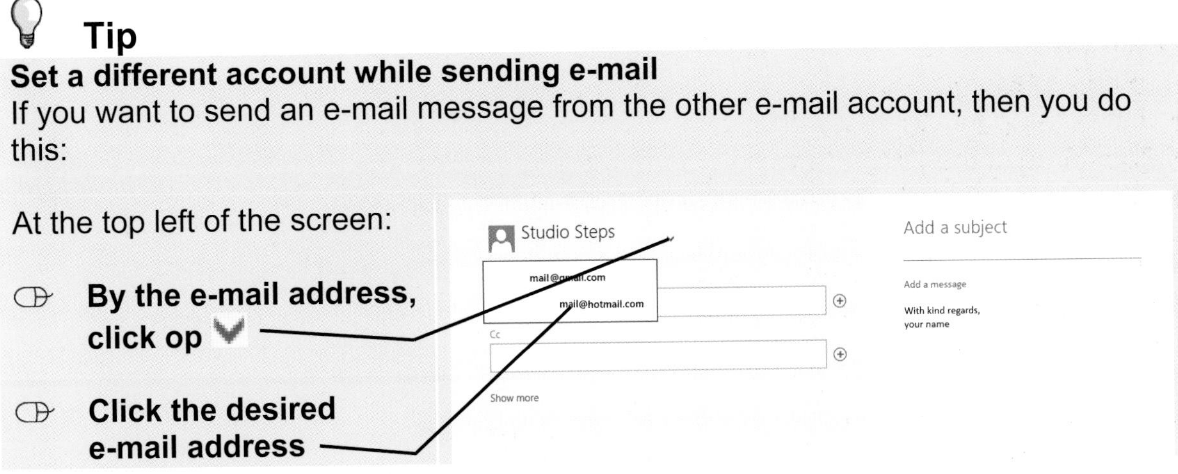


At the top left of the screen:

- **By the e-mail address, click op** ⌄
- **Click the desired e-mail address**

## Tip

**Print an e-mail**

If you want to print an e-mail message:

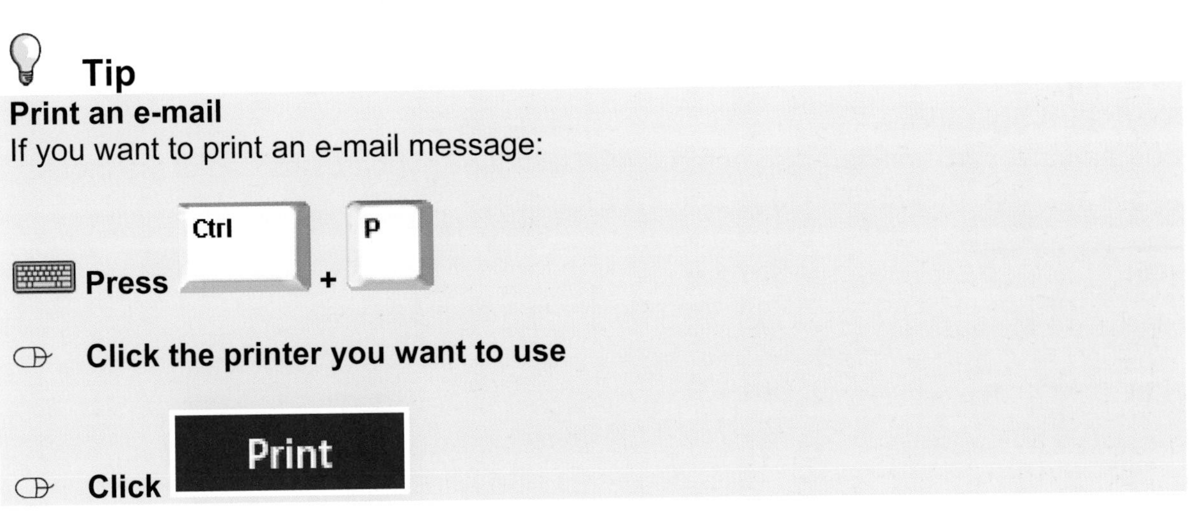

Press **Ctrl** + **P**

- **Click the printer you want to use**
- **Click** **Print**

## Tip

**CC and BCC**

There are several ways of sending e-mail to more than one person. In the message screen you will see a box with CC, below the box with To.

CC

You use *CC* (*Carbon Copy*) if you want to send a copy of the e-mail to other people. In the e-mail it will be visible to whom you send these copies, so the CCs will be displayed too.

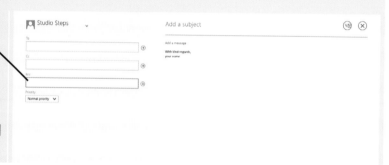

There is yet another option. You will need to display it first:

**Click** Show more

Another box has appeared:

BCC

The recipients in the BCC (*Blind Carbon Copy*) box are invisible to the other people who have received this e-mail too.

## Tip

**Keyboard operations**

For the most part, you can also operate *Mail* with the keyboard, instead of the mouse. Below you will find the main keys and their function.

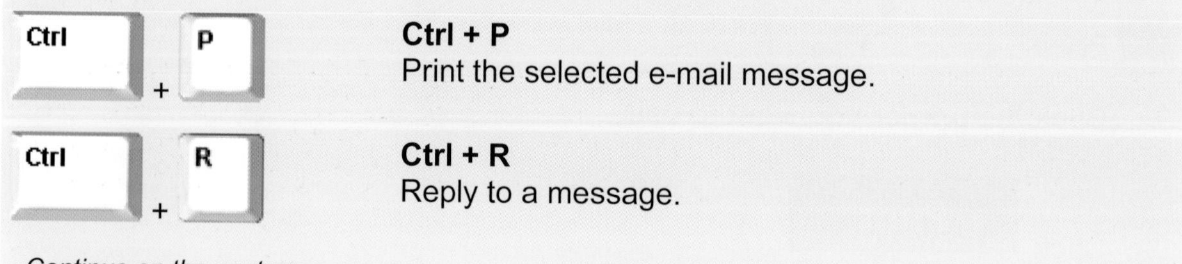


**Ctrl + P**
Print the selected e-mail message.

**Ctrl + R**
Reply to a message.

*- Continue on the next page -*

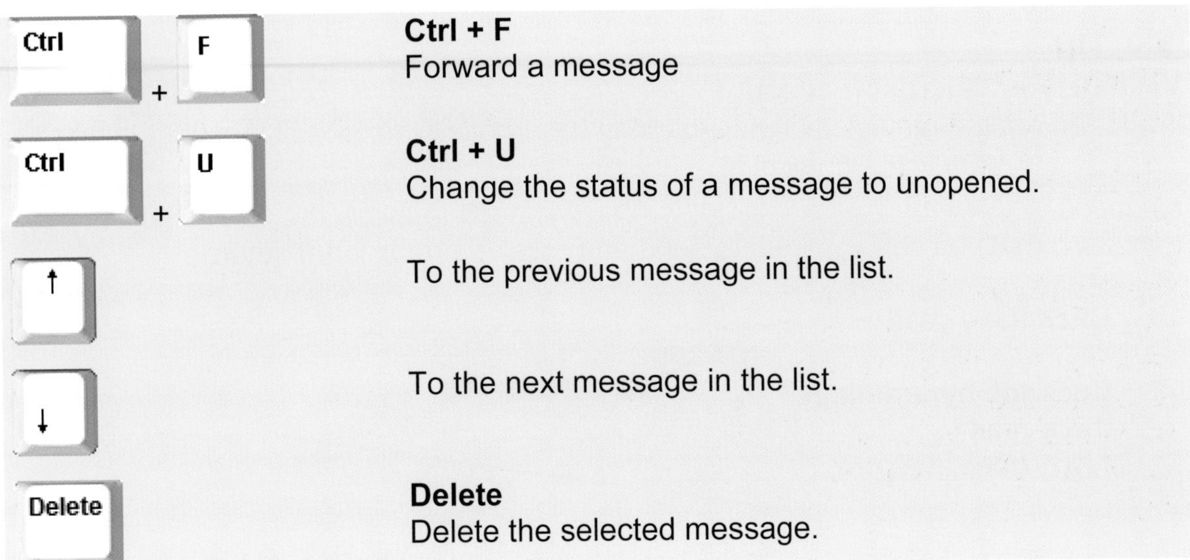

**Ctrl + F**
Forward a message

**Ctrl + U**
Change the status of a message to unopened.

To the previous message in the list.

To the next message in the list.

**Delete**
Delete the selected message.

## Tip

**Change the text formatting**
This is how you can change the font, letter size, and style of the text in the e-mail message. And you can add effects too, such as colors:

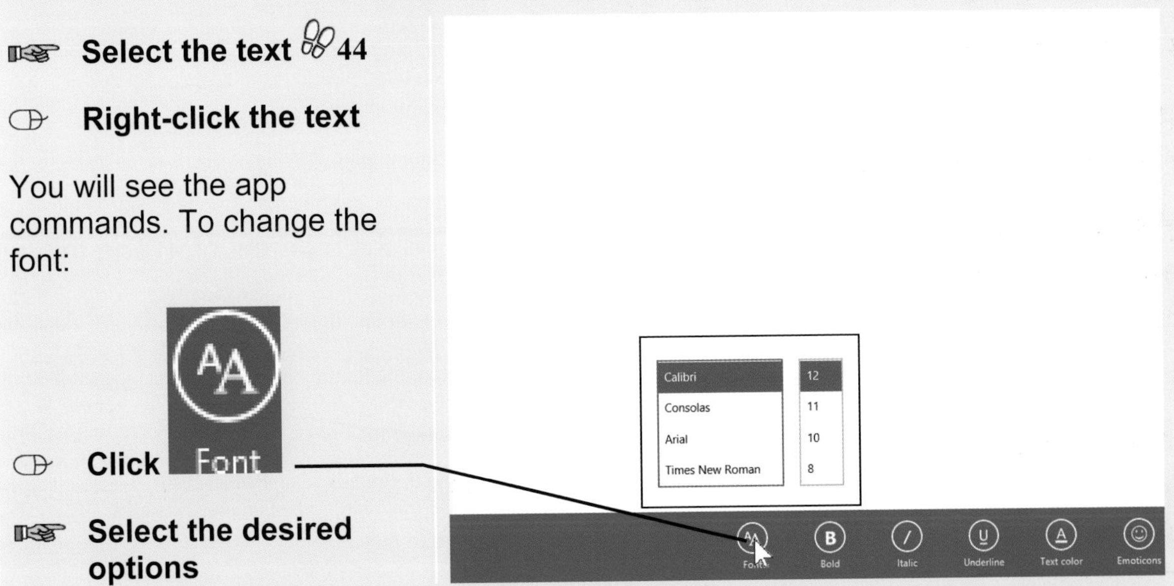


**Select the text** 44

**Right-click the text**

You will see the app commands. To change the font:

**Click** Font

**Select the desired options**

Other options are also shown on this bar. You can make your text bold or cursive. You can also change the color and apply underlining as needed. You can even add emoticons. Emoticons are keyboard characters that symbolize facial expressions. For example, :-) looks like a smiling face when you look at it sideways and :-( is just the opposite.

## Tip

**Validate your Microsoft account**

While receiving e-mail messages, you may have noticed an e-mail message from *Microsoft* Hotmail Member Services Please sign in to your account. You will need to follow the instructions in this e-mail, so that you can continue to send and receive e-mail in the future:

- **Click the e-mail**
- **Click the hyperlink in the e-mail** http://mail.live.com

The *Internet Explorer* app is opened:

The e-mail address is already filled in:

- **By** Password**, type your password**
- **Click** Sign in

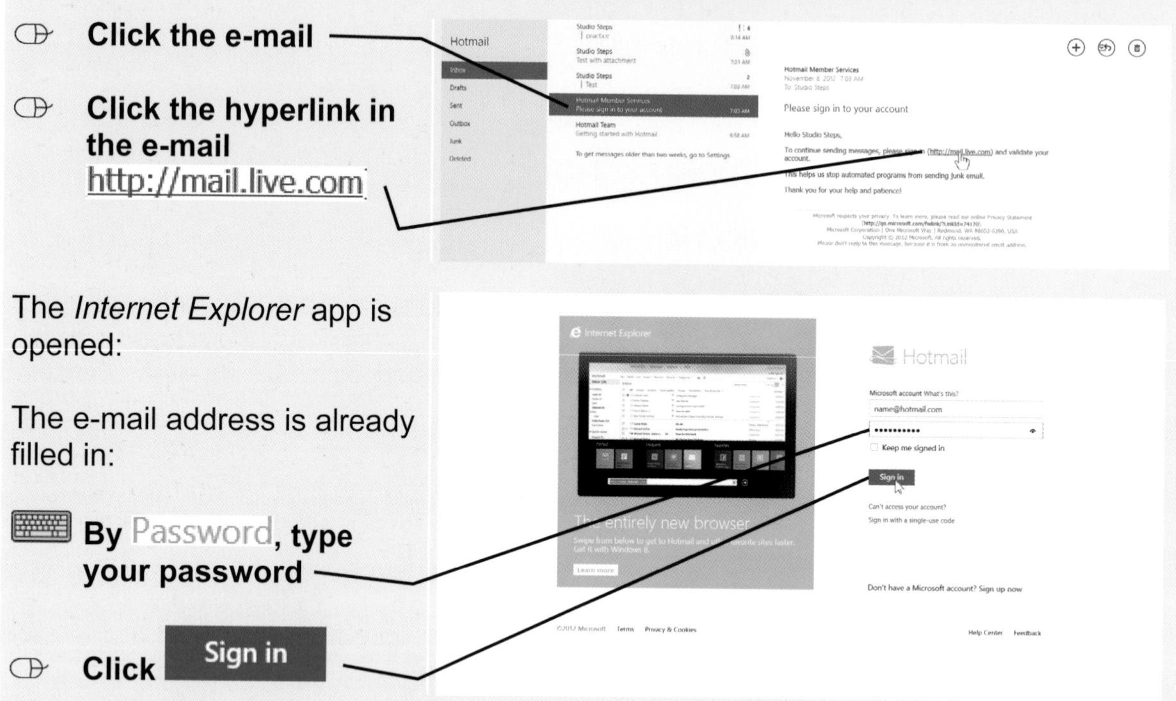


The e-mail will be opened in the *Internet Explorer* app. At the moment of writing this book, no further action was necessary.

At the top right-hand of the screen:

- **Click** sign out

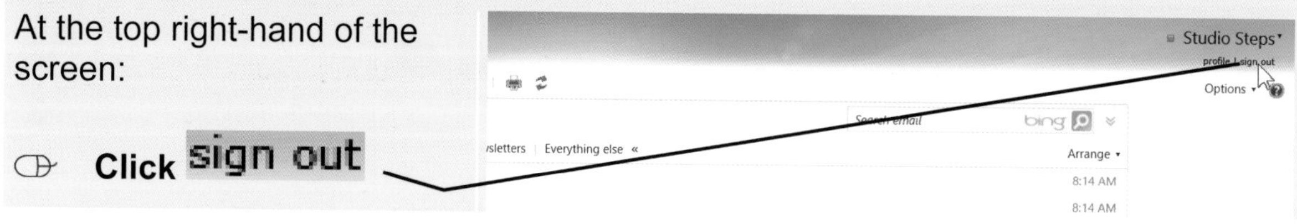

# 6. Downloading and Printing

There is a vast amount of information on the Internet that you can copy onto your own computer. This copying is called *downloading*. The opposite of *downloading* is *uploading* (sending files from your computer to the Internet).

You can download just about anything: computer programs, music, video films and more. After you have downloaded something, you usually save it to your computer's hard drive so that you can use it again later.

For computer programs, the second step after downloading is usually installing the program onto your computer. Installation makes the program ready for use so that you can work with it. For example, the program gets added to the Start screen so you can easily open it.

In *Windows 8* you also will be using apps. These are little programs. There are several apps available. In the *Store* you can find thousands of apps, free apps as well as paid apps that you can download and install. In this chapter you will learn how to install a free app.

You can print the web pages you find interesting, and read them a while later. In most cases you can save photos and the open them in a photo editing program to edit them further. Besides, the Internet contains lots of so-called PDF files. These are files that are read-only. You will not be able to alter the content of these files. Many companies use a PDF file to publish their general terms and conditions regarding subscriptions and purchases on the Internet, for example.

In this chapter you will get acquainted with all these types of downloads.

In this chapter you will learn how to:

- download and install a program;
- delete the installation program;
- download and install a free app;
- save an image from the Internet on your computer;
- open a PDF file on the Internet;
- print a web page.

# 6.1 Downloading and Installing a Program

In order to be able to use a program on the computer it needs to be installed to the computer first. This means all the program files have to be copied to the correct folder on the hard disk, and the program has to be included in the list of programs. All these operations are handled by an *installation program*. This is also called a *setup* program.

Some software programs are still issued on a CD or a DVD, and the installation procedure will automatically start when you insert the CD ROM into the computer's CD or DVD player. But nowadays you can download and install most computer programs directly from the Internet.

To practice downloading software, in this chapter you are going to download and install the free photo editing program *Picasa*.

**Open *Internet Explorer* on the desktop** 9

**Open the web page picasa.google.com** 1

Note that you do not need to type www at the beginning of the web address.

On the website you will see a brief introduction to *Picasa*. You are going to download the program:

**Click**

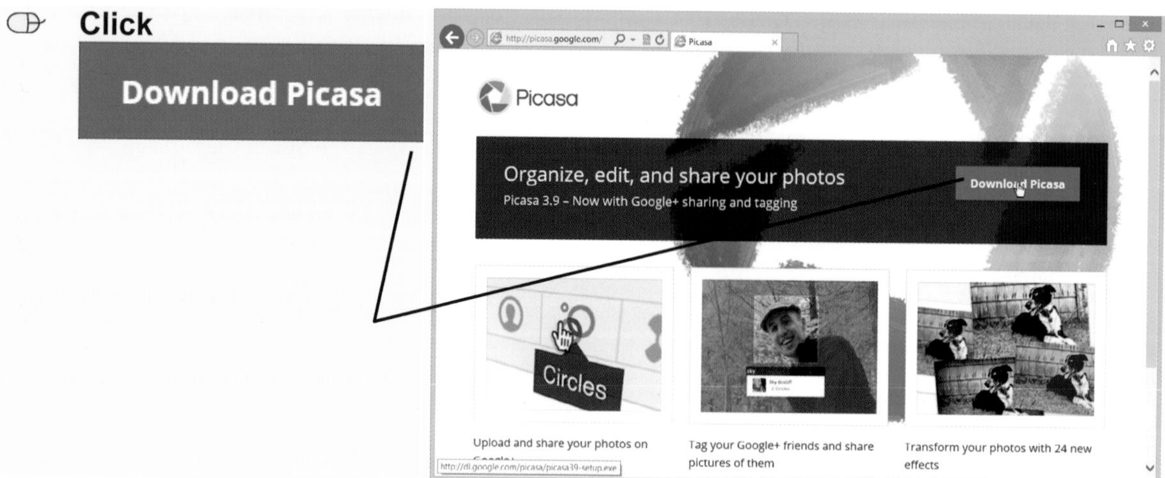

## Please note:

If you download a program in the *Internet Explorer* app it works the same way.

Next, you will see a bar at the bottom of the window, with two possible options Run and Save ▾:

You can choose between:

- run a file. This will directly start the installation program.
- saving the file. This means the program file will first be stored on your computer's hard disk. Afterwards you will need to start the installation program yourself.
- If, on second thoughts, you decide not to download a file, you click *Cancel*.

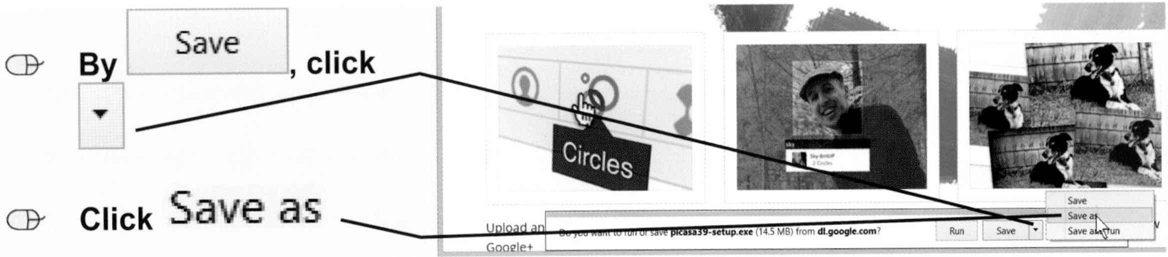


**By** Save **, click** ▾

**Click** Save as

You will see a window where you can select a location to save the file:

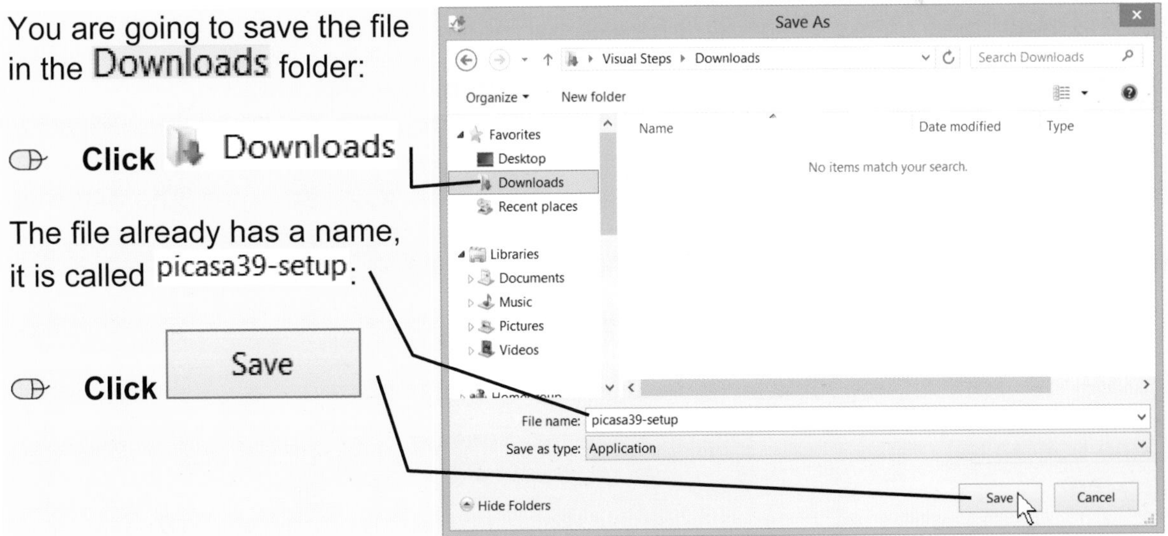


You are going to save the file in the Downloads folder:

**Click** Downloads

The file already has a name, it is called picasa39-setup:

**Click** Save

## Tip

**Save directly**

If you had directly clicked Save in the previous step, the file would automatically have been saved in the Downloads folder too.

After the download operation has finished you see this bar. You can close the bar:

**Click** ✕

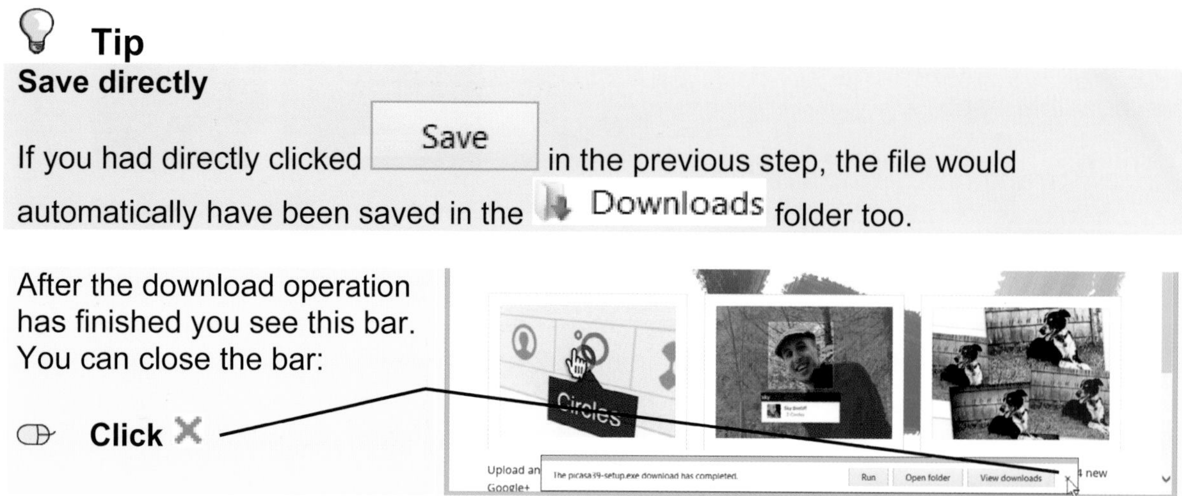


You can close *Internet Explorer*.

**Close *Internet Explorer*** 12

*Picasa* has been downloaded and stored on your computer's hard disk. Now you can install the program to your computer.

## Tip

**Downloads? Always save these in the same folder.**

It is a good idea to save the files you have downloaded in the same folder, for example in Downloads. It makes it easier to find your files later on.

Most computer programs contain several parts. In order for the program to work properly, all these parts have to be correctly installed on your computer. The different parts are then copied to the right place on your hard drive and the program name is added to the list of apps and programs in *Windows*. All this work is done by the installation program.

To open the *Downloads* folder:

At the bottom left of the desktop:

**Click**

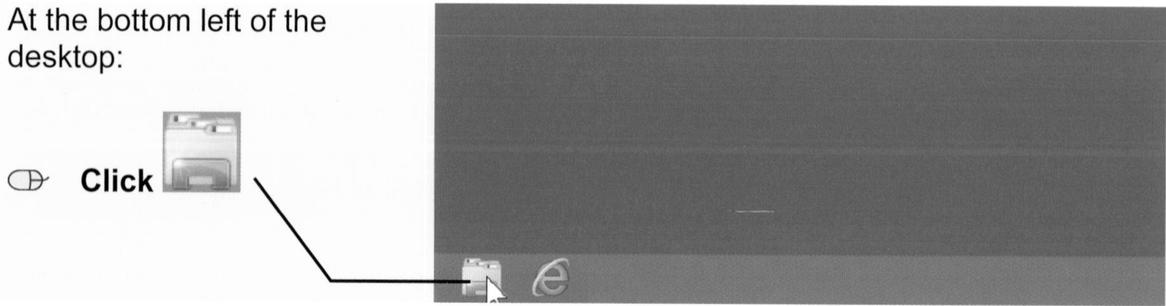

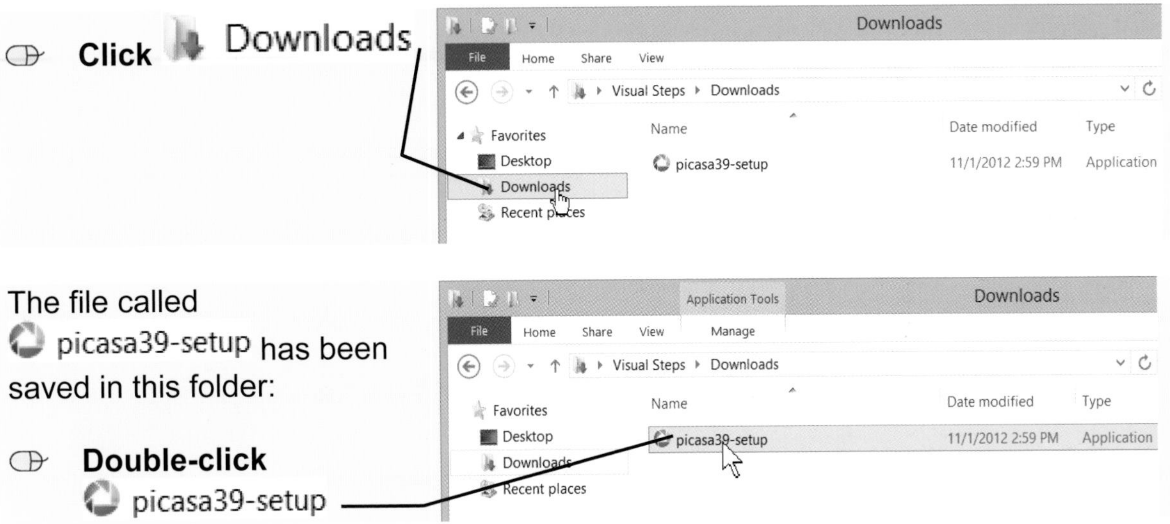


Click Downloads

The file called picasa39-setup has been saved in this folder:

Double-click picasa39-setup

Maybe your screen will now turn dark. In this window you will need to give permission to continue.

**Give permission to continue**

In the next window you will need to agree to the license agreement:

**Click** I Agree

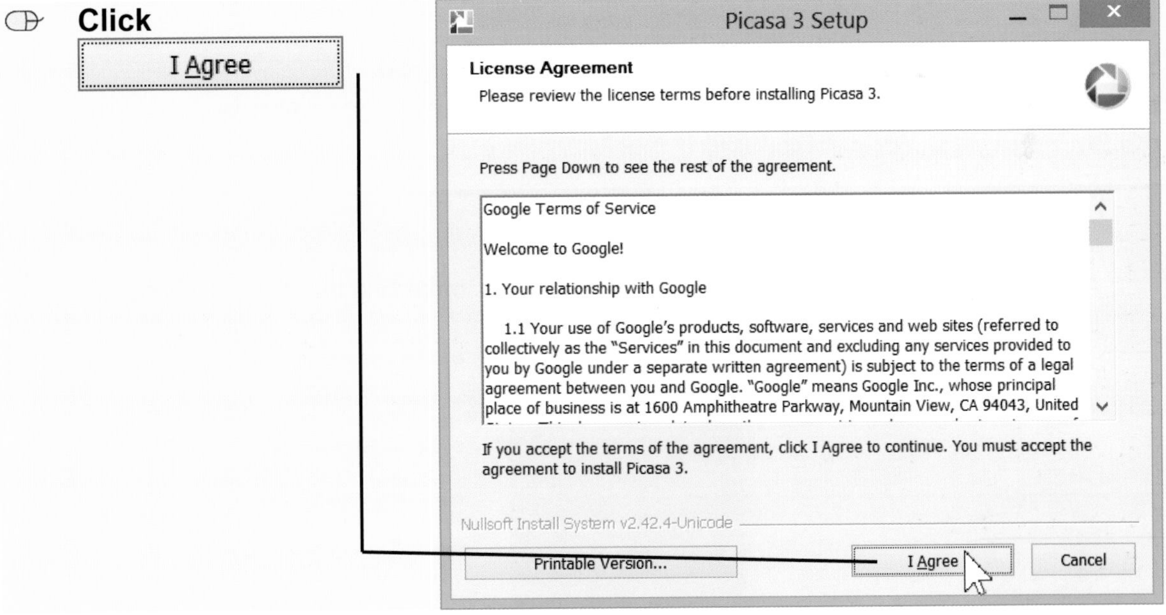

Here you will see the folder in which the program will be installed:

If you want to install the program to a different folder, click Browse... and open the folder you want to use.

Click Install

Picasa 3 Setup

**Choose Install Location**

Choose the folder in which to install Picasa 3.

Setup will install Picasa 3 in the following folder. To install in a different folder, click Browse and select another folder. Click Install to start the installation.

Destination Folder

C:\Program Files (x86)\Google\Picasa3

Browse...

Space required: 63.6MB

Space available: 859.7GB

Nullsoft Install System v2.42.4-Unicode

< Back Install Cancel

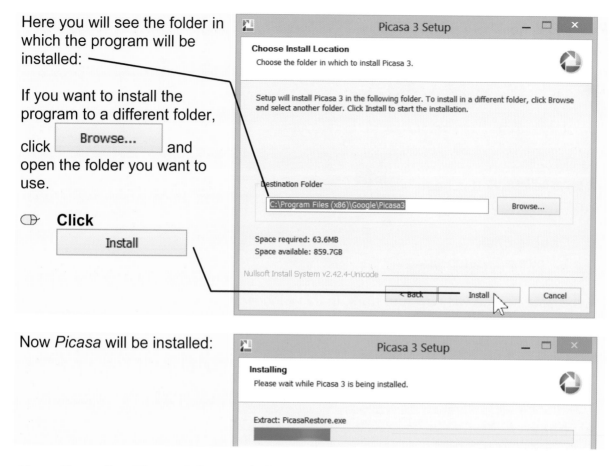

Now *Picasa* will be installed:

Picasa 3 Setup

**Installing**

Please wait while Picasa 3 is being installed.

Extract: PicasaRestore.exe

You will see the *Picasa 3 Setup* window. Many programs offer extra features or additional options. You can disable these for now:

**Uncheck the boxes** ☑ **next to**
Add Shortcut to Quick L
Set Google as my default
Send anonymous usage
**and** Run Picasa 3

**Click** Finish

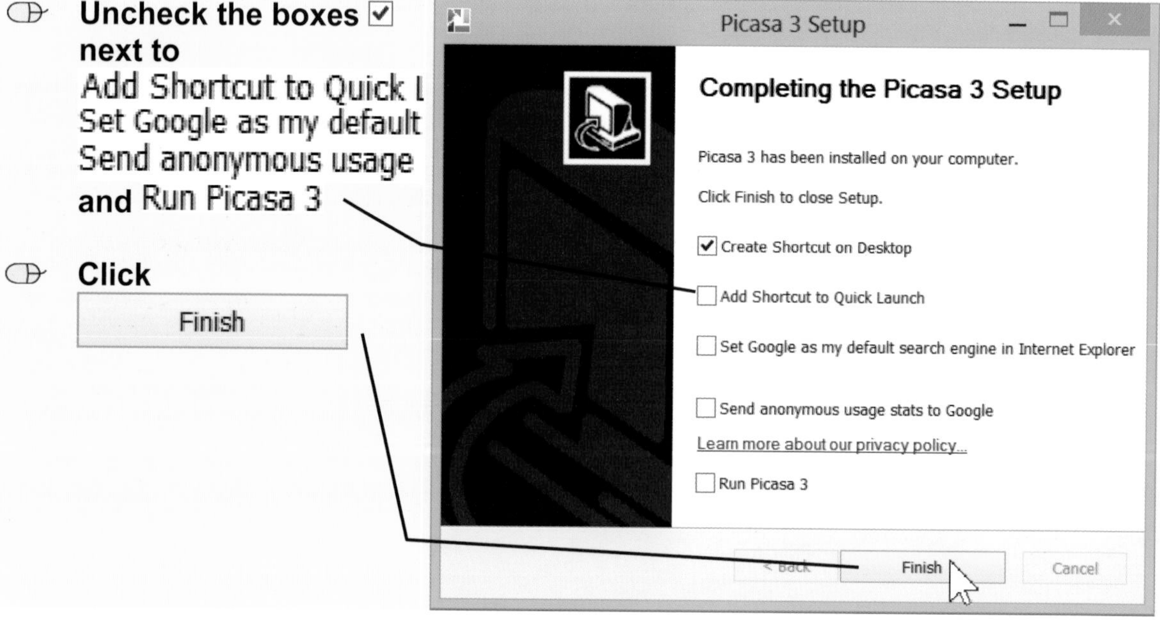

*Picasa* has now been installed on your computer. You can close the *Downloads* window:

**Close the *Downloads* window** 12

On your desktop you will see the *Picasa* icon:

The program has also been added to the Start screen. You are going to check this:

**Go back to the Start screen** 3

You see that the program has been added to the Start screen:

The program in this example placed two tiles on the Start screen.

You will no longer need the *Picasa* in this book. In the next section you can read how to delete this program again. If you do not want to delete the program, then just read through this section.

## Tip

**Learn more about working with Picasa**
In this chapter you have read how to download and install the Picasa photo editing program. In *Picasa* you can manage your photos and edit them very easily.

Do you want to learn more about *Picasa*? Then this title will surely interest you.

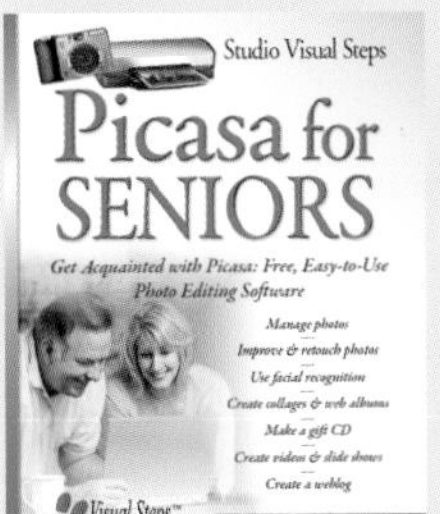


**Picasa for Seniors**
ISBN 978 90 5905 246 8

See for more information:
**www.visualsteps.com/picasa**

## 6.2 Deleting a Program

You can delete a program on your computer if you no longer use it, or if you want to free up space on your hard disk. This is how you delete a program from the Start screen:

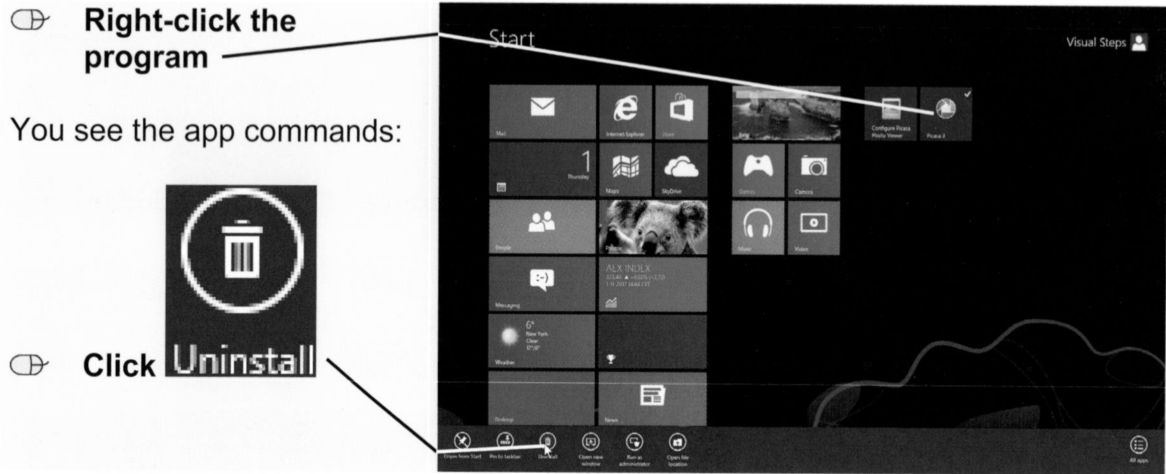


**Right-click the program**

You see the app commands:

**Click** Uninstall

The *Control Panel* is opened:

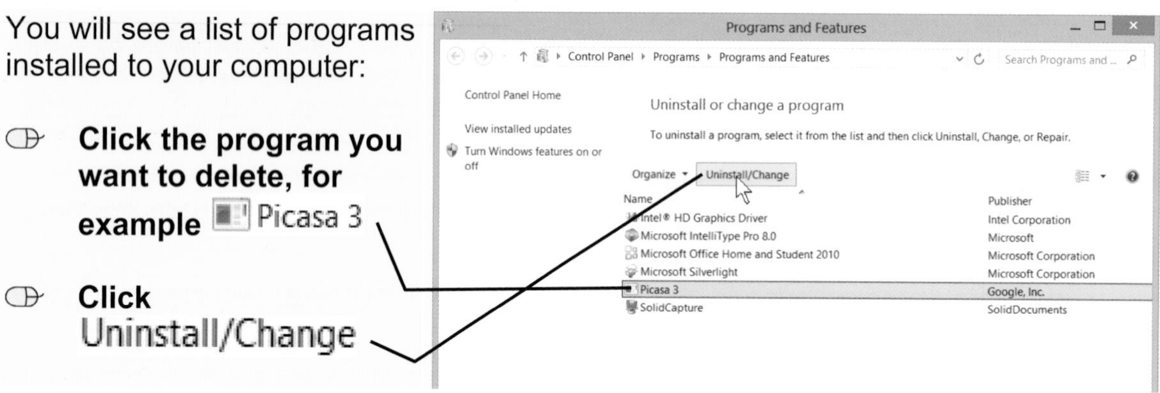


You will see a list of programs installed to your computer:

**Click the program you want to delete, for example** Picasa 3

**Click** Uninstall/Change

Maybe your screen will now turn dark. In this window you will need to give permission to continue.

**Give permission to continue**

You see the *Picasa 3 Uninstall* window:

At the bottom of the window:

Click **Uninstall**

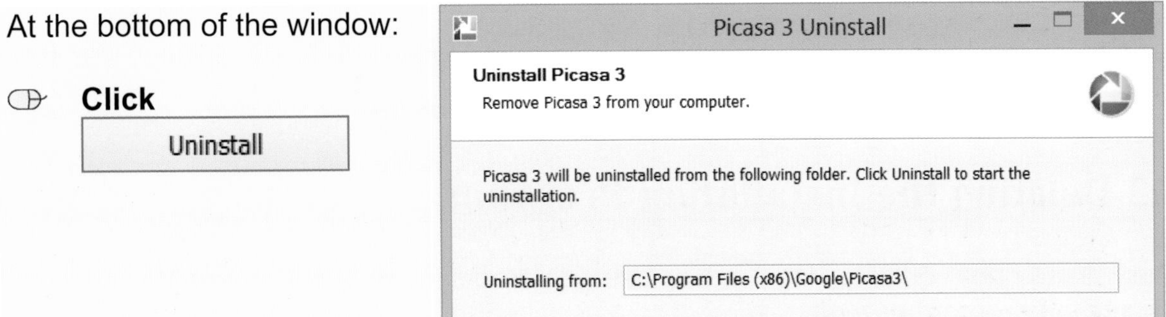


You will be asked if you want to delete the *Picasa* database. If you have not done anything else with *Picasa*, you can go ahead and delete it.

Click **Yes**

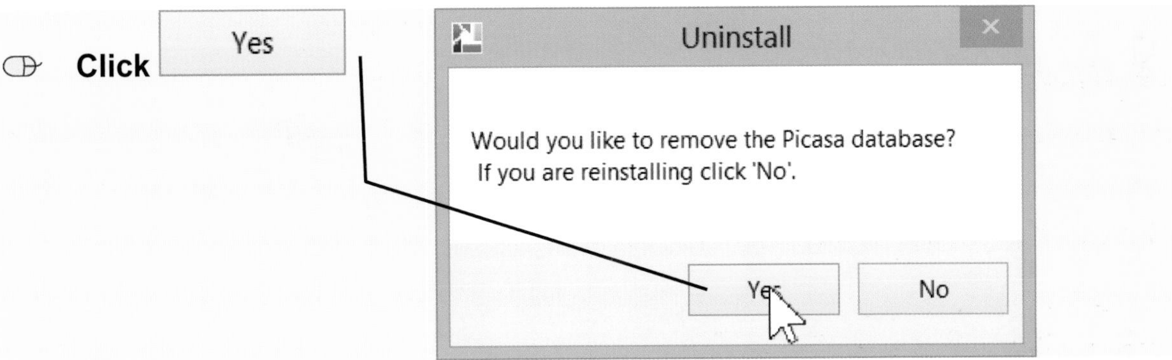


*Internet Explorer* is opened and you see a message by *Picasa*. You can close this window:

**Close *Internet Explorer*** 12

You still need to complete the delete operation of the *Picasa* program.

At the bottom of the window:

Click **Finish**

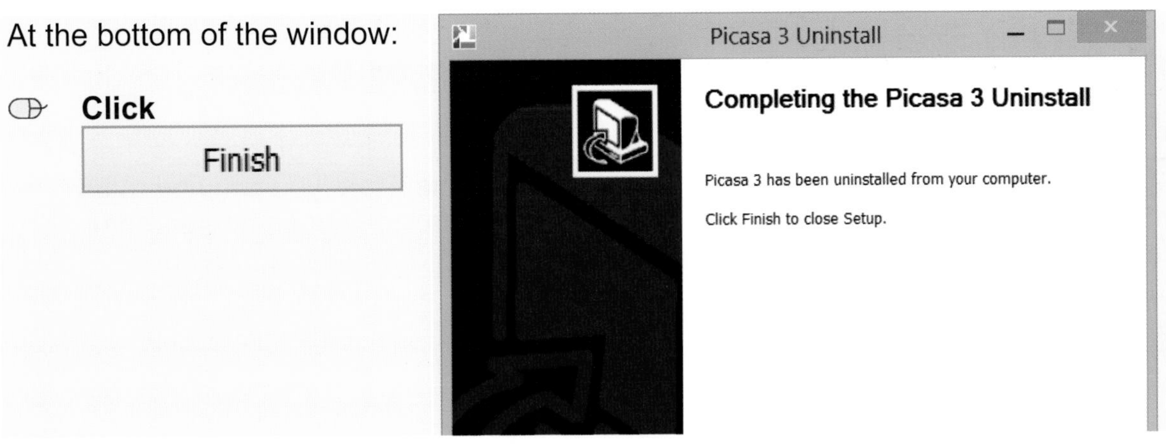

Now the program has been removed from your computer. Both tiles are deleted from the Start screen as well.

**Close the *Programs and Features* window** [12]

# 6.3 Deleting the Installation Program

The *Picasa* photo editing program has been deleted. Now you can delete the installation program as well:

**Open the *Downloads* folder** [37]

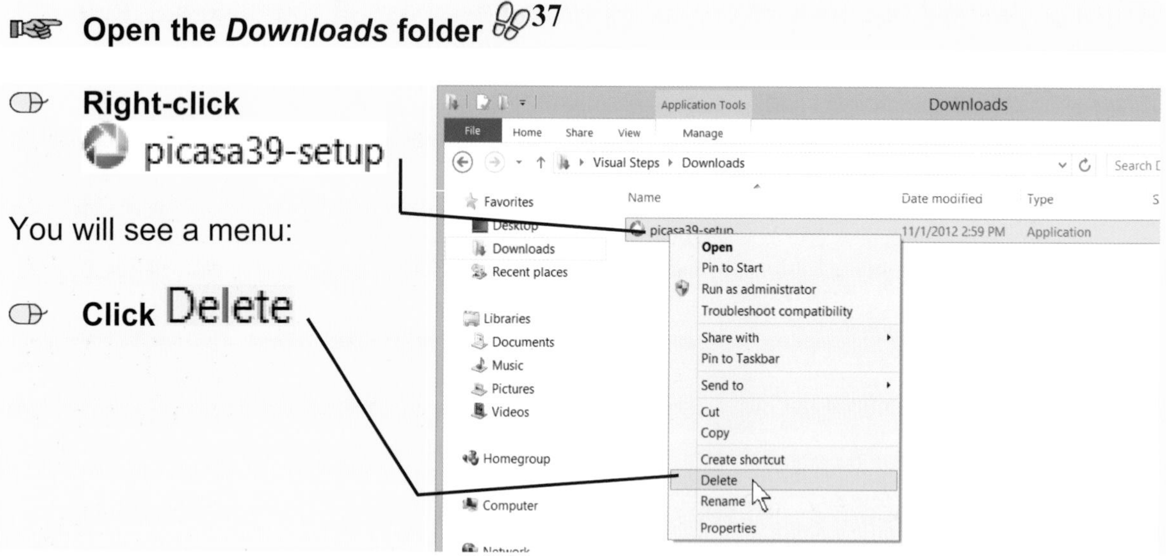

**Right-click** picasa39-setup

You will see a menu:

**Click** Delete



The installation program has been deleted.

**Close the *Downloads* folder** [12]

# 6.4 Downloading and Installing a Free App

In the previous chapters you have already gotten to know some of the apps that are a regular part of the *Windows 8* operating system. In the *Store* you can find many more apps (programs) that you can download and install to your computer, some for free and some at a fee. In this section you are going to download a free app:

**Go back to the Start screen** [3]

To open the *Store* where you can find the apps:

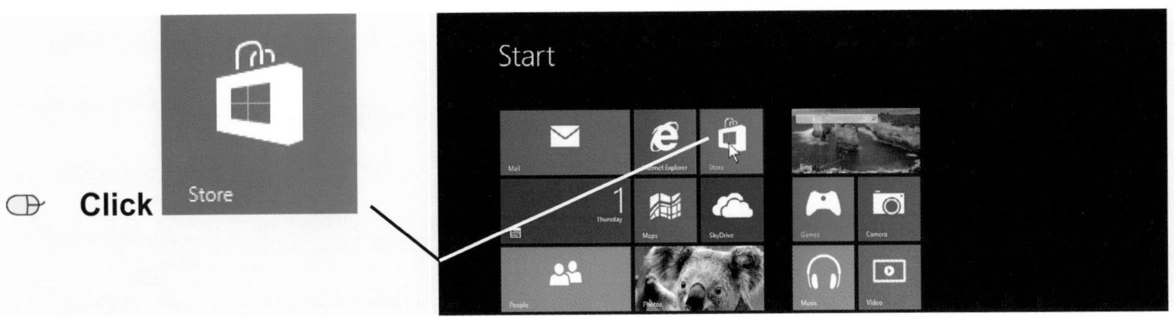


Click Store

Now the *Store* is open. This store is divided into various categories. With the scroll bar at the bottom of the screen you can view these categories. For now you are just going to look for an app:

**Display the charms bar** 8

Click Search

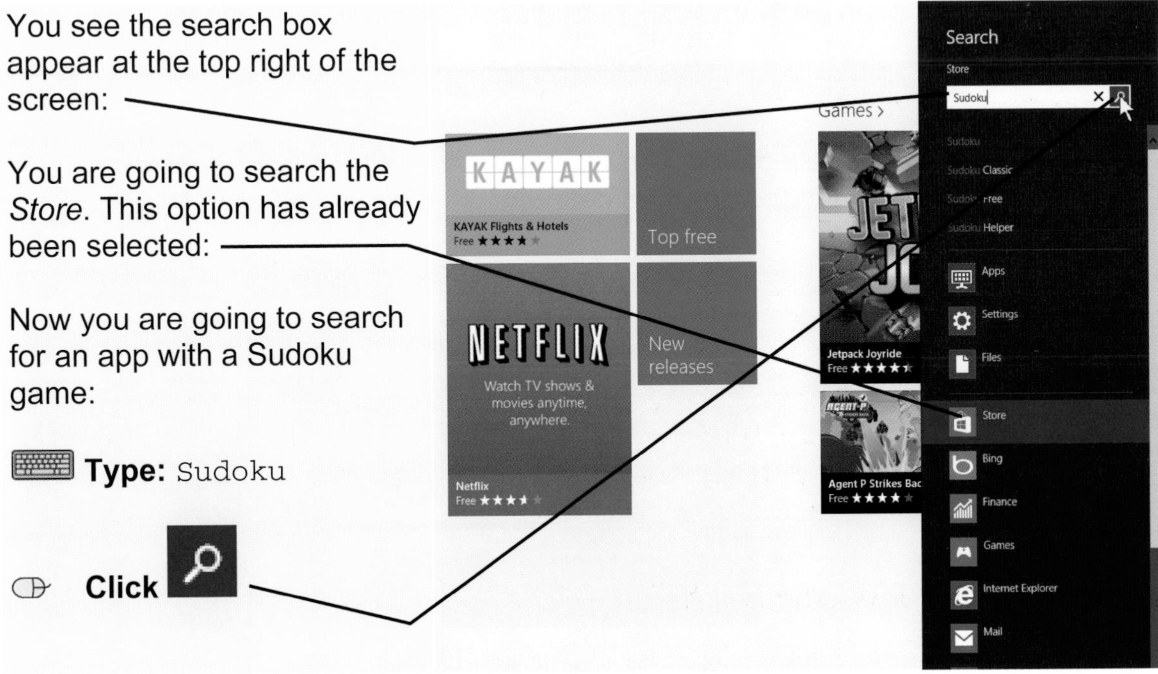


You see the search box appear at the top right of the screen:

You are going to search the *Store*. This option has already been selected:

Now you are going to search for an app with a Sudoku game:

**Type:** `Sudoku`

Click

There are various results for Sudoku.

- **Click one of the results, for example**

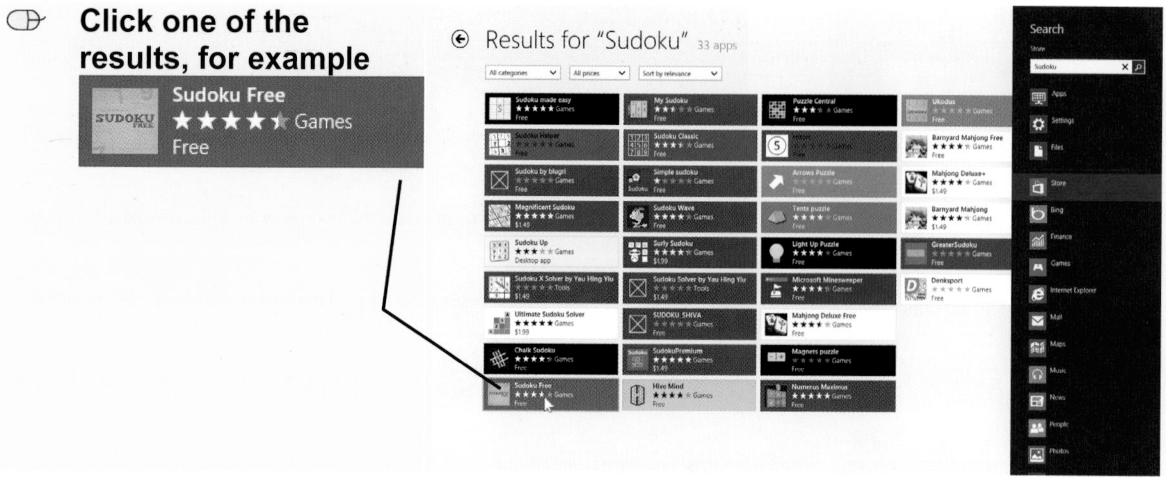


On the right side of the screen you see more information on the app:

This is how you download this app:

- **Click**

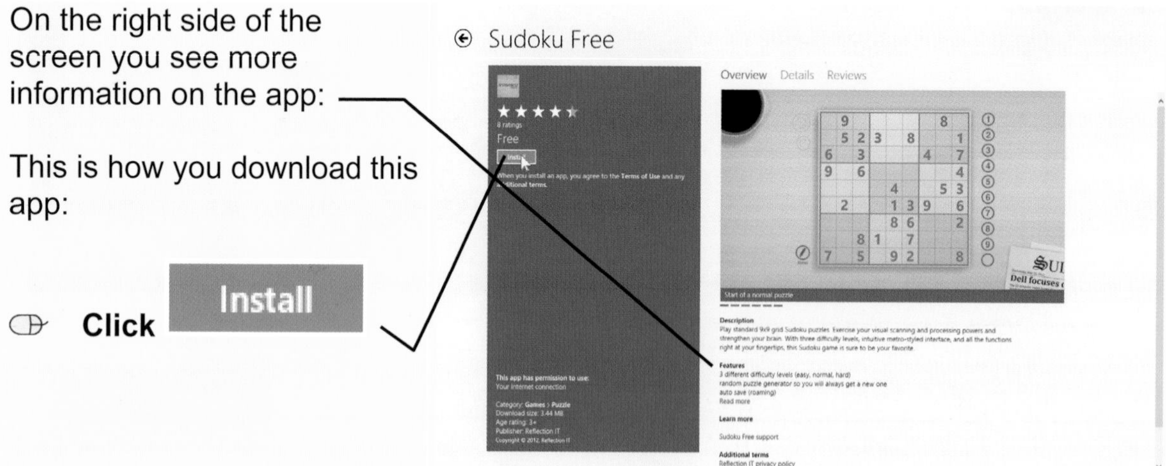


Before the app can be installed you need to sign in with your *Microsoft* account. You have created this account in the previous chapter.

- **Type your e-mail address**
- **Type your password**
- **Click**

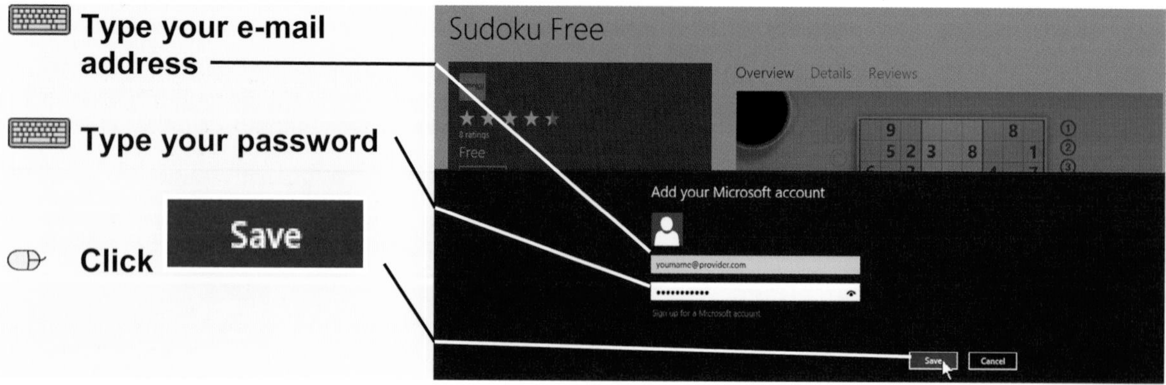

## HELP! I do not have a Microsoft account.

If you do not (yet) have a *Microsoft* account, you can read how to create a *Microsoft* account in *section 5.1 Opening and Setting Up the Mail app*.

You have signed in with the *Store*. The *Sudoku* app is downloaded:

After a while you can see that the app has been installed, by the message in the screen in the upper right-hand corner:

**Close the *Store*** 5

The app has been added to the Start screen:

To open the app:

**Click**

You can select a difficulty level:

After that, you can start the game.

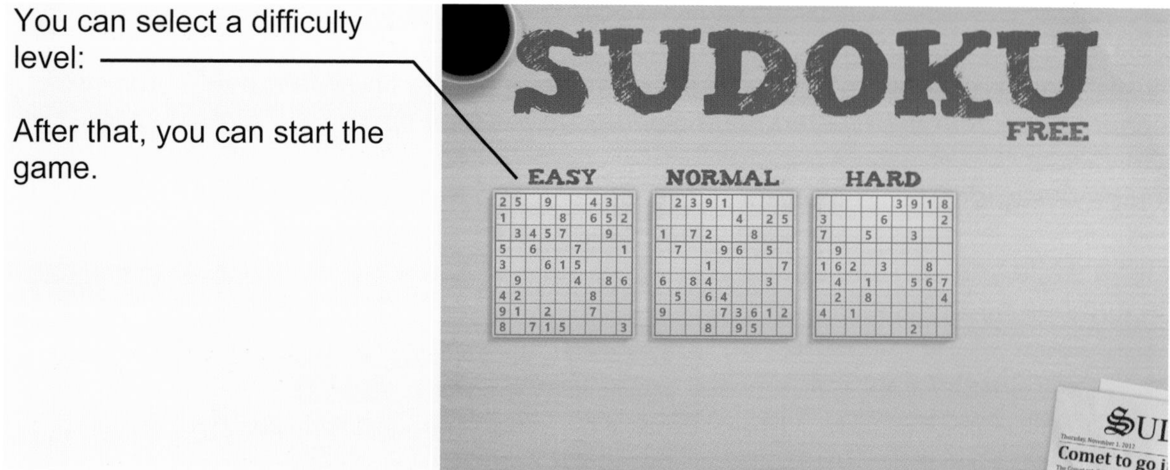


For now, you close the app:

☞ **Close the *Sudoku Free* app** [5]

In this way you can download lots of apps from the *Store*. For some apps you need to pay a fee. In such a case you will see a price somewhere near the app. You can find more information about purchasing apps in *Bonus Chapter Downloading Apps* on the website accompanying this book: **www.visualsteps.com/internet8.** You can read how to open this bonus chapter in *Appendix B Opening the Bonus Online Chapters* at the back of this book.

In the *Tips* at the back of this chapter you can read how to delete an app from the computer.

## 6.5 Save an Internet Image on the Computer

You can directly save an image from a web page on your computer. Later on, you can open the image you saved in you favorite program. This is how you directly store an image:

☞ **Open *Internet Explorer* on the desktop** [9]

☞ **Open the web page www.visualsteps.com/internet8/practice** [1]

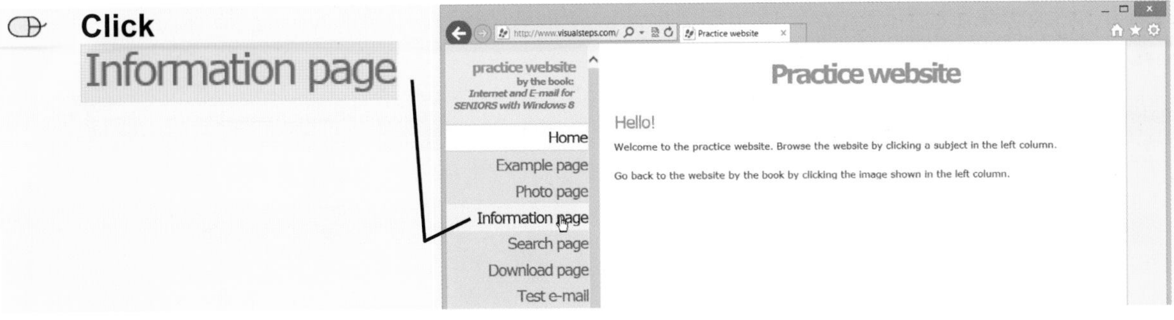


**Click** Information page

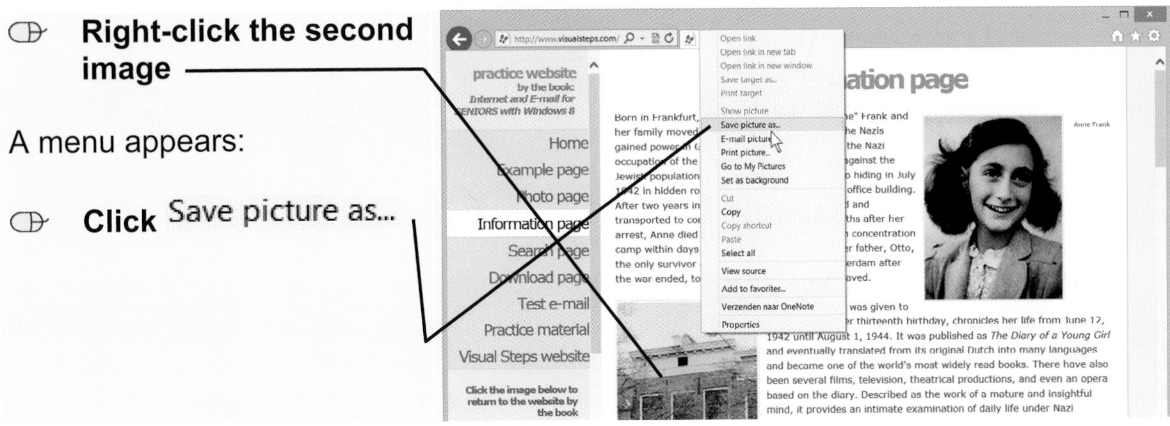


**Right-click the second image**

A menu appears:

**Click** Save picture as...

If you want to be able to quickly retrieve stored photos, it is a good idea to save image in the same folder every time. By default the images that are saved in *Windows 8* are stored in the *Pictures* folder.

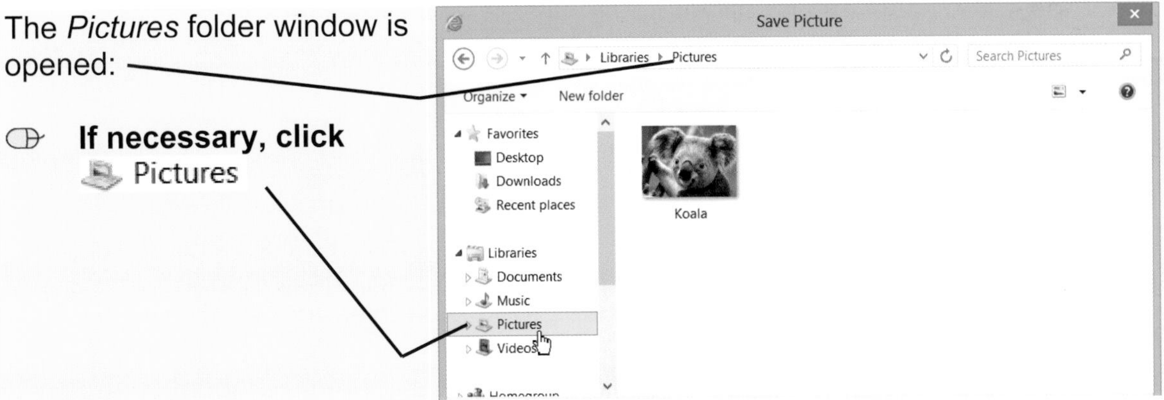


The *Pictures* folder window is opened:

**If necessary, click** Pictures

## HELP! My window looks different.

If you do not see the folders in the navigation pane on the left-hand side:

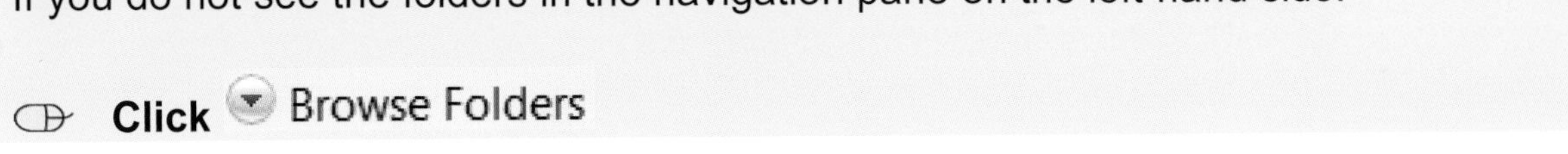

**Click** Browse Folders

The image already has a name *AnneFrankHouseAmsterdam*. You can also name this image yourself.

**By** File name:**, type:**
`Photo House of Anne Frank`

**Click** Save

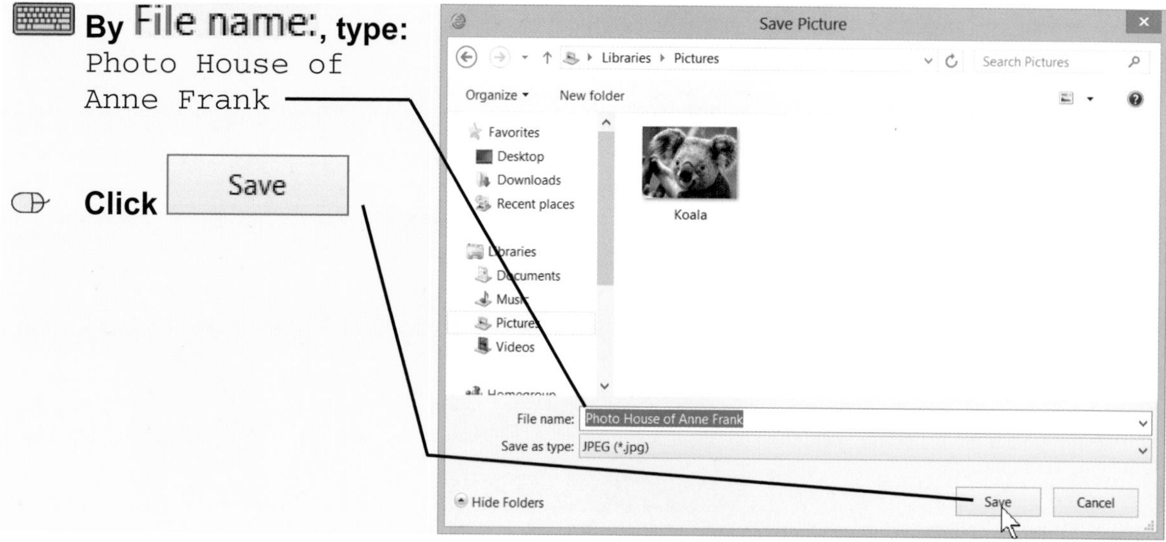


Now the photo has been stored on your hard disk. You can open it later on and use it in a different program, or send it as an attachment to an e-mail message.

# 6.6 Opening a PDF File

The *Reader* is a useful app for viewing PDF files. PDF is short for *Portable Document File*. This file format is often used for information you can download from companies and organizations or institutions.

 **Please note:**

You may have used the *Adobe Reader* program, if you have previously worked on a computer with *Windows 7*, *Vista* or *XP*. You no longer need this program on a *Windows 8* computer. By default, the *Reader* app has been installed to the computer, and can perform the same tasks as the *Adobe Reader* program.

On the website accompanying this book you will find a computer tip about changing the desktop background, displayed as a PDF file.

You are going to view this file with the *Reader* app:

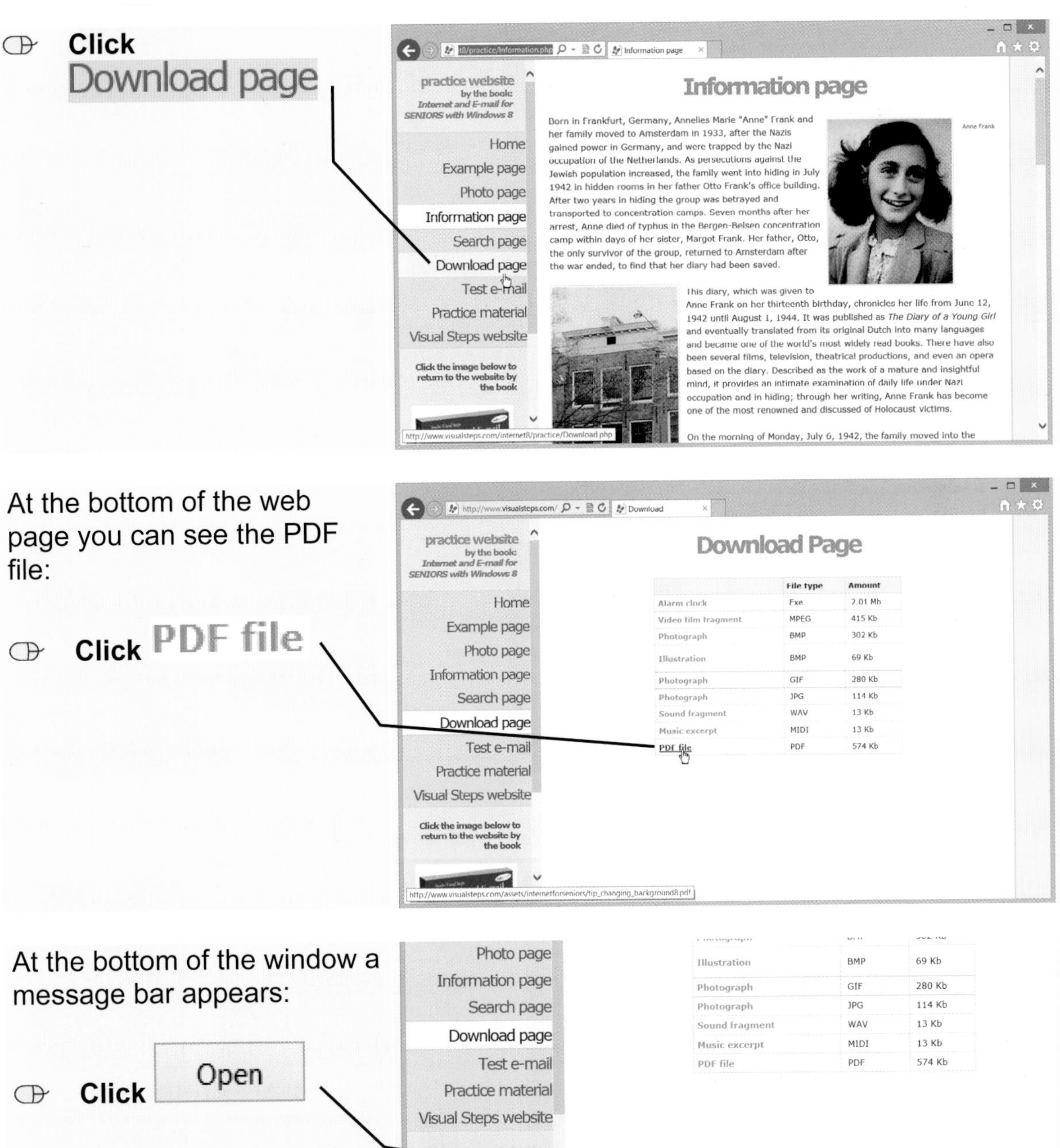

Click
Download page
At the bottom of the web page you can see the PDF file:
Click PDF file
At the bottom of the window a message bar appears:
Click Open

The *Reader* app is opened:

The document is displayed in the screen:

You can leaf through the document by dragging the scroll bar:

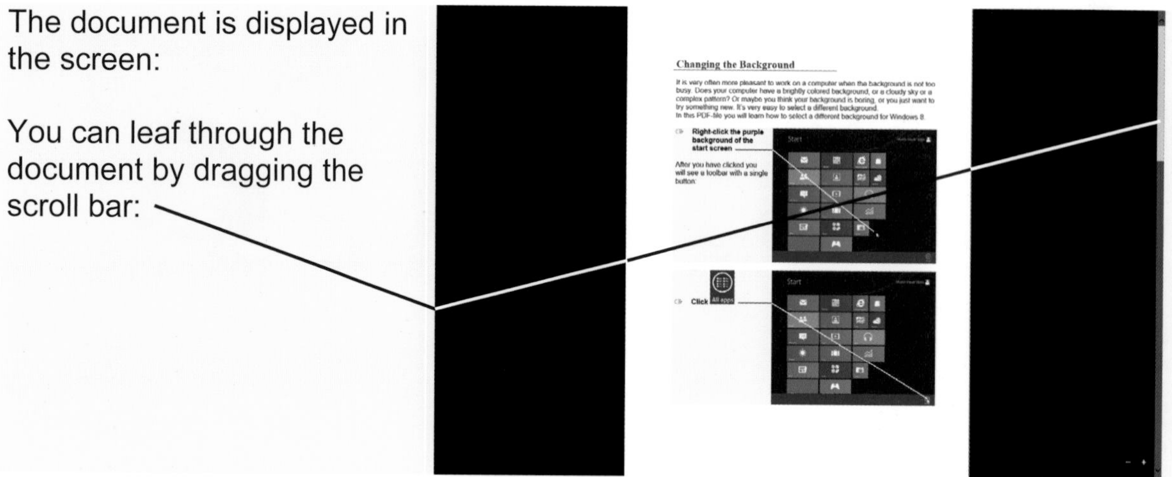


In the *Reader* app you can easily zoom in and out:

At the bottom right of the screen:

Click ➕

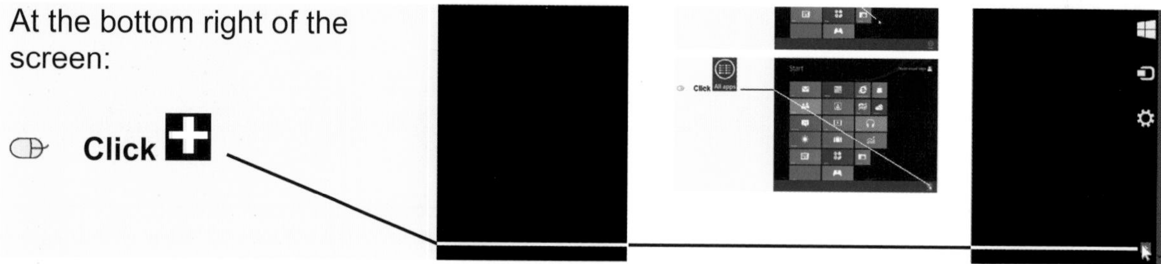

The text is displayed larger. Now you zoom out again:

At the bottom right of the screen:

Click ➖

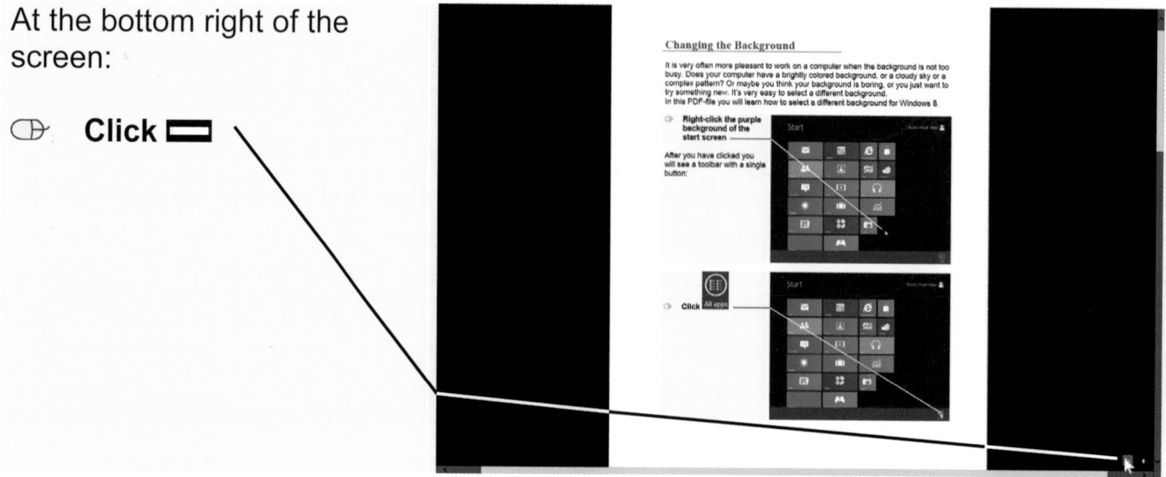

You can display a PDF file in several ways. For example, you can display two pages at once. This is how you do it:

- **Right-click an empty area on the screen**

The app commands appear on the screen:

- **Click** Two pages

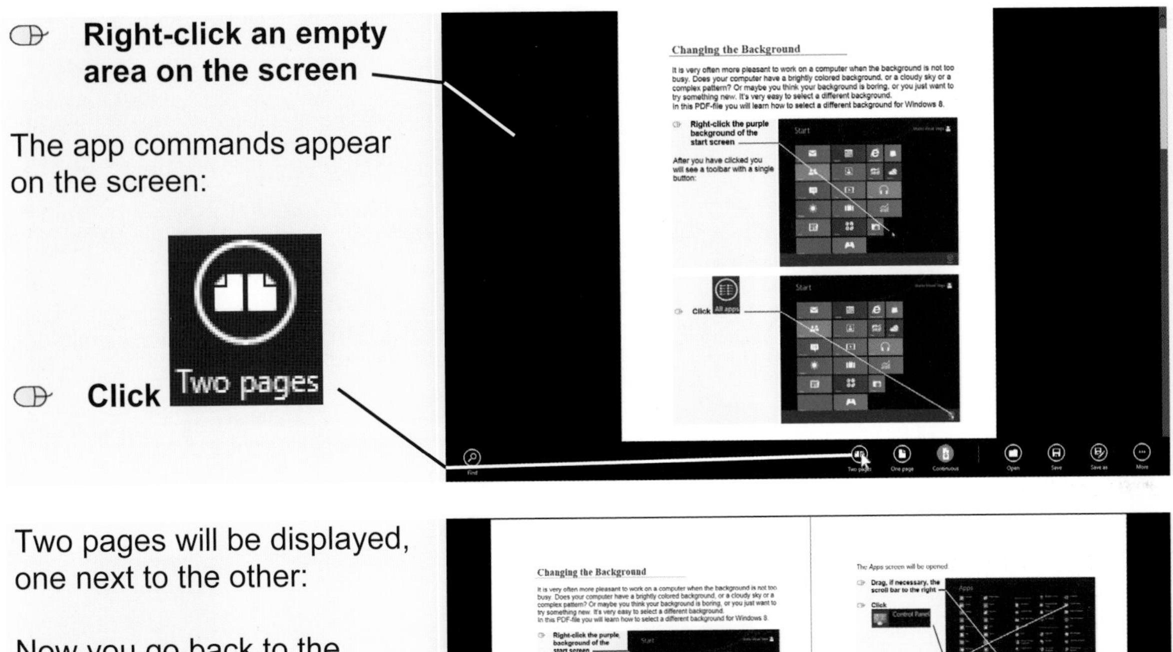

Two pages will be displayed, one next to the other:

Now you go back to the previous view:

- **Click** Continuous

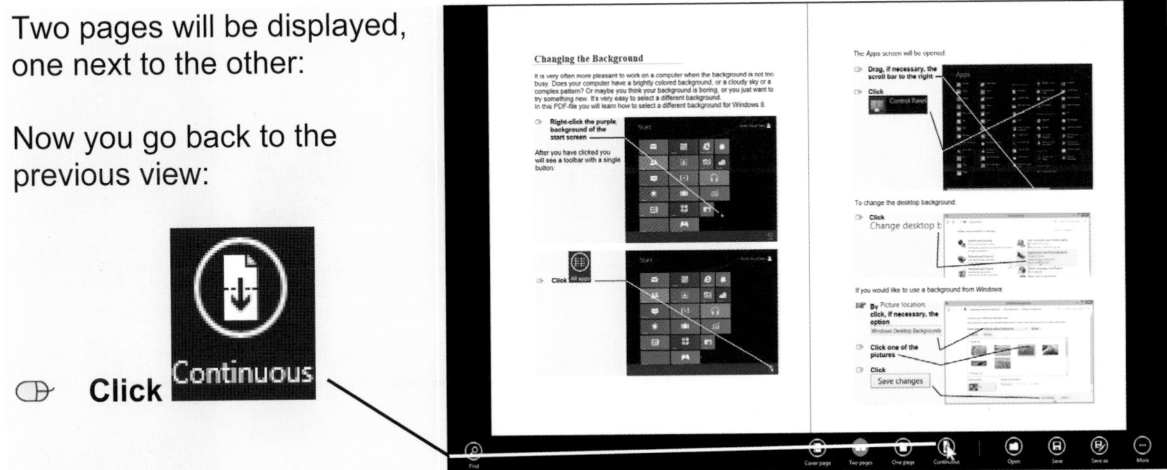

You will see the file in the previous view again. If you wish, you can save a PDF file on your computer's hard disk. This is how you do it:

- **Click** Save as

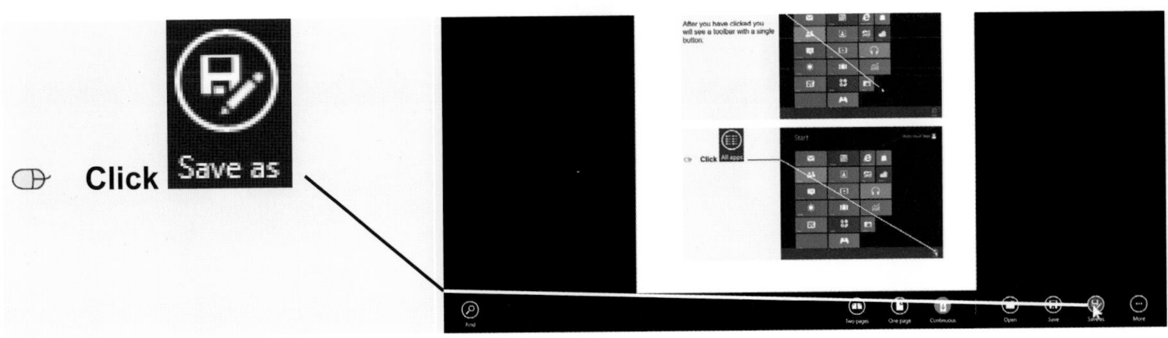

You will see the following screen:

If you want, you can select a different location for storing the PDF file and give the file a different name. In this example you are not going to save the file:

Click **Cancel**

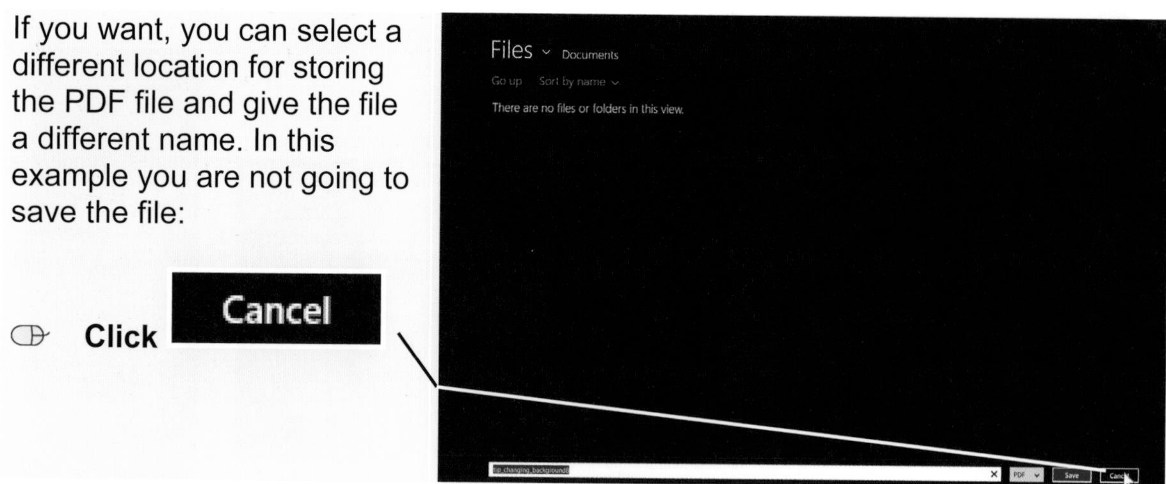


You can print the PDF file. This is how you do it:

**Display the charms bar** 8

**Click** Devices

**Click your printer, for example** Dell 1130n Laser Pri

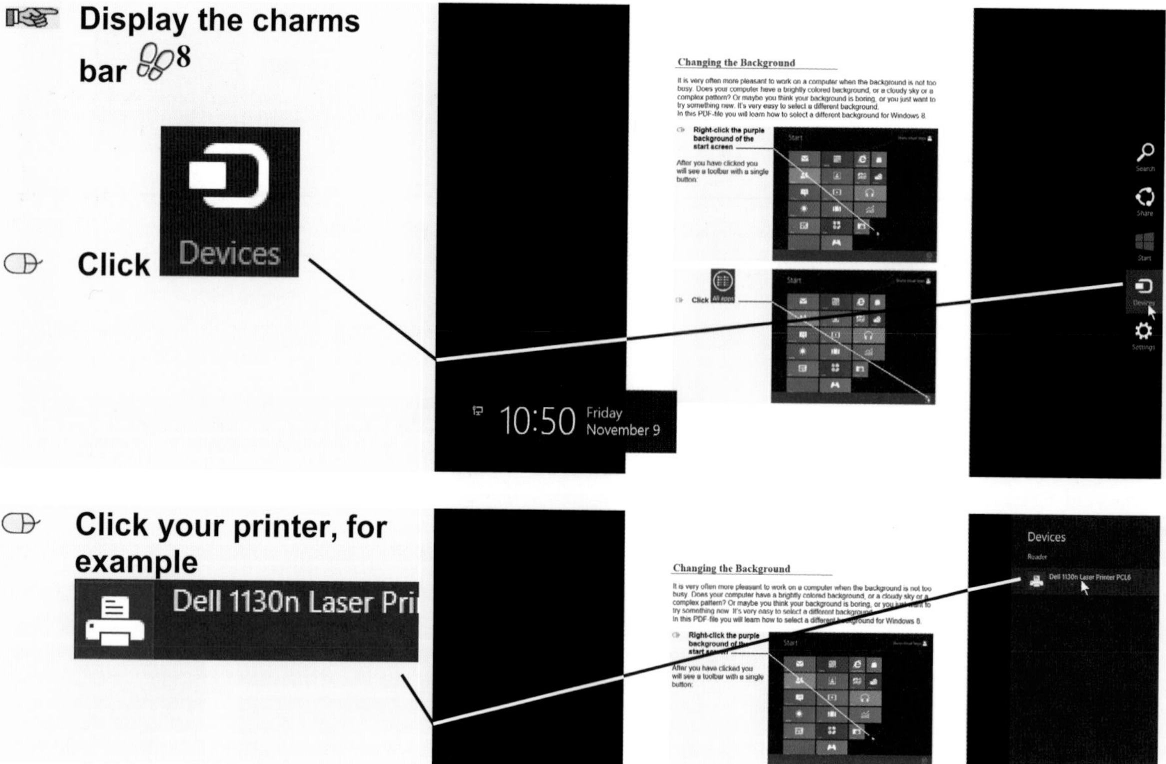

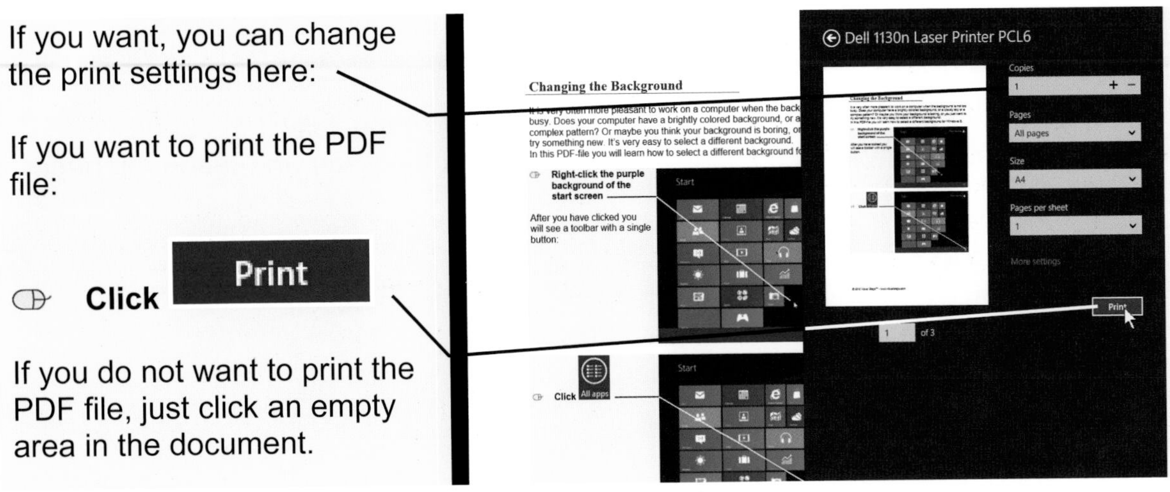

If you want, you can change the print settings here:

If you want to print the PDF file:

Click **Print**

If you do not want to print the PDF file, just click an empty area in the document.

You are going to close the PDF file:

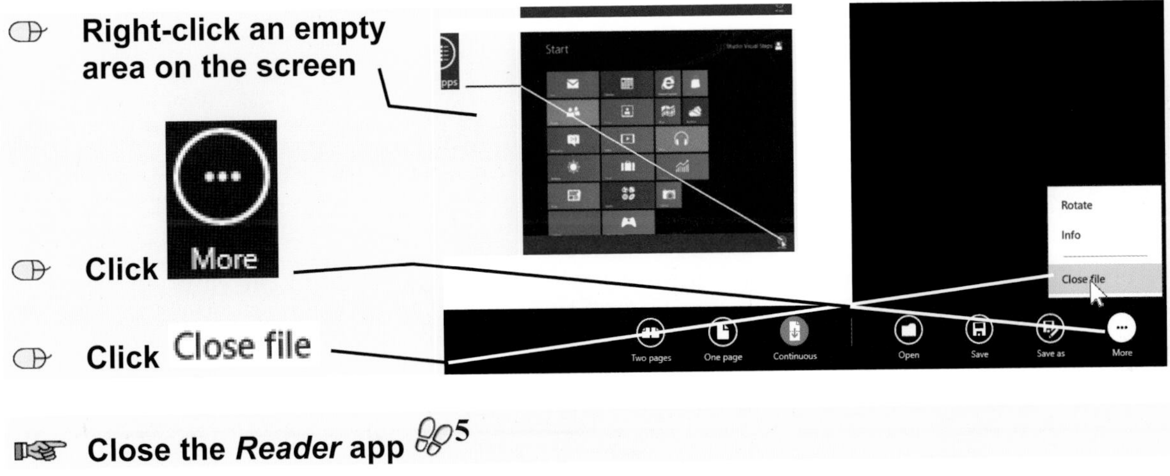

**Right-click an empty area on the screen**

**Click** More

**Click** Close file

**Close the *Reader* app** 5

**Open *Internet Explorer* on the desktop with the switch list** 55

In the next section you are going to print a web page.

## 6.7 Printing a Web Page

It is not always easy to read a web page on the screen, especially if the page contains a lot of text. In such a case you can also print the page and read it on paper.

**HELP! I do not have a printer.**

If you do not have a printer, you can just read through this section.

**First, check if the printer is turned on**

Go back to the Information page:

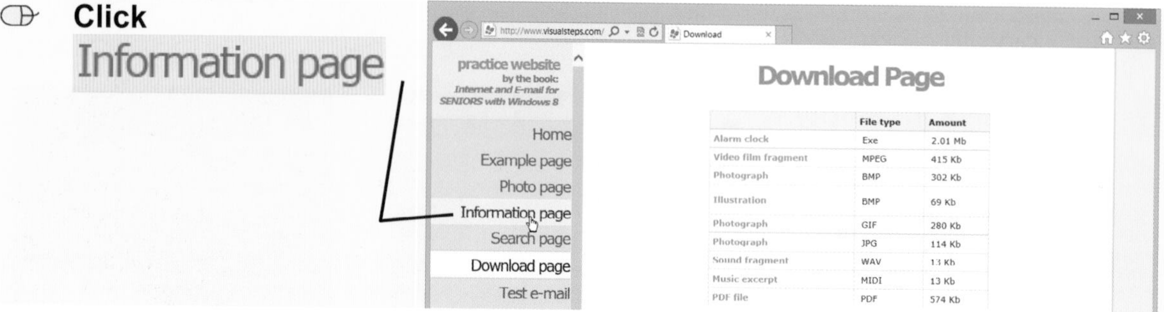


Before you print this page you are going to take a look at the print preview, in order to see what the print will look like on an A4 size paper:

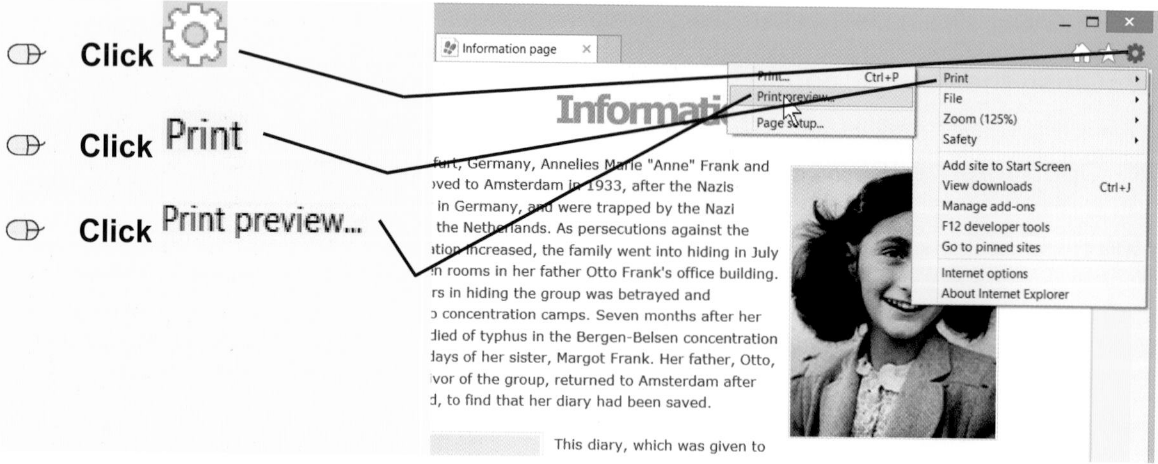

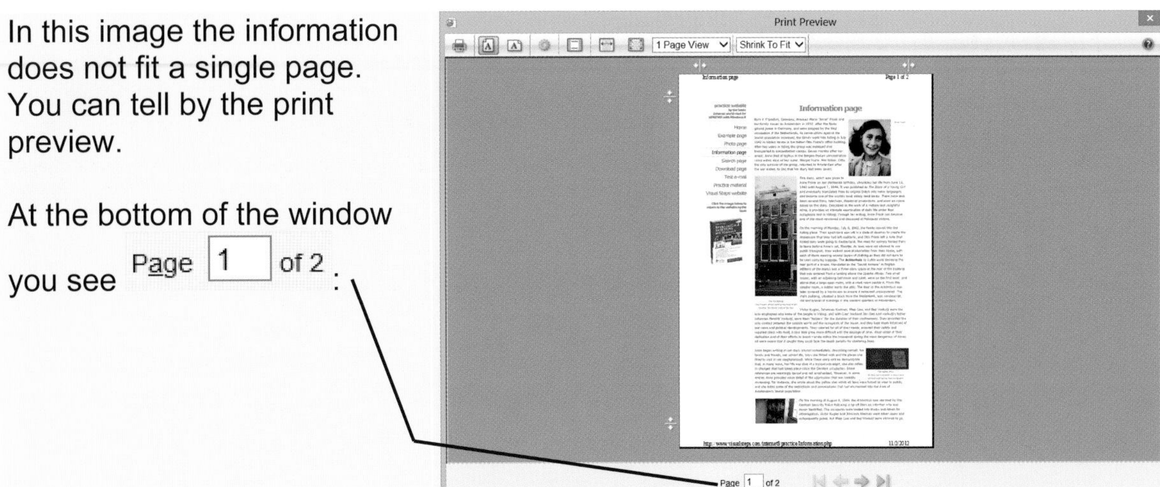


In this image the information does not fit a single page. You can tell by the print preview.

At the bottom of the window you see Page 1 of 2 :

The page contains a header and a footer. It would be a pity to print these texts, so you decide to remove this text:

Click

The headers and footer have disappeared.

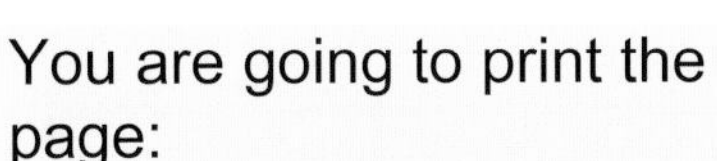

You are going to print the page:

Click

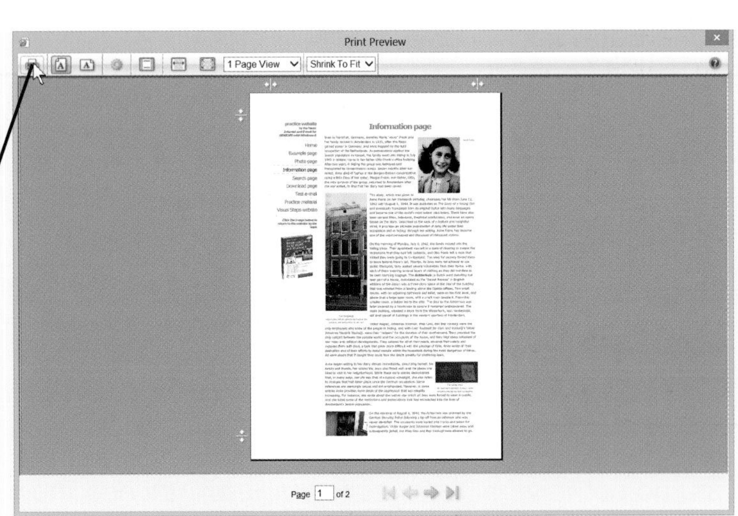

If you want, you can change some settings:

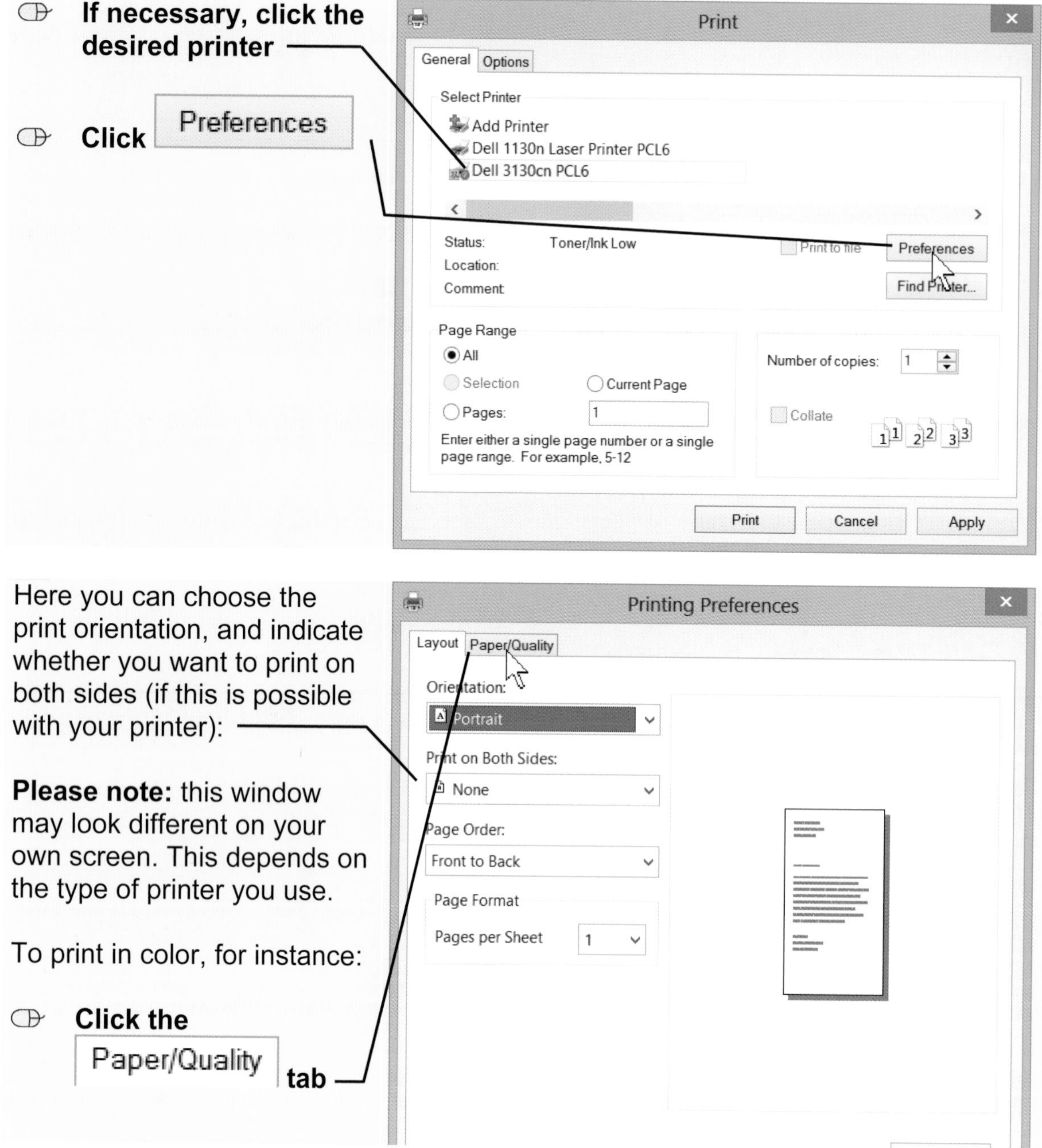


**If necessary, click the desired printer**

**Click** Preferences

Here you can choose the print orientation, and indicate whether you want to print on both sides (if this is possible with your printer):

**Please note:** this window may look different on your own screen. This depends on the type of printer you use.

To print in color, for instance:

**Click the** Paper/Quality **tab**

If you do not have a color printer, you will not see the following option.

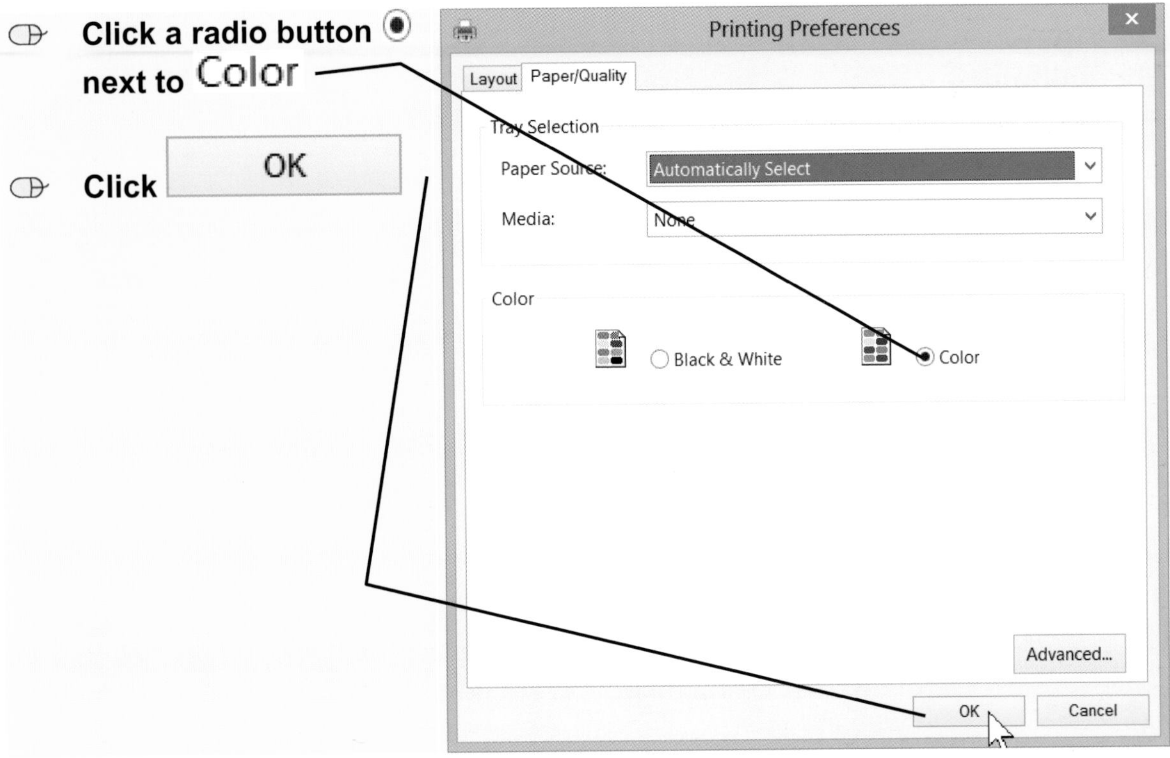


You will see the *Print* window again:

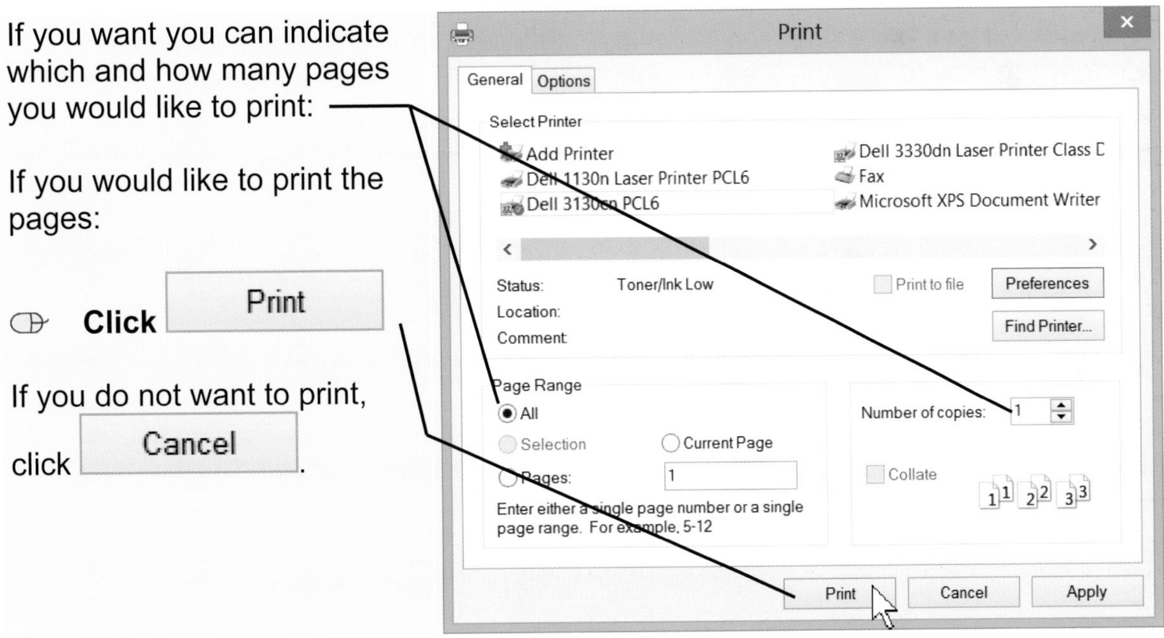


Now your printer prints the page. The print preview is automatically closed.

## Tip

**Other buttons**

The other buttons in the *Print preview* window have the following functions:

  Print the page in landscape/portrait orientation.

 Open the *page settings* window.

 Turn headers or footers on or off.

  Display full width/Display full page.

 Adjust margins.

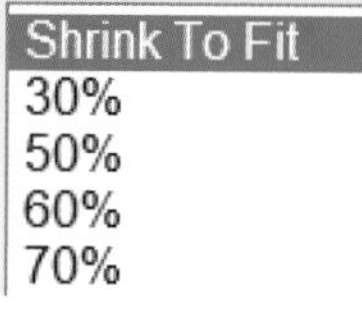


Enlarge/diminish the content of the page by a certain percentage. For example, select 150% if you want to print text and images in a larger format. Remember you will need to use more pages to print the website.

☞ **Close *Internet Explorer*** [12]

In this chapter you have downloaded and installed programs and apps. Also, you have learned how to use the *Reader* app to open PDF files, and you have printed a web page.

## 6.8 Exercises

Have you forgotten how to do something? Use the number beside the footsteps to look it up in the appendix *How Do I Do That Again?*

## Exercise 1: Downloading

In this exercise you are going to download different types of files.

☞ Open *Internet Explorer* on the desktop. 9

☞ Open the web page www.visualsteps.com/internet8 1

☞ Click **Practice website** .

☞ Click Download page.

☞ Open the video file fragment (MPEG). 38

*Windows Media Player* will be opened:

☞ Close the program. 12

☞ Open the photograph file (JPG). 38

You will see the file in *Internet Explorer*:

☞ Go back to the previously visited web page. 6

☞ Open the photograph file (GIF). 38

You will see the file in *Internet Explorer*:

☞ Go back to the previously visited web page. 6

☞ Open the music file (MIDI). 38

*Windows Media Player* will be opened:

☞ Close the program. 12

☞ Close *Internet Explorer*. 12

☞ Go back to the Start screen. 3

## Exercise 2: Downloading an App

In this exercise you are going to download the *ABC Player* app. If you want, you can use this app to watch TV programs broadcasted by the television network.

☞ Open the *Store*. 4

☞ If necessary, click ←.

☞ Search for the *ABC Player* app. 39

☞ Install the app. 54

☞ Close the *Store*. 5

☞ Open the *ABC Player* app. 4

☞ Click a program.

☞ Click ▶ to play the program.

☞ Close the *ABC Player* app. 5

# 6.9 Background Information

**Dictionary**

| | |
|---|---|
| **BMP** | *BMP* was developed by *Microsoft* and is the native graphics format for *Windows* users. The files are usually not compressed and can be quite large. Also known as *bitmap*. |
| **CDA** | Filename extension for a small (44 bytes) file generated by *Microsoft Windows* for each track on an audio CD. Tells where on the disc the track starts and stops. The music files purchased in a store (on CD) have the CDA file type. |
| **Download** | Copying a file from the Internet. A movie or music file, for example. |
| **EXE** | An extension for a filename of an executable program. This is a program that can be installed or executed on your computer. |
| **Footer** | Text that is printed at the bottom of a web page. |
| **Header** | The text that is printed at the top of a web page. |
| **Installation** | In order for a program to work properly, all parts have to be correctly installed on your computer. This means that the different parts are copied to the right place on your hard drive and the program name is added to the *Apps* screen in *Windows*. All this work is done by the installation program. How you add a program depends on where the installation files for the program are located. Typically, programs are installed from a CD or DVD, from the Internet, or from a network. |
| **Installation program** | Also called *setup program*. An auxiliary program that takes care of installing a program in the correct way. |
| **JPG, JPEG** | Filename extension for compressed image files such as photographs, in the format developed by the *Joint Photographers Experts Group*. |
| **MPG, MPEG** | Filename extension for compressed video files, in the format developed by the *Moving Pictures Experts Group*. |

*- Continue on the next page -*

| | |
|---|---|
| **MP3** | Filename extension for compressed audio files, in the *MPEG Audio Layer 3* format. MP3 is the most popular way for compressing audio files and exchanging them on the Internet. |
| **PDF file** | PDF stands for *Portable Document File*. This file format is often used for information booklets you can download from company and organization websites. |
| **Print preview** | The print preview shows a picture of what the (web) page will look like when printed on paper. |
| **Printer** | A device that prints text and images on paper. |
| **Reader** | An app that is used to view PDF files. |
| **Setup** | Installation. |
| **Setup program** | Also called *installation program*. An auxiliary program that takes care of installing a program in the correct way. |
| **WordPad** | *WordPad* is a simple text editor that is supplied as a standard program with the *Windows* software. A text editor is a computer program with which you can create, edit, and print text documents. |

*Source: Windows Help and Support, Wikipedia*

**Types of software**

Various types of software are available on the Internet:

- Freeware: This software may be freely used and copied. It is sometimes also called *Public Domain* software.
- Shareware: The program may be used free of charge for a period of time so you can try it out. If you would like to keep using it after the trial period, you must pay.
- Cardware: Similar to shareware, but the maker wants you to recognize that this is his or her intellectual property. The user is expected to send a postcard indicating that he or she is using the program. Also called postcardware.
- Demos: Demos are free software in which some functions have been disabled. The functions that still work give a good idea of the software's capabilities. Sometimes the demo works fully, but only for a limited time.
- Updates: These are additions, patches or improvements to existing software. They are often provided free of charge to people who have a license for the original program.

**Saving photos on the computer**
You may wonder how it is possible to store a photo on the computer's hard disk. There are several methods for this. Of course, you can copy photos from the Internet and save them on your hard disk, as you have practiced in this chapter. But you need to keep in mind that the quality of the images displayed in web pages is often not high enough to guarantee a good quality print on paper. The requirements of a printer for printing a clear image on paper are much higher than the requirements for displaying a nice picture on the screen.
Nowadays, lots of people use digital cameras. These photos have a much better quality. The image is digitally stored, right away. The photos are stored in the camera, on a small memory card. You can connect the camera to the computer, by cable, and transfer the photos to the computer. Some computers are equipped with a built-in cardreader, in which you can insert the camera's memory card.
A photo that has already been printed can be copied with a *scanner* and then save it on the hard disk. The photo is placed on the glass plate of the scanner, the cover is closed and then the photo is copied by the scan program. This is also called *digitizing*. You can store this digital file on your computer's hard disk. Some types of scanners can also scan dispositive and other transparent materials (negatives).
If you still have any photos left on your old film roll, you can let the film developing company transfer these photos directly to CD. Most companies offer such as service nowadays. You can view the CD with the photos on your computer. The photo files on the CD are digitized. Afterwards, you can edit them on your computer.

**Pixels**
Computer images (drawings or photos) consist of thousands of dots. These dots are called *pixels*. When you enlarge such a photo you will see the grid with all the colored dots:

A professional term for such a grid is a *bitmap,* a map full of dots. You may encounter this term in *Windows* once in a while. The quality of the photo depends on the number of dots used. If a lot of pixels are used for a photo, this photo will be very clear and sharp. If fewer pixels are used, the photo will become less well-defined and more blurry.

*- Continue on the next page -*

Digital photo cameras indicate the quality of their photos by stating their resolution. This resolution is often expressed in megapixels. This indicates the resolution (or the number of pixels) that the optical sensor of the camera can handle.

Apart from that, the quality is also defined by the number of colors used. The more colors, the more realistic the photo will come across. Currently, 16 million colors is a common number used on a regular computer. But professional pictures use many more colors.

| Color depth | Number of possible colors | File size of BMP |
|---|---|---|
| 1-bit | 2 colors | 59 kB |
| 4-bit | 16 colors | 235 kB |
| 8-bit | 256 colors | 470 kB |
| 24-bit | millions of colors | 1407 kB |

For use on the Internet, BMP images are impracticable, because of the enormous file sizes. It would take far too much time to send these images over the Internet.
That is why two other file formats have been developed. Both show fine results but still use acceptable file sizes. The first file type, *GIF*, is often used for colorful images such as drawings. GIF files use .gif as a file extension. The other file type, *JPEG*, is used for photos and can be recognized by the .JPG extension.

**Copyright and images on the Internet**
By copyright, we usually mean the rights of the creator of an original piece of work. This work can be a photo, a book, an article, composition, painting, or a CD recording. Someone who has produced such a work can call it his or her 'intellectual property'. Obviously, such a person is entitled to an appropriate reward. That is why it is forbidden by law to copy another person's 'intellectual property'. You will often see the © sign to indicate that the work is copyrighted. But even if the © sign is absent, you are still not allowed to copy the work without permission.
Clearly, this restriction is valid on the Internet too. A good rule of thumb is to assume that nothing may be copied, unless it is clear that copying is permitted, and the conditions are stated.
Internet has numerous websites where all kinds of materials are offered, for free or at a price: images, photos, texts, computer programs, sounds, MP3 files (music), or even entire music CDs.
These websites often allow or even encourage copying, sometimes on condition that you mention the source if you want to use these materials yourself. For example, if you want to publish a photo on your own website.
Sometimes, people offer materials on websites to which they are not entitled, since they do not own the copyright. In such a case, both offering and copying are illegal activities, against which the rightful claimants actively fight.

## 6.10 Tips

### Tip

**Selecting, copying, and pasting texts from the Internet into documents**

You can save the text that appears on your screen when you open a web page on your own computer. Handy, for instance, if you want to get some information off the Internet and use it in a club magazine. You can do this by copying the text and pasting it in another (text editing) program.
But keep in mind that you are not allowed to copy and paste all possible items from the Internet. The information published on the Internet may be subject to copyrights.

If you want to copy an item, you need to *select* it first. You do this by *dragging* the mouse.

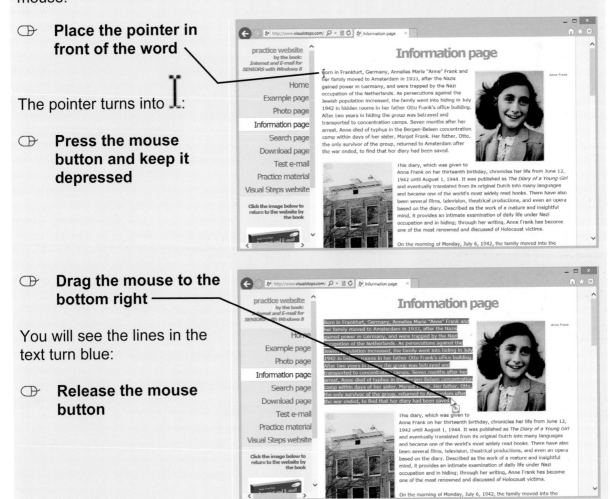

**Place the pointer in front of the word**

The pointer turns into I:

**Press the mouse button and keep it depressed**

**Drag the mouse to the bottom right**

You will see the lines in the text turn blue:

**Release the mouse button**

- Continue on the next page -

The text has been selected. Now you can copy it:

**If necessary, press** Alt

**Click** Edit

**Click** Copy

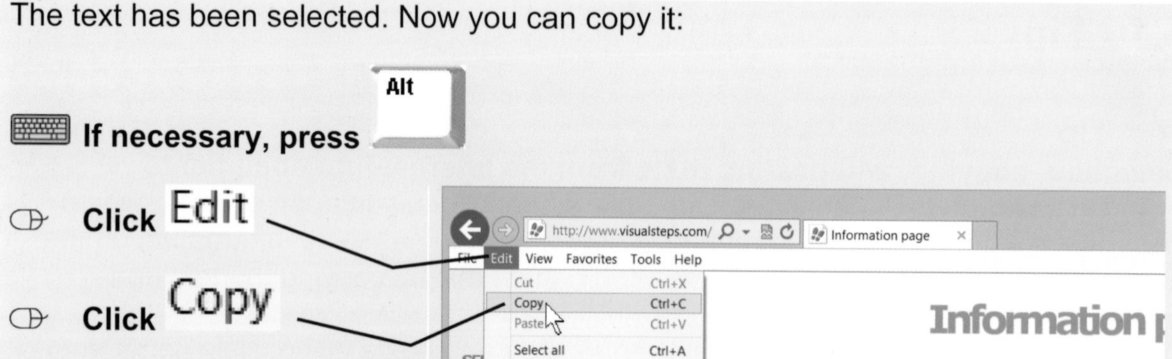


You may not see anything happen, but the text has been copied to the *Windows Clipboard*. Now you can paste the text in another program. For example, in *WordPad*:

**Go back to the Start screen** 3

**Right-click an empty area on the screen**

**Click**

**Click** WordPad

Now the *WordPad* is opened. This is a program you can use for editing texts.

The copied text is still stored on the *Windows Clipboard* (not visible to you). Now you can execute the paste command, to paste the text in the document:

**Click**

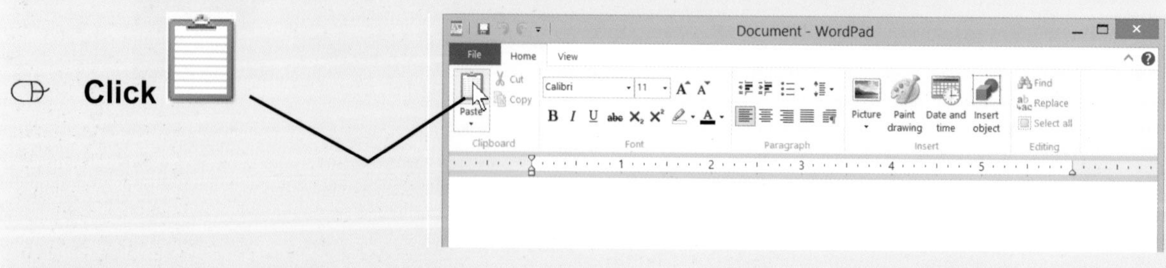


- Continue on the next page -

The copied text has been pasted in the document:

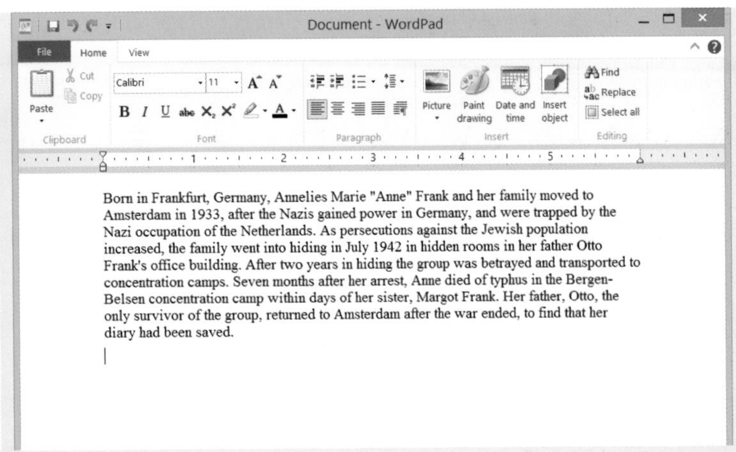


In this way you can copy any text from the Internet and use it in a different program. Just like any other text, you can edit and store such a text on your computer.

If you want to select the entire web page, then you click Edit and Select all on the menu bar.

## Tip

**Printing from the Internet Explorer app**

You can easily print a web page after you have opened it in *Internet Explorer*:

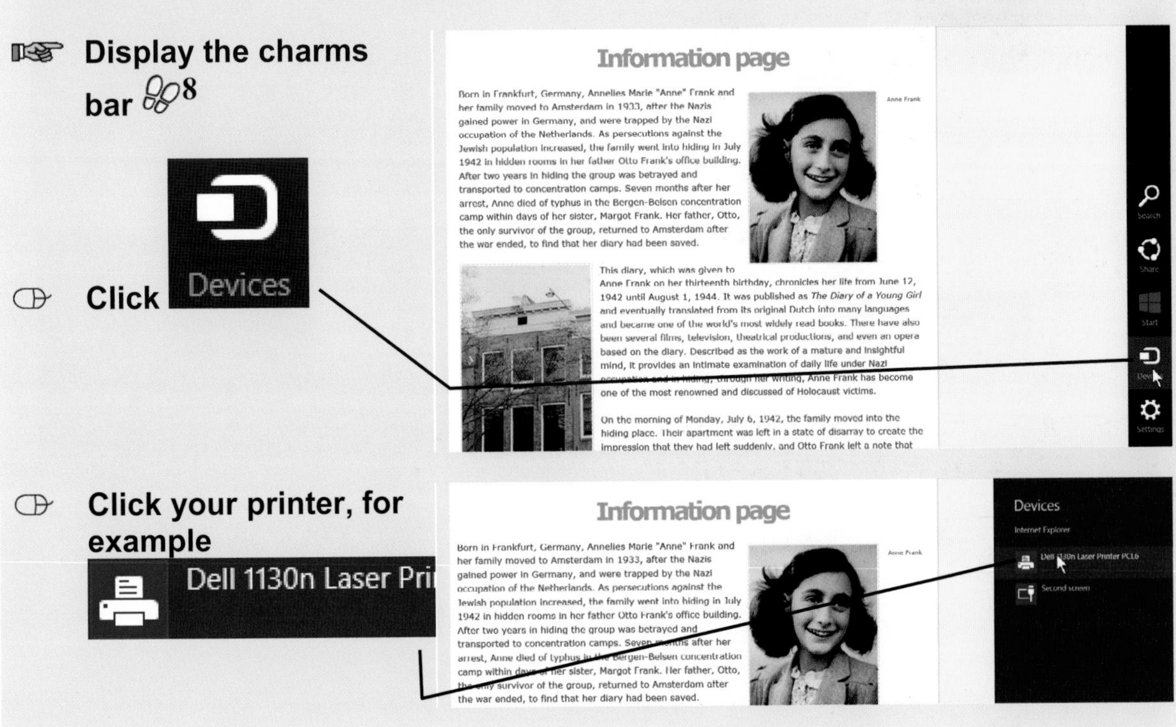


**Display the charms bar** 8

**Click** Devices

**Click your printer, for example** Dell 1130n Laser Pri

*- Continue on the next page -*

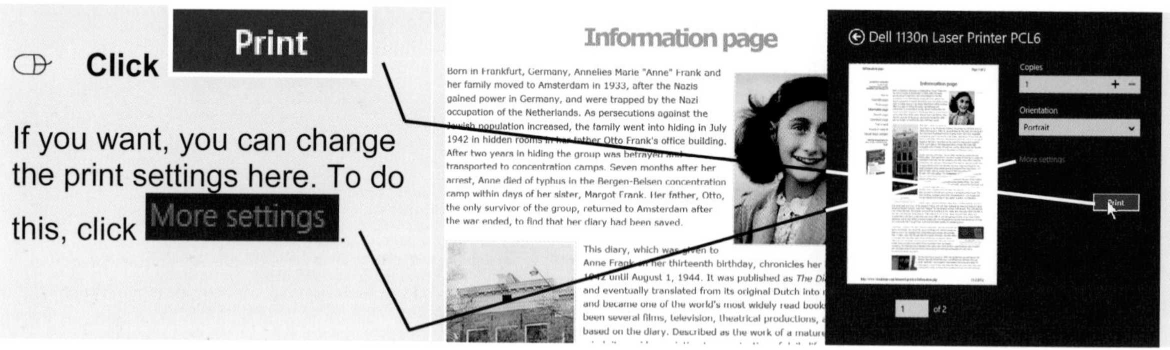


Click **Print**

If you want, you can change the print settings here. To do this, click **More settings**.

## Tip

**Delete an app**

You can remove an app from your computer if you no longer use it. This is how you delete an app on the Start screen:

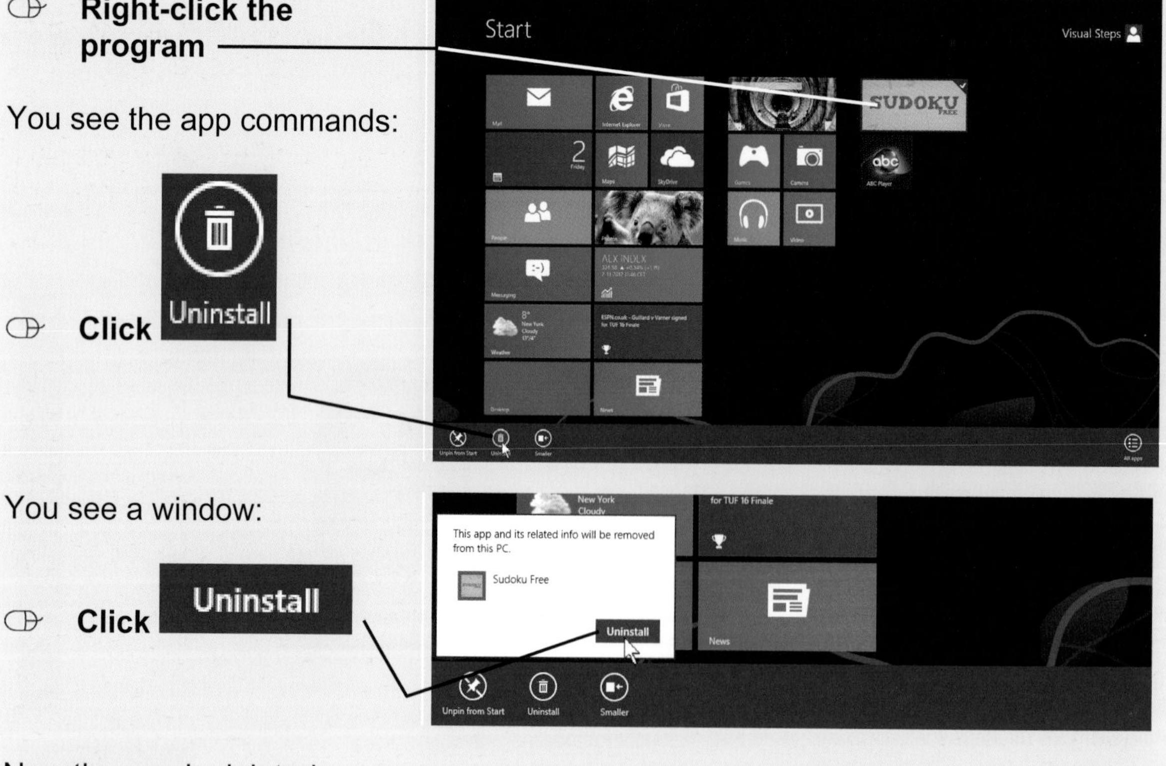


**Right-click the program**

You see the app commands:

Click **Uninstall**

You see a window:

Click **Uninstall**

Now the app is deleted.

# 7. Security and Privacy

In this book you have gained a lot of experience with using the Internet. Security is essential for computers that are regularly connected to the Internet. A good security system reduces the risk of viruses or other harmful software on your computer.

An infected computer can be very frustrating: not only for you, but also for others. If your computer is infected with harmful software, it could in turn infect other computers. This could happen when you send an e-mail, but also when sharing a file on a CD, DVD or USB stick. As a computer owner you are therefore responsible for making sure your computer is protected. *Windows 8* can help you with this, with *Windows Defender*. This is a program that offers complete protection against computer viruses and other unwanted software. In this chapter you can read how the real-time-security features of *Windows Defender* protect your computer, and how it scans your computer for viruses or other harmful software.

Another security tool in *Windows 8* is the *Action Center.* In the *Action Center* you can check the security settings for *Windows 8* on your computer and adjust them, if necessary.

In this chapter you will learn how to:

- adjust the security and privacy settings in *Internet Explorer*;
- recognize phishing and phishing e-mails;
- use the *SmartScreen filter* in *Internet Explorer*;
- check and report a suspicious website;
- manage pop-ups and add-ons in *Internet Explorer*;
- restore an e-mail message that has unjustly been marked as junk;
- use the *Action Center*;
- keep *Windows 8* up-to-date with *Windows Update*;
- update apps;
- use *Windows Firewall*;
- use *Windows Defender*.

**Please note:**

In order to be able to execute all the operations in this chapter, you will need to use an administrator's account. If you do not have such an account, you will not be able to change certain settings. In such a case, *Windows* will display a message. If this happens, you can just read through the relevant section, or you ask the computer administrator to grant you access.

# 7.1 Security Settings in Internet Explorer

In *Internet Explorer* you can select a security level for Internet access. This way you can determine how *Internet Explorer* interacts with various types of websites.

**Open *Internet Explorer* on the desktop** 9

You are going to take a look at the security settings:

**Click**

**Click** Internet options

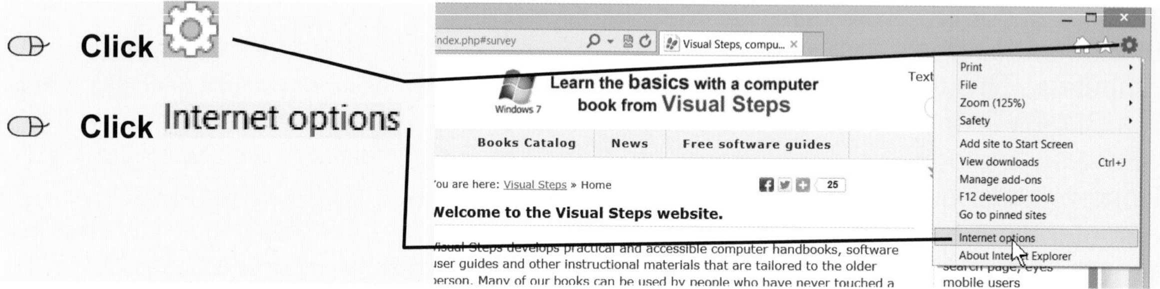


You see the *Internet Options* window:

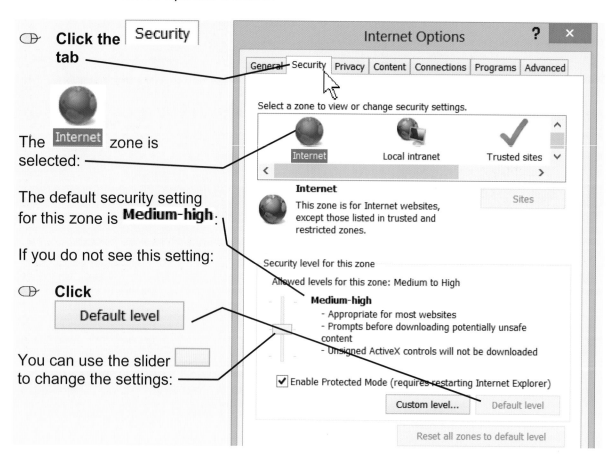

**Click the** Security **tab**

The Internet zone is selected:

The default security setting for this zone is **Medium-high**:

If you do not see this setting:

**Click** Default level

You can use the slider to change the settings:

You can choose between three levels: *High*, *Medium-high* and *Medium*. You can read the description for each level next to the slider.

If necessary, you can choose a different security setting for specific websites you trust and do not trust. Take a look at the *Trusted sites* zone:

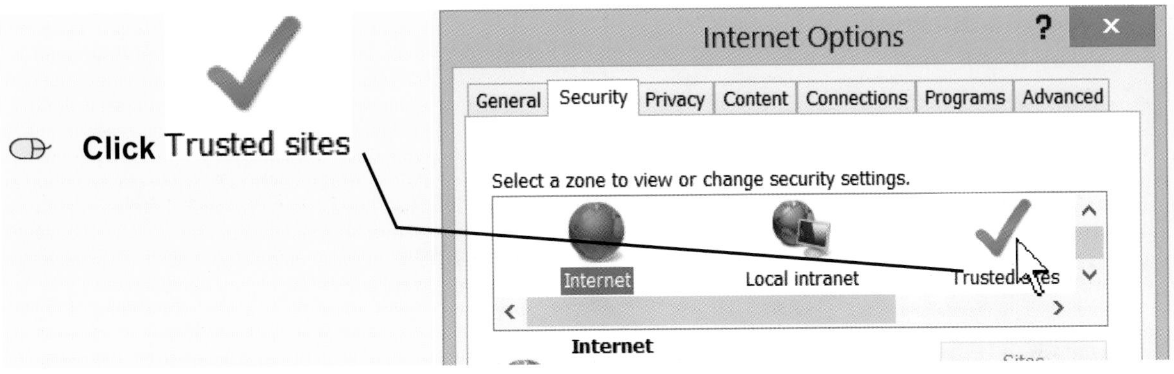


Click Trusted sites

You will see that the default security level for this zone is **Medium**:

Again, you can use the slider to change the settings. You can choose between five levels: *High*, *Medium-high*, *Medium*, *Medium-low* and *Low*.

The *Low* setting is exclusively intended for websites you fully trust.

To add a website to the *Trusted sites* zone:

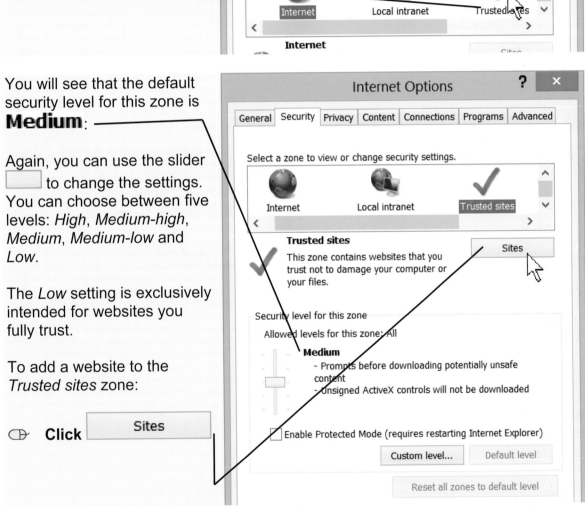

Click Sites

*Internet Explorer* assumes that you want to add the website that is currently displayed to the *Trusted sites*, and has inserted it in the *Add* box. However, you are going to add a different website, for example, the website of your online bank:

**By** Add this website to the z **type the address of your bank, for example** `https://www.bankofamerica.com`

**Click** Add

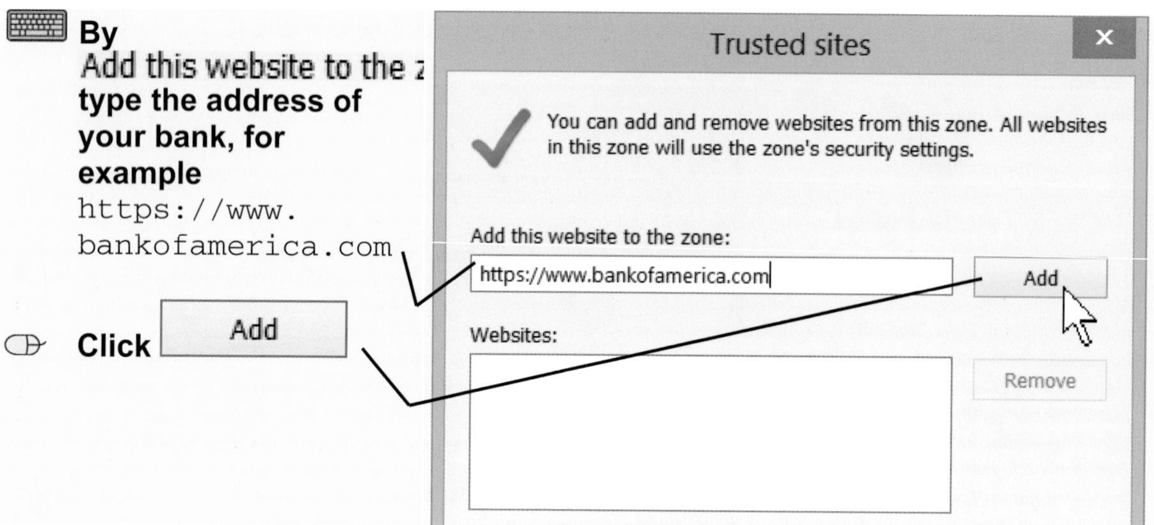


## Please note:

The default setting Require server verification (https:) for all sites in this zone means that sites you add to the *Trusted sites* zone must have the **https://** prefix. This prefix assures a secure, encrypted connection. The information that is exchanged between such a website and your computer will be encrypted and cannot be read by others.

There may already be some trusted websites in the list on your computer.

To remove one of these websites:

**Click** https://www.bankofam

**Click** Remove

You can close this window:

**Click** Close

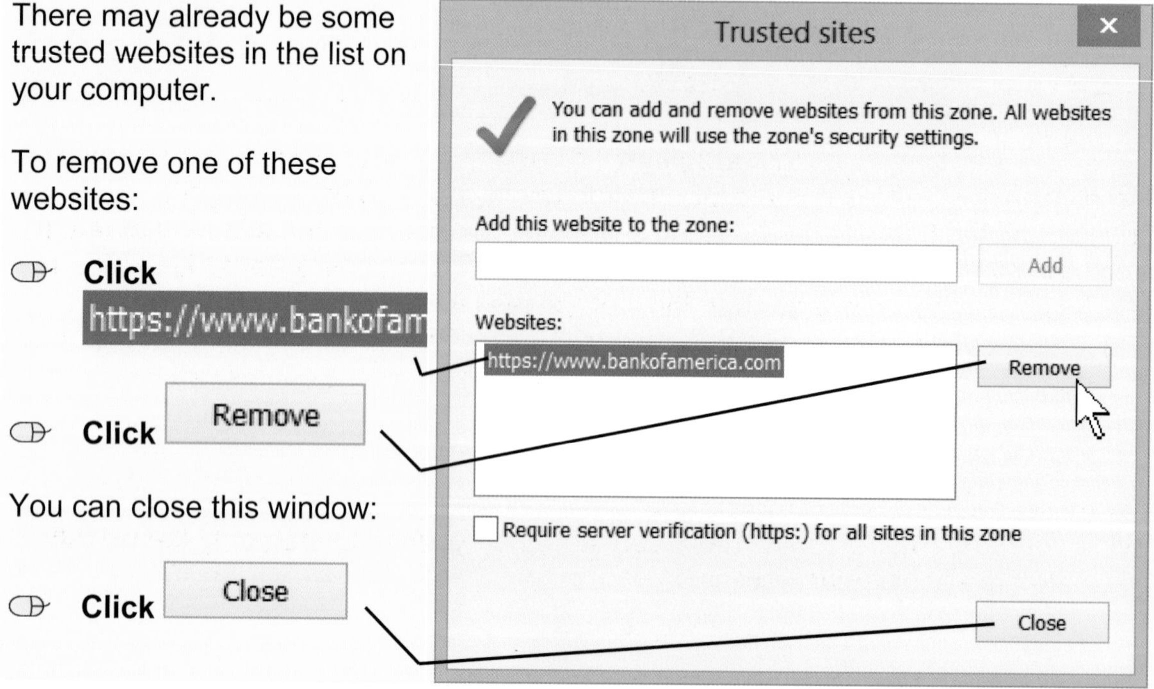

Now you will see the *Internet Options* window again:

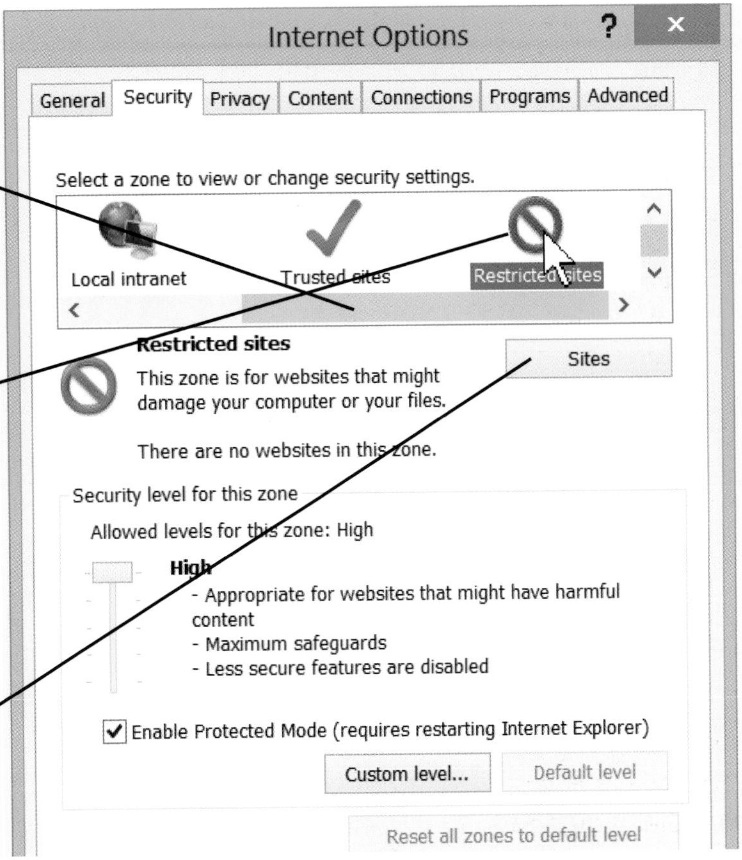

- **Drag the scroll bar to the right**

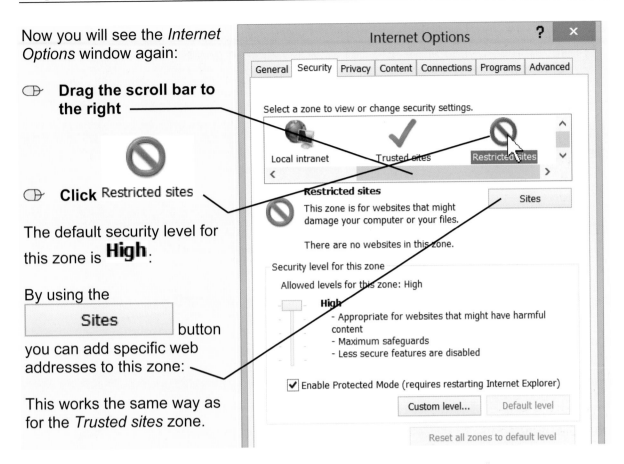

- **Click** Restricted sites

The default security level for this zone is **High**:

By using the Sites button you can add specific web addresses to this zone:

This works the same way as for the *Trusted sites* zone.

The settings you adjust here will also be used in the *Internet Explorer* app.

## 7.2 Privacy Settings in Internet Explorer

*Cookies* are small text files that are placed on your hard drive while you surf the Internet. These little files contain information about data you have entered.
If you look at flight details on an airline's website, for example, the site may create a cookie containing the dates and cities you entered. This makes it possible for you to leaf forward and backward through the web pages without having to enter all your travel details over and over again. Note that the text files cannot be executed on your computer (these are not programs), and their maximum size is quite small.

**Please note:**

Cookies are not dangerous. A website has access only to the information you provide yourself. After a cookie has been stored on your computer, only the website that created the cookie can access it.

If you want, you can set *Internet Explorer* to block cookies. Although you need to consider that blocking cookies may limit the functions of the website.

- **Click the** Privacy **tab**

The default privacy setting is **Medium**. Under the heading you can read what this setting means.

If you do not see **Medium**:

- **Click** Default

To see more settings for handling cookies:

- **Click** Advanced

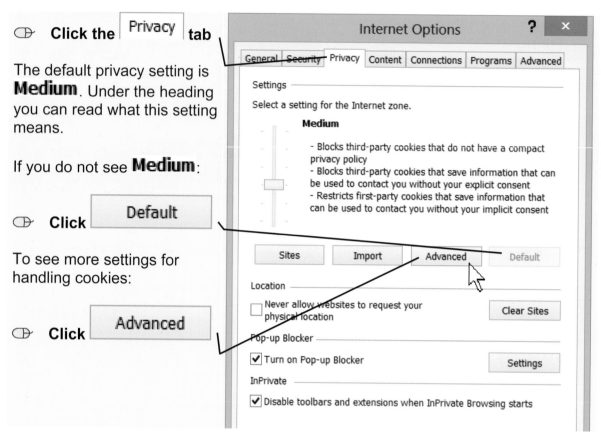

Now you will see the *Advanced Privacy Settings* window:

In this example the handling of cookies is set to override automatic cookie handling.

You can change this setting:

- **Check the box** ☑ **by** Override automatic cook

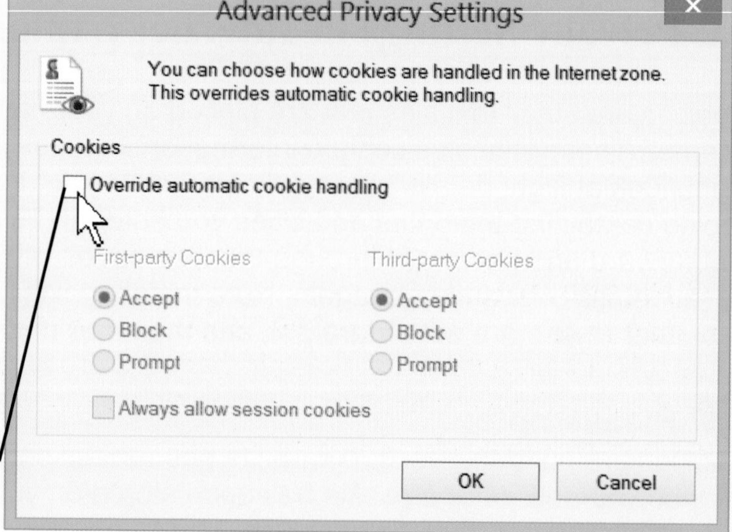

Now you can take a better look at the options. You can specify what you want to do both with *first-party* and *third-party* cookies:

- Accept: cookies will automatically be processed.
- Block: not a single cookie will be accepted.
- Prompt: you will be notified with each cookie, and asked to accept or block the cookie.

*First-party cookies* originate from the website that you are viewing and can be either *permanent* or *temporary*. A temporary cookie is removed when *Internet Explorer* is closed. A permanent cookie is stored on your hard drive and stays there. This means the cookie can be read by the website that created it on your next visit to this website.

*Third-party cookies* originate from other websites' advertisements (such as pop-up or banner ads) on the website that you are viewing. Websites might use these cookies to track your browsing behavior for marketing purposes.

It is better to select the default setting again:

**Uncheck the box ☑ by** Override automatic cook

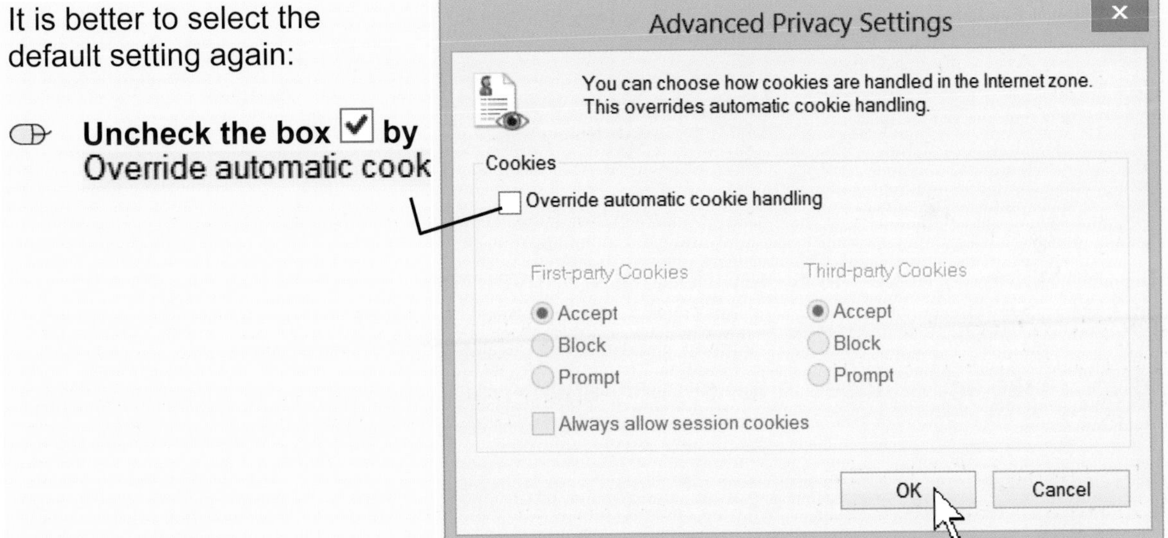

**Please note:**

You may prefer to block all cookies. Keep in mind that if you do, there is a chance you might not be able to view certain websites properly. Of course you can experiment with different settings. It is very easy to return to the default settings if you do not like your new settings.

## Tip

**Always allow session cookies**
Some websites use cookies while you are visiting the site, but remove them afterwards. These are called *session cookies*. Session cookies are also called *temporary cookies*, because they are removed after *Internet Explorer* is closed. Session cookies are used for online banking, for example. If you have specified that all cookies should be blocked, including session cookies, you will not be able to login to that website anymore. You will see a warning message from the website.

For this reason, always check the box ☑ by Always allow session cookies

Even if you block the other cookies.

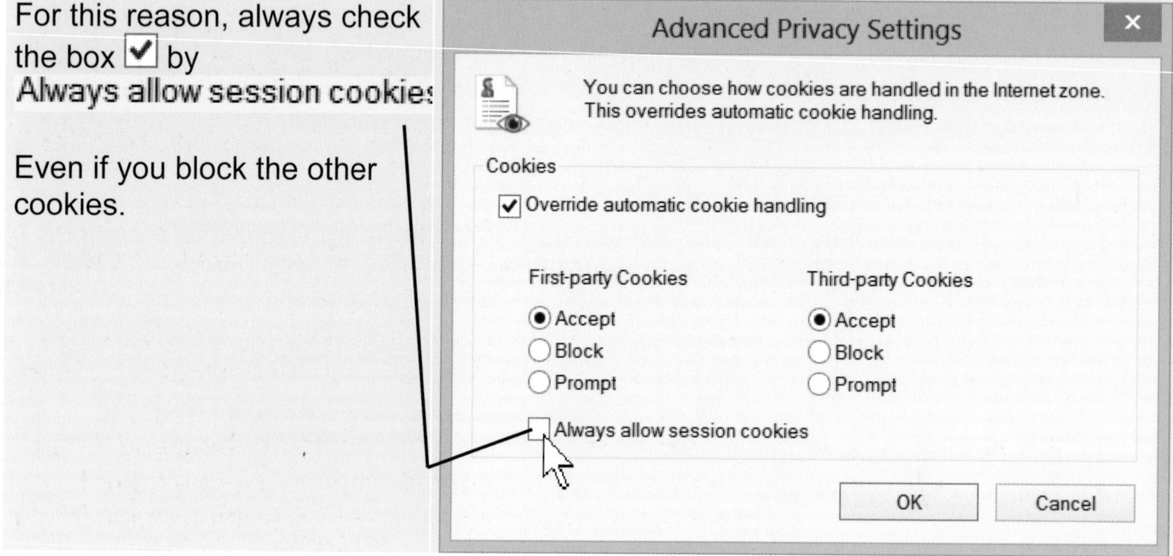


You can easily remove the stored cookies from your hard drive. In the next sections you can read more about it.

Did you make any changes in the security and privacy settings in the *Internet Options* window?

**Click**

If you did not make any changes:

**Close the *Internet Options* window** 12

# 7.3 Deleting Your Browser History

As you browse the web, *Internet Explorer* stores information about the websites you visit, as well as information that you are frequently asked to provide (for example, your name and address). The browsing *History* consists of various items, amongst others:

- **Temporary Internet files and website files**: web pages are stored in a temporary Internet files folder, the first time you view them in your web browser. This speeds up the display of pages you frequently visit or have already seen, because *Internet Explorer* can open them from your hard disk instead of from the Internet.
- **Cookies and website data**: small text files that websites put on your computer to store information about you and your preferences.
- **History**: a list of all the websites you have visited.
- **Form data**: information that you have entered in forms on websites, or on the address bar (like your name, address, and website addresses).
- **Passwords**: each time you type a password on a webpage, *Internet Explorer* asks if it should be saved. These saved passwords can also be deleted.

Usually, it is helpful to have this information stored on your computer because it can improve web browsing speed or automatically provide information, so you do not need to retype it over and over again. You might want to delete that information if you are cleaning up your computer. If you are using a public computer and do not want to leave any of your personal information behind you can delete everything too.

This is how you delete the browser *History*:

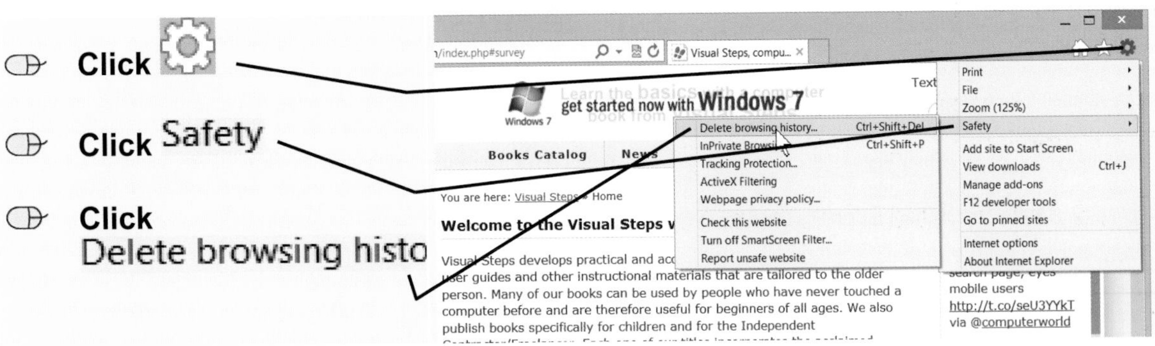

In this window, you can choose which part of your browsing *History* you want to delete. At the same time, this history will be deleted in the *Internet Explorer* app as well.

The items that are checked ☑ will be deleted, except the option at the top:

- **If necessary, check the boxes ☑ by the desired items**
- **Click** Delete

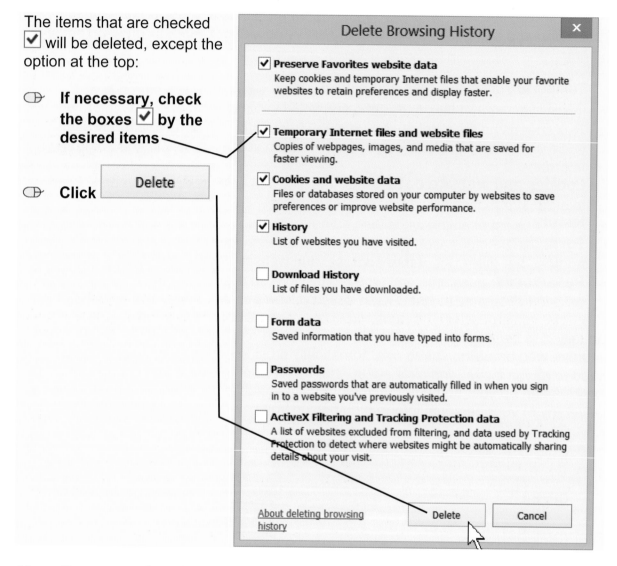

Delete Browsing History

☑ **Preserve Favorites website data**
Keep cookies and temporary Internet files that enable your favorite websites to retain preferences and display faster.

☑ **Temporary Internet files and website files**
Copies of webpages, images, and media that are saved for faster viewing.

☑ **Cookies and website data**
Files or databases stored on your computer by websites to save preferences or improve website performance.

☑ **History**
List of websites you have visited.

☐ **Download History**
List of files you have downloaded.

☐ **Form data**
Saved information that you have typed into forms.

☐ **Passwords**
Saved passwords that are automatically filled in when you sign in to a website you've previously visited.

☐ **ActiveX Filtering and Tracking Protection data**
A list of websites excluded from filtering, and data used by Tracking Protection to detect where websites might be automatically sharing details about your visit.

About deleting browsing history | Delete | Cancel

You will see a confirmation message. You can close it:

- **Click** ×

**Tip**

**Delete part of the History**

You can also remove individual website from the *History*. This is how you do it:

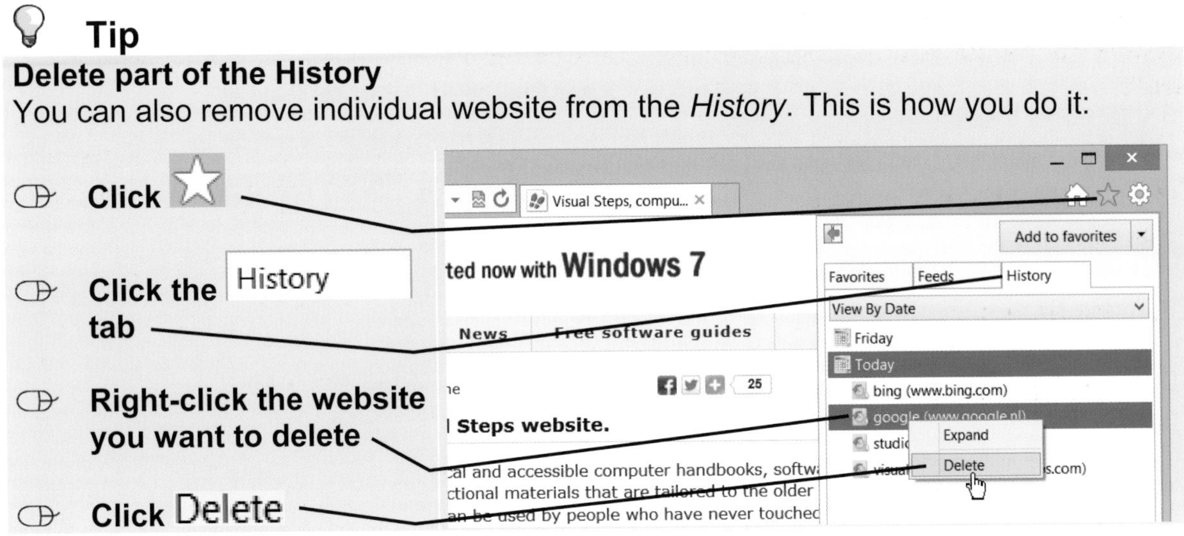


## 7.4 Setting the Number of Days

In the *Internet Options* window there are some other settings you can adjust. For example, you can select the number of days that previously visited web pages should be saved in the *History*.

**Open the *Internet Options* window** 50

On the General tab:

By Browsing history, click Settings

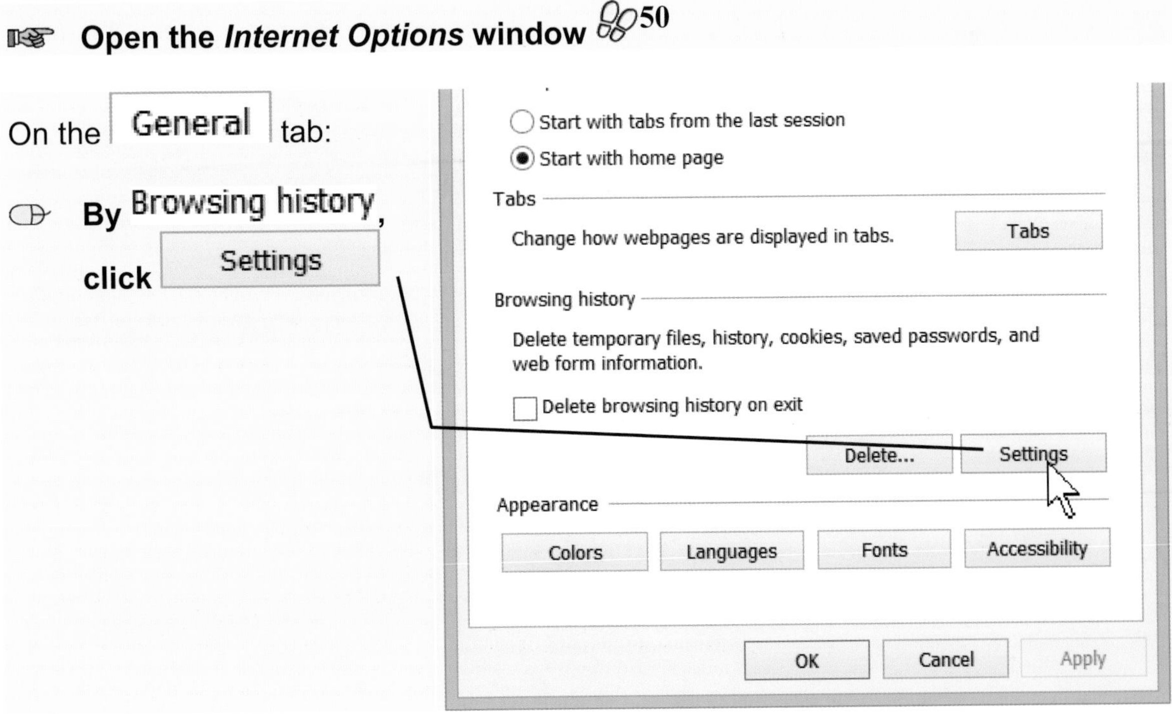

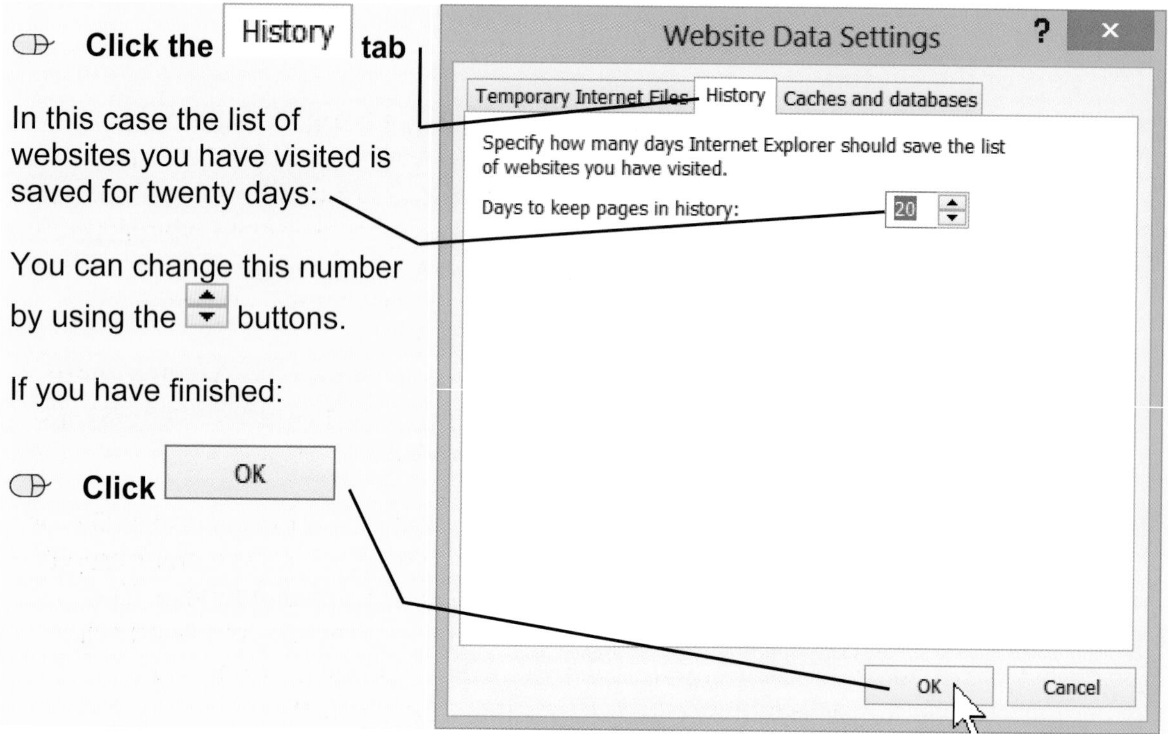


Click the History tab

In this case the list of websites you have visited is saved for twenty days:

You can change this number by using the buttons.

If you have finished:

Click OK

Close the *Internet Options* window 12

Once you have cleared your *History*, the folder will be empty. You can check this for yourself:

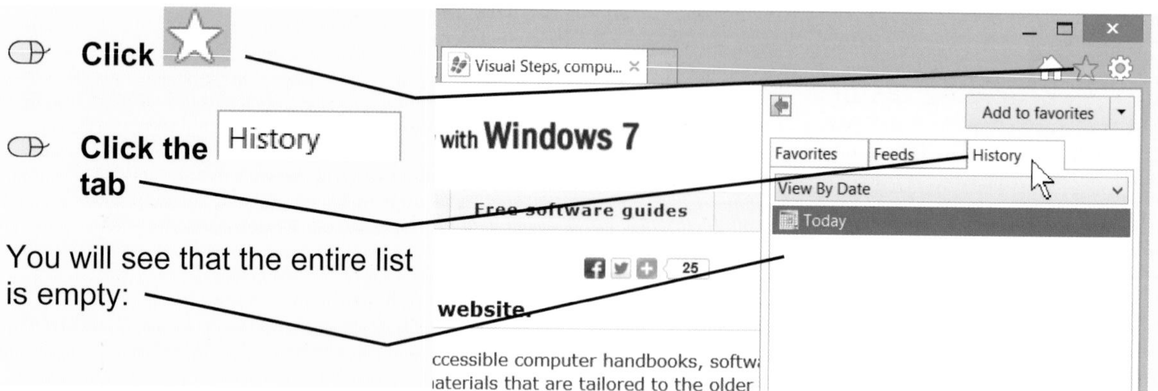


Click

Click the History tab

You will see that the entire list is empty:

All the websites you have recently visited have been erased from memory.

# 7.5 Phishing

The Internet is used more and more these days: for online banking, shopping, ordering your favorite pizza, purchasing airline tickets, selling your old furniture, studying a new subject, etcetera. It seems like almost anything can be done on the Internet. Along with these useful, pleasant, even rewarding activities however, have come some rather unsavory practices. Criminals have found their way to the Internet. One of the latest scams is known as *phishing*. But what exactly is *phishing?*

Online phishing (pronounced like the word *fishing*) is a way to trick computer users into revealing personal or financial information through a fraudulent e-mail message or an innocent looking website. Phishing is in fact 'fishing' for information.

A common online phishing scam starts with a fake e-mail message that looks like an official notice from a well-known trusted source. This can be your bank, your credit card company, or an online shop or auction site you have dealt with before. The same message is sent randomly to thousands of e-mail addresses. In the e-mail message, recipients are linked to a website where they are asked to provide personal information, such as their account number or password.

Once you fall for the trick and enter your personal information, this information is directly sent to the criminals who have set this trap for you. Then they will start using your personal data to buy things, open new credit card accounts in your name, or otherwise assume or abuse your identity. These e-mails and the websites they link to seem so official that many people think they are real. Often, the official bank logo is used in the e-mail, and the websites are meticulously copied.

Here is an example of such a phishing e-mail:

You can see that the text of the e-mail is in bad English. The criminals will ask you to log in or download something through the hyperlink. If you click this link and enter your data on the website, the information will directly be forwarded to the criminals.

From: FraudAddressHere
Sent: 10/17/2012 4:10:17 P.M. Central Daylight Time
Subj: Urgent security update regarding your chase account!

CHASE

Chase Bank Online® Department Notice

You have received this email because you or someone had used your account from different locations.
For security purpose, we are required to open an investigation into this matter.

In order to safeguard your account, we require that you confirm your banking details.

UPDATE NOW

Sincerely,
Jennifer Myhre
Senior Vice President

E-mail Security Information

E-mail intended for your email

*Windows 8* offers protection against online phishing in *Internet Explorer*. In the next section we will tell you more about this subject.

**Please note:**

Criminals no longer restrict themselves to online phishing alone. There are more and more cases known where the victim is phoned at home, by a so-called bank employee who is part of the non-existing '*Windows Maintenance Team*' at *Microsoft*, or from some other seemingly official instiution.

Such a person will ask the victim (usually in badly spoken English or French) to change certain things on their computer. The pretext is usually that the computer security is not up to date. Sometimes the victim has to change the settings himself, but in other cases the so-called employee uses a program to change the settings by remote control, while the victim watches. Often the employee asks for personal codes and passwords for internet banking services without the victim noticing it.

**Do not go into these calls!** Employees of the *Microsoft* company, or from *Windows* support desks will never phone you at home, regarding computer problems. And neither will your bank; they will never ask you to change your computer settings, or give them your personal codes for Internet banking.

**Please note:**

Apart from this, you need to take into account that banks will become much sterner when dealing with Internet banking fraud. If they can clearly demonstrate that you yourself have given a criminal access (unintentionally) to your personal codes or your computer. They may refuse to compensate you for the damage.

So make sure that you always watch what you do and secure the computer with a good and up-to-date antivirus program.

## 7.6 The SmartScreen Filter in Internet Explorer

In *Internet Explorer*, the *SmartScreen Filter* helps to detect phishing websites. *SmartScreen* will also protect you against downloading or installing malware (harmful software).The *SmartScreen Filter* uses three methods to help protect you from phishing scams and malware:

- It compares the addresses of websites you visit against a dynamic list of reported phishing sites and malware websites. If the website you visit is on the list of reported phishing websites, *Internet Explorer* will display a warning web page and a notification on the address bar, which states this website has been blocked for your protection.

- It analyzes the sites you visit to see if they have the characteristics common to a phishing website. If any suspect web pages are found, you will see a message from *SmartScreen* telling you to pay attention, and you can give feedback.

- *SmartScreen* checks the files you download on the basis of a list of reported websites containing harmful software and programs that are known to be unsafe. If any similarities are found, *SmartScreen* will display a warning message which tells you the download operation has been blocked for your own safety. *SmartScreen* also checks the files you download by comparing them to a list of well-known files that are often downloaded by other *Internet Explorer* users too. If the file you want to download is not in this list, *SmartScreen* will display a warning message.

Besides, you can ask *Microsoft* to check whether a certain web address is on the most recent list of phishing websites. And you can report a suspicious website.

This is how you check if the *SmartScreen filter* is turned on your computer:

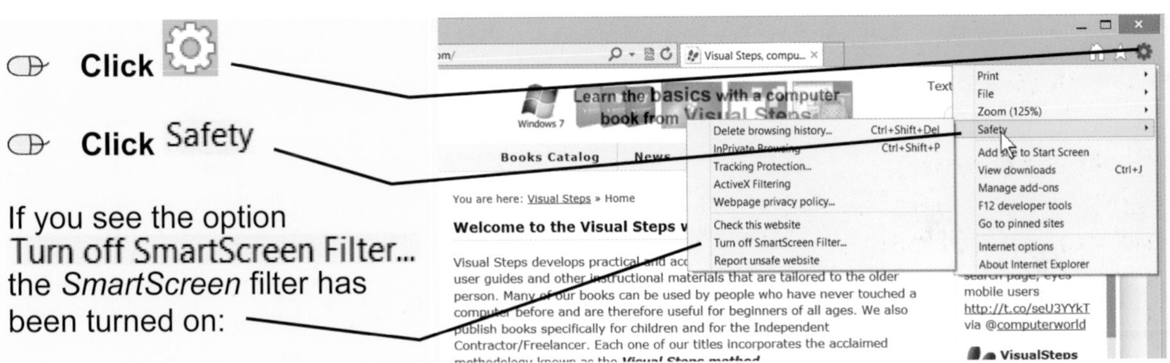


Click [gear icon]

Click Safety

If you see the option Turn off SmartScreen Filter... the *SmartScreen* filter has been turned on:

If the *SmartScreen* filter has not been turned on your computer:

Click Turn on SmartScreen Filter...

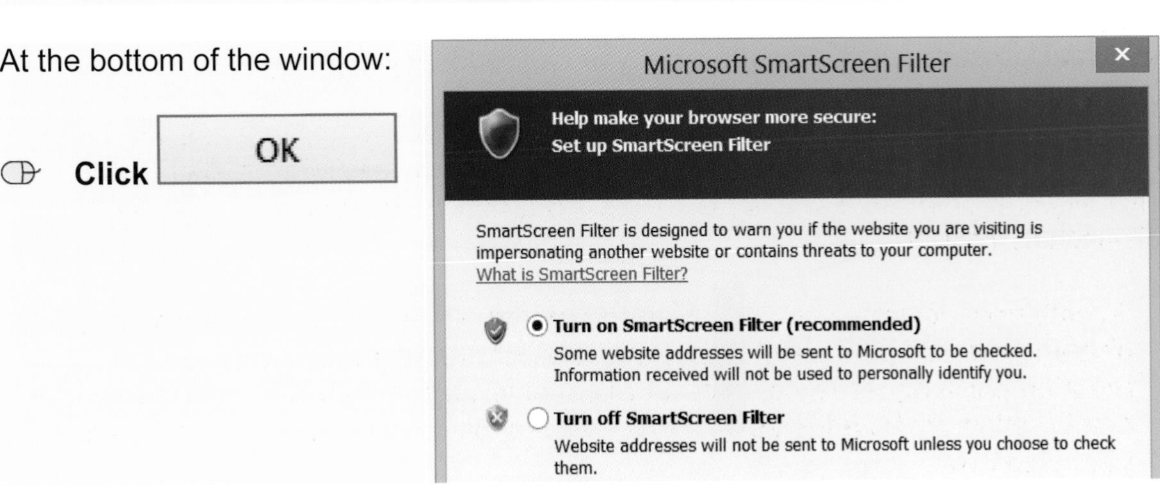


At the bottom of the window:

Click OK

# 7.7 Checking or Reporting a Suspicious Website

If you visit a website you do not trust, you can have it checked by *Microsoft*:

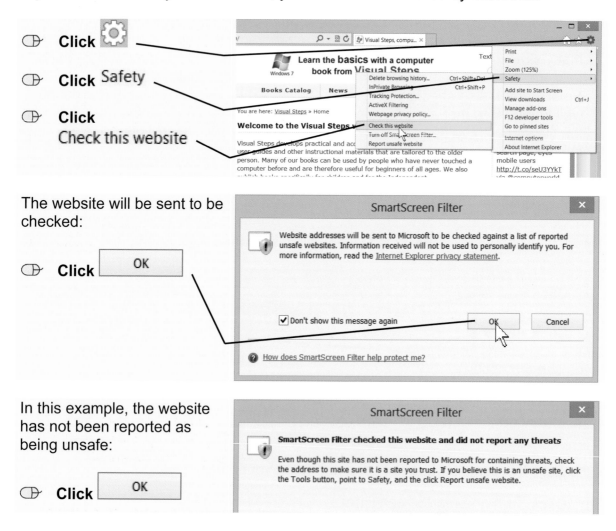

Click ⚙

Click Safety

Click Check this website

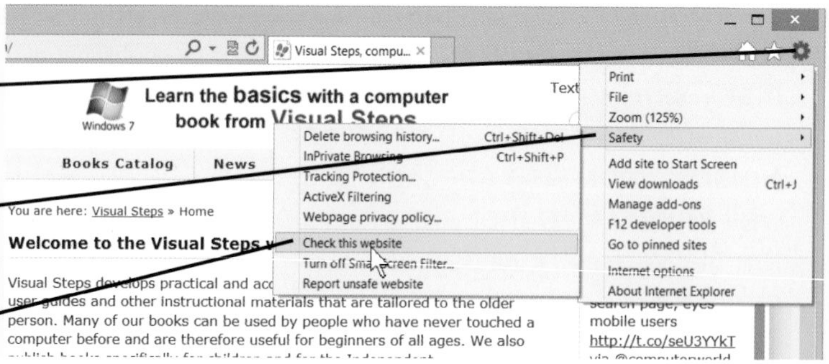

The website will be sent to be checked:

Click OK

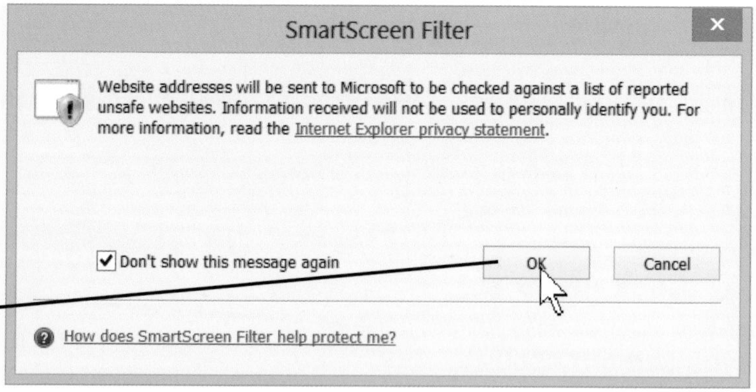

SmartScreen Filter

Website addresses will be sent to Microsoft to be checked against a list of reported unsafe websites. Information received will not be used to personally identify you. For more information, read the Internet Explorer privacy statement.

☑ Don't show this message again  OK  Cancel

How does SmartScreen Filter help protect me?

In this example, the website has not been reported as being unsafe:

Click OK

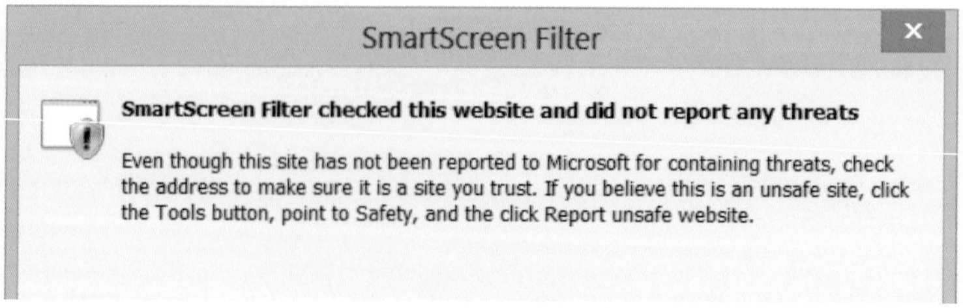

SmartScreen Filter

**SmartScreen Filter checked this website and did not report any threats**

Even though this site has not been reported to Microsoft for containing threats, check the address to make sure it is a site you trust. If you believe this is an unsafe site, click the Tools button, point to Safety, and the click Report unsafe website.

If you think a certain website is unsafe, you can report it like this:

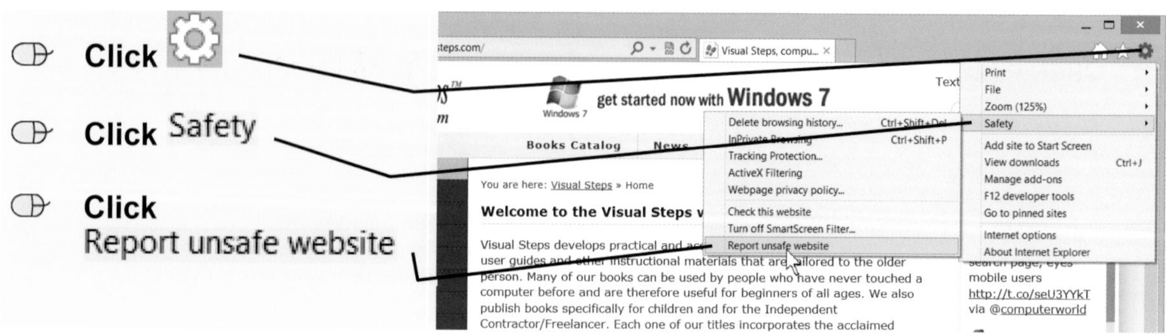

You will see a new window with a form you can use for reporting the website:

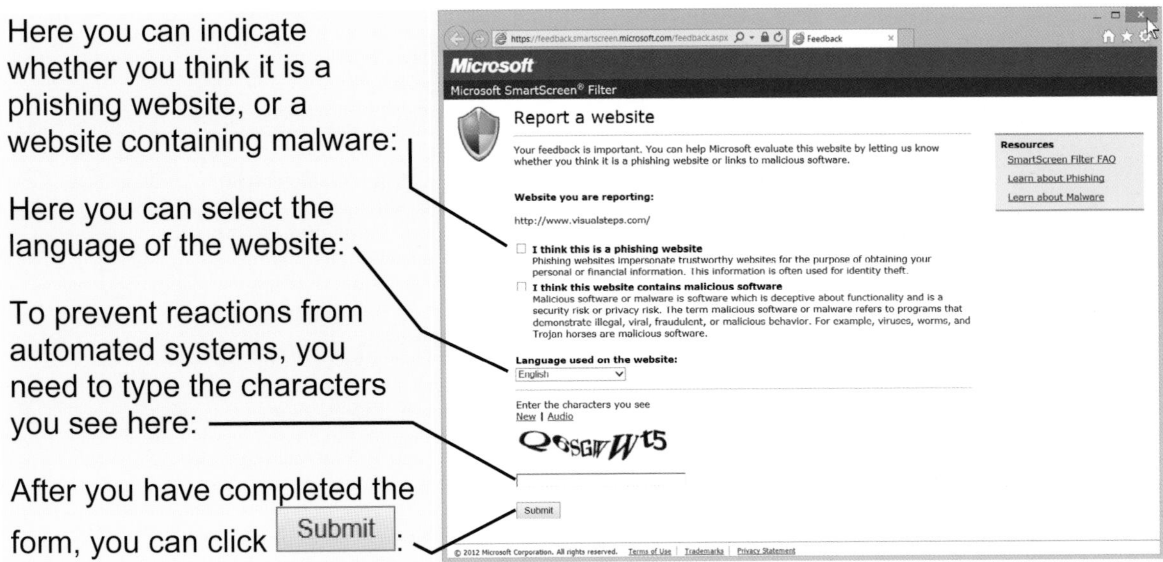


Here you can indicate whether you think it is a phishing website, or a website containing malware:

Here you can select the language of the website:

To prevent reactions from automated systems, you need to type the characters you see here:

After you have completed the form, you can click Submit:

For now, you can close the window:

**Close the window** 12

## 7.8 Pop-up Blocker

*Pop-ups* are very annoying for Internet users. A pop-up is a small web browser window that appears on top of the website you are viewing. Pop-up windows often open as soon as you visit a website and are usually created by commercial companies, for promotional uses.

*Pop-up Blocker* is a feature in *Internet Explorer* that lets you limit or block most pop-ups. When *Pop-up Blocker* is turned on and a pop-up is detected, a little message will be displayed. You are going to see how this works:

**Open the web page www.visualsteps.com/internet8/practice** 1

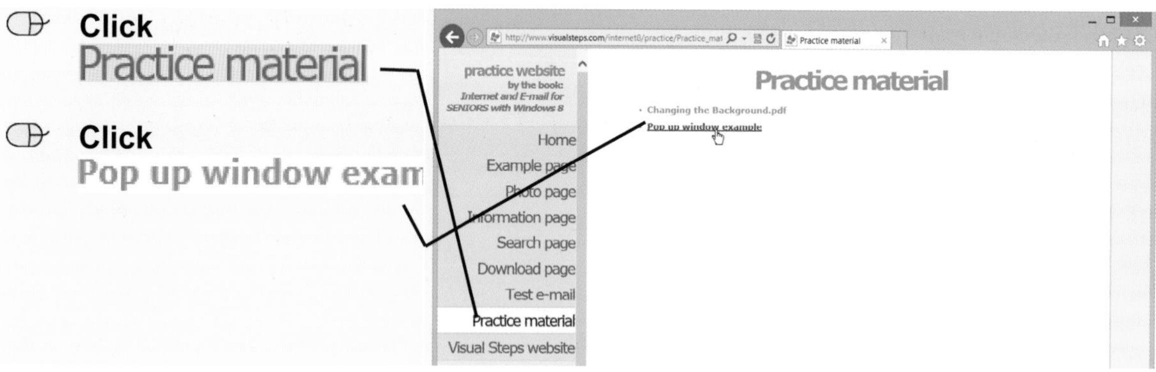


This website tries to show a pop-up window and you will see a message at the bottom of the window:

You can choose the level of blocking you prefer, ranging from blocking all pop-up windows to allowing all pop-ups.

In this case the filter level is set to Medium. This means most pop-ups will automatically be blocked.

Click Medium: Block most autom

Here you see the other two filter levels:
High: Block all pop-ups (Ctrl+Alt to c
and
Low: Allow pop-ups from secure s

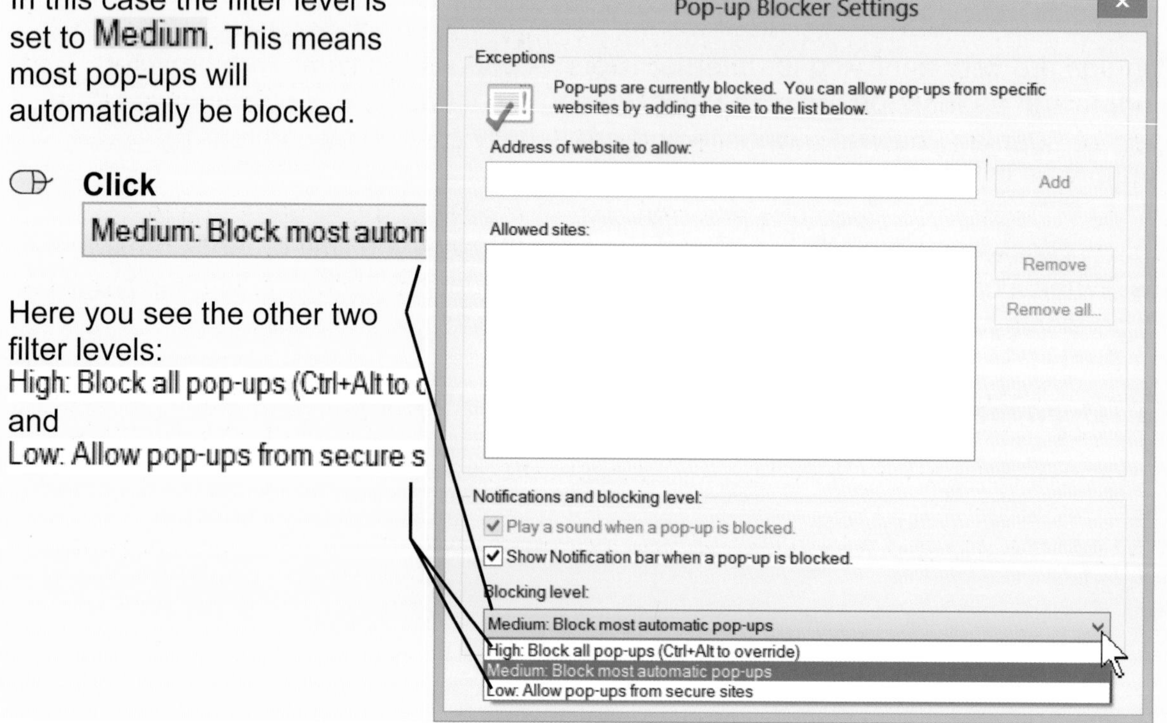

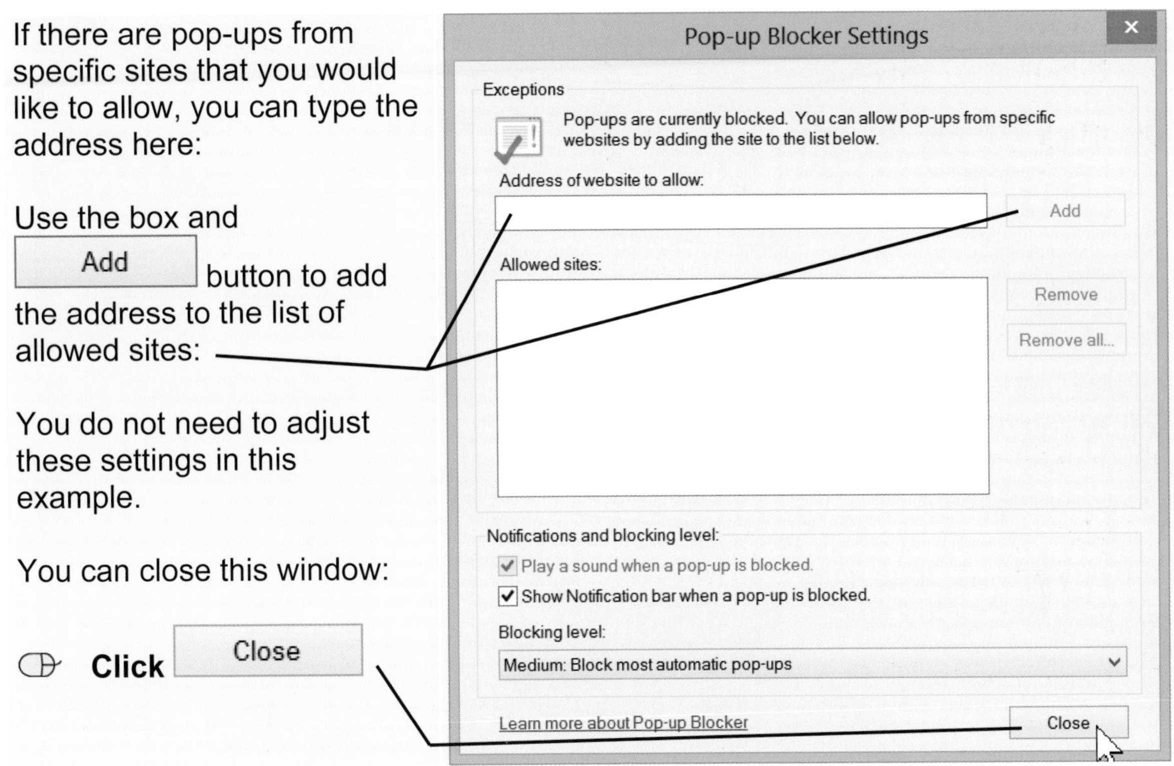


## 7.9 Managing Add-ons in Internet Explorer

An *add-on* is a program that adds extra functionality to a web browser like *Internet Explorer*. Examples of add-ons include extra toolbars, animated mouse pointers, and programs that block pop-up windows. Add-ons are also known as *ActiveX controls*, *Plug-ins*, *Browser extensions*, or *Browser Helper Objects*.

On the Internet, many add-ons are available. For most of them, you have to give permission before they are downloaded to your computer. Some add-ons, however, are downloaded without your knowledge. This could happen if the add-on is part of a program you have installed. Some add-ons are installed with *Windows 8.*

An add-on can be used without any problem most of the time. Sometimes the add-on can cause *Internet Explorer* to close unexpectedly. This could happen if the add-on was poorly designed or was created for another version of *Internet Explorer.*

Now you are going to take a look at the add-ons that are already installed to your computer.

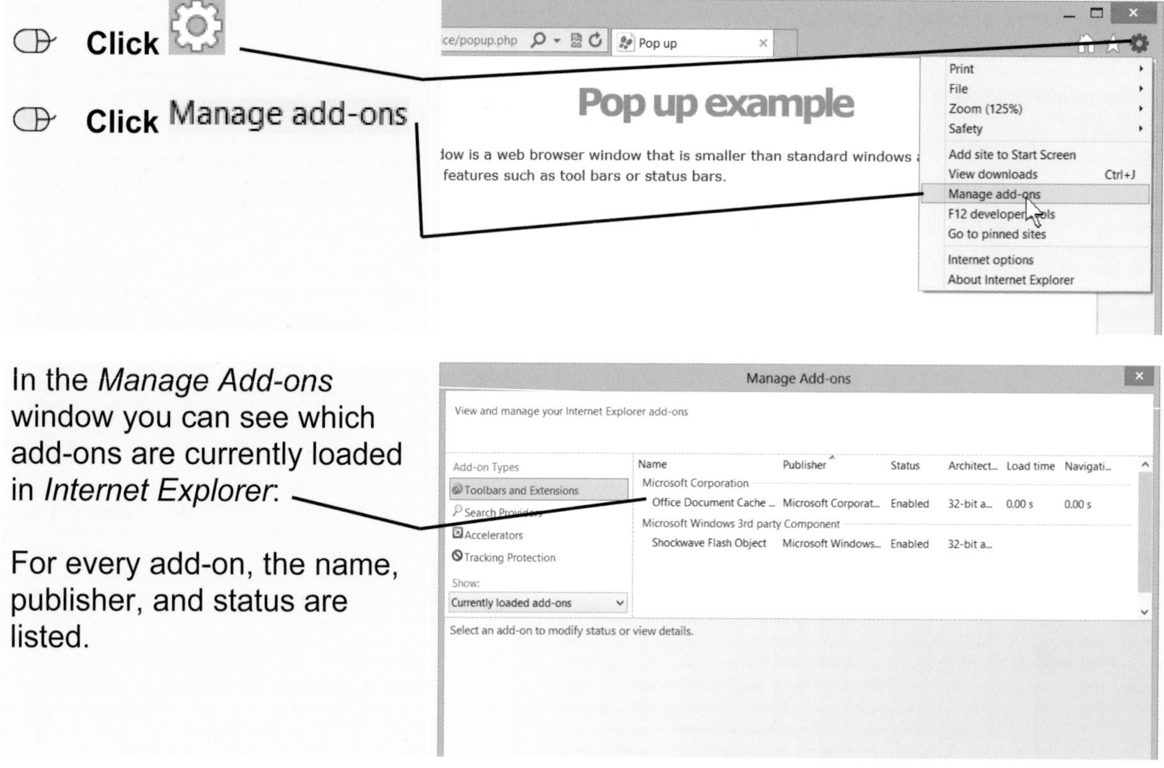


Click

Click Manage add-ons

In the *Manage Add-ons* window you can see which add-ons are currently loaded in *Internet Explorer*:

For every add-on, the name, publisher, and status are listed.

Of course, the list in this example will look different from the list on your own screen.

If you do not trust or do not want to use an add-on, you can disable it:

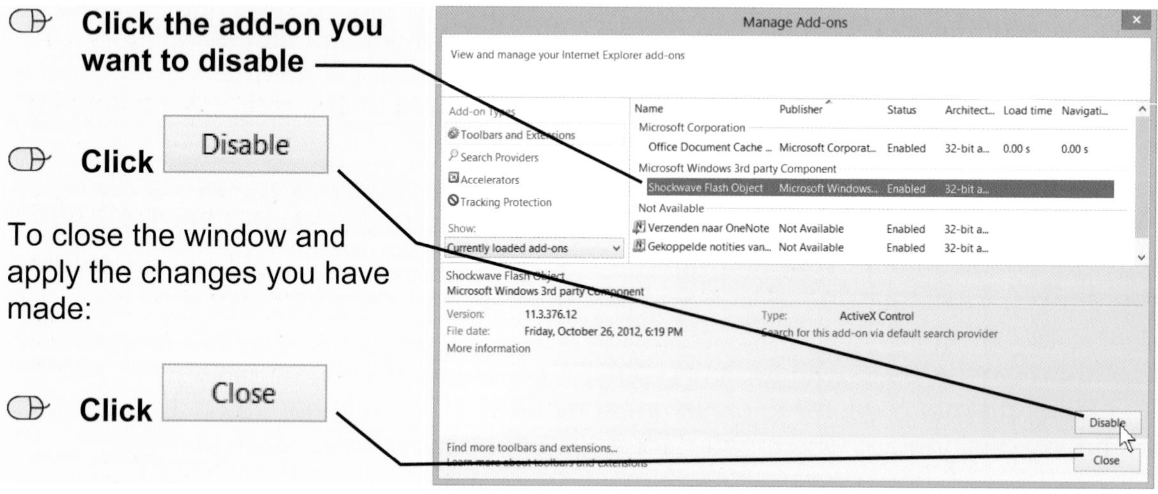


**Click the add-on you want to disable**

**Click** Disable

To close the window and apply the changes you have made:

**Click** Close

To complete the operation you need to close *Internet Explorer* and then open the program again:

**Close *Internet Explorer*** 12

**Open *Internet Explorer* on the desktop** 9

If you want to start using the add-on again, you can enable it once again:

Click

Click Manage add-ons

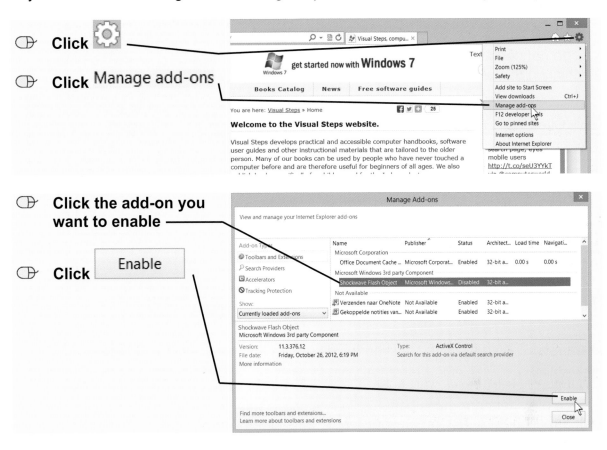

Click the add-on you want to enable

Click Enable

Before closing the window, you will now take a look at the add-ons on your computer which can be used by *Internet Explorer*:

Click Currently loaded add-ons

Click All add-ons

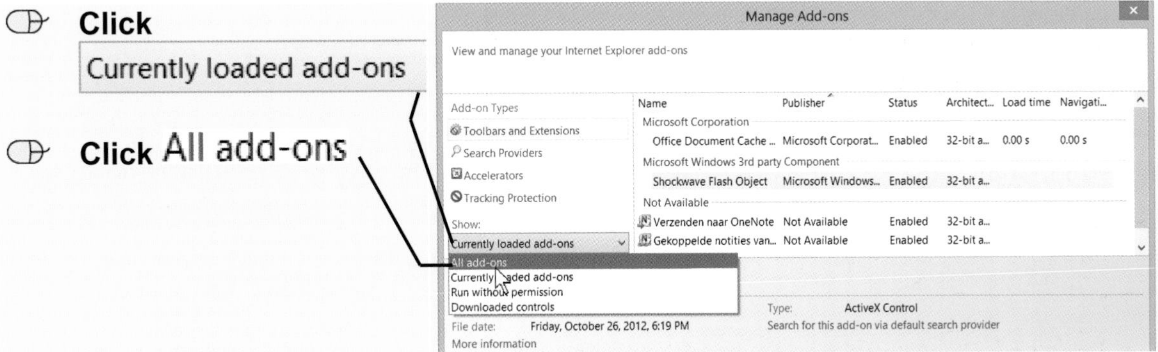

Now you will see the complete list of add-ons for *Internet Explorer*.

The list in this example will probably look different from what you see on your screen.

You do not need to change anything in this window:

**Click** Close

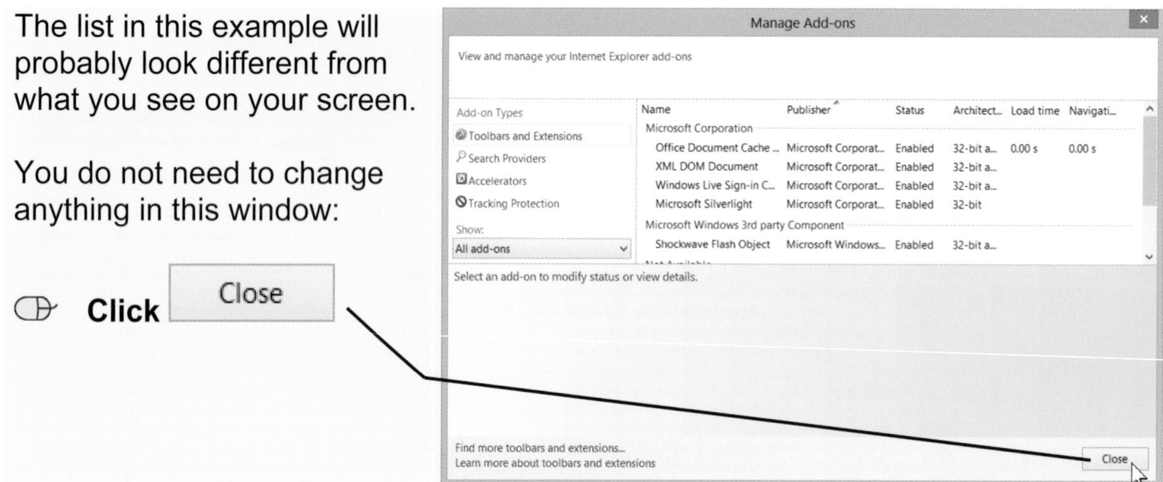


**Close *Internet Explorer*** 12

## 7.10 Junk E-mail

In *Chapter 5 Working with Mail* you have seen that you can set up multiple e-mail accounts in the *Mail* app. In this app you cannot use any settings to handle unwanted, junk e-mails. This is becoming much less of a necessity, since Internet service providers are much better able to stop phishing e-mails and other types of junk e-mail, before they reach your *Inbox*. Messages that are identified as junk e-mail will automatically be moved to the *Junk* folder.

If the e-mail message is suspect, you will see this message in the *Junk* folder:

**This message is marked as junk mail.**
All links, images, and attachments have been disabled to help protect you. If you trust the sender, move the message out of junk e-mails and we'll put it back the way we found it.

The spam filter cannot always tell the difference between unwanted e-mail or phishing e-mail, and an innocent e-mail message. That is why you regularly need to check the *Junk* folder.

Has an e-mail message unjustly been moved to this folder? This is how you can move the selected message to your *Inbox*:

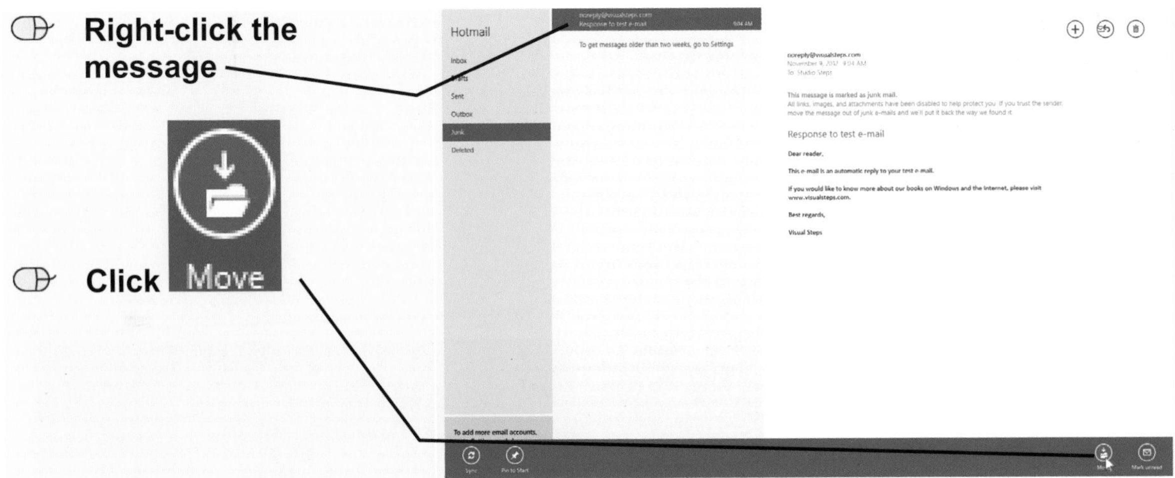


**Right-click the message**

**Click Move**

**Click the Inbox folder**

The message will be moved to your *Inbox*. The links, images, and/or attachments will be enabled again. In the *Tips* at the back of this chapter you will find more tips to better protect you against junk e-mail.

## Tip

**More about e-mail**

In the *Outlook.com* e-mail program you have a lot more options for managing unwanted e-mail messages. For example, you can flag an individual e-mail message as junk, or as a phishing e-mail.

If you want to know more about *Outlook.com*, then read the *Bonus Chapter Outlook.com* on the website accompanying this book and you will find out more about this program. In *Appendix B Opening the Online Bonus Chapters* you can read how to open this Bonus Chapter.

# 7.11 Action Center

The *Action Center* in *Windows 8* checks the security settings for your computer and keeps track of the *Windows 8* updates. Also, you can see and control the maintenance status of your computer in the *Action Center*, and solve any computer problems.

This is how you open the *Action Center*:

**Go back to the Start screen** 3

**Right-click an empty area on the Start screen**

The app commands appear:

**Click** All apps

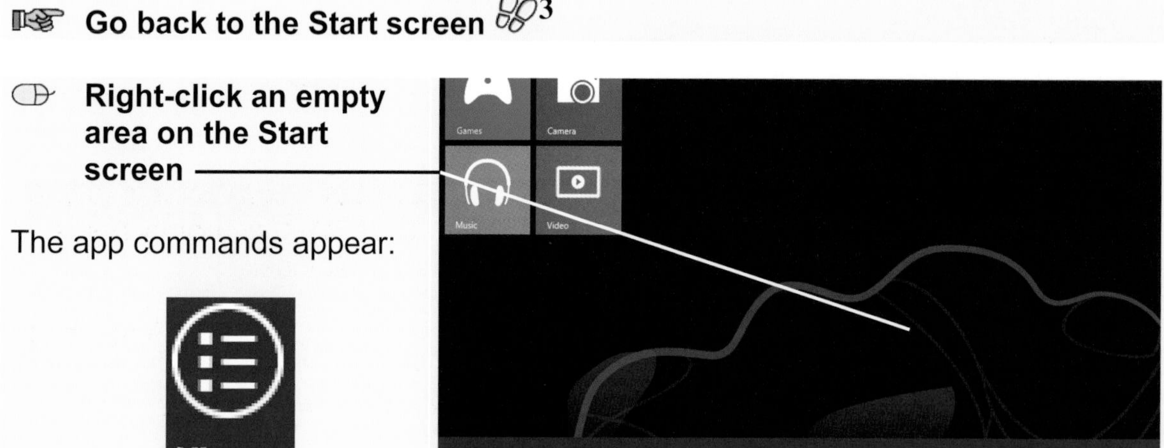


**Click** Control Panel

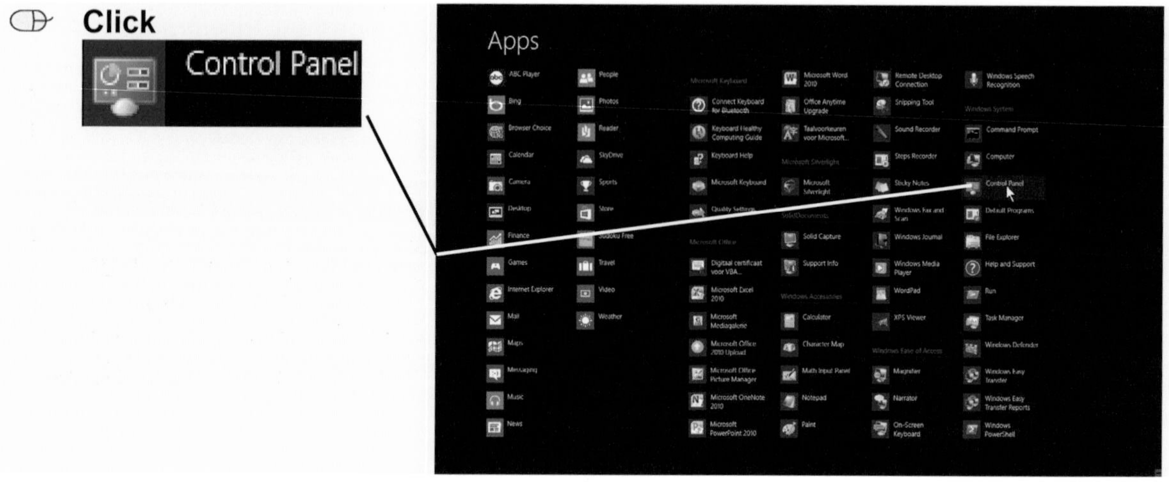

The *Control Panel* will be opened. This is the gateway for settings on your computer.

**By** System and Security**, click** Review your computer's s

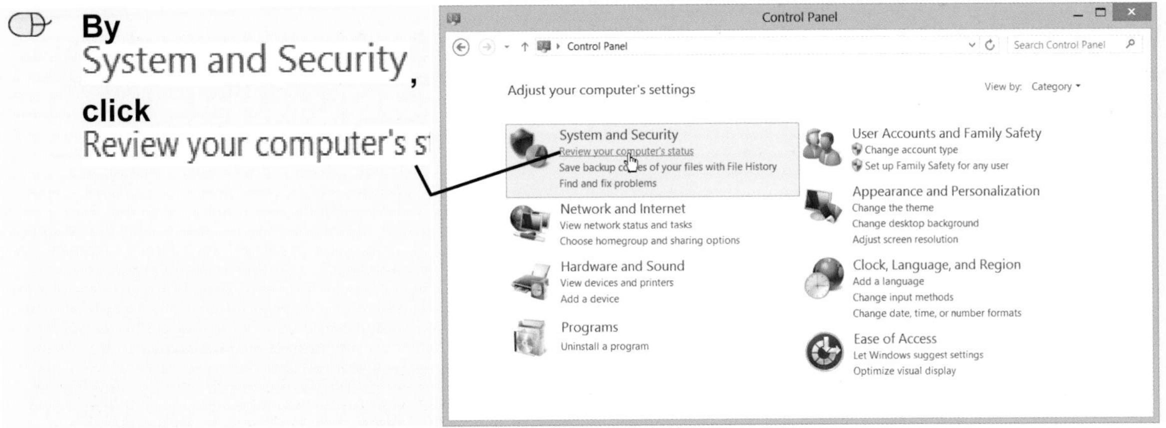


In the *Action Center* you will see the status of the most important components of your computer's security, such as the firewall, *Windows Update*, protection from viruses, spyware and unwanted software and various other security settings:

**Click** Security

You will see the statuses:

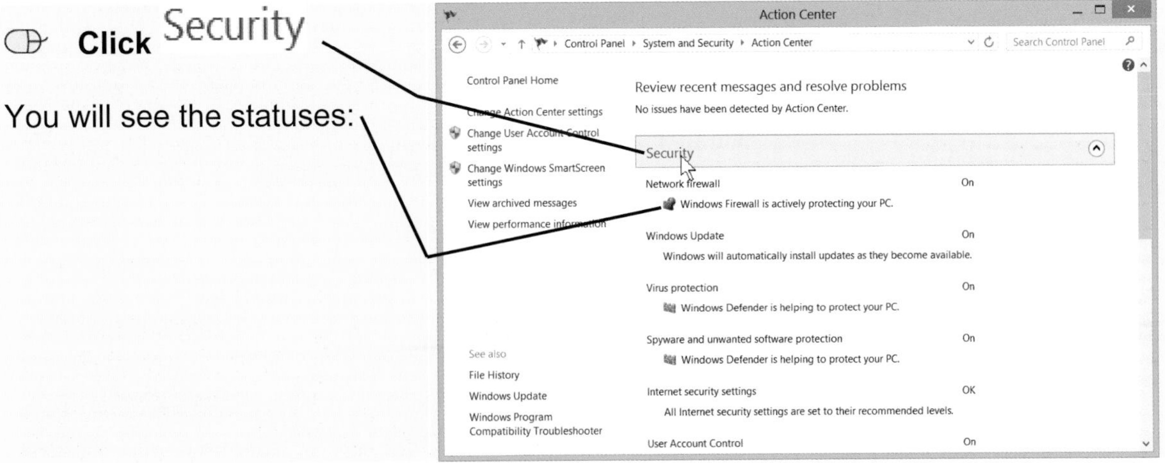


At a single glance you will be able to see if there are any current problems on your computer. The problems are indicated in red or yellow. The red color indicates a problem that needs to be solved immediately, such as enabling anti-virus protection. The yellow color indicates a maintenance task you might need to execute, such as updating the computer with *Windows Update*.

## Please note:

Your computer's settings may differ from the settings in this example.

**Close the *Action Center*** 12

## Tip

**Spot a problem through the taskbar**

On the taskbar you can immediately see whether there are any problems with the security or maintenance of your computer. If you see an icon with a flag and a red cross  on the right-hand side of the taskbar, this means a problem has been spotted:

- **Place the pointer on**

You will see a message with a brief overview of the problems:

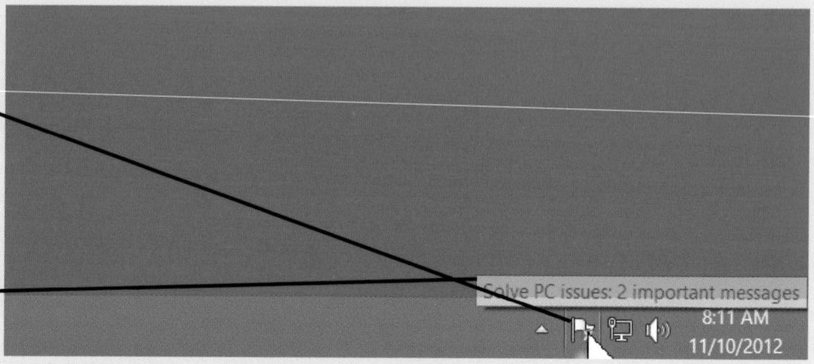

- **Click**

Now you see a separate window with a more lengthy description of the problems:

Here you can click a link which will lead you directly to a window where you can solve the problem:

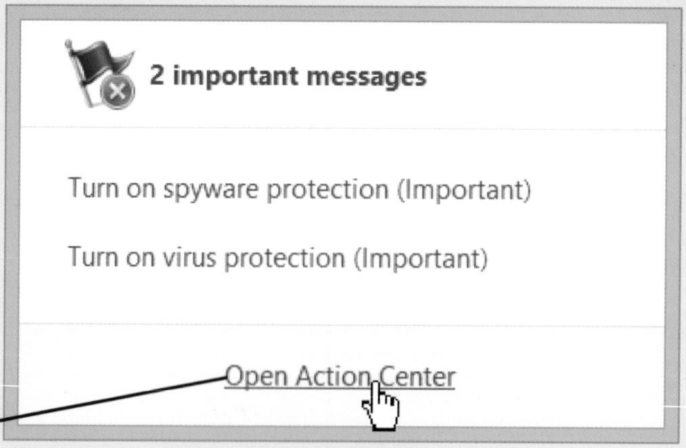

- **Click** Open Action Center

You see the *Action Center*:

You can spot the problems right away:

Additional options for problem solving:

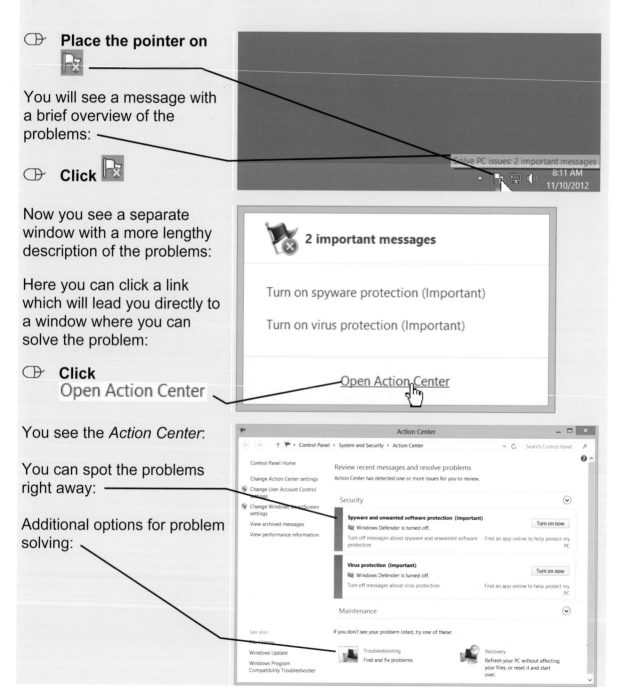

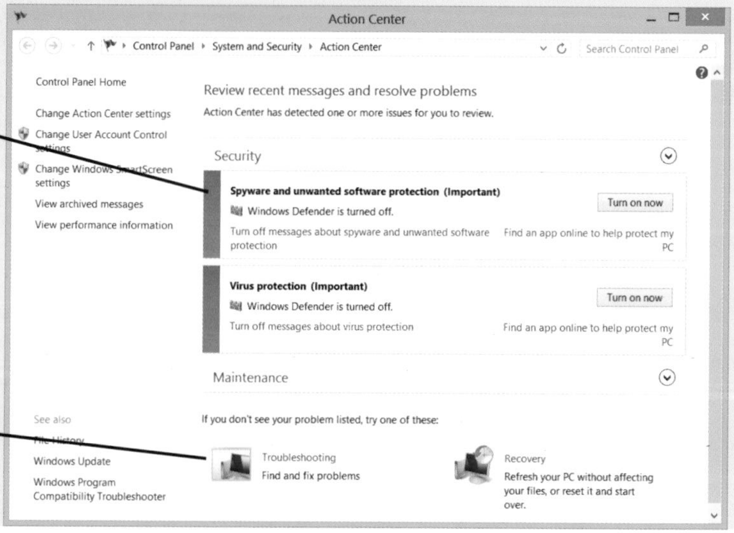

# 7.12 Windows Update

A very important part of the *Action Center* is *Windows Update.* This is a system that checks if you are using the most recent version of *Windows 8. Windows 8* is constantly being modified, expanded and made more secure. The additions and fixes for known security leaks and any (programming) errors are dispersed by *Microsoft* in the form of software *updates*.

**Please note:**

*Microsoft* never sends software updates by e-mail. Anyone who receives an e-mail claiming to contain *Microsoft* software or a *Windows* update is strongly advised not to open the attachment. Immediately delete the e-mail and do not forget to delete this message from the *Deleted* folder too. Such e-mails are sent by criminals who try to install harmful software on your computer.

Open the *Control Panel* again:

**Open the *Control Panel*** 51

If you want to make sure your version of *Windows 8* stays up to date, you should make sure *Automatic Updating* is turned on. This is how you do it:

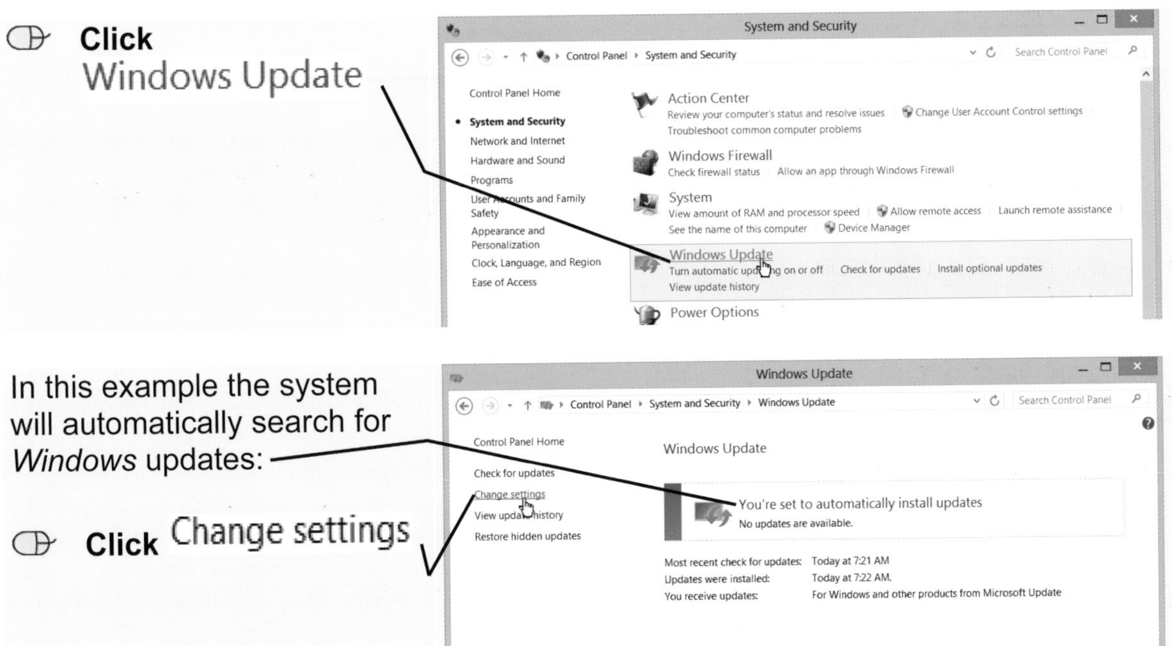

Here you will see your computer's current settings:

Click Updates will be automati

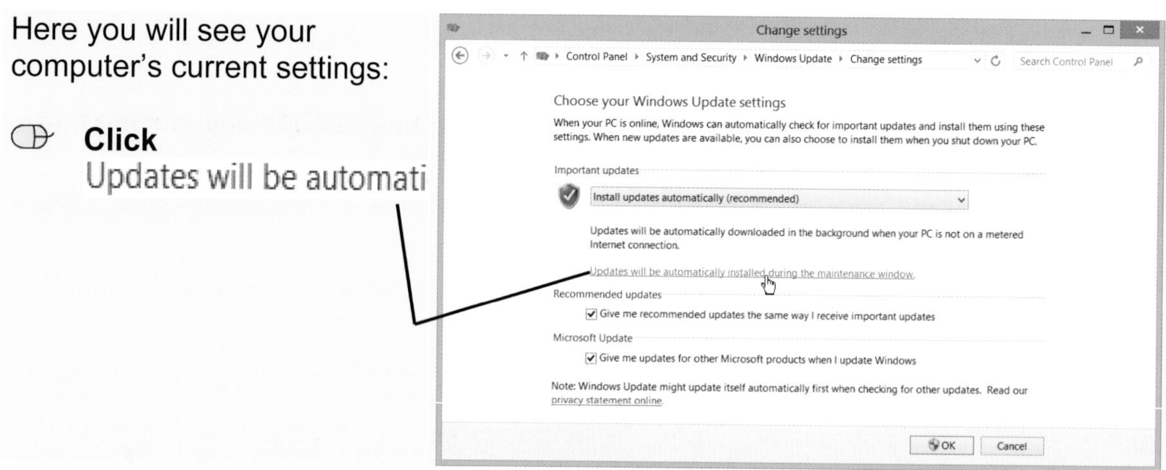


In this example, *Automatic updates* will check for updates every day at 03:00 p.m. If the computer is switched off at that time, the system will check for new updates at startup. The available updates will automatically be downloaded and installed to your computer. *Windows* will usually display a message at the bottom of your desktop, but in most cases you will be able to continue using your computer. In case of major updates it may be necessary to restart your computer.

At the bottom of the window:

Click Cancel

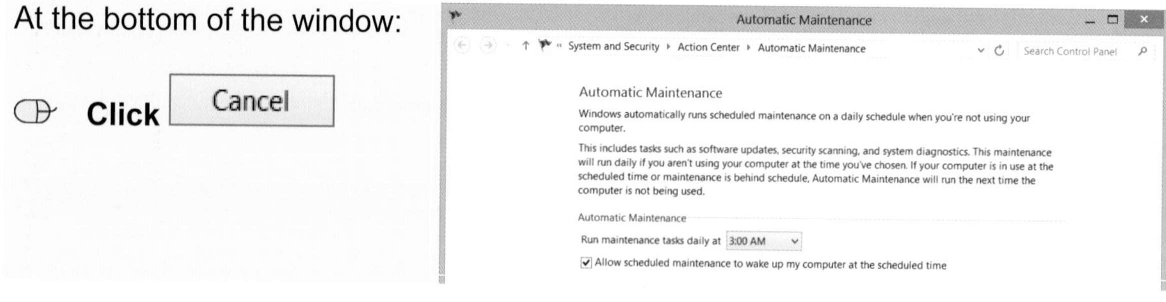


It is a good idea to select the Install updates automatically (recommended) option. You can modify the time settings and select the time you prefer.

If you have modified a setting:

Click OK

If you have not changed anything, you click Cancel.

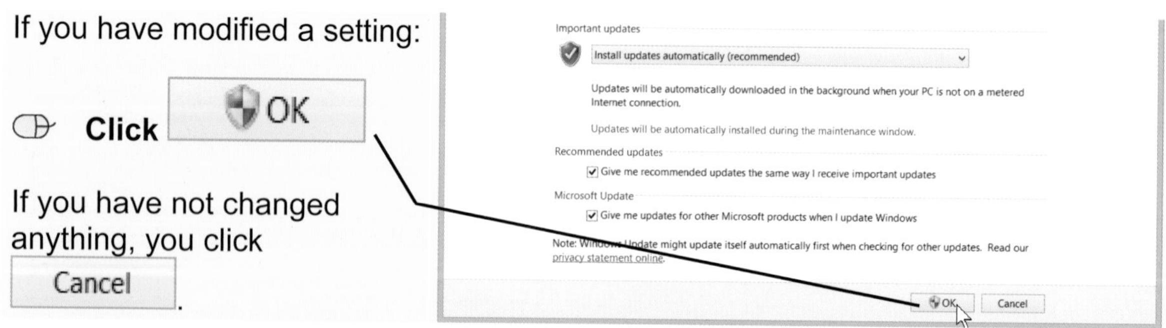


**Close the *Control Panel*** 12

# 7.13 Updating Apps

*Windows Update* will only update your computer's operating system. Sometimes, the individual apps need to be updated too.

You can tell by the number that appears on the *Store* tile on the Start screen:

Maybe you see a different number on your own screen, or there may not be any updates available yet. In this example there are fifteen updates available for various apps:

Click Store 15

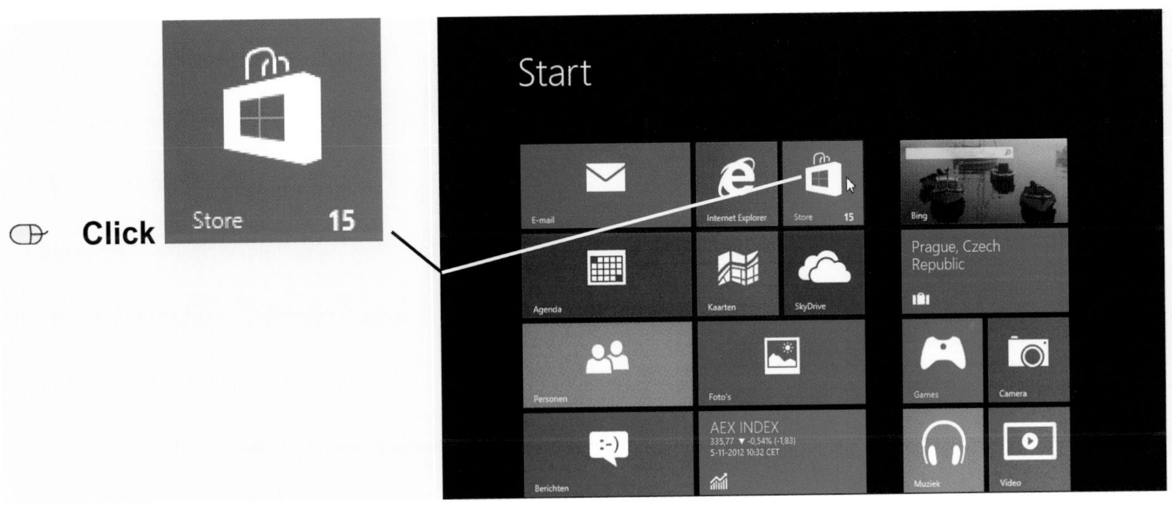


This is how you install the updates:

At the top right of the screen:

Click Updates (15)

You see the apps for which an update is available:

- Click Install

The updates are installed. You will see the progress of the operation:

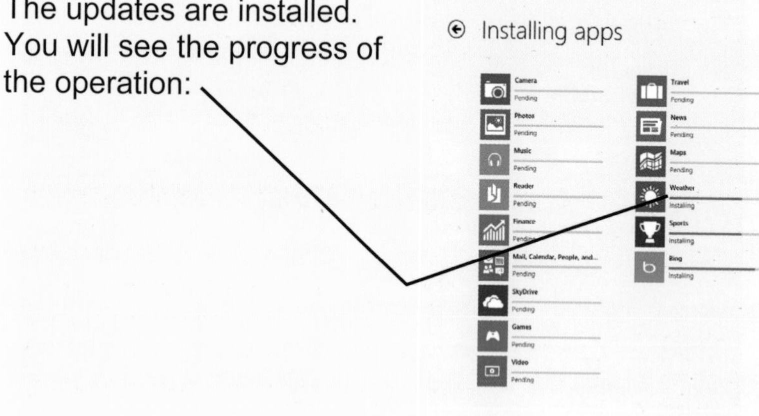


The updates that have been completed will disappear from the screen. After all the updates have been installed you will see this screen:

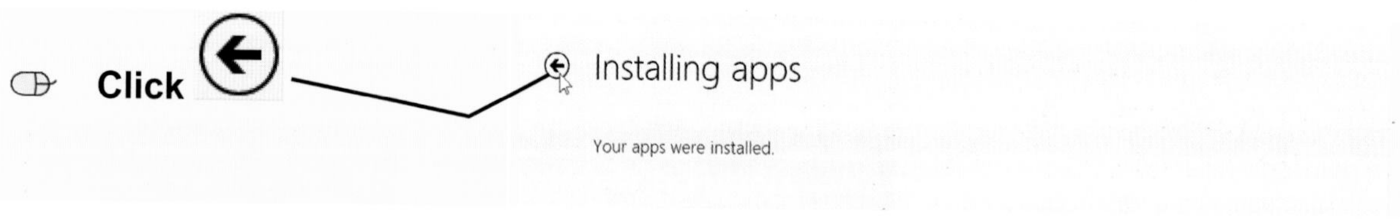


- Click

- **Close the *Store*** 5

# 7.14 Windows Firewall

A *firewall* is software or hardware that checks information coming from the Internet or a network, and then either blocks it or allows it to pass through to your computer, depending on your firewall settings.
The word *firewall* sounds safer than it actually is: a firewall does not protect you against computer viruses. If your e-mail program is allowed access to the internet through your firewall, you can still receive an e-mail with an attachment that contains a virus. This means the firewall does not check the content of the data traffic.

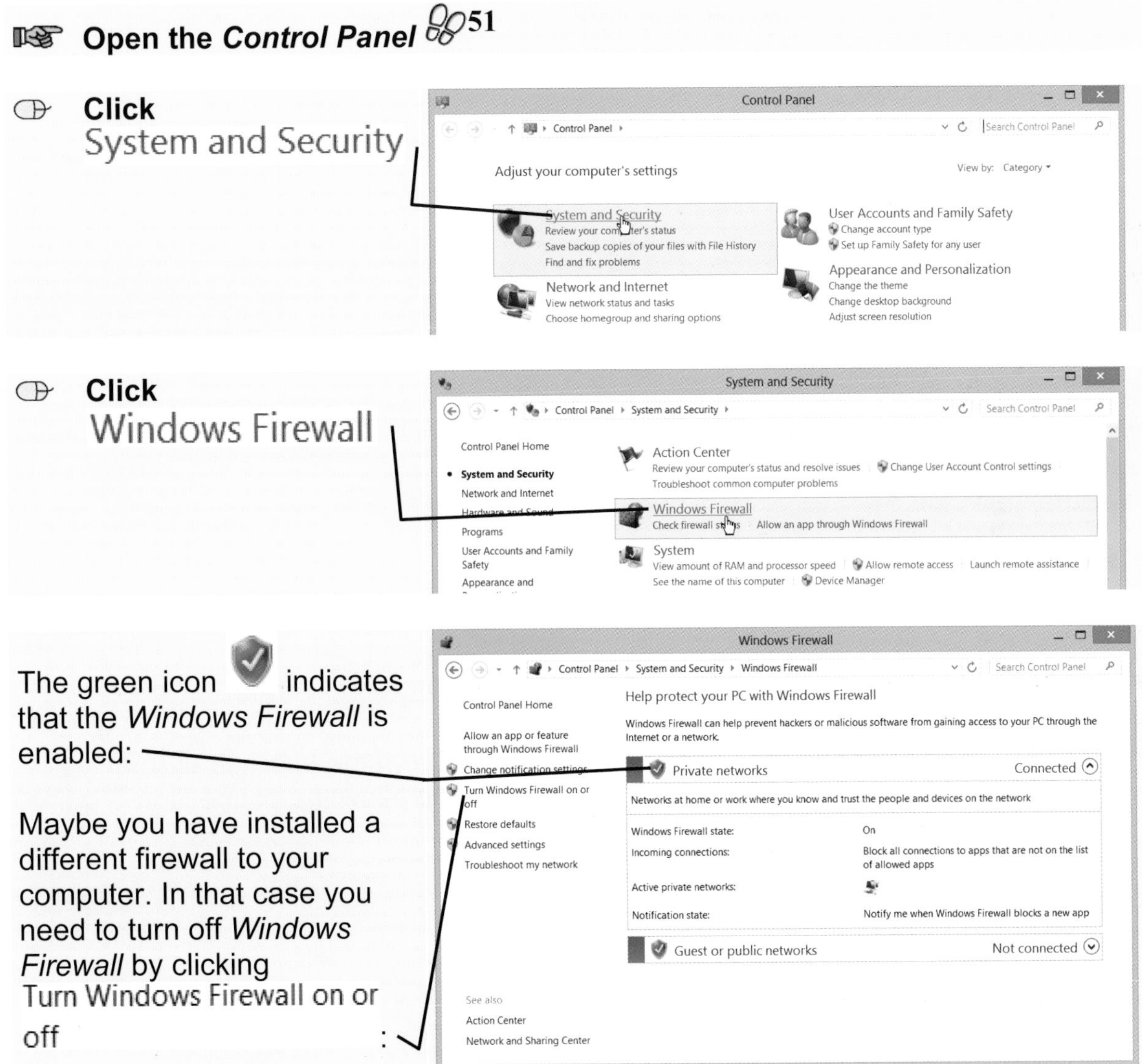

**Open the *Control Panel*** 51

**Click**
System and Security

**Click**
Windows Firewall

The green icon indicates that the *Windows Firewall* is enabled:

Maybe you have installed a different firewall to your computer. In that case you need to turn off *Windows Firewall* by clicking Turn Windows Firewall on or off:

Using two separate firewalls simultaneously will cause problems.

You can also change the settings for the *Windows Firewall*:

**Click** Change notification setti

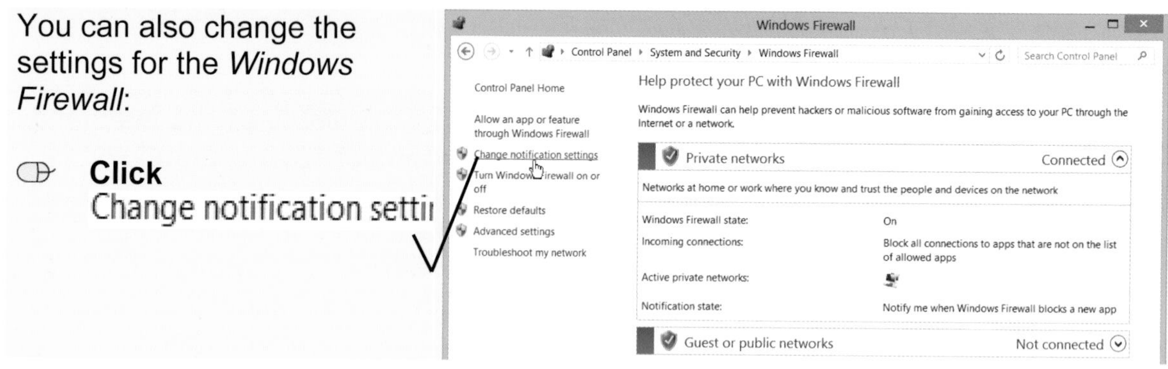


Maybe you need to give permission to continue:

**Give permission**

Now you will see the *Customize Settings* window:

You can turn on a firewall for different types of networks:

You can block all programs, for instance in a public wireless network and you can send a notification for a blocked, new app:

Usually, the default settings will suffice.

**Click** Cancel

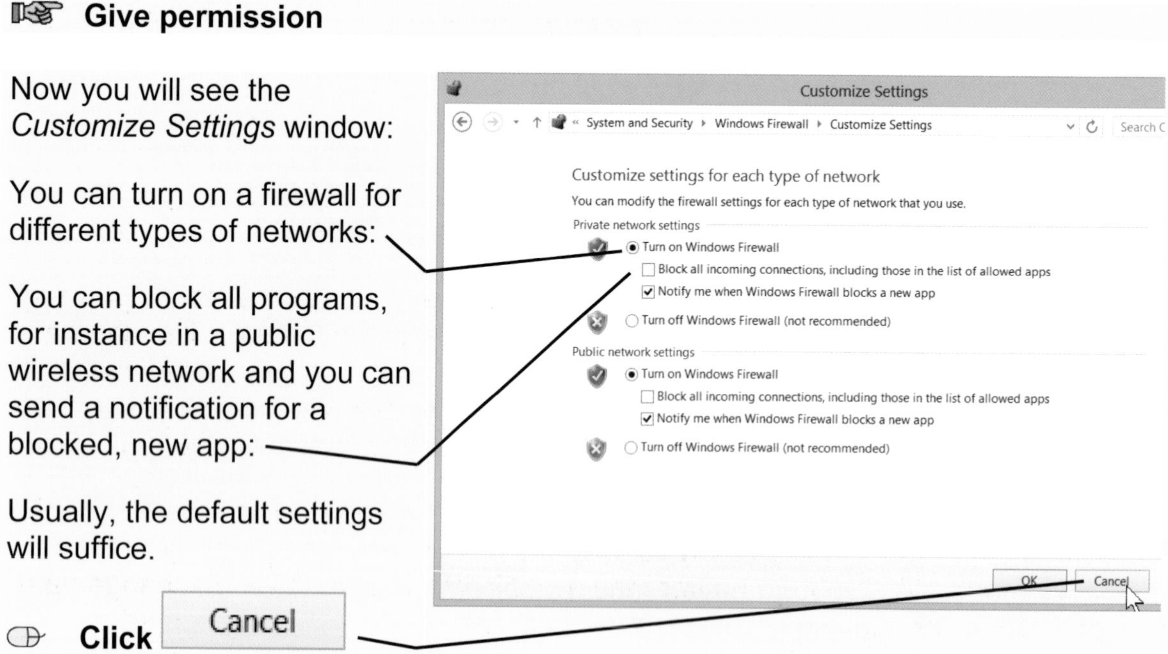


If you are using a program that needs to receive data from the Internet, or from another network, the firewall will ask your permission to allow the connection. You can define the settings in this window:

**Click** Allow an app or feature through Windows Firewall

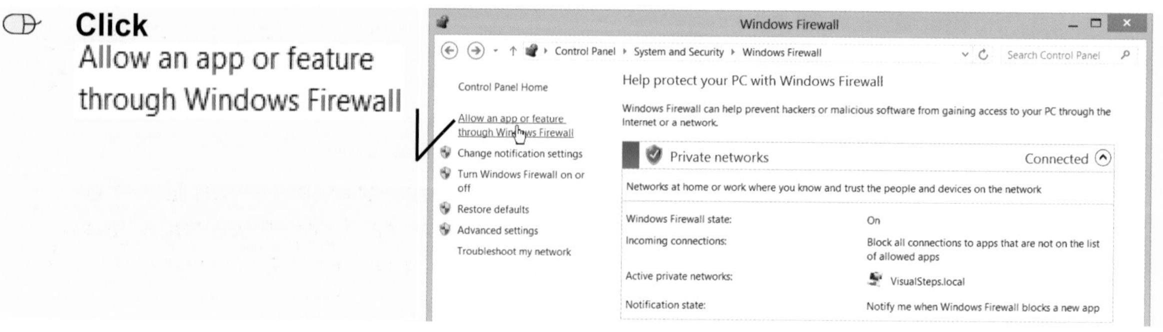

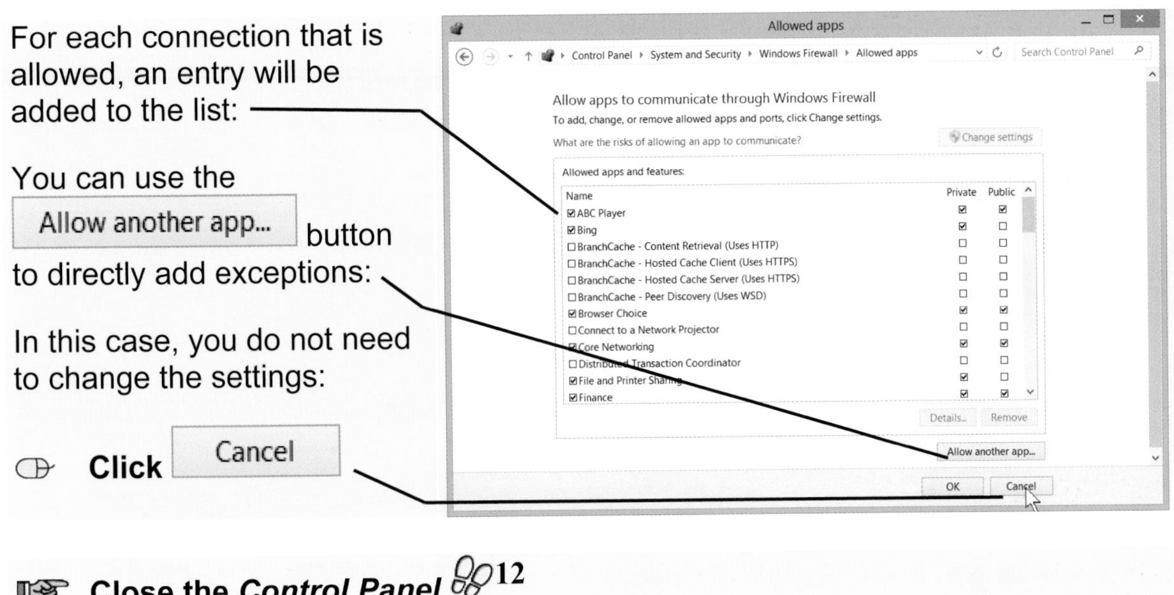


For each connection that is allowed, an entry will be added to the list:

You can use the Allow another app... button to directly add exceptions:

In this case, you do not need to change the settings:

Click Cancel

Close the *Control Panel* 12

## 7.15 Protection from Viruses with Windows Defender

A virus is a well-know term, but actually, viruses are just a part of the rapidly growing threats that can assault any computer that is connected to the Internet. The general term for this kind of software is *malware*. Malware is short for *malicious software*. This is software that is especially developed to damage your computer. Viruses, worms, spyware, and Trojan horses are all examples of unwanted and harmful software.

The computer can be infected by an attachment to an e-mail, or by a program you have downloaded. But your computer may also be infected when you exchange data through USB sticks containing malware, or CDs, DVDs, or other storage media. Some malicious software might just be programmed to be executed on unexpected moments, and not just during installation.
*Windows Defender* comes with *Windows 8* and helps you remove harmful software from your computer, in two ways:

- **Real-time security**
  With *Windows Defender* you are warned if malicious software tries to install itself, or is installed to the computer. And you will also be warned when an app tries to modify important settings.
- **Scan**
  With *Windows Defender* you can scan your computer, whenever you like. For instance, if your computer does not function properly, or if you have received a suspicious-looking e-mail message. In such a case you can run a scan to check whether you have not unintentionally downloaded any malware.

This is how you open *Windows Defender*:

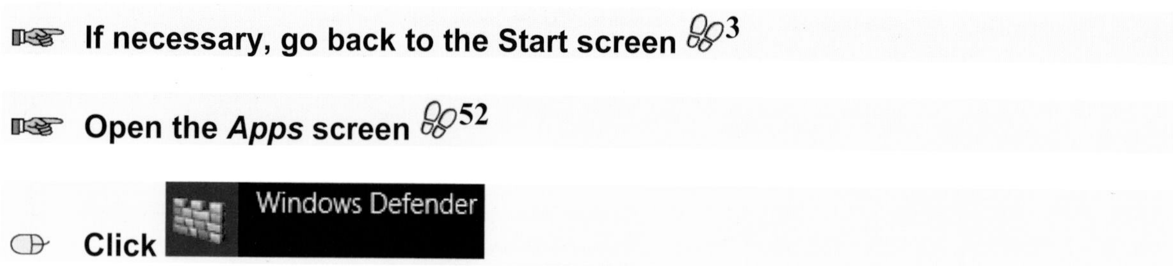

**If necessary, go back to the Start screen** [3]

**Open the *Apps* screen** [52]

**Click** Windows Defender

The *Windows Defender* home screen appears.

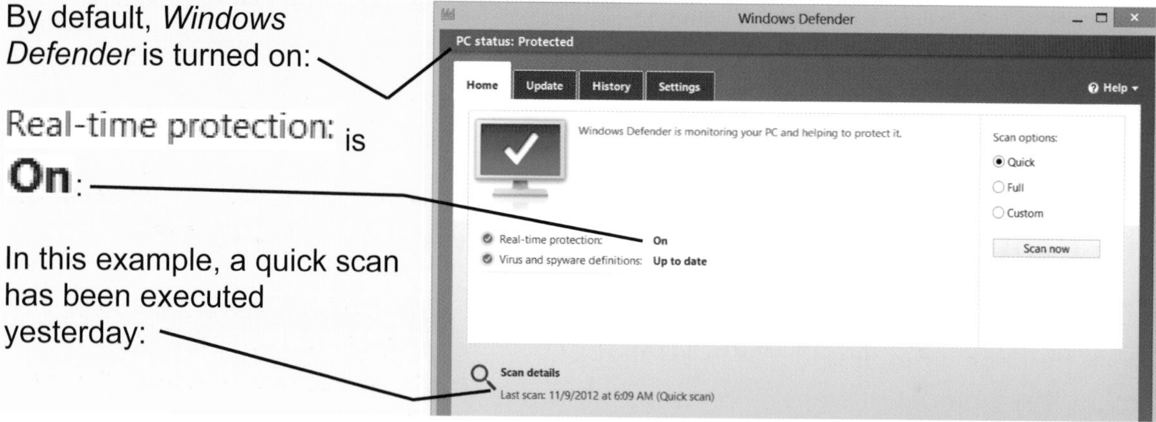


By default, *Windows Defender* is turned on:

Real-time protection: is **On**:

In this example, a quick scan has been executed yesterday:

*Windows Defender* closely cooperates with *Windows Update*. As soon as new spyware and malware definitions are available, these will automatically be downloaded and installed. This way, the program will always be able to use the most current information. By default, the program will run an additional updates check before a scan is executed. You can also update *Windows Defender* yourself:

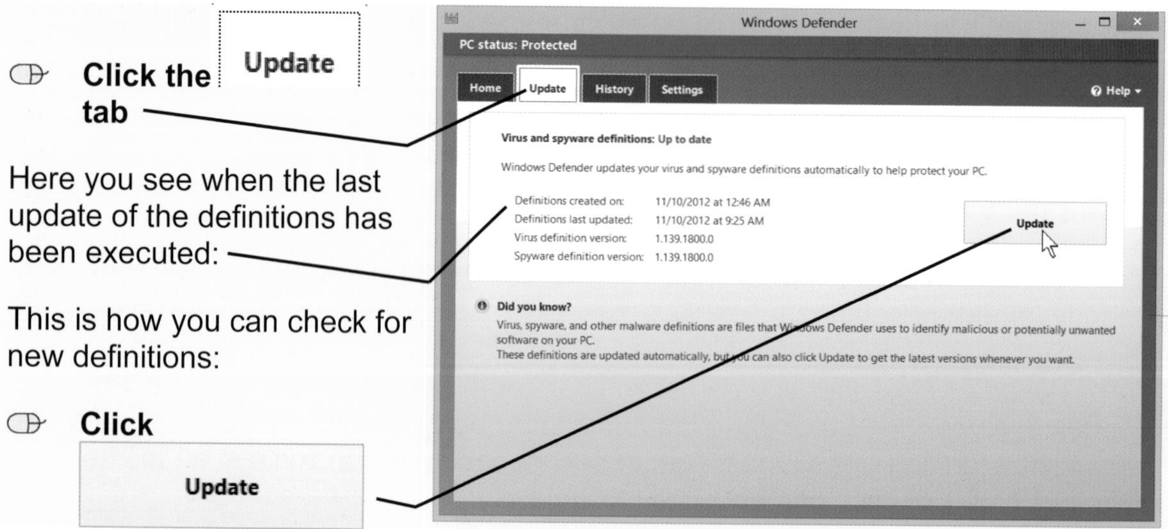


**Click the** Update **tab**

Here you see when the last update of the definitions has been executed:

This is how you can check for new definitions:

**Click** Update

If new definitions have been found, *Windows Defender* will immediately be updated:

In this example you can see the progress of the install process of the new definitions:

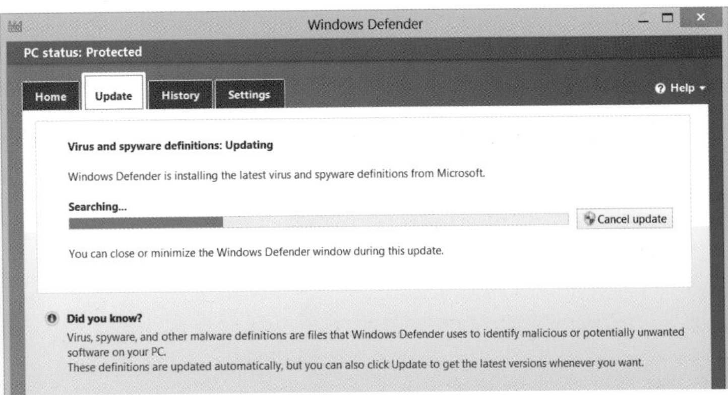


# 7.16 The Real-time Protection of Windows Defender

The real-time protection of *Windows Defender* will warn you immediately, as soon as it detects spyware or malware that is trying to install itself on your computer.

As soon as *Windows Defender* detects harmful software, you will see a message in the upper right-hand corner of the screen. The harmful software is immediately placed in quarantine, so it cannot be executed. You can take a look at it later on, to decide whether you want to delete or restore the item. This is how you do it:

To protect the privacy of the user, you will not immediately see which items have been placed in quarantine:

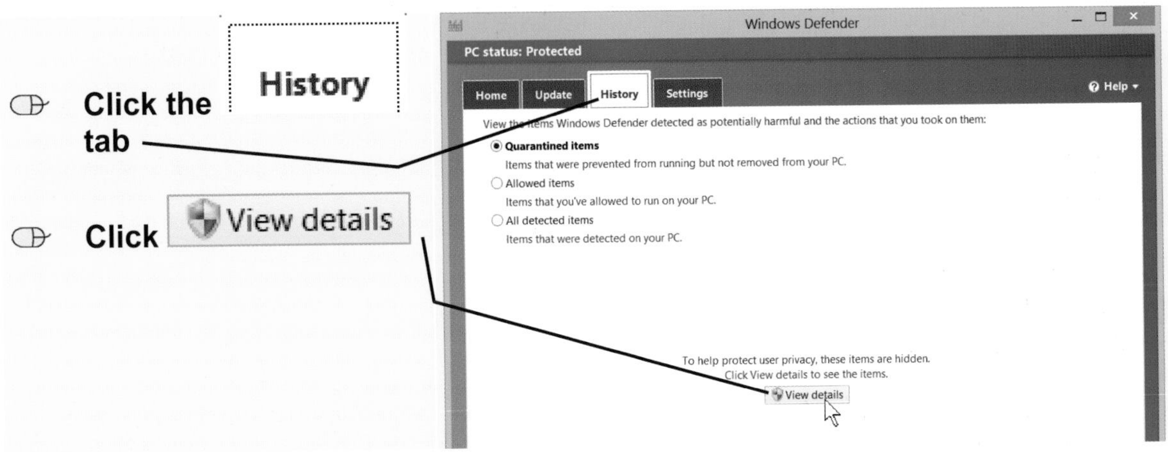


Maybe you need to give permission to continue:

**Give permission to continue**

You will see an overview of the items that have automatically been placed in quarantine. In the next section you can read more about quarantine. Possibly the list on your own computer is empty.

If this list contains an item you know not to be harmful, you can check the box next to it and restore the item by clicking the Restore button:

This is how you delete everything:

Click Remove all

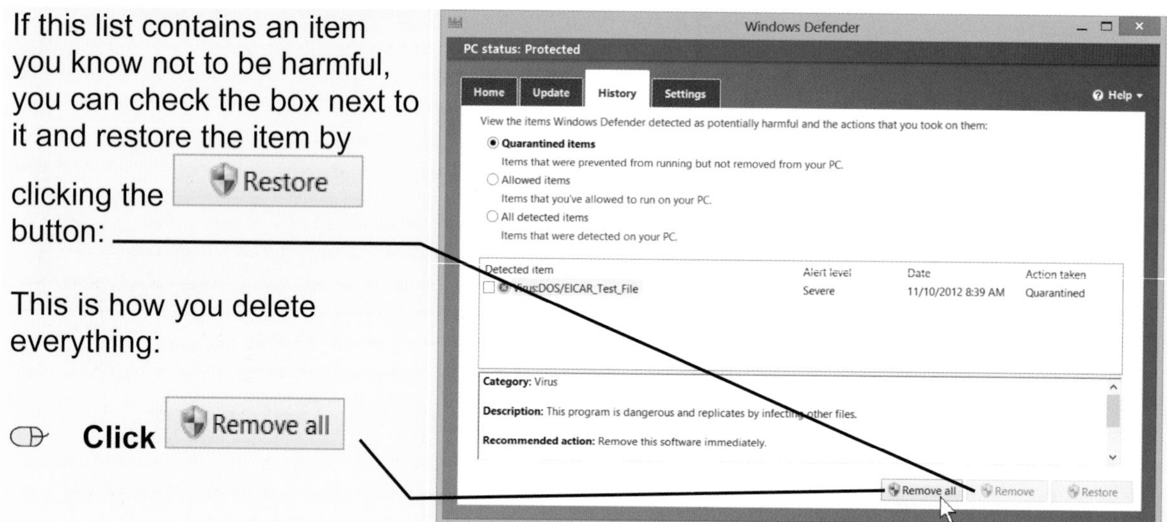


Now all harmful software has been removed.

## 7.17 Scanning Your Computer with Windows Defender

You can scan your computer with *Windows Defender* whenever you want. For example, if your computer does not work properly, or if you have received a suspicious-looking e-mail message. In order to be sure that your computer has not been infected by a virus or other unwanted software, you can execute a scan of your computer.

You can choose between three scan types:

- Quick: only scans the locations where unwanted software is often found.
- Full: scans all files and folders on your computer.
- Custom: only scans the folders you specify.

To get an idea of how a scan works, you are going to execute a quick scan.

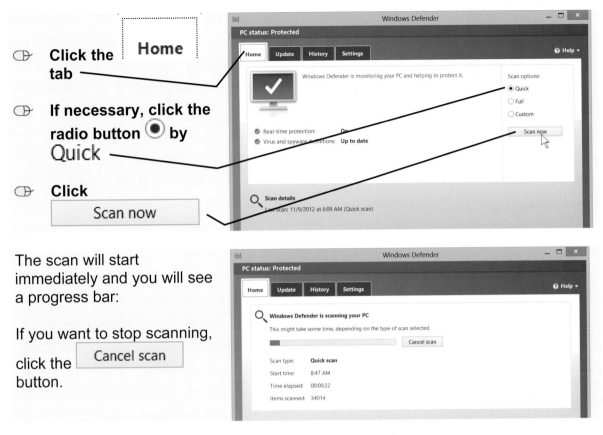

- **Click the Home tab**
- **If necessary, click the radio button ◉ by Quick**
- **Click Scan now**

The scan will start immediately and you will see a progress bar:

If you want to stop scanning, click the Cancel scan button.

A full scan may take fifteen minutes, or up to half an hour, depending on the speed of your computer and on the number of files. The quick scan is much faster.

After the scan has finished you will see a scan report.

In this example no suspicious files have been found:

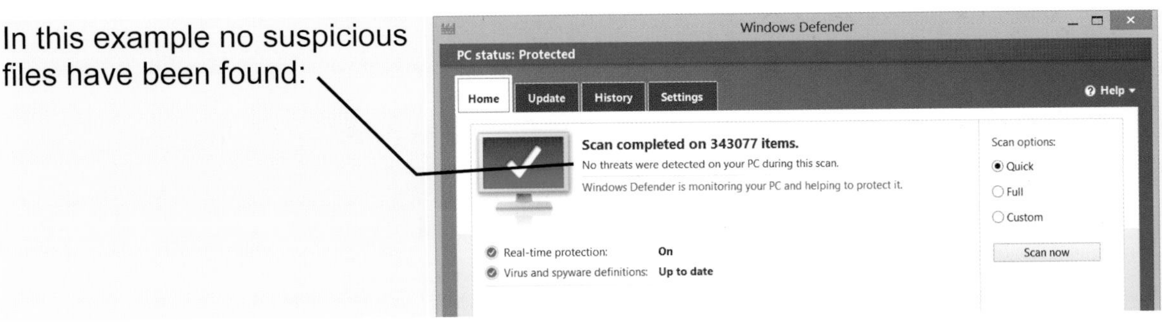


If you do not open unknown e-mail attachments or use suspect programs, there is a small chance that any unwanted programs will end up on your computer. However, *Windows Defender* will still find a suspect file once in a while.

If something is found, you will see a message. You will see a description of the harmful software, information on how serious the threat is, and the advice of *Windows Defender* on how to proceed.

There are several possible options:

- Remove: the infected file or virus is removed from your computer. This means the content of the file will be lost if you do not have a backup copy. This is the usual action if there is no other solution to the problem.
- Quarantine: the item is stored in a folder where it cannot do any damage. If you appear to need this item after all, you can restore it. Select this option if you are not sure about an item.
- Allow: this item will no longer be shown in future scans. Select this option if you are familiar with the item and you are sure you want to keep it.

If no suspicious files have been found on your computer, you can just read through the next part of this section.

If a harmful program has been found, you will see this window:

You can view the details:

**Click** Show details

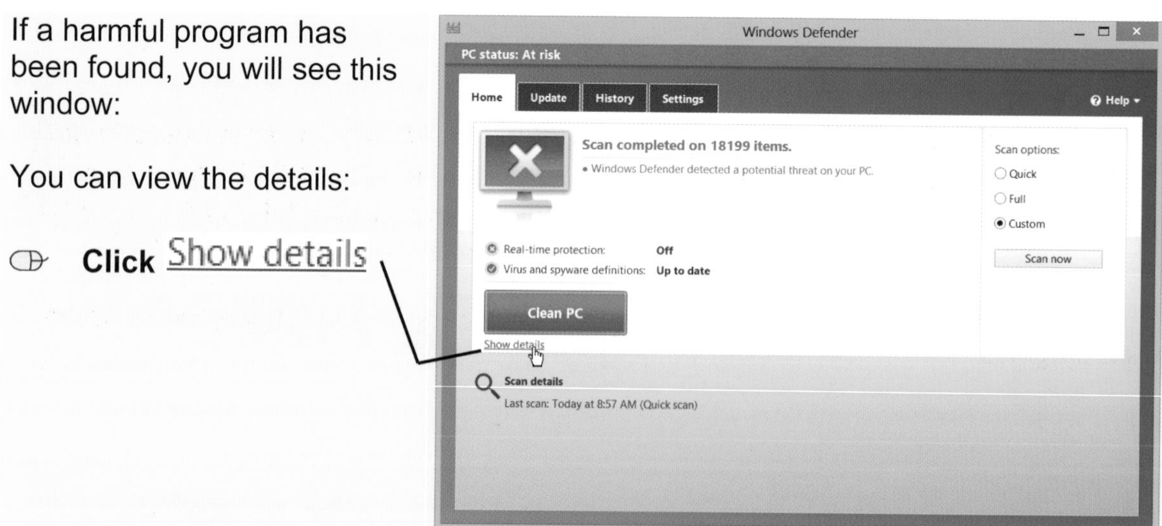


*Windows Defender* advises to Remove the file:

This is how you do it:

**Click** Apply actions

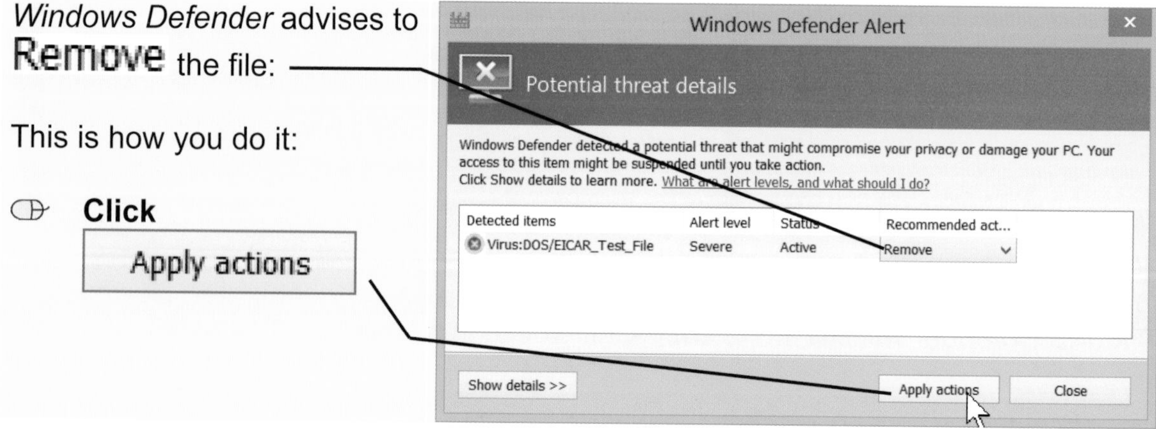

The computer will be cleaned up.

You can close the window:

**Click** Close

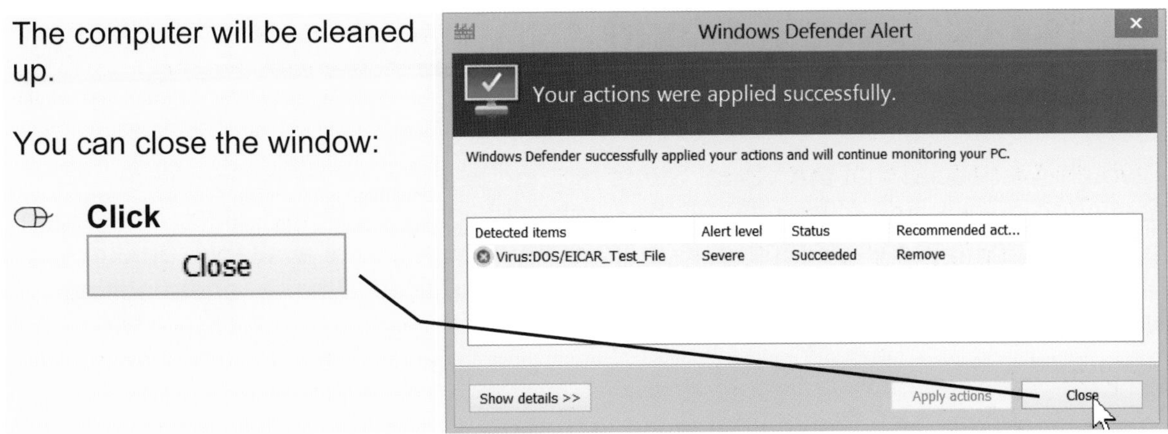


You have learned to know some of the options of the program. Now you can close *Windows Defender*:

**Close *Windows Defender*** 12

## Tip

**Make regular back-ups**

Your computer is filled with files that are important to you, such as precious photos, e-mail messages of family and friends, important documents, the addresses of your favorite websites, and addresses of your contacts. Surely, you would hate to lose all these files, even part of them, because of a virus or other computer problems? Create a back-up of your files from time to time.

Although *Windows Defender* offers good protection against viruses, it is better to be safe than sorry.

## 7.18 The Visual Steps Website, Newsletter, and Follow-Up Books

So you have noticed that the Visual Steps method is a great method to gather knowledge quickly and efficiently. All the books published by Visual Steps have been written according to this method. There are quite a lot of books available, on different subjects. For instance about *Windows*, *Mac OS X*, the iPad, iPhone, photo editing, video editing, *Facebook* and several other topics.

**Website**
Use the blue *Catalog* button on the **www.visualsteps.com** website to read an extensive description of all available Visual Steps titles, including the full table of contents and part of a chapter (as a PDF file). In this way you can find out if the book is what you expected.

This instructive website also contains:
- free computer booklets and informative guides (PDF files) on a range of subjects;
- separate web pages with information on photo and video editing;
- a large number of frequently asked questions and their answers;
- information on the free *Computer certificate* you can obtain on the online test website **www.ccforseniors.com**;
- free 'Notify me' e-mail service: receive an e-mail when books of interest are published.

**Visual Steps Newsletter**
Do you want to keep yourself informed of all Visual Steps publications? Then subscribe (no strings attached) to the free Visual Steps Newsletter, which is sent by e-mail.

This Newsletter is issued once a month and provides you with information on:
- the latest titles, as well as older books;
- special offers;
- new, free computer booklets and guides.
- contests and questionnaires with which you can win nice prizes.

As a subscriber to the Visual Steps Newsletter you have direct access to the free booklets and guides, at **www.visualsteps.com/info_downloads**

With this book you have acquired the basic skills for working with the Internet and e-mail on a computer with *Windows 8* installed, and you have learned how to use the *Internet Explorer* and *Mail* apps, among others.
But you can learn much more. Visual Steps offers various titles in the *Windows 8 for Seniors* series, but apart from that there are countless books to be read in the other series.
And remember this: almost every Visual Steps book has been written according to the same step-by-step method, with accompanying screenshots. If you can work with a book written for seniors, you will also manage to work with nearly all the other books published by Visual Steps.

For more information on these and other books, visit **www.visualsteps.com**

The **Internet and E-mail for Seniors with Windows 8** book has taken you through all the Internet features. Now you can download software, personalize your e-mail, send, receive, open and save attachments. Interested in gaining more skills? Try the following Visual Steps books in the SENIORS series:

**Windows 8 for SENIORS**

*For senior citizens who want to start using the computer*

ISBN 978 90 5905 118 8
**www.visualsteps.com/windows8**

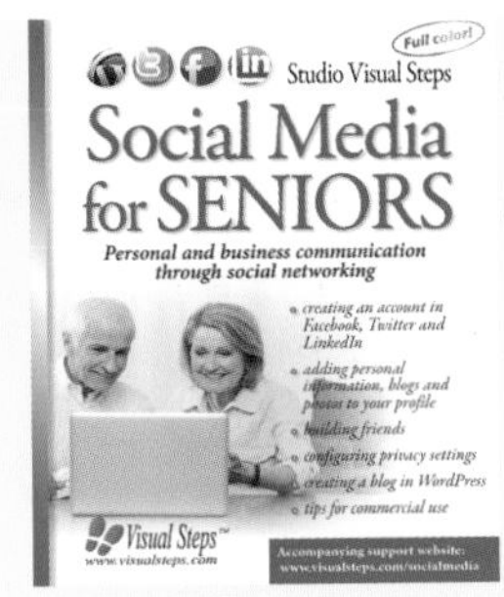


**Social Media for SENIORS**

*Personal and business communication through social networking*

ISBN 978 90 5905 018 1
**www.visualsteps.com/socialmedia**

**Google for SENIORS**

*Get Acquainted with free Google Applications*

ISBN 978 90 5905 236 9
**www.visualsteps.com/google**

**Picasa for SENIORS**

*Get Acquainted with Picasa: Free, Easy-to-Use Photo Editing Software*

ISBN 978 90 5905 246 8
**www.visualsteps.com/picasa**

If you would like to know more about these books, please visit our website, **www.visualsteps.com**

## 7.19 Background Information

**Dictionary**

| | |
|---|---|
| **Action Center** | System that checks your computer's security settings and keeps track of updates to *Windows 8*. |
| **Add-on** | A program that adds extra functionality to a web browser, such as *Internet Explorer*. |
| **Browser History** | The traces you leave on your computer when you browse the Internet. In *Internet Explorer*, the complete browsing *History* consists of the temporary Internet files, cookies, *History*, form data and passwords. |
| **Cookies** | Small text files that are placed on your hard drive by the websites you visit while you surf the Internet. |
| **Custom scan** | Option in *Windows Defender* to scan only the folders you specify yourself. |
| **Firewall** | Software or hardware that checks information coming from the Internet or a network, and then either blocks it or allows it to pass through to your computer, depending on your firewall settings. |
| **First-party cookies** | Cookies that come from the website you are viewing at that moment. They can be permanent or temporary. Websites can use these cookies to store information they can use when you visit the site the next time. |
| **Form data** | Information that you have entered in forms on websites, or typed in the address bar. |
| **Full scan** | Option in *Windows Defender* to scan all files and folders on your computer. |
| **Https://** | This prefix denotes a secure (encrypted) Internet connection. |
| **Junk e-mail** | Unsolicited commercial e-mail. Also known as *spam*. |

*- Continue on the next page -*

| | |
|---|---|
| **Malware** | Short for *malicious software*; software that is designed to deliberately harm your computer. Viruses, worms, spyware and Trojan horses are examples of malware. |
| **Permanent cookies** | Cookies that are stored on your hard drive, to be read by the website that created it when you visit that site again. These cookies make sure you can open the website much quicker, if you have visited it once before. |
| **Phishing** | Online phishing is a way to trick computer users into revealing personal or financial information through a fraudulent e-mail message or an innocent looking website. Often the online method of phishing starts with an e-mail message that appears to be sent by a trusted source. The recipients are coerced into disclosing personal information, on a fake website.<br>A new method of phishing starts with a phone call by a so-called bank employee, by someone from the non-existing 'Windows Maintenance Team', or from some other seemingly official institution. This person will try to gain access to your computer, or to get you to disclose personal information. |
| **Pop-up** | A pop-up is a small web browser window that appears on top of the website you are viewing. Pop-up windows often open as soon as you visit a website and are usually created by advertisers. |
| **Pop-up blocker** | A feature in *Internet Explorer* that lets you limit or block most pop-ups. |
| **Quick Scan** | Option in *Windows Defender*. By running this scan, only the locations where malware is often found are scanned. |
| **Real-time security** | This function makes sure that *Windows Defender* will constantly monitor all the activities while you surf the Internet. Any attempts at installing malware to your computer will be blocked. |
| **SmartScreen filter** | In *Internet Explorer*, the *SmartScreen Filter* helps detect phishing websites. If the site you are visiting is on the list of reported phishing websites, *Internet Explorer* will display a warning webpage and a notification on the address bar. |
| **Spam** | Unsolicited commercial e-mail. Also known as junk e-mail. |

*- Continue on the next page -*

| | |
|---|---|
| **Spyware** | Malicious software that can display advertisements (such as pop-up ads), collect information about you, or change settings on your computer, generally without appropriately obtaining your consent. |
| **Temporary cookies** | Cookies that are removed when *Internet Explorer* is closed. Also known as session cookies. Websites use these cookies to store temporary data. For example, the items you have put in your shopping basket in a web shop. |
| **Temporary Internet files** | When you view a web page, *Internet Explorer* saves a temporary copy of that page; this way, the page can be displayed more quickly if you open it again later, since the page can now be opened from the hard disk. |
| **Third-party cookies** | Indirect cookies that come from pop-up windows or banner ads on the website you are currently visiting. |
| **Trojan horse** | Program that contains or installs a malicious program. The program may appear to be harmless, useful or interesting, but is actually harmful when executed. |
| **Unwanted software** | Programs that are designed to harm your computer. |
| **Virus** | A program that attempts to spread from computer to computer and either cause damage (by erasing or corrupting data) or annoy users (by displaying messages or changing the information on the screen). |
| **Windows Defender** | Complete solution for your Internet Security, packaged with *Windows 8*. The program protects your computer against all sorts of malware, such as viruses and spyware. |
| **Windows Update** | System that checks if you are using the most recent version of *Windows 8*. |
| **Worm** | Malware in the form of a self-replicating program, just like a virus. By using a worm, criminals can take over your computer, for example. |

*Source: Windows Help and Support*

**Safe surfing**

In this chapter you have taken a look at various security settings in *Windows 8.* But remember, your own actions play a very large part in your security.

Here is a summary of things you can do to avoid mishaps:

- Always make sure that *Windows Defender* or another good antivirus and antispyware program is up-to-date and enabled.
- Always make sure that *Windows Firewall* or another good firewall is installed and enabled.
- Always make sure that *Windows* and the installed apps are up-to-date.
- Have *Windows Defender* or your other antivirus and antispyware programs scan your computer regularly.
- If something strange happens while you are surfing, break the connection immediately. In the *Tip Disconnecting from the Internet* you can read how to do this.
- If you do not need access to the Internet for a longer period of time, break your connection. This reduces the chance that others can break into your computer.
- Protect yourself from pop-ups, junk mail and phishing attempts by using the measures discussed in this chapter.
- Download files and programs from trustworthy websites only.
- Enter as little personal data as possible on websites.
- Do not click hyperlinks in e-mails and chat messages sent by strangers, and do not click suspicious links. Visit websites by typing the well-known address in *Internet Explorer's* address bar.
- Pay attention to the address and safety features of the website when you are doing your online banking or when you are buying something. The address (URL) should be exactly the name you expect and start with https://. Do not enter credit card or bank information, PIN codes or passwords unless you are absolutely sure you are on a secure website.
- Be careful when entering your e-mail address on websites. Some websites try to gather e-mail addresses to be able to flood them with spam later. It is a good idea to create an extra e-mail account with a free provider like *Hotmail* or *Gmail* for use on the Internet. Use that e-mail address to register on websites for example. If this address attracts a lot of spam you can always use a different address later on.

**Safe e-mail behavior**

A regular e-mail message containing only text is not a big risk. But attachments to e-mail messages can be dangerous. Fortunately, different types of potentially dangerous attachments are already blocked by the real-time protection of *Windows Defender*. But it is still very important that you carefully examine every message before you open it.

Pay attention to these points:

- Always make sure that *Windows Defender* or another good antivirus program is up-to-date and enabled.
- Curiosity killed the cat! Never open unfamiliar messages or messages from unknown senders. Delete them immediately.
- Do not click hyperlinks in e-mails sent by strangers.
- Does the message contain an attachment with a strange name or of a strange type? Do not be curious: delete it right away.
- Does the subject of the message seem familiar? Viruses sometimes use old messages and send them to random addresses in the address book on the infected computer. If you think it is an old message, or a message that is not meant for you, delete it immediately. You can also contact the sender by phone first and check if he actually sent the message.
- Does the message offer you spectacular offers, prizes or wonder drugs? Do not respond to the message or click on an *unsubscribe* link. By doing that, you confirm to the sender that your e-mail address is real. This will result in even more spam.
- Not every phishing message is caught by the *SmartScreen filter*. Never respond to messages from banks, credit card companies or online shops that ask you for confidential financial information. Remember, these e-mail messages and the websites they link to can resemble the real website very closely. Your bank will never ask you for your password or PIN code through e-mail. Call the company or organization, if you have doubts about a message.
- Regularly check your bank and credit card statements.
- Remember that deleted e-mail messages are stored in the *Deleted* folder. This folder should be emptied from time to time.

On your bank's website, and on websites such as www.microsoft.com you can find more information on phishing and well-known phishing methods.

## Hoaxes and Chain Letters

*Hoaxes* and *chain letters* are e-mail messages written with one purpose: to be sent to everyone you know. The messages they contain are usually untrue.

Hoaxes are usually e-mails that warn of virus threats. Sometimes these e-mails give detailed descriptions of how you can detect and remove a particular virus file from your hard drive. Often these are *Windows* system files. If you were to follow these instructions, *Windows* would no longer function properly. Other e-mails warn about e-mails with attachments that are sent out. Never carry out the instructions and never forward these virus hoax e-mails to others.

This is an example of such a hoax:

*Subject: IMPORTANT-VIRUS ALERT!!!*
*Hi everybody, I just wanted to let you know you should check your computers by following the procedure that's next... I don't remember getting an e-mail with that file attachment, but I found it in my system. Since I found the dumb little bear in my computer, I'm sending you the info. The virus is called jdbgmgr.exe and it transfers automatically through Messenger and also through your address book and since I have all of you in my address book I have to send everyone this info. I'm sorry if this causes any problems. It certainly wasn't intentional. The virus isn't detected by McAfee or Norton and it remains in the folder for 14 days before activating and harming the system. It can be erased before it eliminates the files in your computer. To do so, follow these steps: (...) If you find this virus in your computer, please send this message to all the people in your address book before it causes any damage.*

Other hoax messages contain stories about someone who is sick or needs your help. By sending the message to other people, money is supposedly raised to help this person. These messages are always untrue.

Chain letters have the same purpose as hoaxes. These messages generally offer money or good luck to anyone who passes the message on. And of course, bad luck if you refuse to do that. Chain letters are often used to collect e-mail addresses and sell them to commercial organizations.

You usually receive a hoax or a chain letter from a friend or an acquaintance. That will make you more inclined to believe the story. You should always do some research to find out whether the information in the e-mail is correct. A good source of information is hoaxbusters.ciac.org. On this website you find an index of known hoaxes. You can search the database with a few keywords from the suspected hoax message you have received.

Always let the person who sent you the hoax know that it is a fake virus warning or a fake story and point him or her to this website.

**Shopping and paying on the Internet**

As with any other type of financial transaction, buyers and sellers on the Internet demand a secure, reliable and fraud-free transaction. The customer wants to be sure he gets what he has paid for and in turn the merchant wants to make sure he gets paid. The merchant will request information from the customer. He needs to know where the order should be sent and where he can recover his losses if anything goes wrong.

To help consumers, a company called *ShopSafe* has developed online directories that list companies worldwide that practice "safe shopping". ShopSafe independently reviews the companies and lists only those that meet its criteria for safe shopping.

**How can I pay online?**

- **Credit Card or Bank Debit Card**
  You provide the online merchant with your credit or debit card data.
- **Check or Money Order**
  You place your order online, then send your paper check or money order by regular mail to the address listed on the merchant's website.
- **Electronic Funds Transfer or Electronic Check**
  You provide the online merchant with your bank account number and routing number, and authorize him to deduct the funds directly from your account.
- **PayPal**
  This is an increasingly popular alternative for individuals and small businesses accepting payments over the Internet.
- **C.O.D.**
  You place your order online and pay the delivery person at the door when you receive it. Many merchants no longer accept this kind of payment.

# 7.20 Tips

 **Tip**

**Other antivirus software**
*Windows Defender* is integrated in *Windows 8* and offers real-time protection against viruses, spyware, and other malicious software. But of course there are other good antivirus programs available on the market.
The most widely known programs are *Norton* and *McAfee*. But lesser known programs such as *Norman* or *Panda* also perform very well. These programs offer free downloads for a 15, 30 or 60-day trial period.
For more information check these websites:

- *McAfee*: us.mcafee.com
- *Norton*: shop.symantecstore.com
- *Norman*: www.norman.com
- *Panda*: www.pandasoftware.com

 **Tip**

**Recognizing a secure website**
When you buy something on the Internet, you should always check if you are on a secure website before you enter your credit card details.
The most important difference between a secured and an unsecured website is that on a secured website information is transferred using encryption technology. The user enters his or her data, such as a credit card number. This information is encrypted using special software and then transferred to the seller, who decrypts the information. Only specially authorized parties are capable of doing so. This way you can prevent hackers from stealing and using the information when it is sent over the Internet.

The easiest and fastest way of recognizing a secure website is by means of the website address. When this starts with “https://” rather than simply "http://", you are on a secure website. The extra “s” stands for “secure”. Here you see an example:

Another sign is the small padlock icon which will be shown in the address bar as soon as you enter the website. If this icon is missing, then the chances are that the website is probably unsecured. Only enter your personal data and credit card information if you are absolutely sure you are visiting a secure website that guarantees safe methods of communication.

**Please note:** many websites have both secured and unsecured areas. For example, when you are looking for a book on www.amazon.com, the pages are unsecured. As soon as you log in to order and pay the book, you are directed to a secure area.

## Tip

**Disconnecting from the Internet**

If something strange happens while you surf the Internet, it is wise to break the connection immediately. This is how you do it if you have a wireless connection:

On the desktop:

- **Click** (wireless network icon)

You will see an overview of the wireless networks in your neighborhood:

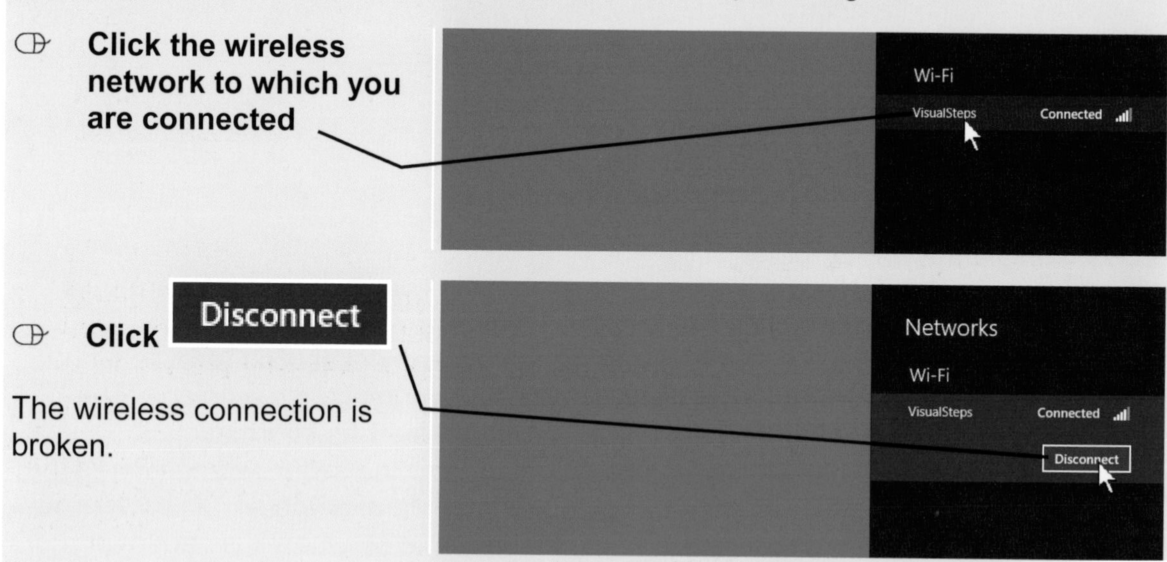


- **Click the wireless network to which you are connected**

- **Click** Disconnect

The wireless connection is broken.

If you are using a wired Internet connection, then you break the connection like this:

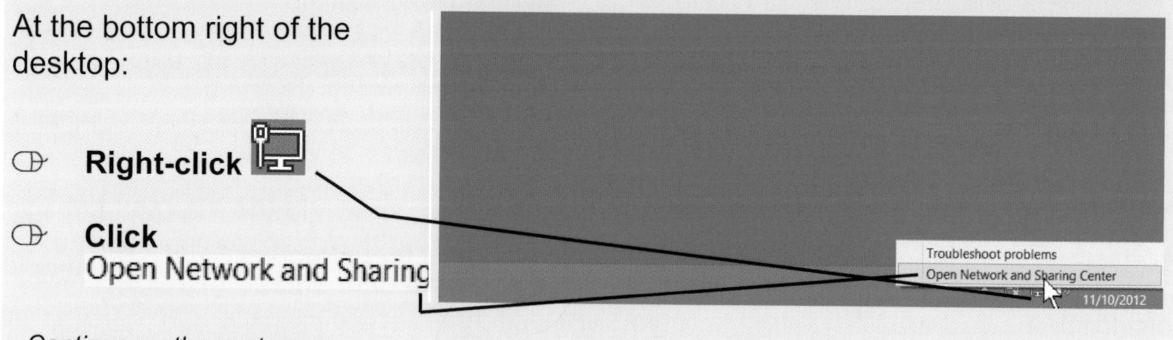


At the bottom right of the desktop:

- **Right-click** (network icon)
- **Click** Open Network and Sharing

- *Continue on the next page* –

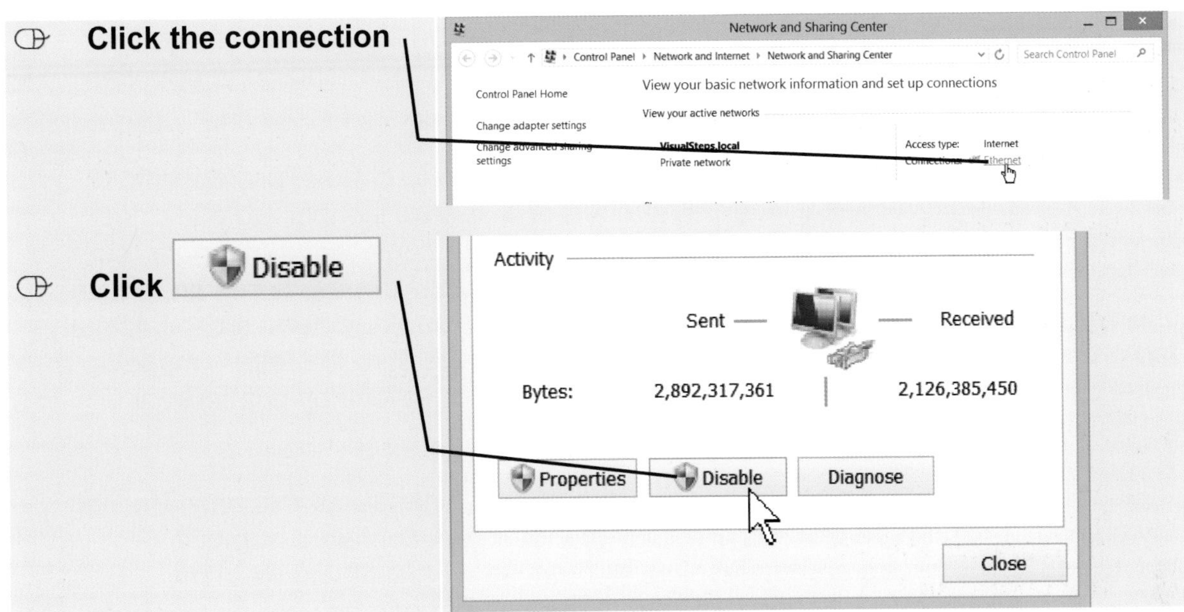

Click the connection

Click Disable

## Tip

**User names and passwords**

If you regularly surf the Internet, you will notice that many services require a user name and a password. For example, if you want to order or buy something, if you want to play online games, or if you want to comment on a message posted on a forum or news site.

Usually, you enter your e-mail address and a user name:

When creating the account, pay attention if there are any messages regarding the Privacy Notice of the website:

If you look at the privacy statements, check whether the owner of the website reserves the right to supply third parties with your e-mail address.

Make sure not to use the exact same combination of e-mail address and password on all the other sites. It is better to use multiple (free) e-mail addresses I you need to create online accounts.

*- Continue on the next page -*

If you use strong passwords, you will be better protected against hackers and malicious software. This way, you can safely surf the Internet and do your online shopping.

Unfortunately, many online services do not require you to choose any specific or difficult passwords. A capital letter, a number, or a special symbol are often not required. It is very tempting to choose a password you can easily remember, such as your grandchild's name, or your birthday. These types of passwords are unsafe. It is better to choose a password that consists of letters and numbers, a capital letter, and preferably some special character too, and to make sure the letters make up a non-existent word. Such a password is very difficult to retrieve by criminals or special password-breaking programs.

A password can be safe and still easy to remember. What about this one: Mccnbc (My computer cannot be cracked)? Although it does not contain a number.
Or Iywmg82! The letters are the first letters of these words: 'If you were my girlfriend', a well-known hit song by Prince. The number can be your former home number, for instance. And at the end you add a special character, such as an exclamation mark, for instance. Of course you can also change the order of the characters by putting the numbers or the exclamation mark in the middle of the letters. The longer the password is, the safer it becomes.

Fortunately, there are some online services that require your password to be strong and safe. As soon as you choose a password that does not meet the requirements, you will see a message with the requirements for the password.

## Tip

**Delete browser History in the Internet Explorer app**

If you want to delete (part of) the browser *History* in *Internet Explorer*, these data will also be deleted in the *Internet Explorer* app. This is how you can quickly delete the full browser *History* in the *Internet Explorer* app:

☞ **Display the charms bar** 8

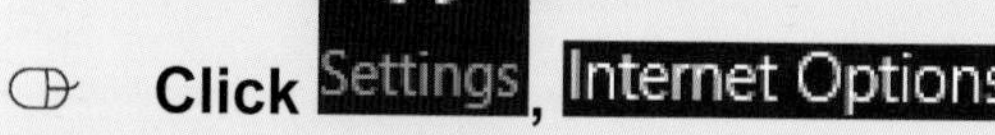


**Click** Settings, Internet Options

**By** Delete Browsing History**, click** Delete

Now the browser *History* is deleted, for the app but for the full version of the *Internet Explorer* program too.

# Appendices

# A. How Do I Do That Again?

In this book you will find many exercises that are marked with footsteps. 1
Find the corresponding number in the appendix below and see how to do something.

1 **Open a web page**

- Click the address bar
- Type the web address
- Press 

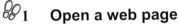

2 **Open the tabbed menu**

- Right-click an empty area on the web page
- Click 

3 **Go back to the Start screen**

- Place the pointer at the bottom left-hand corner of the screen
- Move the pointer into the corner as far as possible, until it disappears from view

*When you see a button of the Start screen:*

- Click 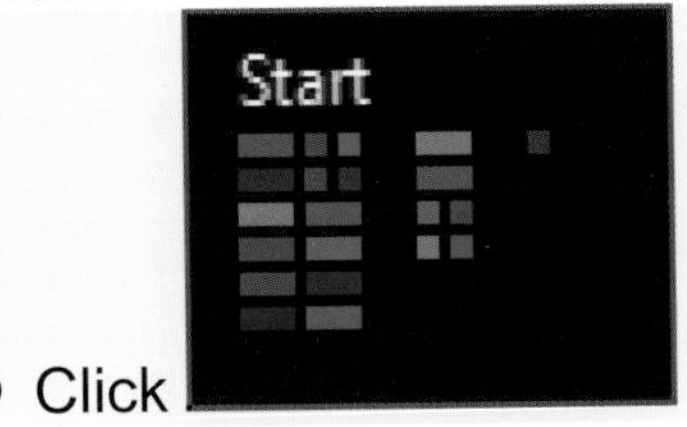


4 **Open an app on the Start screen**

- Click the desired app, for instance 

5 **Close an app**

- Place the pointer on the top border of the screen
- Drag the border of the screen downwards
- Drag the app to the bottom of the schreen
- Release the mouse button

6 **View a previously visited web page**

- Click 

7 **View a web page visited after the current one**

- Click 

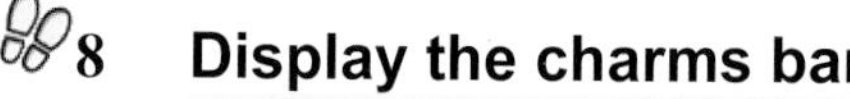

8 **Display the charms bar**
- Move the pointer into the top-right hand corner of the screen, as far as possible

9 **Open *Internet Explorer* on the desktop**
- If necessary, click Desktop
- Click 

10 **Refresh a web page**
- In the address bar, click 

11 **View the bottom of a page**
- Drag the scroll bar down

*Or:*
- Use the mouse wheel

12 **Close a window and/or the program on the desktop**
- Click ×

*In Internet Explorer, if multiple tabs have been opened:*
- Click Close all tabs

13 **Open a new tab**
- Click

14 **Open a link in a new tab**
- Press Ctrl and keep it depressed
- Click the link
- Release Ctrl

15 **Minimize a window**
- Click

16 **Open a window from the taskbar**
- Place the pointer on the button on the taskbar
- Click the miniature

17 **Close a tab**
- If necessary, click the tab
- Click ×

18 **Open a website from the address bar**
- Click the address bar
- Type the beginning of the web address
- Click the desired website

19 **Make a website a favorite**
- Click
- Click Add to favorites
- Click Add

**20 Open a website from history**

- Click
- Click the History tab
- Click the day
- Click the folder of the website
- Click the desired web page

**21 Open a favorite**

- Click
- If necessary, click the Favorites tab
- Click the desired web page

**22 Make a web address a favorite and save it in a folder**

- Click
- Click Add to favorites
- Click
- Click de desired folder
- Click Add

**23 Open a favorite in a folder**

- Click
- Click the folder
- Click the website

**24 Delete text**

- Click the box three times
- Press Delete

**25 Search for information**

- Type the search term in the address bar
- Press 

**26 View web pages**

- Click the name of the web page

**27 Begin a new search**

- Click the address bar

**28 Send an e-mail message**

- Click 

**29 Create a new e-mail message**

- Click 
- By To, type the e-mail address
- Type the e-mail address
- Click Add a subject
- Type the name of the subject
- Click Add a message
- Type the message

**30 View the *Inbox***

- Click Inbox

**31 Open an e-mail**

- Click the message

**32 Delete an e-mail**

- Click the e-mail to be deleted
- Click

*Permanently delete e-mail:*

- Click Deleted
- Click 

**33 Save an e-mail**

- Click
- Click Save draft

**34 View the *Drafts* folder**

- Click Drafts

**35 Add an attachment**

- Right-click an empty area on the screen
- Click 

- Select the desired file
- Click Attach

**36 Open an attachment**

- Click the name of the attachment
- Click the miniature image of the attachment

- Click Open

**37 Open *Downloads* folder**

- Click 
- Click Downloads

**38 Download and open a file**

- Click the file name

**39 Search for an app**

- Place the pointer in the right-hand corner of the screen
- Click 

- Type the app name in the search box
- Click 

**40 Save a photo from a web page**

- Right-click the photo
- Click Save picture as...

**41 Name a photo**

- By File name:, type the name
- Click Save

**42 Display the menu bar**

- Press Alt

**43 Display the app commands**

- Right-click an empty area on the screen

**44 Select text**

- Click the text three times

**45 Go back to start screen of an app**

- Click

**46 Save data**

- Click

**47 Sign in with your *Microsoft* account**

- Type your e-mail address
- Type your password

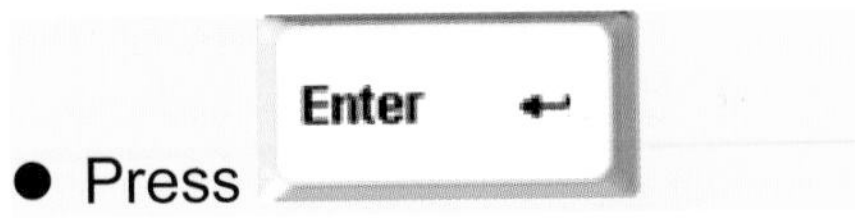


- Press

*Of:*

- Click Save

**48 Select desired folder**

- Click the folder

**49 Open *Settings* in an app**

- Move the pointer into the top-right hand corner of the screen, as far as possible

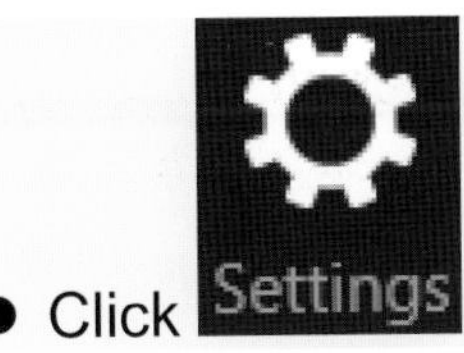


- Click

**50 Open the *Internet Options* window**

- Click
- Click Internet options

**51 Open the *Control Panel***

- Right-click an empty area on the Start screen

- Click

- Click

**52 Open the *Apps* screen**

- Right-click an empty area on the Start screen

- Click

**53 Switch to another tab**

- Click the tab

### 54 Install an app

- Click the app
- Click Install
- If necessary, type your e-mail address and password
- If necessary, click

### 55 Open apps with the switch list

- Move the pointer into the top-left hand corner of the screen as far as possible
- Move the pointer downwards
- Click the miniature of the app or program

# B. Opening the Bonus Online Chapters

This is how you open the bonus online chapters on this book's website:

☞ **Open *Internet Explorer* on the desktop** 9

☞ **Open the web page www.visualsteps.com/internet8** 1

You will see the website that goes with this book:

**Click** Bonus Online Chapters

Now you will see this webpage:

To open the bonus chapter:

**Click** Start downloading »»

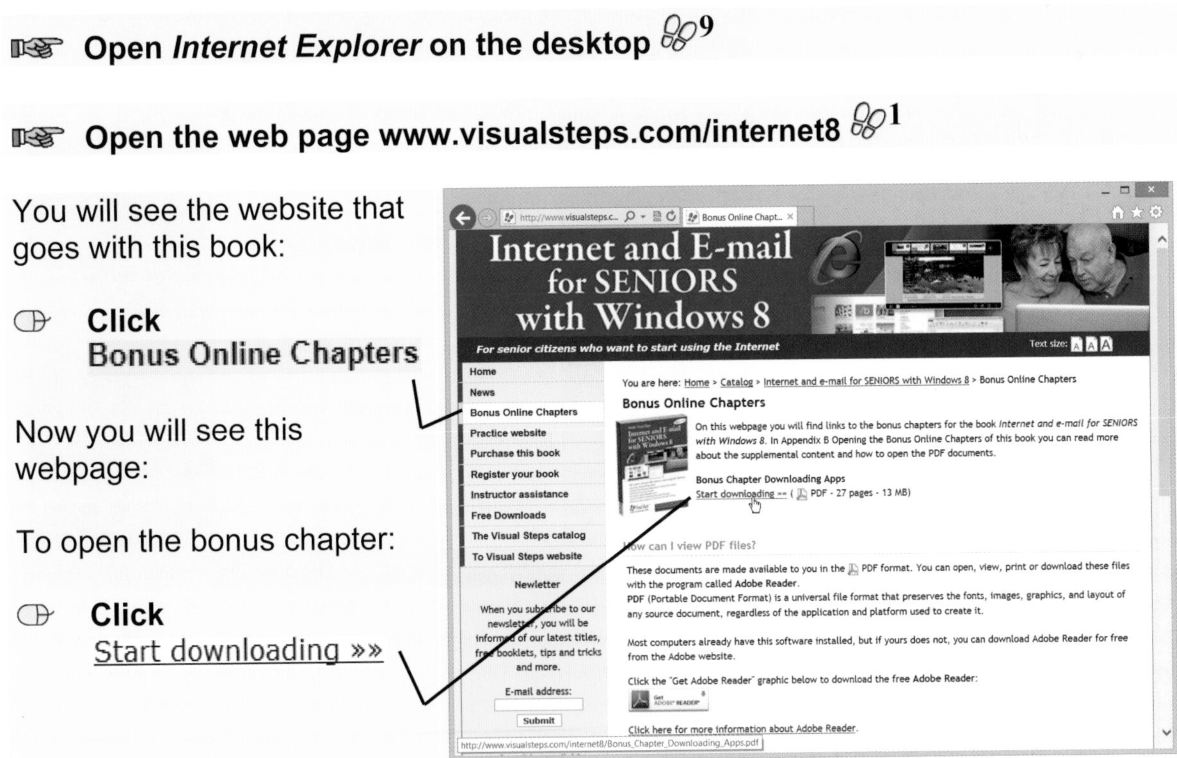


The PDF files are secured by a password. To open the PDF files, you need to enter the password:

A message bar appears at the bottom of the window:

**Click** Open

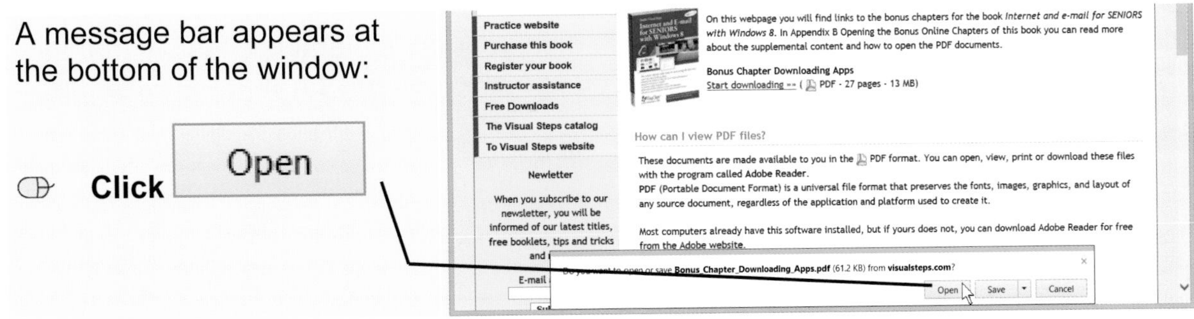


You can use the *Reader* app to open these PDF files. This app allows you to view the files and even print them, if you wish.

You need to enter the password to open the PDF file:

**Type:** `55987`

**Click** Open

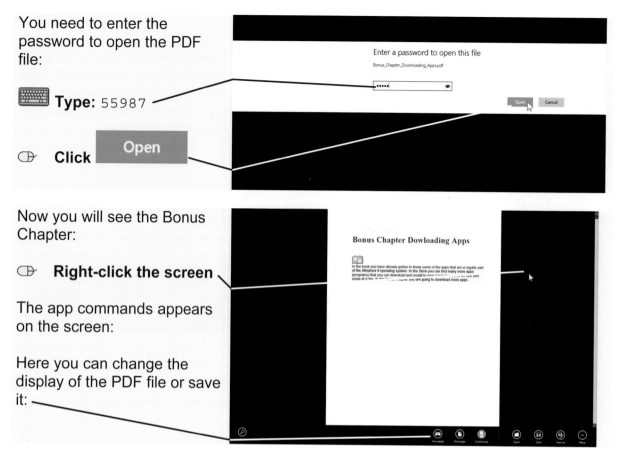

Now you will see the Bonus Chapter:

**Right-click the screen**

The app commands appears on the screen:

Here you can change the display of the PDF file or save it:

In *section 6.6 Opening a PDF File* you have learned how to print a PDF file. You can work through this online chapter in the same way you have worked with the chapters in the book. After you have read or printed it, you can close the window.

**Close all apps** 5 **and windows** 12

## HELP! I see a different program.

When the program *Adobe Reader* is installed on your computer it is possible that the PDF file will be opened by this program. You can also use this program to view the PDF file. If you wish to print the document, click .

# C. Index

## P



## Q



## R



## S

# Picasa for SENIORS

**Picasa for SENIORS**
*Get Acquainted with Picasa: Free, Easy-to-Use Photo Editing Software*

**Author**: Studio Visual Steps
**ISBN**: 978 90 5905 246 8
**Book type**: Paperback
**Number of pages**: 264
**Accompanying website**:
www.visualsteps.com/picasa

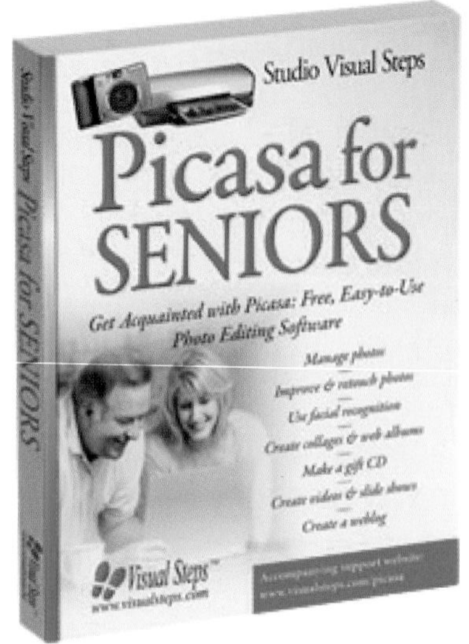


Are you looking for a handy and free photo management program? In that case the popular *Picasa* is an excellent choice! *Picasa* offers extended functionality for organizing and presenting your photo collection. It also offers several useful editing options. With just a few mouse clicks you can improve color quality and remove undesirable "red eyes". You can crop or straighten photos in a few seconds, print them or create a slide show. In order to safeguard your photos you can burn them to a CD or DVD. You can make internet web albums or publish your photos to your own blog. In other words, Picasa offers exactly what you are looking for: an easy way to manage, edit and present your photo collection.

**Characteristics of this book:**

- practical, useful topics
- geared towards the needs of the self-employed, independent contractor or freelancer
- clear instructions that anyone can follow
- handy, ready-made templates available on this website

**You will learn how to:**

- manage photos
- improve and retouch photos
- create collages and web albums
- make a gift CD
- create videos and slide shows
- create a blog